Navy Pier

*Grant
Park*

Soldier Field

McCormick Place

Illinois
Inst of
Technology

d

LAKE

MICHIGAN

90

94

CTA Green Line

VIVIAN HARSH PARK

ORIGINAL PANCAKE HOUSE

**HYDE
PARK**

41

SOPHY HOTEL

*Washington
Park*

CLOISTERS APARTMENTS

Dorchester Ave

Univ of
Chicago

Museum of Science
and Industry

MIDWAY PLAISANCE

*Jackson
Park*

OAK WOODS CEMETERY

**GREATER
GRAND
CROSSING**

E-Z TREE RECYCLING

CTA Red Line

**SOUTH
SHORE**

**SOUTH
CHICAGO**

Dorchester Ave

Yates

former US Steel
South Works

Dan Ryan Expwy

Cottage Grove

Stony Island

Chicago Skyway

*Calumet
Park*

Chicago State Univ

41

Praise for *Unforgiving Places*

"Ludwig thinks more deeply about the causes of American gun violence than anyone, and his policy solutions have been proven to work. *Unforgiving Places* is the best book on American violence I've ever read."

STEVEN LEVITT, coauthor of *Freakonomics*

"An extraordinarily important book that challenges conventional wisdom about one of the most vexing problems in the United States: gun violence. *Unforgiving Places* is provocative, compelling, and essential."

MELISSA S. KEARNEY, author of *The Two-Parent Privilege*

"If you thought you understood the origins of gun violence, think again—this book might just be the key to saving millions of lives."

KATHRYN J. EDIN, coauthor of *The Injustice of Place: Uncovering the Legacy of Poverty in America*

"This book accomplishes an extremely rare feat: providing a new perspective on an old problem. And it does so for one of the biggest problems plaguing society: gun violence. It is a must-read for every person struggling to make sense of the violence around them."

SENDHIL MULLAINATHAN, MIT

"A brilliant, engaging, and highly accessible analysis of the causes of gun violence in the United States, enriched with real-world examples from Ludwig's experience studying crime in Chicago. *Unforgiving Places* offers a promising foundation for finally making headway at reducing gun violence in America. It is a must-read for anyone worried about the level of gun violence in our country—and especially those motivated to actually reduce it."

CECILIA ELENA ROUSE, Princeton University

"On the list of challenges facing American cities, gun violence may be the most pressing. *Unforgiving Places* portrays the problem in deeply human and actionable terms. It is the most important book I've read on this quintessentially American challenge. Ludwig knows this work, and he knows what works."

MICHAEL NUTTER, mayor of Philadelphia 2008–2016

"Ludwig's book is a must-read for all Americans, including and especially those who understand that our biggest current tragic failure as a country is our inability to protect our children from gun violence."

CHARLIE BECK, former chief of the Los Angeles Police Department and former superintendent of the Chicago Police Department

UNFORGIVING PLACES

UNFORGIVING PLACES

THE UNEXPECTED ORIGINS OF AMERICAN GUN VIOLENCE

JENS LUDWIG

THE UNIVERSITY OF CHICAGO PRESS

Chicago and London

The University of Chicago Press, Chicago 60637
The University of Chicago Press, Ltd., London
© 2025 by Jens Ludwig
Published 2025
Printed in the United States of America

34 33 32 31 30 29 28 27 26 25   1 2 3 4 5

ISBN-13: 978-0-226-82813-8 (cloth)
ISBN-13: 978-0-226-83948-6 (e-book)
DOI: https://doi.org/10.7208/chicago/9780226839486.001.0001

Library of Congress Cataloging-in-Publication Data

Names: Ludwig, Jens, author.
Title: Unforgiving places : the unexpected origins of American gun violence / Jens
    Ludwig.
Description: Chicago : The University of Chicago Press, 2025. | Includes
    bibliographical references and index.
Identifiers: LCCN 2024033883 | ISBN 9780226828138 (cloth) | ISBN 9780226839486
    (ebook)
Subjects: LCSH: Urban violence—United States. | Urban violence—United States—
    Psychological aspects. | Urban violence—Illinois—Chicago. | Gun control—
    United States. | Criminal behavior—United States.
Classification: LCC HV6493 .L83 2025 | DDC 303.609173/2—dc23/eng/20240909
LC record available at https://lccn.loc.gov/2024033883

♾ This paper meets the requirements of ANSI/NISO Z39.48-1992
(Permanence of Paper).

For Annika and Willa,
whom Mom and I love more than life itself.
A small effort to make the world you inherit at least a little bit better.

To know that one knows what one knows,
and to know that one doesn't know
what one doesn't know, there lies true wisdom.

CONFUCIUS

CONTENTS

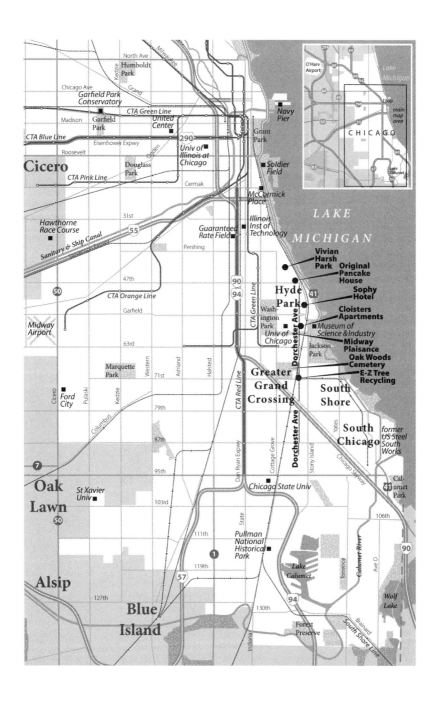

PREFACE

Dorchester Avenue runs right through the heart of Chicago's South Side. At its northern end is Kenwood, an upscale neighborhood that's been home to some of the city's most influential Black residents, including Senator Carol Moseley Braun, Muddy Waters, Louis Farrakhan, and Muhammad Ali. At 47th Street is the Original Pancake House, for my money the best breakfast spot in Chicago. Across the street is the Dunkin' Donuts that is my older daughter's favorite because there's never a line on the customer side of the bulletproof glass.

Just south of Kenwood is Hyde Park, one of the most diverse neighborhoods in a city that is still overwhelmingly segregated. Hyde Park is where I live with my family, and it's also home to the University of Chicago, where I work.

At 58th Street is the Cloisters, a high-rise apartment building that claims to have housed more Nobel Laureates than any other apartment building in the world.

At 59th Street, Dorchester crosses the Midway, a mile-long, one-block-wide strip of manicured green space designed by the same landscape architect behind New York's Central Park. The Midway separates Hyde Park from Woodlawn, the predominantly Black neighborhood to the south. For much of the twentieth century, Woodlawn was a thriving middle-class area, home to a stretch of clubs along 63rd Street where some of the world's most famous musicians played. Many of those buildings are demolished now, leaving stretches of 63rd vacant and Woodlawn residents divided over concerns about redevelopment and gentrification.

South of Woodlawn, some 10 miles before Dorchester Avenue ends by the abandoned steel mills along Lake Calumet, is a sign for a small mulching business, E-Z Tree Recycling (slogan: "A tree is a terrible thing to waste"). This sign at Dorchester and 71st Street is the unofficial but highly consequential border designation between two Chicago neighborhoods: South Shore to the east, stretching all the way to Lake Michigan, and Greater Grand Crossing running to the west, along a portion of 71st that was renamed for local resident Emmett Till.

At first glance, Greater Grand Crossing and South Shore appear quite similar. They're next-door communities in the same American city, mostly indistinguishable in their economic conditions and in the racial and ethnic makeup of the people who live there.

But the two neighborhoods are dramatically different in one important respect: On a per-capita basis, there are about twice as many shootings in Greater Grand Crossing as in South Shore.

Whatever you believe about the causes of gun violence in America, those beliefs almost surely fail to explain why Greater Grand Crossing would be so much more of a violent place than South Shore. How, in a city and a country where guns are everywhere, does gun violence occur so unevenly—even across such short distances, in this case literally right across the street? If we can't explain even the most basic questions of where and why gun violence occurs, no wonder the US has made so little progress solving this long-term public policy and public health crisis.

I've worked for thirty years to try to understand the puzzle of gun violence in America. I come to the problem as someone who is technically not from here: I was born in Germany and immigrated to the US with my family when I was three. My father's first job was as a dishwasher, which he took over from his father. I grew up hearing stories from my parents about living on potatoes and dandelion soup after the war. My mom learned English from watching *Sesame Street* with my sister and me. Her English eventually got good enough for a subscription to *Time* magazine, which I'd then pore over when she was done. Growing up in the 1970s and 1980s as violent-crime rates surged, I could see the coverage in *Time* becoming more anxious. President Ronald Reagan blamed violence on what he called the age of "the human predator."[1] By the 1990s, in the rhetorical arms race of the time, this label evolved into "super-predators."[2]

As a first-generation college-goer I stumbled into economics because that's what my freshman roommate happened to study. But I was never really that interested in the stock market or GDP; I wanted to use what economists know about data to answer questions about what I thought of as the real world. I went to college in New Brunswick, New Jersey, in the late 1980s, as the crack-cocaine epidemic and the shootings that came with it swept over that city. As a volunteer soccer coach for local kids, whose team would field as many players as could fit into my Ford Escort, I saw what gun violence does to a neighborhood. Now as someone trying to do something about that gun violence, I've met too many people who have lost loved ones to this problem. My goal has been to use data and the insights it can provide to identify policies capable of preventing gun violence by developing a better understanding of why gun violence happens in the first place.

For most of my career, that's meant looking at whether fixing America's many social problems—including poverty, racism, social isolation, inadequate schools, under-resourced neighborhoods, and gaps in the social safety net—could reduce the country's problem with gun violence. If America were better at supporting and caring for its people and equalizing opportunity, would it become a less violent place?

After three decades of studying these dynamics, I'm sure the answer is yes. But I am *also* sure that we are, unfortunately, not anywhere close to fixing those problems as a society. Neither are we close to reining in the availability or lethality of guns, which, despite all the well-intentioned legislative efforts to the contrary, remain a ubiquitous part of American life.

Waiting and hoping for a better world—one free of injustice, free of illegal guns on the streets—is not a real plan. By continuing to treat gun violence as something that will get better once we fix everything else that's wrong with society, we perpetuate levels of pain and loss that seem unacceptable for a country like the United States.

This book provides a new way of thinking about gun violence, because I fear the traditional way of thinking about it has proven too limited and unproductive. A new perspective, a new understanding of the problem, can give us new ideas about solutions and renewed hope that the daily headlines of lost lives and shattered families are not intractable parts of American life.

Eighteen years ago, I moved to Hyde Park to become a professor at the University of Chicago. I started a research center, the University of Chicago Crime Lab, to partner with the government and nonprofits to help reduce gun violence out in the real world—including on the South Side, a place caricatured by some as a hothouse of American lawlessness run amok. But the South Side isn't just a politicized talking point about crime policy: it's where I live, in a city I've come to love. I haven't just spent a lot of time looking at data, I've also seen these problems up close, firsthand: countless hours spent in schools, parks, playgrounds, housing developments, courtrooms, jails, police stations, police cars, and lots and lots of McDonald'ses.

It's hard to solve a problem we don't understand.

Having gone down my share of dead ends in trying to understand gun violence myself, I can say that many of our assumptions about this problem have inadvertently made, and continue to make, the problem worse. So-called criminal behavior turns out to be—surprisingly—not that different from everyday human behavior: bad decisions made under stress in difficult situations. Approaching violence with the insights of the rapidly developing field of behavioral economics provides a new way to understand—and, to the extent possible, solve—this quintessentially American problem.

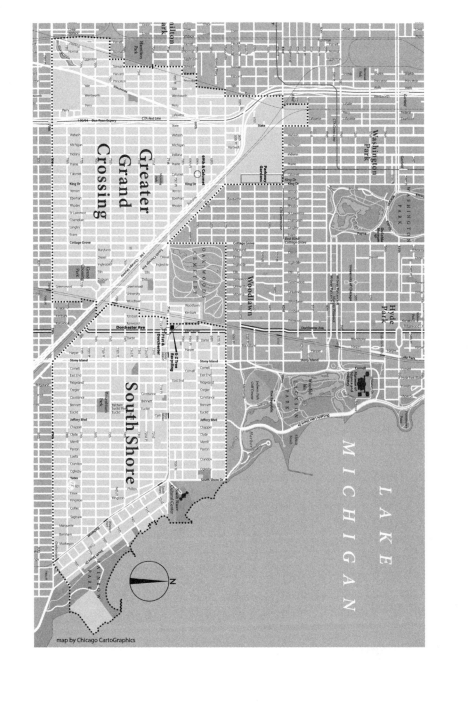

Greater Grand Crossing

South Shore

Woodlawn

Washington Park

Hyde Park

LAKE MICHIGAN

N

map by Chicago CartoGraphics

1

A NEW IDEA

Calumet Avenue and 69th Street cross in the heart of the Greater Grand Crossing neighborhood here on Chicago's South Side. The intersection sits a few blocks west of the Chicago Skyway, an elevated highway that connects Lake Shore Drive to northern Indiana. Popular legend holds that the Skyway was originally built to make it easier for Chicago's first Mayor Daley—Richard J.—to get to his family's beach house in Michigan.[1] The real story is, if anything, even weirder: In the 1950s, when President Eisenhower was shelling out billions of dollars for superhighways to evacuate cities in case of nuclear war, the city of Chicago and state of Indiana planned their highway routes . . . without coordinating with one another. The Skyway was hurriedly built to prevent the doomsday scenario of thousands of cars exiting the Indiana highway and spilling onto Chicago's surface streets.[2] The lesson, not the first for Chicagoans, was that the people in charge sometimes don't know what they're doing.

The intersection also sits just a few blocks south of Parkway Gardens, the apartment complex where Michelle Obama lived briefly as a child. That complex was later made famous by drill-rap artists like King Von, Chief Keef, and Fredo Santana, who helped coin its gang-related nickname, "O-Block." The *Chicago Sun-Times* called it "the most dangerous block in Chicago."[3]

It was at 69th and Calumet at 10:00 p.m. on Halloween Eve, 1996, when Brian Willis, age 18, was arguing with Alexander Clair, 23, about a used beige two-door Ford LTD parked in front of Little Hobo's restaurant. Clair had sold Willis the car a few days earlier and complained that Willis hadn't paid for it yet. Willis was angry that Clair had reportedly entered the car earlier that night and tried take it back.

Regarding payment, Willis told Clair, "I'm not going to give you shit." Regarding adherence to the transaction's terms, Clair replied, "If I catch you in the car—if I see the car or I catch you in the car—I'm going to burn the car up."

The two argued in the street for another ten minutes.[4]

Eventually Willis broke off and ran across 69th, past the car and behind the building at 352 East 69th Street. Clair followed. Meanwhile Clair's girlfriend, Jewel Washington, 25, was trailing behind when she heard two loud gunshots. Those would turn out to be the gunshots that killed Clair, fired from a short-handled, 12-gauge pump-action shotgun with one shotgun blast to Clair's stomach and one to his head.

Washington turned and tried to run back toward Calumet Avenue. Willis, still holding the shotgun, yelled, "Where do you think you're going, bitch?" and then again, "Where the fuck do you think you're going, bitch?" A witness would later report hearing a high-pitched voice outside her window pleading, "Please don't, please don't." Three more shotgun blasts and Washington was dead along with Clair.[5]

Brian Willis was later convicted of two counts of first-degree murder and sentenced to life in prison. In effect, three lives, not just two, were lost that night.[6]

In terms of its impact on American life, gun violence *is* America's crime problem. Property crimes like shoplifting, bike thefts, and burglaries are maddening. Gun violence is devastating. Moreover, gun violence victims aren't the only victims. The trauma radiates outward to families and entire communities. And since everyone in the United States lives under the *threat* of being a victim of gun violence, it leads to large-scale social disruption as people and businesses flee impacted neighborhoods and cities. Shootings account for fewer than 1 percent of all crimes but nearly 70 percent of the total social harm of crime.[7]

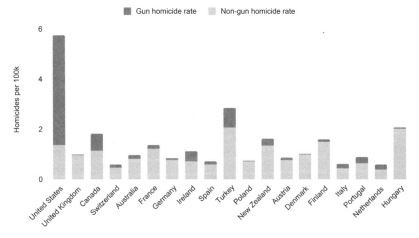

FIGURE I.I. Murder rates per 100,000 people by country by weapon

Mass shootings are an important part of this burden, the kind of shocking, terrifying, heartbreaking event that has become synonymous with American gun violence. But in terms of frequency, mass shootings account for a modest share of all the lives lost to interpersonal gun violence every year in America. Most gun violence victims lose their lives as part of the daily tragedies that typically don't make news headlines— what the mayor of Milwaukee once referred to as "slow-motion mass murder."[8] That will be my focus here.

This type of violence is unheard of in any other rich country in the world. America's murder rate on a per-capita basis is about five times that of the United Kingdom, for example (figure I.I).[9] Almost all the difference is due to the US's far higher rate of murders committed with guns.

It's natural from that fact to conclude that gun violence in America can be traced to one simple origin: guns. And it's true that the US has, alongside its exceptionally high rate of murders, an exceptionally high number of guns: 400 million guns for a country of 330 million people. But these two facts are not *inevitably* linked. For example, both Canada and Switzerland have above-average rates of gun ownership, like the US, but unlike the US, those countries *don't* have particularly high rates of murder.

The challenge of understanding and reducing gun violence is thus complicated by the fact that *guns* and *violence* are overlapping but ultimately discrete issues.[10] Guns alone aren't catastrophic, as the relatively modest murder rates in relatively high-gun countries like Canada and Switzerland illustrate. Violence alone isn't catastrophic; the UK has high rates of violent crime overall (assaults, robberies, etc.) but practically no guns, and so it has a relatively low murder rate. It's the *combination* of lots of guns *and* lots of violence that's catastrophic. The causes of gun violence, in other words, can be summarized by a simple formula: Gun violence = guns *plus* violence.

That simple formula has implications not just for understanding the problem but also for solving it—because the implication is that there are *two* ways to solve gun violence, not just one. If, for better or worse, the four hundred million firearms in the US aren't just going to disappear anytime soon, if major nationwide gun control is unlikely in the foreseeable future, then progress on gun violence can—or maybe *must*—come from figuring out how to reduce the tendency of people to use those widely available guns to harm one another. Figuring that out begins with questioning some of the things we tell ourselves about gun violence in the first place.

THE TWO CONVENTIONAL WISDOMS

For most Americans, the tragedy at 69th and Calumet in Greater Grand Crossing can be explained in one of two ways.

The first is that shootings like this one stem from characterologically bad people. Whether born bad or raised badly, the perpetrators of gun violence in this view have no moral compass or fear of the justice system. "I cannot say it any clearer—it is the good guys against the bad guys. These bad guys are violent, they carry guns, and the symbol of our public safety, which is that police uniform, they have total disregard for." That's from the mayor of New York City.[11] These narratives of "bad guys" or "wicked people" are usually accompanied by calls for greater vigilance: for the government to deter or incapacitate criminals by putting more police on the streets; for the building and filling of more prisons; for private citizens to protect themselves by arming themselves.

A second perspective is that gun violence stems from root causes—that is, from a set of social conditions that fuel gun violence. In this view, violence grows where human flourishing doesn't. "Violence is an expression of poverty" is how a recent mayor of Chicago put it.[12] This narrative often leads to calls to fundamentally transform American society: to desegregate our cities; to end the social isolation of the most vulnerable; to take greater steps to end poverty; to dismantle the prison-industrial complex; to defund the police and the military and channel those resources back into social programs instead.

The data confirm that most Americans believe that crime and violence are due to some version of one of these two conventional wisdoms. In focus groups, Americans say crime is due to "something inherently wrong within the lawbreaker, such as lack of moral fiber, or due to ecological considerations that influence or force individuals to break the law, such as lack of money."[13] We see the same thing in surveys. In 1994, around the time President Clinton signed the largest crime bill in US history, seven of ten Americans were telling Gallup pollsters that crime was due to amoral criminals and the failure of the criminal-justice system to stop them. The next-most-common explanation was poverty. Of course, these aren't literally the *only* ideas out there. But they're clearly the ones driving the conversation.

It's not just policymakers and members of the general public who believe these conventional wisdoms. They're what I, the person who studies crime for a living, long believed, too. I grew up reading about Ted Bundy and John Wayne Gacy and the Son of Sam killings in *Time* and, later, in books like *In Cold Blood* and *Helter Skelter*—violence committed by predators and lunatics. Later, as an economics major in college, I read University of Chicago economist Gary Becker's argument that criminals are rational actors responding to incentives—that crime is a kind of market response to other, less good options.[14] I was also reading the biographies of people like Robert Kennedy and Martin Luther King Jr. and Malcolm X, which was to read the stories of lives lost to the violence epidemic, the root causes of which these men were trying to stamp out. These two coexisting schools of conventional wisdom about what causes violence aren't just entrenched; they're unavoidable.

And there is indeed some truth to both ideas.

There *are* bad people in the world. These are people who lack empathy, are narcissists with a grandiose view of themselves, are pathological liars, have a constant need for stimulation, are manipulative, fail to feel remorse or guilt, and refuse to take responsibility for anything. Many of them show signs of problem behavior in their early years and then engage in antisocial or violent behavior for most of their lives. Some estimates suggest that perhaps 1 percent of all men in America fall into this group. They can be found in every walk of life: on the street corner, in a police car, teaching in a university classroom, at an investment bank or church, in a Boy Scout troop, or sometimes even in the very highest of political offices. An outsized share of these individuals wind up in prison, although most people who are incarcerated are *not* in this category. Psychiatrists call them psychopaths.[15]

There is also evidence that the threat of punishment can indeed deter some criminal behaviors. We know this from studying what social scientists call natural experiments, changes out in the world that manipulate policies in a nearly random way akin to the sort of randomized controlled trial that provides gold-standard evidence in medicine. Consider the 2006 mass pardon in Italy, in which 40 percent of all inmates in the country were released from prison all at once. Their release came with a condition: If rearrested, people would have to serve out the remainder of their original sentence. The released prisoners varied greatly in how much time they had left on their original sentence (from one to thirty-six months), depending on the luck of the draw as to how far into their prison sentence they were when the pardon was issued. Thus, similar "types" of people were released facing different punishment levels for committing exactly the same crime. The data showed that those who were facing stiffer penalties engaged in less violence.[16]

Meanwhile, the people who believe violence is borne of the persistent unfairnesses of American society, including its inequality, discrimination, and segregation, are also right. Turn on the news and see where the violence happens; it's rarely in the fancy neighborhoods.

This phenomenon is neither recent nor limited to the American context: Wherever groups of people are treated as less-than by a society, crime often follows. A hundred years ago, three of Chicago's earliest immigrant enclaves were populated by nationalities historically subject to discrimination: the Irish (depicted as "ape-like" and alcoholic by British writers of the era[17]), Polish (a common European saying was "drunk as a Pole on payday"[18]), and Italians ("Just a little worse than the Negro, being if anything filthier in their habits, lawlessness, and treacherous," according to Louisiana's governor in the 1910s[19]). So when University of Chicago sociologists catalogued the city's gangs in the 1920s, guess which three groups accounted for the largest share of gang members?[20] Similar dynamics of disadvantage and crime and violence can be observed all around the world: In Brazil it is the favelas; in Paris it is the banlieues, where many people from France's former colonies live; in Cape Town, it is the outlying Cape Flats area, where the government forced Black people to move during apartheid.

The root causes of violence, in other words, stem from both economic disadvantage and social disadvantage, including racial and ethnic discrimination. What do the consequences of this disadvantage and discrimination look like in modern-day America? They look like the five Chicago neighborhoods that together account for fewer than one in ten city residents but experience fully one in three of the city's homicides.[21] It's no accident that these neighborhoods are located in the most disadvantaged, socially isolated, racially segregated, predominantly Black areas of Chicago's South and West sides. In the US as a whole, Black Americans are 13 percent of all residents but 27 percent of all victims of police shootings, 33 percent of all prison inmates, 33 percent of those arrested for violent crimes, and 54 percent of all murder victims.[22]

THE LIMITS OF CONVENTIONAL WISDOM

The conventional wisdoms that gun violence is caused by either bad people or bad economic opportunities have produced no shortage of policy proposals. The history of these policies illustrates the limits of how we've traditionally characterized the problem and its solutions.

"Get tough" policies (enforcement, imprisonment, public vigilance) have helped improve safety to a degree but only by imposing tremendous harm along the way. For example, the data show that imprisonment can reduce violence. But the growth in American prisons in the 1970s, and the harms that prisons impose on incarcerated people's health, families, and livelihoods,[23] occurred at a rate that had no historical or international precedent. The growth in police spending has helped reduce violent crime,[24] but the frequent gravitation toward "zero-tolerance" policing has generated substantial human costs as well. The decisions of private citizens to arm themselves has contributed to a flood of gun stores and used guns that make firearms more likely to wind up being used in crimes. All these harms are disproportionately concentrated in the same disadvantaged, segregated communities that suffer the most from gun violence itself.

Meanwhile, reforms meant to stem the root causes of violence—attempts at fixing society's most complicated challenges through policy change—typically run aground when their political proponents reach office.[25] Diminishing political and social returns—ideas that start from good intentions only to end in frustration and disillusion—seem to plague most attempts at addressing America's structural problems, which remain and persist. While poverty in America has decreased by some measures, inequality in both income and wealth have increased. In Chicago, the city's challenge with gangs shows few signs of being resolved. Racial segregation in the city has barely changed for forty years. In the face of such minimal gains from earnest attempts to fix our biggest social problems, the reflexive "sending thoughts and prayers" approach to US gun violence somehow seems less vapid: Gun violence, like racial prejudice and inequality, often appears to be the kind of problem that only wishes can solve.

The hope of many that the gun problem might be solved with a single stroke of a legislative pen—that some US president and US Congress will do what no previous government has done and radically reorient gun laws in America—has in practice led to few legislative victories.

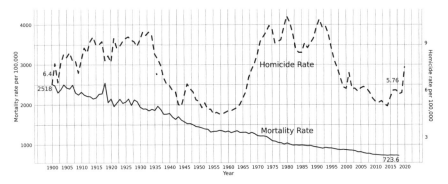

FIGURE 1.2. Trends in US homicide and overall mortality rates per 100,000 people, 1900–2020

Whether that will change anytime soon is far from obvious. As a 2022 *New York Times* headline put it, "As shootings continue, prospects for gun control action in Congress remain dim."[26]

What has this collection of policies suggested by conventional wisdom added up to? The answer is: little long-term progress in reducing gun violence (figure 1.2).[27] This failure is remarkable in part because of how good the US has been at addressing so many other public health problems. Since 1900, death rates per capita have declined by 38 percent for heart disease, 84 percent for strokes, 95 percent for respiratory diseases like influenza and pneumonia, and around 99 percent for tuberculosis.[28] Overall life expectancy has nearly doubled. Yet the rate of murders, most of which are committed with guns, is almost exactly the same as it was 125 years ago.

GREATER GRAND CROSSING AND THE LIMITS
OF CONVENTIONAL WISDOM

Why have the policies of the past not had more impact? The answer is that explanations of gun violence as the result of either bad people or tragic circumstances are deeply incomplete.

Consider Greater Grand Crossing and South Shore, communities separated only by Dorchester Avenue. They're adjacent neighborhoods

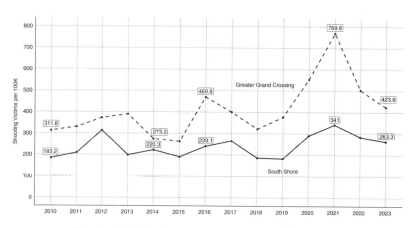

FIGURE 1.3. Shooting victimization rates per 100,000 people for South Shore and Greater Grand Crossing, 2010–2023

in the same part of Chicago, which means many of the policy variables that we think of as determining public safety are identical in both places. Both neighborhoods are served by the same police department and court system, the same jails and prisons, and regulated by the same federal, state, and city gun laws.

The neighborhoods are sociodemographically similar, too, having been shaped by the same larger social forces over Chicago's history. Greater Grand Crossing and South Shore both "tipped" racially in the middle of the twentieth century; today more than nine of every ten residents in both places are Black. Since the local steel mills started closing in the 1970s, both areas have struggled economically. At the end of the twentieth century, median household incomes in both places were about 70 percent of the national average; today they're more like 45–50 percent.[29]

Given these similarities, the fact that Greater Grand Crossing has so much more gun violence than South Shore (figure 1.3)[30] tells us there must be *something* else—not just evil people, not just social injustice—that drives violence. If that weren't the case, then Greater Grand Crossing would have to be twice as evil, or subject to twice as much injustice, as South Shore, which seems both inconsistent with the available data and implausible as a matter of common sense.

The fact that gun violence varies enormously across neighborhoods with similar levels of concentrated poverty and racial segregation tells us there's a lot we don't know. Violence, it seems, is driven in large part by other factors.

We can see the same limits of conventional wisdom by looking more closely at specific acts of gun violence. Like many stories about violence in Chicago, news reports on the shooting at 69th and Calumet in Greater Grand Crossing looked like bad people acting in dire circumstances. After all, the confrontation centered on an unpaid debt. Brian Willis, the man convicted of the two murders, verbally menaced his two victims before killing them. One of the victims, Jewel Washington, begged for her life. Willis went ahead and shot her three times.

While it is possible that Willis was the kind of antisocial "superpredator" that some commentators warned Americans against, after being sentenced to life in prison Willis got not only his college degree but a master's degree.[31] Neither does it seem that economic desperation drove the shootings. The 1996 Blue Book value for the two-door 1986 Ford LTD at the center of the disagreement was $3,500.[32] The statistical chances Willis would get caught for murder were about 50 percent.[33] What person, no matter how economically desperate, would be willing to flip this coin: Heads, you get out of paying for a $3,500 used car; tails, life in prison? The benefit versus cost sides of this ledger are wildly unequal. For an 18-year-old like Willis who might live another sixty years, that deal pays off just $60 for every year risked behind bars.[34] In our search to understand the motives here, conventional wisdom leaves us largely lost.

Other details about the case are similarly challenging for conventional wisdom to explain. Every person involved was young, with a shooter in his teens and two victims in their twenties. This is a recurring pattern: One of the strongest predictors of gun violence is age—or rather, lack of it. Here again this pattern contradicts how we usually think violence occurs. If violence is perpetrated by bad people, why would it be that young people are so much more violent than older ones? People's fundamental moral character doesn't change with age.

(And anyone who thinks it does wouldn't be pushing for three-strikes-
and-you're-out laws, as many proponents of the bad-people narrative
have often done.) Neither can this pattern be explained by changing
economic burdens over the life course, since survey data suggest that
people tend to feel like these burdens, if anything, get *heavier* as we
get older.[35]

The disagreement that preceded the murders in the Willis case began at 10:00 p.m. on the night before Halloween. This timing, too, is
predictable based on violent-crime patterns: Violence is much more
likely to happen late at night. It's also more likely to happen when
it's warmer—in the summer rather than in the winter, or, in the case
of October 30, 1996, on an unusually mild fall day by Chicago standards.[36] Gun violence is more common on weekends and holidays (like
the night before Halloween) than during the regular workweek. None
of these patterns can be explained by what we think we know about
violence. People aren't less moral (or less poor) in June than they are in
January, or at night versus during the day, or on Thursday versus Friday.

It is hard to solve a problem that we don't understand.

A DIFFERENT VIEW OF HUMAN BEHAVIOR

This book offers a very different explanation for gun violence.

In American politics, the Right and Left disagree about lots of things
but do have one point of (implicit) agreement: They assume that shooters are *acting rationally*. Both sides believe that before anyone pulls a
trigger, they've carefully thought through the pros and cons.

For those on the right, shooters are bad seeds, suffering from some
combination of personal deficits (morality, empathy) and insufficient
fear of punishment. The assumption of rationality shines through in
the heavy emphasis policy has placed on deterrence—changing the
incentives for criminal behavior through things like longer prison sentences. Moreover, those policies are typically imposed without much
effort to ensure everyone knows about them—without widespread
publicity campaigns—which is another "tell" about the assumption of

rationality: "Criminals" are usually just assumed to find out on their own, as if they have perfect information.

For those on the left, shooters are economically desperate people for whom the monetary benefits of crime loom too large in the face of poverty. Simply reducing the incentives to commit crime by reducing economic desperation is widely thought to be sufficient for reducing crime.

Both conventional wisdoms essentially assume people are always perfectly rational, benefit-cost calculators: Their decisions to do bad things are based on a weighing of options. The main point of disagreement is simply whether the solution is more sticks or better carrots.

But the underlying assumption here is incorrect: In the real world, normal human beings are *not* always perfectly rational benefit-cost calculators.

My personal epiphany about human behavior came as the result of a near-death experience I had a few years ago: I almost killed myself by stepping in front of a bus. I'm sure my obituary would have focused on the *why* of it: *He had so much to live for—a beautiful wife, two amazing daughters, a good job as a professor at the University of Chicago. He was tall, handsome, athletic*—(I assume obituary writers take some licenses)—*No one saw it coming.* The questions, in other words, would have centered on what my rational self was wrestling with at the time. Was I under stress at work? Was there a financial scandal? The focus would have all been on *me*.

But here's another thing to know about my near-death experience: I was in London. That's relevant because, as it turns out, Londoners drive on the wrong side of the road. So in that moment, I found myself doing something simple (crossing the street) that looked identical to something I've done every day of my life in America. My brain made an implicit assumption: This was routine street-crossing as usual, so my routine strategy for doing it—*look left*—would work just fine. But that assumption, which works fine in Chicago, nearly got me killed in London. This near disaster wasn't about me as a *person* so much as about my *situation*.

Behavioral economics, which seeks to better understand human decision-making, has helped reveal why all people are so vulnerable to situational influences. If human cognition were perfect, my being in London instead of Chicago shouldn't have mattered. I am, after all, a cultured man of the world: I've read the *Harry Potter* books to my kids. I've seen not only *Paddington* but *Paddington 2* as well. A perfectly rational optimizing person with the benefit of this cultural capital would have remembered that driving in England is screwed up.

But a key lesson from behavioral economics over the past fifty years is that we are all, in a sense, of two minds. The sort of deliberate, conscious thought that people normally refer to as "thinking" takes real effort. For this reason, all people tend to rely on automatic responses developed to effortlessly deal with situations we see routinely. These responses, happening below the level of consciousness, are usually adaptive and automatic ("Look left when crossing the street") but can lead to trouble when overgeneralized. Usually-useful-but-sometimes-overgeneralized automatic responses can lead to gaps between our deliberate intentions and our actual actions. An obituary writer would have looked at my actions and assumed that my intent was "I can't take it anymore." But my actual thought was "Jesus Christ, where did that giant red bus come from?" I felt less like an idiot when I realized what good company I was in; Winston Churchill was nearly killed in 1931 when hit by a taxi crossing the street . . . in New York.[37]

Daniel Kahneman won a Nobel Prize for his study of these two lanes of human thought: the automatic responses, which happen fast; and the deliberate responses, which happen slowly.[38] The fast thinking, which Kahneman labeled System 1, is a kind of autopilot; the slow thinking, called System 2, requires more effort but is more analytical. The human reliance on System 1 for most everyday functioning means that people are not always perfectly rational; we're imperfectly rational, or *boundedly rational*. Because we're so often on System 1 autopilot, we can make mistakes—decisions that our rational, deliberate System 2 selves would not endorse if we just stopped and thought carefully about things just a bit more. We're all especially vulnerable when faced with novel, difficult, high-stakes situations.

This explanation for human behavior extends even to those actions that we most closely associate with morality, right and wrong, good and evil.

In a canonical study from the 1970s, a team of social psychologists enrolled forty students from the Princeton Theological Seminary and asked them to walk across campus to another university building to deliver a talk on the parable of the Good Samaritan.[39] In the biblical story, a man is robbed and left injured at the side of the road; he is then ignored by a passing priest before being cared for by a passing good Samaritan. In the study, the subjects encountered a person (a plant of the researchers) slumped in a doorway, not moving, eyes closed, who would cough and groan as the subject went by—a person, in other words, in need of help. Yet only 40 percent of the seminary students stopped to help the person in need. As the researchers observed, "On several occasions, a seminary student going to give a talk on the parable of the Good Samaritan literally stepped over the victim as he hurried on his way."

What distinguished the subjects who helped from those who didn't? Was it something about their character, like their level of religious devotion? It turns out that how religious subjects were explained little about who stopped to help and who didn't. The most important factor? Whether the subject was in a hurry. Some were randomly assigned to be told they were late to give their talk, while others weren't. Those who were in a hurry helped far less (10 percent) than those not in a hurry (63 percent). The lesson of the Bad Samaritan is not so much about the effects of hurrying per se. It's more general: For helping behavior, the situation mattered far more than the person.

If Kahneman's work showed that all humans have a uniform capacity for something less than perfect rationality, the Bad Samaritan study illustrated that these tendencies don't lessen with individual goodness or altruism, and in fact can shape the degree to which any of us manifest what *looks* like individual goodness and altruism—or their opposites. Even the best of us navigates life with imperfect tools. This point also turns out to be relevant, as we will see, to how gun violence happens.

GUN VIOLENCE IS HUMAN BEHAVIOR

Experts who study crime estimate that only something like 20 percent of gun violence is motivated by profit. These profit-motivated shootings are gang wars over drug turf, robberies, carjackings, murders, and the like, animated and premeditated for reasons of personal gain. Shootings based on these sorts of motives tend to dominate the news coverage.

But that's not what most shootings in America are. An estimated 80 percent seem to instead be crimes of passion—including rage. They're arguments that could be defused but aren't, then end in tragedy because someone has a gun. Most violent crimes are the result of human behavior gone temporarily haywire, not premeditated acts for financial benefit. In *The Better Angels of Our Nature*, Harvard psychologist Steven Pinker lamented the "dubious belief about violence . . . that lower-[social]-class people engage in it because they are financially needy (for example, stealing food to feed their children) or because they are expressing rage against society. The violence of a lower-class man may indeed express rage, but it is aimed not at society but at the asshole who scraped his car and dissed him in front of a crowd."[40] While the criminal-justice system may treat crimes of passion the same as crimes driven by profit, the two have very different underlying causes.

Who gets into arguments? You. Me. Everyone. Conflict is normal human behavior. And if you don't think you're susceptible to it, just think about the last time you were surprised by something that made you angry.

My family's dog, Aiko, is a seventy-pound mix of hound dog and German shepherd. She's built like a moose but acts like a lap-cat. Her favorite place in the house is wherever one of her humans is. Anyone who sits on the couch will find Aiko right next to them, either asleep with her snoot resting in their lap or lying on her back looking at them with her big brown eyes, showing her belly in a "you-know-what-to-do" sort of way. Aiko is a lover, not a fighter.

Every morning I take Aiko out for a walk around the University of Chicago campus. On Wednesdays I do that while having a weekly check-in call with the leadership team of my research center. One Wednesday I had leashed up Aiko, put in my AirPods and patched into my weekly work call. I was walking down the sidewalk when a neighbor's dog came barreling down their driveway, barking, snarling, and baring its teeth, then attacked Aiko.

What to do?

If I were operating with my rational System 2 thinking, I would have realized that I could have just put myself between the other dog and mine. Or I could have picked up Aiko and gotten her out of harm's way. Or I could have reminded myself that the worst-case scenario of my dog getting attacked would ultimately have amounted to just an unexpected visit to the vet.

Sadly, my rational System 2 self was nowhere to be found in that moment. I did none of these things.

Because System 2 is mentally taxing, we rely more on System 1 when our mental bandwidth is depleted. In their book *Scarcity*, MIT economist Sendhil Mullainathan and Princeton psychologist Eldar Shafir show that the extra stress and trauma found in some neighborhoods can deplete mental bandwidth, leading people to lean more heavily on System 1 in ways that often compromise their decision-making. I live in Hyde Park, a well-resourced neighborhood, so my day-to-day community environment doesn't *normally* deplete my mental bandwidth from trauma or stress. But in that moment, my bandwidth was depleted because I happened to be talking on the phone about something stressful for work.

While my rational self probably would have played it cool, my *actual* self took this scenario in a different direction. My System 1, as all of our System 1s tend to, gravitated toward the most negative possible interpretation of the situation (this dog owner's an irresponsible jerk who intentionally let this happen). That same System 1, in its haste to come up with quick responses, tends to engage in dichotomous, black-and-white thinking: It considers only two options in assessing the situation, "no big deal" versus "end of the world." This situation wasn't the former, so System 1 concluded it must be the latter, thereby making this negative event even more negative than it was (a process known as "catastrophizing"). System 1 decided that it—that *I*—was ready to risk it all because my dog got attacked by this other dog.

Here is a brief transcript of how I articulated those feelings to the owner of the other dog:

> JESUS CHRIST CONTROL YOUR FUCKING DOG MOTHERFUCKER. WHAT THE FUCKING HELL IS WRONG WITH YOU—THIS BETTER NOT EVER FUCKING HAPPEN AGAIN. THIS IS UN-FUCKING-ACCEPTABLE. KEEP YOUR FUCKING DOG ON A FUCKING LEASH.

If letting my dog be attacked is literally the end of the world, then by definition any other course of action would be less bad than that. So I didn't even bother to consider the consequences of other candidate actions, or the consequences of the course of action I wound up taking. Luckily for me, the leadership team of my research center was still on the phone with me, so they could hear every word—*including when my neighbor jumped on his bike to chase after Aiko and me, then confronted us again.*

Here is where everyone involved got lucky: Hyde Park is chock full of what journalist Jane Jacobs famously called "eyes on the street,"[41] people around who enforce a shared set of social norms. Being near the University of Chicago, round two of our disagreement occurred in an area patrolled by campus security guards. As we were screaming at one another, one of the guards drove by, stopped, and asked, "Everything OK?"

I jumped at the lifeline. I yelled to the security guard, "This guy jumped off his bike and got in my face!" The security guard stopped his car and picked up his radio to call the campus police. That led the neighbor to hop on his bike and ride off—giving me the double bird as he went.

Afterward, I worried there might be something wrong with me: Was I more of a hothead than I realized? Do I have some self-control problem? But then I told this my-dog-got-attacked story to a very distinguished, civically engaged rich guy here in Chicago. "Oh, that happened to me once," he said cheerfully. "I picked up the other dog and body-slammed it to the ground."

My neighbor and I here in Hyde Park were also lucky during this incident that neither of us had a gun. It's not that a gun *causes* altercations, but placing a gun into the middle of an argument greatly increases the chances someone winds up dead. That is, guns stored away in people's closets or basements aren't such a big problem; it's when they get carried out in public that leads to the biggest trouble. Gun carrying turns in-the-moment System 1 mistakes into tragedies.

The conventional wisdom that violence is caused by villains and hardship doesn't explain any of this insanity. Neither my neighbor nor I are psychopathic super-predators: We're both middle-aged dads who love our families. And I didn't yell at my neighbor, and he didn't yell at me, because of economic desperation. But just because conventional wisdom can't explain it doesn't mean it didn't happen: There I was, in a very real sense completely outside myself in that moment, acting increasingly stupid until the calm security guard stepped in and interrupted us.

Behavioral economics, in contrast, *can* explain all these actions. My System 1 misconstrued the situation and focused on the most negative possible interpretation; it then catastrophized in thinking through what to do and concluded that nothing was worse than having my dog attacked, and so by implication any course of action was justified. Meanwhile the neighbor's System 1 did the same thing, concluding there was nothing worse than being yelled at in front of his own house.

What saved me from my System 1's mistakes in that case is that I live in a neighborhood with lots of eyes on the street—other people around to step in and interrupt our argument. Behavioral economics explains why that's so important. If gun violence were really motivated by deliberate, conscious, premeditated, rational System 2 cognition, as conventional wisdom claims, that motivation would be *persistent*. So long as the powerful forces in the background are there (moral poverty, actual poverty), the motivation for violence is there. But in contrast, under the behavioral-economics perspective, the fleeting nature of System 1 motivations (including shooting someone when you're mad at them) can evaporate in the face of even just a bit more deliberation. Whether someone is around to step in and interrupt can be the difference between an argument and physical conflict. And, for that matter, the same logic implies that behavioral economics can explain why gun carrying is so important: Whether someone has a gun with them or not in the moment can be the difference between a fistfight and a life-altering tragedy.

To make this claim is not to equate a dog being attacked with the loss and trauma of gun violence. It is simply to illustrate: In situations where our brains are overwhelmed or surprised in stressful, novel situations, when the stakes are particularly high, when we need our rational selves the most, we often become versions of ourselves that are *not* perfectly rational. And when that happens, it's very often our surroundings that determine what happens next.

THE MYSTERY OF DORCHESTER AVENUE, EXPLAINED

Why is there so much more gun violence west of Dorchester Avenue than east of it?

Not because the people are so much different on one side of the street than the other, but rather because the complexity and stakes of the decision-making environment are.

Greater Grand Crossing and South Shore are sociodemographically similar today but have over their histories developed in ways that led to different built environments. Relative to Greater Grand Crossing, South Shore's location alongside Lake Michigan led it to develop more densely, with more people and businesses interspersed with one another. It's exactly this sort of mixed-use community that Jane Jacobs thought was conducive to social control—lots of neighbors walking to local stores, eyes on the street to interrupt conflict before it escalates. Sociologists call this phenomenon "collective efficacy." Criminologists call it "informal social control." Whatever you call it, the data shows there seems to be more of it in South Shore than Greater Grand Crossing.

Lack of social control within a neighborhood makes daily life unpredictable. That creates challenges for System 1, which is designed to deal with the routine and predictable.

Lack of social control can lead to counterproductive policy responses. For example, in Greater Grand Crossing there seems to be more zero-tolerance policing. That makes it harder for System 1 to get the sort of feedback it needs to learn how to navigate a given social environment, which we all learn how to do in part through trial and error.

Lack of social control and the extra stress and trauma it brings can deplete people of mental bandwidth.

And lack of social control also leads people to rely more on self-protection—including being more likely to carry a gun, as the data suggests seems to be the case in Greater Grand Crossing.

Under the behavioral-economics perspective, the other puzzling trends illustrated in the 69th and Calumet shooting make more sense as well. Why does gun violence vary so much with age? Because for most of us, as we get older, we get wiser. Why is there so much more gun violence at night versus the day, or during warmer periods, or on holidays and weekends compared to weekdays? Because at times like warm summer weekend nights there are relatively more social interactions among young people—more opportunities for conflict—and relatively fewer responsible adults (that is, eyes on the street) around who can step in if arguments escalate to violence.

HOW TO SOLVE A POLITICIZED PROBLEM

I realize how radical it is to claim that there is an *entirely new idea* that explains a major part of one of America's most pressing public health and public policy problems.* The notion that there might be a big new

---

*By "entirely new idea," I do not mean to imply that this is the first time gun violence has been linked to behavioral economics. All the ideas here can be deduced from first principles from Daniel Kahneman's *Thinking, Fast and Slow*. Aaron Beck links violence to ideas in psychology (derived from a clinical psychologist's perspective, rather than the theoretical perspective of the dual-systems model of cognition) in *Prisoners of Hate*. Steven Pinker's *The Better Angels of Our Nature* also includes many of these ideas interspersed within his explanation for the long-term decline in all sorts of violence over the course of human history. Rather, by "entirely new" I mean "previously almost

idea is especially radical in the case of gun violence, which (along with other criminal-justice topics like mass incarceration) stirs up strongly held feelings in many people. It's a topic divided by people's politics and opinions.

But amid the noise of these debates, important questions of *fact* are not being addressed. I believe this omission has contributed to our lack of progress.

The traditional understanding of gun violence can't account for why shootings happen more during certain times of year, at certain times of day, or among people of a certain age, or in some countries (or neighborhoods) than others. A scientific approach—a systematic, experiment-driven approach to proving or disproving an assumption—can explain these anomalies.

Imagine we relied on this shoot-from-the-hip approach in, say, medicine. We would have had people doing things during the global COVID-19 pandemic like taking ivermectin (used to prevent heartworm and other parasites in horses), drinking colloidal silver, or injecting bleach into their bloodstreams. The bulwark against that madness was our sixty-year-old scientific approach to drug testing and development—the requirement by the federal government's Food and Drug Administration (FDA) that any new drug or medical device be subject to a randomized controlled trial (RCT) to ensure its effectiveness before being sold to patients.[42] Before that, the drug companies themselves basically got to decide what constituted evidence of effectiveness. The perverse incentives of this less-scientific era are what gave rise to the term "snake oil."

RCTs are useful in medicine because they are one of the few ways to reliably establish cause and effect: Did a drug really produce improvements in a given health condition, or did the improvements occur

---

entirely absent from the policy and public conversation about gun violence." The contribution of this book is in some ways to try to make the connection between these different ideas and America's challenge with gun violence more clearly and directly than they have been made before, and also to present rigorous new empirical evidence in chapter 8 testing this explanation.

due to other factors? By randomly assigning patients to experimental groups (who get the new drug) and control groups (who get sugar pill placebos), RCTs create two groups that are, on average, comparable in every way *except* for receipt of the new drug. This experimental structure helps isolate the independent effects of the drug from the effects of all the other health determinants that normally vary out in the world.

RCTs remove the difficulties of subjectivity and motivated reasoning, one of the most powerful of all cognitive biases, from the study of a problem. The power of motivated reasoning was illustrated by one classic study that asked Dartmouth and Princeton students questions about the annual Dartmouth-Princeton football game like "How many fouls in the game were committed by Dartmouth players?" That is a factual question with an objective answer; we'd expect everyone to give the same answer. But after rewatching the game film, Princeton students counted over twice as many fouls by Dartmouth players as Dartmouth students did (9.8 versus 4.3), an "illustration of the old, established truth that when anybody with a preference watches [an event], he sees only what he prefers to see."[43] One Dartmouth alumnus heard about all the Dartmouth fouls from a Princeton friend; after getting a copy of the game film in the mail he wired his friend back: "Preview of Princeton movies indicates considerable cutting of important part please wire explanation and possibly air mail missing part."[44]

Unfortunately there is no FDA for public policy that forces government to test policies before they're implemented at large scale. That's one reason for all the unintended policy consequences we see over and over. Kansas cut taxes dramatically to spur economic growth and increase tax revenue, only to have to reverse course a few years later after slow growth and huge deficits. The federal government's Department of Housing and Urban Development eventually spent billions of dollars to tear down what it had a few decades before spent billions to construct: high-rise public housing, dreamed up originally by progressive housing reformers. China's one-child policy, designed to solve a demographic problem, may lead to economic calamity. The British tried to reduce deaths from venomous snakes in Delhi by offering a reward for each dead cobra someone turned in. That policy unintentionally incentivized the breeding of cobras, ultimately *increasing* the wild cobra population. Backfires like this one are so common there's a term for it: "Goodhart's law."[45] In a complicated world, good intentions alone aren't enough.

This unruliness in public policy's "marketplace of ideas," the inability of that marketplace to consistently weed out snake oil, is especially consequential with a problem like gun violence. That represents a missed opportunity since the RCT evidence on gun violence offers all kinds of valuable insights—including many that run counter to our inherited narratives about the problem.

For starters, we have RCTs of policies that try to strengthen social control in communities. These policies try to get more eyes on the street by cleaning up vacant lots, fixing up abandoned buildings, improving street lighting, opening more stores, or even hiring private unarmed security guards. Conventional wisdom predicts these policies shouldn't really matter much for gun violence; few of them have anything to do with increasing the chances (or severity) of punishment, and none of them is about ending big, structural root causes like poverty or segregation or social isolation. Yet these different aspects of social control are all still situational factors in their own right as well—they're just easier to change than things like poverty and segregation. While conventional wisdom claims these policies shouldn't matter, the RCTs show that each of these policies can help prevent violence from happening in the first place.

Of course one might be able to come up with some alternative explanations for why those policies reduce violence that are unrelated to the behavioral-economics perspective on gun violence. So it's noteworthy that we have data on a second type of policy as well: social programs where literally all they do is help people learn to be a little less System 1 and a little more System 2 during novel, high-stakes situations. They basically teach people to "self-interrupt" in fraught social interactions. The RCT evidence shows that these programs can lead to reductions in violent crimes, weapons offenses, and sometimes even robberies as well. And the *size* of these effects is noteworthy—sometimes just ten or fifteen hours in a program can reduce violence by as much as 50 percent.

In the sixteenth century, everyone thought the sun revolved around the earth. Copernicus pointed out the evidence didn't fit that explanation nearly as well as one in which the earth rotates around the sun. People eventually changed their minds. Similarly, many of the most important facts about gun violence fit better with the behavioral-economics explanation than they do with conventional wisdom. Maybe it's time to change our thinking about gun violence, too.

AN UNFORGIVING PLACE

One tragedy of America's misunderstood gun-violence problem is that the policies enacted over the past fifty years, often motivated by concerns about characterologically bad people, have too often made the problem worse. The US has built the world's largest prison system, which has hollowed out many communities of some of their greatest resources: adults who could help strengthen their communities by serving as eyes on the street. The frequent use of zero-tolerance policing has made it harder for people in impacted neighborhoods to get the sort of feedback that helps them learn the right response to different situations. Widespread gun ownership for protection against crime has made it easier for people to get illegal guns that they then carry in public to commit crimes, which increases the costs of System 1 mistakes. The cure has an effect of adding to the disease, especially for the most disadvantaged Americans.

We have, in other words, created far too many unforgiving places.

I don't mean "unforgiving" in the sense of what society does *after* a shooting happens (though one would be reasonable in saying as much). I mean unforgiving in the sense that normal human frailty—including the deficiencies of momentary misjudgments—can become starkly more consequential based on an individual's surroundings and circumstances.

Criminal behavior, even gun violence, is human behavior. Most violence stems from a remarkably common way human beings interact with one another: conflict. Most shootings start with words. When

System 1 unwittingly takes over, it can produce behavior that System 2 will later regret. Anyone can fall into these traps. What determines the outcome—what separates people in the US from becoming the victim or perpetrator of gun violence or not—is not necessarily (or merely) their morality or poverty, but whether their circumstances are forgiving or unforgiving. In America, the answer to that question winds up depending a great deal on someone's zip code.

The behavioral-economics perspective makes clear why moral appeals so often fail to reduce gun violence: Given the way the offender construes their situation in the moment, in their mind they are *already* doing the morally right thing. As the psychologist Aaron Beck put it, a common feature of most violence is that "the victim is perceived as the Enemy, and the aggressor sees himself as the innocent victim."[46] The sociologist Donald Black described moralistic violence, which seems to account for most violence, as a form of "self help. . . . From this standpoint, it is apparent that capital punishment is quite common in modern America . . . though it is nearly always a private rather than a public affair."[47]

The good news is that with the right understanding of the problem, gun violence turns out to look much more *preventable* than conventional thinking has allowed us to believe.

Steven Pinker has shown that over the long arc of human history—starting at least around 1200 CE, when records are available, through around 1900 CE—violence has become dramatically less common. He argues that this trend is due in part to the implicit training of System 1 via the growing sophistication of human society: the growing role of the state, the industrialized economy, and more formalized social interactions.[48]

The fact that this long-term progress on violence seems to have slowed down since 1900 suggests we might have reached the limits of relying on the inadvertent anti-violence effects of naturally occurring, gradual societal changes. There may be value in policies that more deliberately try to solve the challenges of System 1 in novel, high-stakes, difficult situations.

To the pessimist, these ideas might be dismissed as a kind of magical thinking: Achieving large-scale change of this kind simply doesn't happen. But here, the recent histories of America's two largest cities, New York and Los Angeles, provide proof to the contrary. While neither place has *explicitly* adopted behavioral economics as the guiding principle behind its policies, the key ideas of behavioral economics are reflected in the emphasis on violence prevention and interruption, and on policies to teach people to self-interrupt. There are RCTs and natural experiments showing the efficacy of many of the individual component parts of their policy responses. But the cumulative aggregate effect is what's particularly impressive: results so dramatic no one imagined they were remotely possible before they happened. From 1991 to 2019 (the last pre-pandemic year), murder rates didn't just decline, they plummeted. Los Angeles's murder rates fell by nearly 80 percent; New York's fell by nearly 90 percent.

The benefits of dramatic declines in gun violence are greatest for the most economically disadvantaged communities of color in these cities, the places most disproportionally affected by gun violence. The decline in shootings then becomes an important tailwind for the economic development of disadvantaged areas, which in turn delivers downstream improvements in most every phase of life and economy.

WHAT THIS BOOK SHOWS

This book examines the scientific evidence for what drives gun violence in the United States. As with any problem of human behavior, the problems themselves and their determinants are complicated. And indeed, it's exactly those complications that have contributed over the last century to our fundamental misunderstanding of the problem.

It's also why the tools of data science and behavioral economics are so important. Using the powerful methods and insights they provide, gun violence can be broken down in a way that our usual form of storytelling doesn't. When we do that, we see a problem to be solved, not simply a crisis to be tolerated.

In chapter 2, I discuss why focusing on gun control alone is unlikely to solve America's problem with gun violence. If gun violence = guns + violence, given the difficulty the country has had (and will continue to have) figuring out what to do about guns, there would be tremendous benefit from figuring out how to solve the violence part of the equation.

In chapter 3, I consider the common right-of-center explanation for violent behavior: characterologically bad people unafraid of the criminal-justice system. This hypothesis might not have been unreasonable in the 1970s when it began to dominate public conversation, given what was known at the time. But we've learned a lot since then, and what we've learned shows us how deeply incomplete this explanation is.

The main alternative explanation for gun violence has been root causes—poverty, inequality, discrimination, segregation, social isolation—as I discuss in chapter 4. Most of these root causes have proven very difficult to solve in practice. The idea that gun violence can only be solved by solving every other problem first can leave people feeling that gun violence is a problem too big to fix.

One way to see why conventional wisdom is so limited as an explanation for gun violence is because most shootings are different from what conventional wisdom assumes they are, as I show in chapter 5. The data suggest that most shootings are not carried out by psychopaths in some killing spree, nor are they motivated by economic considerations. Most stem from arguments.

Chapter 6 argues that a lot of gun violence happens because people are acting quickly and viscerally. The canonical economic model of crime by University of Chicago Nobel laureate Gary Becker assumes that people's behavior, including violent behavior, stems from rational benefit-cost calculation. The insights of another University of Chicago Nobel laureate, Richard Thaler, note that people *don't* always act this way—they don't always optimize perfectly, they can rely on biased beliefs, and they can respond to seemingly irrelevant factors.[49] That is, a key insight of behavioral economics is that people's mistakes have predictable structure, which helps better explain how and why people behave as they do. It's not that Becker's view is wrong; it's that it's incomplete. One might say incentives + predictable mistakes = behavioral economics.

I focus here on one specific framework that is particularly useful for understanding the predictable mistakes that drive gun violence: the notion of the automatic, intuitive System 1 and the deliberate System 2. Particularly important for my argument is System 1.* System 1's automatic responses have developed exactly because they can work so well for routine, low-stakes situations we see all the time; as Daniel Kahneman notes, "The automatic operations of System 1 generate surprisingly complex patterns of ideas."† But even System 1 responses that normally work well don't always. And, unfortunately, System 2 might be caught napping in those very moments when it is most needed to catch and correct System 1's responses in high-stakes, nonroutine situations—like fraught moments of potential or actual conflict.

Chapter 7 explains why neighborhoods like Greater Grand Crossing and South Shore can vary so much in the difficulty of the situations people are forced to navigate. Due in part to our past policy decisions, some neighborhoods have less informal social control—fewer prosocial adults around ("eyes on the street") willing to step in and intervene when System 1 makes mistakes and conflict arises. Moreover, behavioral economics explains why System 1 mistakes are more likely in the first place in neighborhoods with less social control: they're more unpredictable rather than routine; they're more stressful (and so deplete people's mental bandwidth, which makes it even more likely that System 2 is napping when needed most); they engender policy responses like zero-tolerance policing that make feedback hard to get;

---

* For expositional purposes, I sometimes use System 2 as a stand-in for Beckerian rational benefit-cost calculation, even though these are not entirely synonymous, since System 2 can itself make mistakes. That is, System 2 cognition is a necessary but not sufficient condition for perfectly rational, Beckerian benefit-cost-calculating behavior.

† Kahneman, *Thinking, Fast and Slow*, 20. To emphasize the point that there *is* some logic to these adaptive System 1 responses (i.e., they usually develop for a reason), for expositional purposes I sometimes describe these System 1 responses as if they have reasoned out the right way to navigate a situation, rather than developed via the automatic learning of if-then rules through trial and error and feedback. This is intended to be something like the behavioral economics analog to Milton Friedman's proverbial pool player, whose behavior can be predicted as if they are relying on the laws of physics—even those players who can't spell "physics."

and they prompt private responses like public gun carrying that make System 1 mistakes more likely to end in tragedy.

Chapter 8 presents empirical support for the behavioral-economics view. This is not a "just-so" story about gun violence that can't be empirically tested or falsified. I show that a series of RCTs and "natural-experiment" tests of policies that behavioral economics predicts should reduce violence, but conventional wisdom implies should not, suggest that such policies do indeed reduce violence.

Chapter 9 notes that behavioral economics helps explain not only interpersonal gun violence but gun suicide and even police shootings as well. The behavioral-economics perspective suggests not only a new set of policies to try in reducing gun violence but ways to make the policies of conventional wisdom more effective (and humane). These policies have the potential to fix a wide variety of other problems in our cities, given the powerful adverse effects of gun violence in contributing to a community's economic and social disadvantage, and conversely given the powerful *beneficial* effects of public safety in contributing to community development.

For fifty years we've thought of gun violence as a problem of rational benefit-cost calculation by characterologically bad people undeterred by the criminal-justice system, or by people made economically desperate because of a bad economy. But behavioral economics teaches us that gun violence is at least as much about bad in-the-moment decisions made in extraordinarily difficult situations. It is not merely a problem of System 2, but at least as much of System 1.

A few years ago, I was talking to one of the supervisors at the Cook County Juvenile Temporary Detention Center. This center is where the local juvenile justice system holds young people deemed to be at the highest possible risk, drawn mostly from some of the most distressed, under-resourced neighborhoods of Chicago's South and West sides. As the supervisor conceded, some of the kids in the facility were genuinely dangerous: "If you let them out, they'll go on to hurt other people." But for the other 80 percent, the supervisor has a saying he repeats often: "If I could give you back just 10 minutes of your lives, none of you would be here."[50]

2

THE LIMITS OF
GUN CONTROL

A few years ago, I was visiting my parents in New Jersey during the University of Chicago's spring break. On the Thursday of spring break, I received an email from the Home Office of the UK (the ministry in charge of British law and order). The email asked if I could be in London for a meeting at 10 Downing Street on Monday, as in Monday in four days. They were seeking experts to attend an urgent meeting, to be hosted by the prime minister herself, about how to deal with the UK's growing crisis around . . . knife violence.

I said yes—I mean, of course—but I was also *sure* the meeting would be canceled. This was in the middle of some of the most intense negotiations between the UK and the European Union around Brexit; that Monday specifically was even some sort of key interim Brexit deadline for something or other. I was sure the prime minister would have more important things to do. So I booked a fully refundable plane ticket, then sat around playing Yahtzee with my family waiting for the cancelation to come. It never came. So off I went.

I remember there was a little security hut at the entrance to Downing Street off Whitehall. After screening they just turned me loose. I asked the guard where to go. He said, "Number 10, sir."

I had expected this trip to be like the one time I had gone to the White House for a meeting. That one was held in an airplane-hangar-sized space, with a million presenters each getting two minutes to speak. But walking into Number 10 was more like walking into someone's house. I left my phone in a little wooden cubby by the front door and went up to the second floor in search of the million other speakers scheduled to be on the program as well. I saw the Home Office guy there who invited me. I asked, "Where are all the other presenters?" He pointed and said, "He [singular] is over there."

They shuffled us into a meeting room that was *not* a giant airplane hangar; it was a small room, remarkably small, almost like someone's dining room. As one of the only two outside presenters on the schedule, the room was in fact starting to feel uncomfortably small. The guy next to me was from Birmingham. I'm not very good at small talk so I said the first thing that came to mind: "I love *Peaky Blinders*." In a polite British sort of way he said, "Me too."

The prime minister stayed for the whole meeting, well over an hour. She spent the entire time asking good questions. She took careful notes, longhand, on a yellow legal pad. One of the concerns raised by her staff was whether people with violent intent who are trying to avoid getting caught by the police with a knife might resort to using bicycle spokes instead.

The meeting was interesting, of course, but what struck me most about that trip was actually the cab ride from Heathrow to my hotel on the Sunday night beforehand. The driver was beside himself listening to BBC radio: That weekend in London *four people* had been stabbed.[1] He said "How could this happen in *London*? What are things *coming* to?" I didn't know what to say. Over Labor Day weekend in Chicago, a city just one-third London's size, fully fifty-five people were shot.[2] And that wasn't even our most violent weekend of the summer.[3]

This is all to say, America's level of serious violence, most of which is committed with guns, would be truly intolerable in any other rich country in the world. Yet to everyone here in America, it has come to seem normal—inevitable even. We live under a Second Amendment ("A well regulated Militia, being necessary to the security of a free State, the right of the people to keep and bear Arms, shall not be infringed") that the US Supreme Court has recently interpreted as a constitutional

right for individual Americans to own guns. One of the most powerful lobbying groups in Washington is the National Rifle Association
(NRA), founded in 1871 by two Union generals frustrated about the
poor marksmanship of soldiers in the Civil War.[4] Most Americans
alive today only know what it's like to live in a country with more guns
than people.

The contrast between the UK and US suggests something that the
data confirms: Guns and gun laws matter for gun violence. But guns
aren't *all* that matters. Canada and Switzerland, like the US, have an
above-average number of guns, but they don't have much violent crime
overall (assaults, robberies, etc.), so they have relatively few murders.
The UK has a large amount of violent crime overall but not many guns,
so it also doesn't have many murders. The unique problem in the US,
then, is that we have lots of guns *and* lots of violent crime. That combination is what leads to so many devastated families and communities; that is, gun violence = guns + violence. Both components of the
equation matter. But controlling the flow of guns is not as simple as
we like to think.

TWO SHORT, VERY DIFFERENT HISTORIES OF GUN CONTROL

Gun control is about regulating who can own a gun, the conditions under which they can buy one, what type of gun (and ammunition) they
can own, and where and when they're able to carry or use their guns in
different ways.

The UK entered the twentieth century with almost no gun laws on
the books. The UK exited the twentieth century with some of the strictest gun control in the world.[5]

In 1902, at the end of the Boer War, given the "callousness towards
life [the war] engendered," government officials under Conservative
PM Arthur Balfour were concerned about veterans returning home
with their weapons.[6] The result was the 1903 Pistols Act, which prohibited pistol purchases by the underage or "drunken or insane."
Everyone else had to get a license, issued through the post office to

anyone who could pay the ten-shilling fee (about eight pounds in to-day's currency). Those selling guns had to record the date of sale, the name and address of the buyer, and the post office issuing the license.[7] While the law has sometimes been referred to as "toothless" in hind-sight, it was a first step toward creating a licensing system for gun own-ers in the UK. A licensing system for owners, together with a regis-tration system for guns, is what allows the government to keep track of who owns what gun. Without that, it's enormously difficult for the government to regulate what Duke professor Philip Cook terms the "secondary gun market"—the informal market in which used guns change private hands.[8]

In 1918, at the end of World War I, the government under then-PM David Lloyd George was again concerned about the return to Britain of traumatized, armed veterans—now not by the thousands, but rather by the millions.[9] Alongside that worry was concern about what was hap-pening in Ireland ("a state of virtual civil war") and about the founding of the British Communist Party on the heels of the Russian Revolution a few years before.[10] The result was the Firearms Act of 1920, which made the country's gun-owner licensing system much stricter. People who wanted a gun now had to provide a "good reason" to get a firearm certificate from the government, which would be issued at the discre-tion of local police (a later modification in 1937 ruled out self-defense as an allowable reason).[11] Each certificate lasted for three years and specified what gun the holder could have and even how much ammu-nition.[12] The 1920 bill passed by a vote of 254 to 6.[13]

In 1968, under then-Labour PM Harold Wilson, the Firearms Act added a version of an owner's certificate requirement for shotgun own-ers as well. The Act also required guns and ammunition to be stored locked up, which not only keeps guns out of the hands of curious children and despondent family members but also helps prevent gun thefts. The Act also banned people with certain types of criminal re-cords from having guns.

In 1987, a 27-year-old former paratrooper named Michael Ryan went on an eight-hour shooting rampage in Hungerford, a town of eight thousand located about an hour and a half southwest of Lon-

don.[14] He used a handgun and two semiautomatic rifles, legally obtained. Ryan would ultimately wound fifteen people and kill sixteen,
including his mother and himself. A year later, Conservative PM Mar-
garet Thatcher—the so-called Iron Lady who had launched a rightward
political revolution in the UK so sweeping that, in the words of one
historian, she "took one sort of society, and turned it into another"[15]—
helped enact a new set of restrictive UK gun laws that effectively
banned most semiautomatic rifles and pump-action rifles.[16]

In 1996, a 43-year-old named Thomas Hamilton entered Dunblane
Primary School in Scotland with two 9-millimeter semiautomatic
handguns, two Smith and Wesson revolvers, and 743 rounds of ammunition. He killed sixteen students and their teacher before killing
himself. His guns had been legally obtained. The next year, under the
centrist "New Labour" PM Tony Blair, the UK essentially banned
handguns,[17] with a vote in the House of Commons of 384 to 181.[18]
One MP voting in favor told the press: "We are criticized for bringing
an emotional element to the gun debate, but it's the emotional element
which makes us different from other species."[19]

The accumulated result: Handguns (concealable and hence well-
suited for crime) are banned in the UK. So are the deadliest firearms:
large-caliber semiautomatic rifles. Gun owners must have a license[20]
that requires providing a justification (of which self-defense is not an
acceptable one), an interview with the police, approval from the family
doctor, and two separate written character references.[21] Violations can
bring a mandatory five-year prison term. England plus Wales, which
together have around sixty million people, have something like two
million guns.[22]

By contrast, America's gun laws over the twentieth century took
something of a different trajectory.

The concern in America in the early 1900s wasn't armed veter-
ans but rather organized crime. When four members of Al Capone's
South Side Chicago gang shot seven people in cold blood in a Lincoln
Park garage in 1929, gruesome pictures of the Saint Valentine's Day
Massacre were splashed across the front pages of newspapers across
the country. In 1933 John Dillinger's string of bank robberies and jail

escapes became national news.[23] Criminals were increasingly turning their machine guns against the police.[24] In 1933 even the new president, Franklin Delano Roosevelt, couldn't escape the gun violence of the time. In Miami an unemployed bricklayer, Giuseppe Zangara, fired five shots at FDR. Roosevelt survived, but Chicago mayor Anton Cermak wasn't so lucky.[25]

This concern about organized crime led to the National Firearms Act of 1934, which imposed a tax on machine guns and sawed-off shotguns equal to $3,800 in today's dollars. That amount was about 1.5 months' wages for the average worker at the time.[26] One observer called it a "ban disguised as a tax."[27]

But FDR's attorney general, Homer Cummings, had been pushing for more, including a national registration system for handguns: "Show me the man who does not want his gun registered and I will show you a man who should not have a gun."[28] Public-opinion surveys found that a large majority of Americans agreed with Cummings: 79 percent were in favor of a handgun registration system.[29] But there was opposition from the NRA, so handgun registration got dropped. FDR's assistant attorney general, Joseph Keenan, bitterly referred to the exclusion of handguns as "a joke." FDR lost this fight even with congressional majorities almost unheard of in modern times: 313–117 in the House and 59–36 in the Senate.[30]

A few years later, FDR signed the Federal Firearms Act of 1938, which tried to create a two-tier system in which some people (like those convicted of certain felonies) are banned from having guns while everyone else has easy access. The law also required people "in the business" of selling guns to get a federal firearm license.

But here again the initial goal had been more sweeping: to allow the prosecution of manufacturers and distributors who provided guns to prohibited people. Yet political maneuvering led the final law to include scaled-back language: Businesses would only be penalized if they could be proven of "knowing or having reasonable cause to believe" the buyer was ineligible. Since businesses by law weren't required to do anything to actively find out about the buyer's eligibility, as Assistant Attorney

General Keenan pointed out, it would be nearly impossible to prove that a gun dealer acted in violation of the law.[31]

These 1930s federal laws set a floor on gun regulation, not a ceiling. Cities and states were free to enact stricter gun laws if they wanted. But state and local laws were often undermined by how easily guns can be moved across America's open city and state borders in the unregulated secondary market.

That problem became particularly salient in 1963 when the rifle that Lee Harvey Oswald bought through the mail became the focus of national conversation. Eventually, in 1968, President Lyndon Johnson signed the Omnibus Crime Control and Safe Streets Act and the Gun Control Act, which together banned licensed dealers from selling handguns to people who lived in a different state, raised the minimum age for buying a handgun to 21, banned the importation of small, cheap handguns ("Saturday night specials"), and banned guns for convicted felons and people with a history of drug use or mental health problems.[32]

While the Gun Control Act was debated just after the shootings of civil rights leader Martin Luther King Jr. and presidential candidate Robert F. Kennedy, at a time when violent crime was surging nationwide, President Johnson still couldn't get what he was really after: a system of gun registration and gun-owner licensing. At the bill signing he lamented: "This bill—as big as this bill is—still falls short, because we just could not get the Congress to carry out the requests we made of them. . . . The voices that blocked these safeguards were not the voices of an aroused nation. They were the voices of a powerful lobby, a gun lobby, that has prevailed for the moment in an election year." The secondary gun market was again left unregulated.

As one historian's review of these two waves of legislation dryly put it, the gun laws of the 1930s and 1960s "did not put significant restrictions on civilian gun ownership."[33]

In 1981, President Reagan was leaving the Washington Hilton Hotel when John Hinckley fired six shots using a revolver he had bought for $47 from Rocky's Pawn Shop in Dallas, Texas.[34] Reagan was nearly killed by a bullet that ricocheted off the presidential limousine and struck him in the chest; Reagan's press secretary, James Brady, was struck in the right side of the head and left permanently disabled with a brain injury.

In response, in 1986 Reagan did finally sign a national gun law. But the Firearms Owners Protection Act did *not* make it *harder* for people like Hinckley to get a gun. Instead, the Act banned any sort of national registration system for either guns or gun owners.

In 1991, Reagan, by then out of office, had something of a conversion experience on gun control. The president who had been described as the "first true conservative US President in over 50 years"[35] came out in support of the so-called Brady Bill, which required dealers to carry out background checks of gun buyers to verify their histories of prior crimes, drug use, and mental illness and to impose a waiting period of a few days before allowing any customer to buy a handgun. Reagan encouraged his former vice president and successor in the Oval Office, George H. W. Bush, to support it, too.[36] Reagan even wrote an op-ed for the *New York Times* entitled "Why I'm for the Brady Bill."[37] One NRA official at the time told a reporter, while looking at a photo of Reagan on his desk, "Don't do this to me."[38] The NRA official need not have worried; the first President Bush did not push the bill.

In 1993, twelve years after Reagan was shot, President Clinton finally signed the Brady Act. At the time, a crack-cocaine epidemic was sweeping through cities all across the country, contributing to a rate of murders—most of them committed with guns—that were as high as had ever been seen in the twentieth century.[39] Yet the Brady Act, like previous federal laws, only applied to sales by *licensed* gun dealers and left the secondary gun market unregulated. Despite the law's limits, Richard Aborn, president of the Brady gun control organization at the time, noted that "the Brady Bill became one of the most contested issues in the country, dividing gun control supporters and opponents with a vehemence generally reserved for the most contentious social issues."[40]

The next year, in 1994, Clinton signed the "assault weapons ban" as part of the Violent Crime Control and Law Enforcement Act. Pressure for the ban came partly from California Senator Dianne Feinstein after the 1989 shooting in Stockton, California, of a teacher and thirty-four children. One part of the law banned magazines (the storage device that feeds ammunition into a semiautomatic firearm) holding over ten rounds. The law did *not* ban semiautomatic rifles, as in the UK, but instead banned only some specific models of semiautomatic rifles chosen largely based on their military-type styling. Countless functionally equivalent rifles were left on the market. This law was a little like trying to improve traffic safety by banning cars with flames painted on the side. The assault weapons ban was written to sunset in ten years. Senator Feinstein, noting the compromises needed to get the bill through the US Senate, lamented: "I was amazed to see the degree to which the National Rifle Association controls this body."[41]

In 2022, President Biden signed the Bipartisan Safer Communities Act, which provided funding for some anti-violence efforts (school safety, violence interruption organizations, mental health) and added some penalties for people who traffic guns. But this law, like its predecessors, left the secondary market untouched and wasn't able to reinstate the ban on high-capacity magazines. Biden, at the signing ceremony, noted that "this bill doesn't do everything I want . . . I know there's much more work to do."[42]

The result is a country of 330 million people that owns something like 400 million guns, or over one gun per person (compared to one gun per thirty people in England and Wales).[43] America, home to just 4 percent of the world's population, has nearly 50 percent of all civilian-owned firearms.[44]

DO GUNS PRODUCE CRIME?

The debate about gun control starts with a basic question: Do more guns lead to more crime or less crime?

As a conceptual matter the answer isn't obvious; there are logically plausible reasons to think that either outcome is possible, or even that the number of guns is irrelevant to the crime problem. It's tempting to

answer the question through the lens of your own personal politics—
to view it as an ideological question. Plenty of people have done that.
But more useful is to answer this factual question with facts—that is,
data. That answer turns out to be: More guns don't change the number
of crimes overall, but they do make crime more deadly.

The view that the number of guns in America is irrelevant to the
crime problem is captured by the old bumper sticker: "Guns don't
kill people, people kill people." The basic idea is that someone who is
hell-bent on killing someone else will do whatever it takes to make that
happen; they'll persist and persist until the person is dead, regardless
of what sort of weapon is around.

This idea wasn't just an NRA slogan; it's also what leading scholars
of the time thought. That group of leading scholars included Marvin
Wolfgang of the University of Pennsylvania, who served as the research
director of President Lyndon Johnson's Presidential Commission
on the Causes and Prevention of Violence and was the person once
called the "most influential criminologist in the English-speaking
world."[45]

But over time, as more and better data became available, criminologists figured out that a key premise of the gun-irrelevance hypothesis
was wrong: Most people who attempt murder *don't* seem to have a sustained intention to kill the other person. The intent to harm seems to
be more fleeting. That means the lethality of the weapon the person has
ready at hand in that moment matters a lot for whether someone winds
up dead or not. The combination of lethality and effortlessness of guns
versus other weapons like knives and baseball bats makes crime more
deadly.[46] The best summary of what's now called the "weapon instru-
mentality effect" came from Ozzy Osbourne, of all people, in a *New
York Times* interview: "I keep hearing this [expletive] thing that guns
don't kill people, but people kill people. If that's the case, why do we
give people guns when they go to war? Why not just send the people?"[47]

This is why everyone's so worried about guns: They're dangerous.
And this is why so many people are worried about *handguns* in particular: They're not only dangerous, they're also compact enough to carry
around in public where lots of other people are.

But the same deadliness and portability that make handguns useful for crime also make them useful for self-defense. While the number of times guns are used for self-defense every year is hard to measure,[48] even the *threat* of coming across an armed victim might, as a logical matter, dissuade some people from committing crimes—a form of deterrence. This desire for self-protection is what the data show is an increasingly common motivation for owning a gun. Decades ago most people had guns for hunting or sport; now it's much more for self-defense.[49] I saw signs of that shift at a gun show I visited a few years ago downstate in Kankakee, Illinois. The tables were littered with bumper stickers like: "Nothing stops a bad guy with a gun like a good guy with a gun," "Response times—*911 call*: 27 minutes; *AR-15* [a model of assault rifle]: 3,251 feet per second," and "I carry a gun because a cop is too heavy."

Since guns can have both negative effects (increasing the lethality of crime) and positive effects (self-defense and deterrence), how do we figure out which effect on net dominates?

This is the sort of question in the criminal-justice space that so many of us wind up answering based on our politics—we tend to "cheer for our team" and naturally gravitate toward the evidence that supports our side (so-called motivated reasoning, as with the Dartmouth-Princeton football game study mentioned in chapter 1). Public policy motivated by ideology and motivated reasoning often leads to unintended consequences that undermine collective goals. In a world in which policies can have unintended effects, we usually get better policy outcomes settling questions of fact by looking at facts.

On the relationship between guns and crime, economist John Lott wrote a book whose argument is hinted at by the book's title, *More Guns, Less Crime*. Published to some fanfare in 1998, Lott's book compared crime rates at a given point in time across different US counties with very different rates of gun ownership; he found that the counties that had higher rates of gun ownership tended to have lower rates of crime.[50]

But the challenge of comparing counties to one another like this is that they're different in all sorts of ways that might be relevant for crime rates, that go beyond differences in gun-ownership rates. Think of all the differences between a county located in the Mississippi Delta from a county along the California coast or in the mountains of Colorado or the swamps of Florida or the big cities of the Rust Belt. Lott's comparisons likely confound the effect of different gun-ownership levels with all the other ways in which these counties differ from one another in ways that are also relevant for crime.

My frequent collaborator Philip Cook and I weren't sure we believed Lott's answer,[51] so we looked at the question again and tried to answer it in a different way: We took advantage of a "natural experiment" that arises from the fact that gun-ownership rates in different regions of the country seem to be converging over time.[52] From 1980 to 1999, gun ownership declined by 20 percent in the biggest Southern counties but increased by 20 percent in the biggest Northeastern and Midwestern counties. There are lots and lots of reasons why Jackson County, Mississippi, had different crime rates in 1980 from Cook County, Illinois, most of which can't be directly measured in a dataset. But a lot of those crime determinants don't change much over time; they're present in 1980 *and* they're present in 1999, too. So comparing *changes* in both gun ownership and crime within counties over time from 1980 to 1999 implicitly nets out the effects of any unmeasured county-specific features that are stable over time. This "difference-in-differences" approach helps better isolate the effects of only the factors that change over time differentially across counties—like gun-ownership rates.

So what did the data show happened to crime as gun-ownership rates converged across regions? Trends for most crimes didn't show any detectable difference across regions; that's consistent with the idea that more guns on net don't affect crime rates overall. But there was one important exception: murders. We found that as gun ownership converged across regions, murder rates converged as well. That's consistent with the "More guns means more violent crimes turn lethal" hypothesis. The implication is that the harmful effects guns have in making crimes more deadly seems to outweigh whatever benefits guns create in terms of self-defense and deterrence.

So if gun laws *could* limit the number of guns available to people who are at risk of misusing them, there would be fewer murders. Can gun control actually do that?

THE LIMITED EFFECTS OF REAL-WORLD GUN LAWS

While the history of US gun legislation includes a few success stories, the evidence on the effects of gun laws in America, taken as a whole, is sobering in its lack of major impact. This doesn't mean gun control is intrinsically futile. Instead, it's more likely about the important limitations of the laws that wind up getting passed here in the US.

One of the most successful federal gun laws was the 1934 National Firearm Act, which, as noted above, basically banned sawed-off shotguns and machine guns. For a long time after 1934 the use of machine guns in crime in the US was quite rare.[53]

But that's changed in recent years with the introduction of a piece of metal or plastic (a so-called Glock switch) that turns any semiautomatic firearm, which normally fires just once every time the trigger is pulled, into a fully automatic firearm that fires continually, and so allows the gun to be fired at a much faster—and hence more deadly—rate. In practice basically anyone in modern-day America with $50 and an Internet connection can now undo FDR's signature gun law. And in fact we're seeing Glock switches being used more and more often on the streets of Chicago, resulting in a surge in gun-violence fatality rates.[54]

The 1968 Gun Control Act (GCA) among other key things sought to reduce across-state gun sales; unfortunately, there is little evidence it accomplished that goal. If the law did what it was supposed to do, we would have expected to see a relatively larger decline in gun crimes in places where a relatively larger share of crime guns were coming from out of state (since it's that supply of out-of-state guns that the GCA is trying to limit). But we don't see any signs of that pattern in the data.[55]

The Brady Act of 1994 tried to keep guns out of the hands of prohibited people by imposing a waiting period on handgun sales by dealers and requiring dealers to verify that a potential buyer was actually eligible to have a gun. The fact that some states already had their own state-level Brady-like laws in place (and so weren't really affected by enactment of the federal Brady Act) created a sort of "natural experiment":[56] Did gun violence decline more in the affected states (where dealers had to change what they did after Brady) than in the unaffected states? Philip Cook and I found no detectable effect of the Brady Act on gun homicides.

Here again, John Lott got a different answer from the study Cook and I carried out. In *More Guns, Less Crime* Lott claimed that the Brady Act *increased* gun crimes. Why the different results? Lott was looking at gun crimes involving people of *all* ages, including juveniles. This approach failed to account for the fact that trends in gun crimes involving juveniles were already following very different paths (in the Brady-affected states compared to the Brady-unaffected states) even *before* Brady was implemented. Lott's study, in other words, confounded the effects of the Brady legislation with whatever other factors were already causing juvenile crime to trend differently between Brady and non-Brady states. Cook and I, in contrast, found that adult crime rates trended very similarly in Brady and non-Brady states *before* the Brady Act went into effect. So our study focused just on adult crime. Looking at whether trends in *adult* crime between Brady and non-Brady states diverge *after* Brady went into effect told us something about whether the Brady Act itself had any independent, direct effect on gun murders. (It did not.)

The 1994 Crime Bill included a ban on so-called assault weapons,[57] which in practice involved banning selected models of semiautomatic firearms based largely on features that were arguably more stylistic than functional. That is, the ban left lots of functionally similar semiautomatic weapons still on the market. It's not clear that it had much effect on gun crime.[58]

More helpful might have been the ban on high-capacity magazines for semiautomatic weapons, defined as those that hold more than ten rounds (meaning the gun owner would then have to reload after firing ten rounds). Studies of state laws that implemented such bans suggest they help reduce mass shooting deaths by 11–15 percent.[59] That's obviously helpful—that's lives saved. But at the same time, it's also far from a panacea. Since "only" about 10 percent of all murder victims are killed in multiple-victim homicides, high-capacity magazine bans might be expected to reduce gun murders by not more than (10 percent x 15 percent) = 1.5 percent.

The same issue applies to state laws that ban gun ownership for people with a restraining order against them for domestic violence; those restrictions seem to reduce intimate partner homicides by 7 percent.[60] The data suggest that something like around one in five of all murders are intimate partner homicides.[61] So these laws would be expected to reduce total homicides in a state overall by (7 percent x 20 percent) = 1.4 percent.

The impacts of even the strictest possible state and local laws also seem to have been somewhat underwhelming. For example, in 1976 Washington, DC, banned handguns. A widely cited study in the *New England Journal of Medicine* reported that gun homicides and gun suicides both declined by about one-quarter after the handgun ban went into effect.[62] The problem with this interpretation, however, is that gun murders also declined by nearly as much at the same time in nearby Baltimore, which did not ban handguns—which makes it hard to attribute DC's changes in gun violence to DC's handgun ban.[63]

Let me be clear about what I *am* saying and what I am *not* saying. I'm not saying there's no point in passing gun laws. The most successful of these laws do seem to save lives. What I am saying is that, given the modest size of the impacts we see from the sort of fairly modest laws that have been enacted in the US over the past fifty-plus years,[64] getting more of *those* types of gun laws is very unlikely *by itself* to solve the problem of gun violence in America.

THE PROBLEM OF THE SECONDARY GUN MARKET

How do we reconcile the fact that more guns seem to lead to more murders, yet most gun laws in the US seem to have had modest (at best) effects? To me the most plausible answer is that most gun laws don't touch the so-called *secondary market* for guns[65]—sales that don't involve a licensed gun dealer and so are effectively unregulated under federal law.

If you want a gun, going to a licensed federal firearms dealer requires going through a background check. If you are underage or have a disqualifying criminal record or history of mental illness, the dealer will find out and is then supposed to not sell you a gun. Plus, you have to fill out some official paperwork that stays with the dealer and lists you as the buyer of record. That way, if your gun one day in the future winds up at a crime scene, the government can figure out you're the one who originally bought it. They can then show up at your door to ask questions.

Now imagine you wanted to avoid anyone knowing you bought a gun. All you'd have to do is go to a garage sale, or to Facebook, or to a gun show, or find literally anyone who's selling guns but is not technically "in the business" of selling guns as their key source of income (and so is exempt from federal background-check and paperwork requirements). From them you just buy the gun. No questions asked, no background check, no paperwork. The only relevant federal regulation is that the other person can't *knowingly* sell a gun to an ineligible person. But they also don't have to check. So long as you're not wearing a "Rikers Island Alumni" hat to the sale, you're good. As John Feinblatt, president of Everytown for Gun Safety, put it: "Imagine if the TSA had two lines for security—one where you are screened and one where you aren't."[66]

No wonder most crime guns in the US come from the secondary gun market. Lots of people are choosing the "aren't screened" line.

State and local laws have tried to shut down the secondary market in different ways, ranging from licensing and registration systems to outright bans. But those efforts get undermined by the secondary markets in nearby states and townships with looser gun laws.

For example, just look at where the crime guns in Chicago come from: not Chicago. Almost all of them come from places with relatively looser gun laws, either the Chicago suburbs or other states. The top source is Chuck's Gun Shop in Riverdale, Illinois, twenty-three minutes from Hyde Park. The second most common source is Midwest

Sporting Goods in Lyons, Illinois, near the Brookfield Zoo where I take my kids all the time. Together those two stores alone sell 11 percent of all crime guns in Chicago.

The third most common source of Chicago crime guns is Westforth Sports in Gary, Indiana, so close to Chicago, I took my daughter there to get her COVID vaccine. The fourth most common is Cabela's in Hammond, Indiana, so close to Hyde Park that my family drives down there all the time in the summer to get soft serve from our favorite ice cream place, Dairy Belle.[67]

Cities like DC and Chicago are, in other words, islands of restrictive gun laws surrounded by an ocean of four hundred million guns.

If the US *could* somehow adopt some consistent nationwide regulation of the secondary gun market, there's a real chance it could do some good (recognizing that we've never tried that approach, so we don't have any direct data to confirm this hypothesis).

A disproportionate share of America's four hundred million guns are in the closets, nightstands, and basements of people statistically unlikely to use them in crime: middle-class, middle-aged men, more often than not living in some suburban or rural area. In contrast, it's young people who are at highest risk for misusing guns. The goal of regulation would be to make it harder for every new upcoming generation of teens and twentysomethings to get guns. It helps matters that those young people tend to prefer new guns, in part because having a new gun helps them avoid getting caught with a used gun that someone else used to commit a previous crime (and avoid getting blamed for that crime). This preference for new guns by young people makes the big stock of existing older guns at least a little less central to the gun violence problem.

It also helps that the underground market for guns (a durable good) seems to work much less well than the underground market for drugs (a consumable good). In the drug market there are many more transactions—it's a "thick" market—so there are lots of sellers and lots of buyers and it's relatively easy to connect. In the gun market there are many fewer transactions—a "thin" market—so there are fewer buyers and sellers, which in turn makes it hard for them to connect. In work that Philip Cook, Anthony Braga, and I did with ethnographer Sudhir Venkatesh, we found substantial price markups for guns on the streets of Chicago, consistent with the idea that the markets don't work well. We even found a system of brokers developed to facilitate sales, charging $30 to $50 per transaction, and even those brokers can't get a gun in 30–40 percent of transaction attempts.[68]

That's to say: National regulations capable of adding more friction into the secondary gun market—laws seeking to hinder any of the hand-to-hand sales that flow freely in American secondary markets— might have real effects on gun use in crime. Yet given the state of US politics, that sort of law is, for better or worse, unlikely to happen anytime soon.

THOUGHTS AND PRAYERS OF POLITICAL ACTION

If you were a person in favor of more gun control in America, and if you wanted to be optimistic, you might focus on three facts in a search for hope. First, most Americans support almost every gun regulation short of an outright ban on handguns. Second, lots of states have been enacting new gun laws over time. (Set aside for the moment that most of those laws are pretty modest in their scope.) Third, the NRA is going through what one might call a period of transition; one gun control advocate, less diplomatically, described the current state of the NRA as "disarray."[69] The longtime head, Wayne LaPierre, retired from the NRA in 2024, the subject of a civil fraud case related to financial scandals. And news accounts suggest the NRA's budget is a mess.[70]

At the same time there are many, many reasons—both legal and political—for gun control advocates to be pessimistic.

On the legal front, over the past twenty years the US Supreme Court has adopted a new interpretation of the Second Amendment and started striking down lots of gun laws around the country, starting with DC's handgun ban in 2008 (*DC v. Heller*)[71] and then Chicago's handgun ban in 2010. Gun rights plaintiffs hit pause after that since Chief Justice John Roberts, the pivotal fifth vote, was widely viewed as a "Second Amendment squish"[72] (read: a person not to be counted on), but that changed once the court's conservative majority expanded to 6–3 in the Trump administration. In June 2022, Justice Clarence Thomas wrote the decision in *New York State Rifle & Pistol Association Inc. v. Bruen*. That case not only struck down New York's restrictive gun carrying law but also overturned the traditional practice of how the federal courts had understood the Second Amendment since *Heller*. Under the old procedure, courts had essentially balanced some historical reading of the Constitution with some consideration of practical consequences for public safety.[73] Now it is looking as if only history might matter.

On the political front, a structural challenge to nationwide gun control is the US Senate, which gives outsized influence in two ways to rural states with high levels of gun ownership. The first is through how senators are allocated to states; six hundred thousand Wyomingites get the same number of senators as thirty-nine million Californians. Second is through the Senate filibuster custom that requires sixty votes to end debate.[74]

Gun rights supporters also have another powerful structural advantage: They are extremely motivated and extraordinarily politically active, unlike the large majority of (most not very politically active on this issue) gun control supporters.

For most gun control supporters (which is to say, most Americans), their support is usually motivated from a sense of the larger collective good, and gun control is one of a long list of policy issues they care about. They often also care about reproductive rights, education, poverty, homelessness, climate change, LGBTQ rights, democracy, and criminal-justice reform; gun control, in other words, may live at the back of the line of issues for many voters, even those who are politically engaged. When they decide whom to vote for, they're looking at candidates' positions across a full slate of issues.

In contrast, for many gun owners, gun control is *the* issue they care about, often because there's some *personal* sense of self-interest. Some are convinced they need guns for self-defense. Others are convinced they need guns to prevent government tyranny. (This attitude is captured in the popular gun-show bumper sticker, "The Second

Amendment is in place in case they ignore the others.") I remember many years ago I flew to Minneapolis in the middle of a blizzard to testify about some proposed new gun law. I was there to provide a different perspective to that of the other expert testifying at the hearing, John Lott (of *More Guns, Less Crime* fame). I was living in DC and at that time had no idea any place on Earth could ever get quite that cold. Yet the room was totally packed. And almost everyone in the room had a giant orange button showing they were on Lott's side.

Support for gun control—motivated by a sense of the collective good, but not motivated enough to work that hard personally for that collective good—is typically a mile wide and an inch deep. Opposition by the much smaller number of people who feel like they've got a personal stake in unregulated gun rights is intense—they'll do whatever it takes. This dynamic is so common it has a name in social science: the "collective action problem." The collective action problem explains why movements for change (or movements to maintain a status quo) are so often difficult with anything less than zealotry from the people involved.

This idea may also help explain, among other things, why gun control proponents have been losing on one particularly important regulatory issue: gun carrying. This issue is important because a gun in public is much more dangerous than a gun locked away in someone's closet or basement. Fifty years ago, most states gave local government officials a lot of discretion about whether someone who applied for a permit to carry a gun concealed in public would get it (the law said that officials "may" issue one). The result was that in practice officials typically used their discretion to ensure that not all that many concealed-carry permits got issued. But today, forty-five states have some version of a law that says local government officials "shall" issue a permit—reducing their discretion and increasing the number of concealed-carry permits that get issued. The best available research suggests these laws increase violent crime by 20 percent, partly by leading to many more guns out in public places (like cars) getting stolen (gun thefts rise by 50 percent).[75]

What will the future bring? What are the chances of a big federal law that regulates the secondary gun market? We of course can't know for sure. Politics is hard to predict.

But what I do know is that I've been working on this issue for thirty years, and after every mass shooting I have heard claims that in terms of national gun control politics, "this time is different." That was true after the mass shooting at Columbine High School in 1999. After Sandy Hook in 2012. After Las Vegas in 2017. After Parkland, Florida, in 2018. After Uvalde, Texas, and Highland Park (just north of Chicago) in 2022. I heard "this time is different" most recently after a mass shooting at a Christian elementary school in Nashville in 2023.[76] The next day the *Washington Post*'s headline was "In Congress, little urgency to address gun violence with legislation."[77] The *New York Times* headline: "A shared shrug at gun control."[78]

As a data guy, to come up with a forecast about national gun control I'd look at the base rate—that is, the average rate at which new gun laws get enacted in the US. Over the last 243 years of US history, the number of major, restrictive federal gun laws has been (depending on how you count) something like five or six.[79] If the next fifty years are anything like the past 243, the math suggests you should expect at most one or maybe two new federal gun laws, both of which will be modest. More likely, for better or worse, is that federal gun politics will continue to feel a lot like World War I trench warfare: lots of effort expended but little movement.

Even if you have a different view of the odds of a big federal gun law, it seems risky to try to solve the gun violence problem by relying *exclusively* on the hope of more gun control. In the 1950s a University of Chicago–trained economist named Harry Markowitz invented something called "modern portfolio theory": the idea that investors should diversify their holdings to hedge against failures or losses across their bets. It's the same basic principle for why financial advisors tell you never put your entire retirement savings into a single company's stock.

If gun violence = guns + violence, the logic of diversification suggests the country can't put all of its eggs in the gun control basket. We need to *also* be worrying about violence, not just guns.

3

THE ORIGINS OF WICKED PEOPLE

If gun violence = guns + violence and if the national politics around guns are for better or worse largely paralyzed, then progress on gun violence will require making progress on the *violence* part of the equation.

How do we do that? For the last fifty years, America's answer has been largely to build more and more places like the Cook County, Illinois, Juvenile Temporary Detention Center (JTDC), where the juvenile justice system holds teens deemed at highest risk for violence. The JTDC is a giant concrete building that takes up nearly half a city block on Roosevelt Road out on Chicago's West Side. To get inside you have to store everything (watch, wallet, belt, etc.) in a locker, go through a metal detector, have the staff buzz you through a secure door, take an elevator that requires swiping a staff ID, and then finally pass into the residential section where each living unit (or "pod") is separated from the main hallway by another locked, secure door. One of the first weekly dramas on HBO was a dystopian show about an adult prison in the US called *Oz*; I turned it on once and found it to be way too brutal and depressing to watch. One of the nicknames Chicago teens have for the JTDC is "Baby Oz."

The sheer scale of places represented by Oz and Baby Oz is a relatively new phenomenon in America. Through most of the twentieth century the incarceration rate per capita in the US was in line with what we see in other countries around the world. But starting in the 1970s the imprisonment rate exploded to a level with no historical or international precedent.

Any such major social change will obviously be due to many causes. The legal scholar Michelle Alexander in her book *The New Jim Crow* argues that the move toward what has come to often be called "mass incarceration" was a backlash to the civil rights movement of the 1960s. And there is indeed a substantial body of evidence documenting discrimination in different parts of the justice system, contributing to the overrepresentation of Black Americans behind bars (12 percent of all Americans but 33 percent of prison inmates).[1] But race can't be the *only* explanation. Discrimination is ubiquitous around the world, but no other country has a prison system quite like that of America's. And even within the US, the last half-century's boom in prison population has happened even in overwhelmingly white states.

Another key reason for this punitive turn was that Americans increasingly viewed the underlying cause of violence as inherently, characterologically bad people. And, as historian Timothy Crimmins has argued, a major driver of that view of the problem, and what to do about it, was the Harvard political scientist James Q. Wilson.[2] Wilson was one of the leading figures arguing that prevention and rehabilitation don't work, that crime is due to what he called "wicked people," and that the only solution to the problem of widespread crime and violence is incarceration.

Wilson's argument taps into a basic feature of how humans' minds work: We view the causes of other people's behavior as being about them as people rather than about their situations. In a canonical study, researchers told study subjects that a different set of college students had been assigned to write an essay either opposing or supporting Communism in Cuba under Fidel Castro.[3] The subjects were then asked to predict the personal attitudes of the essay authors, knowing that the authors had not themselves picked the positions they were arguing. Yet study subjects nonetheless predicted that those who had been assigned by someone else to write a pro-Communist essay were actually more pro-Communist themselves, even though the subjects knew the essay authors had been assigned the position to argue by someone else![4] This tendency to focus on the person and not the situation occurs partly because people are the things in view that are active: Behavior grabs our "attentional spotlight," while the situation sits static in the background, easy to overlook.[5] This tendency is so common there's a name for it: the "fundamental attribution error."[6]

Wilson's arguments were intuitive, incredibly influential, plausible (based on what was known at the time), and—given what has been learned about human behavior since then—wrong.

WILSON'S THEORY OF THE CASE

James Quinn Wilson grew up in Long Beach, California, in the 1930s and 1940s, then served in the Navy during the 1950s. After he got discharged, he left for Hyde Park to get his PhD in political science at the University of Chicago. He eventually moved to Harvard, where he would become the Henry Lee Shattuck Professor of Government and chair of the Harvard Government Department. His work on bureaucracy got him interested in understanding how police departments work. From there it was a small, natural step to start thinking about crime.

Wilson was a complicated person.

Wilson chaired the White House Task Force on Crime in 1966 for the famously liberal president Lyndon Johnson, who (aside from FDR) did arguably more than any other US president to create America's modern-day social safety net. Yet while on the task force Wilson spent a fair amount of time loudly criticizing its other academics for relying on their political views (mostly left-leaning) rather than their science in coming up with policy recommendations.[7]

A retrospective by Wilson's Harvard colleagues noted, "His practical attitude began to earn him the reputation as a conservative, which he unsuccessfully resisted, for though he was skeptical of gun control, he was also wary of guns."[8] Resist though he might, he would go on to become a conservative hero; the conservative columnist George Will titled his tribute in the *Washington Post* "James Q. Wilson, honored prophet."

At the same time, he was also a longtime friend of Senator Daniel Patrick Moynihan (Democrat, New York). Wilson's obituary in the *New York Times*, which ran on the front page (almost unheard of for an academic), noted that "even his critics acknowledged that he was less an ideologue than a scientist."[9]

Yet one of Wilson's academic colleagues offered a more nuanced view: "What makes reading Wilson exciting is the variety of levels of sophistication and rigor one is likely to encounter at different points in the same text. A reader can make the long journey from scholarship to salesmanship and back in the space of a single Wilsonian paragraph."[10]

Wilson thought of himself as pragmatic and so got frustrated with the academic conversations of the time. Most academic experts were focusing on abstract ideas about how crime stemmed from people's attitudes or larger social processes. There was debate about whether the idea of "free will" made sense.[11] But often it wasn't clear what sort of concrete policies these lines of thinking implied. So it often felt to Wilson like such debate was just talking for talking's sake. Wilson wanted to know what we should actually *do*.

Some people in government around that time were focusing on the root causes of crime—social failings and their contributions to further social failings. But that approach was coming on the heels of the US government having just tried the War on Poverty. Americans had some ambivalence about the effectiveness of government anti-poverty policies,[12] and for that matter even some ambivalence about whether government should be trying to reduce poverty versus leaving people to pull themselves up by their bootstraps.[13] That's to say, it was far from clear the public was in the mood to double down on a new War on Poverty as a crime-fighting strategy.

Wilson offered a different diagnosis of the crime problem and a different cure. His 1975 book *Thinking about Crime* argued that a lot of the crime problem was due to fundamentally bad people: "Wicked people exist. Nothing avails except to set them apart from innocent people."

In his focus on the difference between "criminals" and everyone

else, he was following in the footsteps of people like the Enlightenment philosopher David Hume, who argued that crime was due to the
"character and disposition of the person,"[14] as well as the nineteenth-
century Italian criminologist Cesare Lombroso, who created an elaborate typology of personal attributes that affected crime: not just bad
character but also insanity and (since Lombroso was working in the
middle of the Darwinian revolution) whether someone represented a
somewhat earlier stage of human evolution.[15] In Wilson's 1985 book
with psychologist Richard Herrnstein, he would elaborate on some
of the physical and biological features that he himself thought distinguished criminals from everyone else (gender, age, IQ, body type, and
impulsivity, among others).[16]

Wilson also argued that "many [other] people, neither wicked nor
innocent, but watchful, dissembling, and calculating of their chances,
ponder our reaction to wickedness as a clue to what they might prof-
itably do."[17] That is, some comparison of benefits of crime (monetary
gain or nonmonetary rewards like status or a sense of accomplish-
ment) to the costs (punishment, public disapproval, sense of guilt). To
Wilson, this argument was just common sense: "Such opinions spring
naturally to mind among persons who notice, as a fact of everyday life,
that people take their hands off hot stoves, shop around to find the
best buy, smack their children to teach them not to run out into a busy
street [this was the 1970s, after all], and change jobs when the opportunity arises to earn more money for the same amount of effort."[18]

These two Wilsonian ideas together imply a coherent view of criminal behavior: Crime stems from rational benefit-cost calculation; the
people who choose to commit crime as a result of such calculations
are those who weigh a given set of incentives differently from other
people or who, as Wilson put it, "most likely have a weaker conscience,
worry less about their reputation in polite society, and find it harder
to postpone gratifying their urges."[19] Those whom Wilson called the
"wicked" are people for whom the benefits of crime loom so large it
would be hard to switch their benefit-cost calculation (as an economist
I'd call them "inframarginal," that is, they already think the benefits
of crime and violence so far outweigh the costs that they're far from

the key decision margin—not much will tip them over to a different decision). The "watchful, dissembling and calculating" are those for whom their sense of the benefits and costs of crime leaves them close to the decision margin; a change in expected punishment might, in this view, be the difference that would tip them from one decision to the other.

One of the things that made Wilson so influential was that he could write in plain English. Other academic experts of the time were writing things like: "For nearly two decades no sociologist has formulated a major theory about the *etiology* of crime. The great drought stemmed from a shift in focus (concomitant with the emergence of the labeling perspective) to crime as a reactive phenomenon and from endeavors to demonstrate that 'positivist' criminology is the handmaiden of capitalism."[20] Everything Wilson wrote, in contrast, a normal person could— and might even want to—read.

Wilson's focus on a criminal-justice solution to crime, rather than a social-policy solution, was, he said, not ideological but rather pragmatic. As he noted: "The theory of human nature on which is erected the idea of deterrence (the theory that people respond to the penalties associated with crime) is also the theory of human nature that supports the idea that people will take jobs in preference to crime if the jobs are more attractive."[21] That is, the Left and Right implicitly agreed that crime was due in large part to rational calculation.

Wilson acknowledged that in principle social policy could prevent crime but said that his review of the best available evidence suggested the social policies that had been tried to date had proven incapable of crime prevention. "We do not know how to re-educate or uplift because most young delinquents seem to re-educate themselves no matter what society does."[22]

So where did that leave us? Wilson argued "for a sober view of man and his institutions that would permit reasonable things to be accomplished, foolish things abandoned, and utopian things forgotten."[23] The practical failure of social policy to prevent crime left, in his view, only one other viable solution to the crime problem, a solution simple and mechanical enough so that even government, with its intrinsic limitations, was capable of successfully carrying it out. He described that solution in the title of a 1975 op-ed in the *New York Times*: "Lock 'em up."

THE FACTS OF WILSON'S TIME

Wilson's pessimism about crime prevention and rehabilitation wasn't crazy given what was known back in the 1970s.

President Lyndon Johnson had announced crime prevention as a secondary goal of his War on Poverty: "There are a thousand hacking at the branches of evil to one who is striking at the root."[24] The War on Poverty, together with the booming economy of the 1960s, had succeeded in cutting the official poverty rate in half. But through the first ten years after the War on Poverty was launched, the murder rate doubled and the robbery rate tripled.

Of course, other things were changing over this ten-year time period as well, so the rising murder and robbery rates don't necessarily mean the War on Poverty failed. But at the very least, the War on Poverty as an attempt to solve the root causes of crime wouldn't have struck even a fair-minded observer as an obvious success. As Wilson put it: "In retrospect, we might not have described certain 'Great Society' programs as failures if the problems they sought to remedy . . . had not been suddenly enlarged in scope and altered in character."[25]

There was also other data coming out around this time from research studies that tried to isolate the independent effects of social programs on crime, holding other determinants of criminal behavior constant, and so provided a stronger basis for cause-and-effect conclusions. By the 1970s, lots of rehabilitation programs had been tried: job training, individual counseling, group counseling, prison work experience, changes in the whole institutional environment of prisons, intensive post-prison supervision, etc. A sociologist named Robert Martinson took on the job of reviewing the best available evidence, looking at 231 studies done between 1945 and 1967. He published his conclusion in 1974 in a policy journal called the *Public Interest*: "Nothing works."

For a relatively dry piece of social-science analysis, the essay's impact was striking. Martinson was interviewed by *60 Minutes* and even *People* magazine.[26] Like Wilson, Martinson's politics were hard to pin down. He started off as a Freedom Rider in Mississippi before eventually infuriating many liberals with his "Nothing works" report. On top of that Martinson was a little bit of a loose cannon in interviews. On *60 Minutes* he told Mike Wallace that parole was "almost a Machiavellian attempt" by inmates to "get out." Counseling, he argued, was at best a "good way to pass the time" but had "no effect."[27]

While not all experts agreed with Martinson's conclusions, at the same time he was far from the only expert who was reading the data this way.[28] For example, a decade later a review essay by two leading criminologists of the time (Sheldon Messinger of UC Berkeley and Richard Berk, then at UCLA) would argue: "Numerous preventative programs have sought to affect these 'causes' [of crime.] So far, none has been shown to be particularly effective."[29]

From the perceived failure of prevention and rehabilitation in reducing crime, it's a small step to concluding that criminals are incorrigible. Social programs didn't seem to work. Overall crime rates were surging. And on top of it all, the data showed that fully two-thirds of the people released from prison each year re-offend within a few years.[30] (Since then, new research has pointed out a subtle but important conceptual problem with those calculations that, when addressed, suggests the recidivism rate is much lower—but this problem with the standard recidivism calculations wasn't known in the 1970s.[31])

It all combined to create a sense of futility.

The data available to Wilson at the time, combined with the fundamental attribution error that we're all prone to, made Wilson conclude that criminality must be an essential part of the nature of those who commit crime. This verdict in turn led Wilson to conclude that, as a pragmatic matter, prison's goal can't be to "to turn burglars into Rotarians"—in no small part as "a frank admission that society really does not know how to" do such a thing.

Given Wilson's conclusion that prison is the only way to control crime, he was deeply worried that the criminal-justice system wasn't doing its job. In *Thinking about Crime*, he asked: What are the chances that for a given, say, robbery, the offender winds up imprisoned for the crime? The answer came as a big surprise to many people. Victim surveys tell us that about half (55 percent) of robbery victims reported the crime to the police in the 1970s; 31 percent of reported robberies led to an arrest, and 13 percent of robbery arrests resulted in some prison time. The implication is that (55 percent x 31 percent x 13 percent) ≈ 2 percent of robberies resulted in the offender behind bars.[32]

(As an aside, you might be curious about what that figure is today. The dramatic rise in imprisonment in America since the 1970s has increased the odds that a robbery offender winds up in prison for a given robbery by around 50 percent—from 2 percent up to around 3 percent.)[33]

It wasn't just conservatives at that time who were worrying about the low probability of punishment for crime. As one observer put it, "The odds in favor of the criminal are so high that the constant rise in criminal offenses seems only natural."[34] That quote isn't from some right-wing politician like Ronald Reagan or Richard Nixon but from Hannah Arendt, often considered one of the most important political philosophers of the twentieth century (author of *The Origins of Totalitarianism* and *Eichmann in Jerusalem*) and a longtime professor at the progressive New School university in New York City.

For policy purposes, the relevant question is not "What is the probability a given criminal winds up in prison for a given crime?" but rather "What are the costs and benefits to society from *changing* the incarceration rate and making the probability of prison higher?" If we expand prisons, the benefit is, ideally, less crime. But there are costs, too—money, but also the collateral harms to people, families, and communities. Isolating the crime-reducing benefits of prison in the data is hard for the same reasons isolating the independent effect of guns on crime is hard. The National Academy of Sciences convened a blue-ribbon commission to consider the data in the 1970s[35] and concluded that despite the limitations of the available data and evidence, more prison probably did lead to less crime. So Wilson was following the evidence at that time when he argued that "the best studies of deterrence that manage to overcome many of these [methodological] problems provide evidence that deterrence works."[36]

THE MAKING OF A NEW SHARED WISDOM

Very few academic books have the policy impact that Wilson's did. Soon after the book came out in 1975, he was invited to give a special briefing to Attorney General Edward Levi at the White House. Other top officials of the Ford administration were given copies of the book.[37]

The book's influence wasn't limited to right-of-center politicians. Then–California governor Jerry Brown (a Democrat who would serve as governor again from 2011 to 2019) was using the book's ideas as the foundation for his own speeches on crime at the time.[38] Mark Kleiman, who would go on to get a public policy PhD from Harvard, teach at UCLA and NYU, and serve as an adjunct scholar at the left-leaning Center for American Progress, talked about how reading Wilson's book completely changed his own thinking about crime when he arrived at the US Department of Justice as a young staffer in the late 1970s.[39]

A key tailwind for Wilson's arguments was the substantial rise in violent crime in America that started in the mid-1960s. The murder rate in 1960 was 5 per 100,000 (about what it's been in the US in recent years); by the early 1970s that figure had doubled.

As violent-crime rates rose, news coverage of crime rose as well, as the Cornell political scientist Peter Enns has shown in his book *Incarceration Nation*. Because news media is necessarily in the business of monetizing current events, to maximize readership the news coverage tended to emphasize the most sordid features of the most terrible crimes. Headlines were published like "The Incorrigibles" (*Newsweek*)[40] and "Headless Body in Topless Bar" (the *New York Post*).[41] Detailed descriptions of Jeffrey Dahmer's murders were published at a graphic level of detail beyond anything any reader could previously have imagined, not in some tabloid rag but in the *New York Times*.[42] Two decades of elevated rates of violence culminated rhetorically in a 1995 essay in the *Weekly Standard* by political scientist John DiIulio (a former

PhD student of Wilson's at Harvard),[43] who famously coined a term to describe "super crime-prone young males" who are raised in "abject moral poverty": "super-predators."[44]

The news coverage also tended to focus on the offender and the crime, rather than the offender's social environment (nine mentions of the former for every one mention of the latter).[45] Defendants were frequently described as if criminality were an essential feature of their character: "thrill killer," "career criminal," "fugitive," "serial date rapist."[46]

Newspaper reporters, as susceptible as anyone else to the fundamental attribution error, were writing for an American public that may be particularly prone to the same problem. The reason is that compared to people in other rich countries, Americans are more likely to be religious fundamentalists,[47] which leads adherents to believe people have an inherent moral nature—a "strict division between righteous people and evildoers."[48] For example, while 27 percent of western Europeans said they "believe in God as described in the Bible," that figure is twice as high in the US (56 percent).[49] Those who interpret religious texts literally are more likely to attribute crime to people's bad character,[50] so criminality seems "both incurable and worthy of punishment."[51] In surveys, Protestant conservatives rank almost all crimes equal in moral wrongness. Trespassing, disturbing the peace, assault, and murder are all viewed as falling into the same moral category—"very wrong."[52] When surveys ask people if they believe in absolute good and evil, around a third (35 percent) of Europeans agree with that sentiment, while nearly half (49 percent) of Americans do.

The rise in crime, the rise in news coverage focusing on the terrible people committing these terrible acts, and the predisposition of all of us (but Americans in particular) to attribute people's behavior to their moral character all combined to lead the American public to become more punitive over time. For example, over the 1970s the share of Americans who thought courts were too lenient rose from 65 percent to 80 percent. The share of people who believed the main point of prison is punishment more than doubled (8 percent to nearly 20 percent). Support for the death penalty went from under 50 percent to nearly 70 percent.[53]

In focus groups and surveys, most Americans tend to think crime is due to one of three "types" of people:[54] the *psychopaths*, "born bad"; the *amoral*, made bad by their environments, for whom the benefits of crime loom too large and the costs of crime loom too small; and the *economically desperate*. Historically most people tend to focus on the first two explanations rather than on the last one.[55] For example, by the time President Clinton signed the Crime Bill in 1994, over *two-thirds* of all Americans believed the crime problem was due to something wrong with the criminals (psychopaths or the amoral) or to an insufficiently tough justice system to stop them.[56]

The "wicked people" idea had widely taken hold.

THE LONG SHADOW OF JAMES Q. WILSON

For most of the twentieth century, America's imprisonment rate wasn't all that different from those of most other rich countries, with around 100 people in prison for every 100,000 in the general population. This incarceration rate had been so constant, despite major social changes (the Depression, alcohol prohibition, two world wars, etc.), that social scientists started to write papers about how and why punishment levels would stay stable forever.[57] The 1971 Attica Prison riot even led to calls for a *halt* to prison construction.[58] But starting not long thereafter, America experienced a growth in imprisonment that had no historical or international precedent: Through 2000, incarceration rates quadrupled.

What happened?

For something as complicated and far-reaching as a massive change in the prison system, there will inevitably be multiple explanations (and ongoing debates about those explanations).[59] Some of those explanations fit the data, some don't. But there would seem to be little doubt that an important part of the story here is the shift toward a more punitive American public, a mindset with deep roots in the Wilsonian view of what to do about crime and violence.

Many people believe the massive increase in imprisonment was simply a moral panic about drugs. And it's true that the War on Drugs is part of the story—but just a part. It's far from the whole story. The criminal-justice system did become harsher for drug cases. But it also became harsher for most other crimes as well.[60] By my calculations, the War on Drugs accounts for something like a quarter of the total nationwide increase in imprisonment. Today about 20 percent of all inmates behind bars are there on some sort of drug offense.[61]

Others have argued that "neoliberalism" (academic jargon for privatization) "lies at the root of the carceral state."[62] It's true that in recent years private prisons have grown faster in percentage terms than government-run federal and state prisons (from 2010 to 2016, 47 percent versus 9 percent). But private prisons started off, and remain, a small share of all prison beds. Even after a very large increase in proportional terms, private prisons account for just 9 percent of all prison inmates.[63] So privatization by itself also can't explain the rise in imprisonment.

Michelle Alexander in *The New Jim Crow* suggests racism is the explanation. And indeed the role of race in the US criminal-justice system is hard to miss, given the dramatic overrepresentation of racial and ethnic minorities in the system. There are three types of data that establish the independent causal role of racism and discrimination as contributors to this overrepresentation.[64]

First, behavioral scientists have shown that the tendency to favor in-groups and disfavor out-groups runs deep. Over the course of human evolution, this tendency might have helped close-knit clans survive, but in modern society it leads to discrimination and prejudice. Nor do the personal characteristics that distinguish in-groups from out-groups need to be very distinctive. Consider a study from the 1950s of two groups of middle-school boys at Robber's Cave State Park in Oklahoma. As the two groups started to compete with each other in sports and other events, each group started to be convinced that the boys in *their* group were far superior in every way to the boys in the *other* group. Things escalated to arguments and worse.[65] What is remarkable is that this out-group hostility arose even though there were no *actual* differences across groups. *The two groups were formed by randomly assigning a*

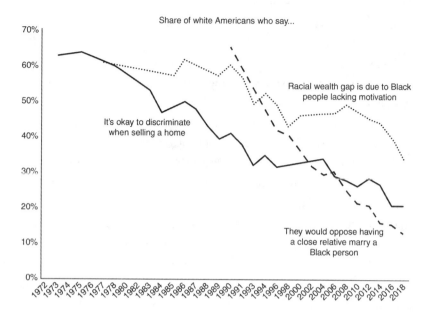

Share of white Americans who say...

FIGURE 3.1. Trends in racial attitudes by white Americans, 1972–2018

homogenous pool of white Protestant boys to each group. All it took for out-group hostility to occur was to pit the two groups against each other in a few small competitions.

Second, there is ample survey data from the real world document-ing explicit bias. There seem to have been large declines in explicit discrimination by whites over time (figure 3.1).[66] But it's still the case that even today, around one in ten white Americans say they wouldn't want a relative to marry a Black person, one in four say that they think it's okay to discriminate when selling a house, and one in three say the racial wealth gap is due to a lack of motivation among Black Americans.[67]

Third, there is a growing body of rigorous natural-experiment studies that isolate the independent role of race in key criminal-justice decisions. For instance, one study looked at what happened when dif-ferent police officers get sent to different neighborhoods purely as a result of the random chance in how 911 calls are assigned. When po-lice get sent to mostly white areas, the odds that the police will use force are similar for officers of all races. But when a 911 call takes police into mostly Black neighborhoods, we see a *much* higher chance of force by white than by Black officers.[68] Other studies show racial bias in other criminal-justice decisions like, for example, whom judges decide to put in jail awaiting trial.[69] The only part of the system that's been studied to date where the best studies *don't* seem to reveal detectable bias is parole.[70]

But race can't be the *whole* explanation. There is discrimination everywhere there are people. Compared to Americans, fewer Germans and Brits would accept a Muslim family member.[71] The French and Spanish are less likely than Americans to think diversity makes their country a better place to live, the Japanese even less so.[72] Yet none of these other countries has a prison system anything like ours.

Within the United States it's true that prison populations over the past fifty years did grow the most in Southern states, the part of the country where in surveys whites on average seem to have the most racist attitudes.[73] At the same time, it's also true that imprisonment grew at a remarkable rate even in overwhelmingly white states like South Dakota (95 percent white in 1970), Colorado (96 percent), Montana (96 percent), Wyoming (97 percent), Idaho (98 percent), and Iowa (99 percent).[74]

A final way we can see that racial discrimination can't be the entire story here comes from the fact that support for increased incarceration came from almost every segment of American society. Prison rates grew dramatically under both Democratic and Republican governors, and under Democratic as well as Republican presidents. Support for getting tough on crime also cut across racial lines, as Yale professor James Forman noted in his book *Locking Up Our Own*. During the 1970s, support for the death penalty rose among Black Americans and white alike.[75] The 1994 Crime Bill was passed with support by a majority of the Congressional Black Caucus.[76] As the Reverend Jesse Jackson Jr. told the *Chicago Tribune* during the onset of the crack-cocaine epidemic in 1980s, "No one has the right to kill our children. I won't take it from the Klan with a rope; I won't take it from a neighbor with dope. We must drive them out."[77] At the peak of the crack epidemic, Jackson said, "This is the new frontier of the civil rights struggle. It's the first time the internal threats and self-destructive behavior . . . eclipses the external threats."[78]

The data suggest another key contributing factor to the punitive turn in American crime policy was the growing Wilson-type view that crime and violence are due to intrinsically bad people. Once one believes crime and violence are due to incorrigibly wicked people whose moral characters can't change, it's a small step to conclude that the only response to crime is incarceration. We can see this connection in the fact that Americans who believe crime is due to characterologically bad people support harsher punishments.[79] We see the same pattern when parole board members are asked to "think aloud" and explain their decisions as they make them.[80]

In *Incarceration Nation*, Enns shows that in states where people became more punitive, prison growth was higher. And one major reason for that turn toward punishment—and a key reason some states became more punitive than others—is the reactions among religious fundamentalists to rising crime.[81] This is the group, as a reminder, that tends to be most inclined to see criminal behavior as due to something wrong with the moral character of the offenders, and to believe that all crime is equally wrong, no matter its severity. The data show enormous variation across parts of the country in the share of people who are religiously fundamentalist, ranging from a high of nearly two-thirds (in the East South Atlantic) to under 5 percent (in New England).[82] The data also show that imprisonment grew the most from the 1970s through 2000 in places where more people are religious fundamentalists.[83]

The result was that many more arrestees were sentenced to prison, for longer and longer prison terms. The US now has more prisoners per capita than China, Russia, and Iran—countries that are not widely regarded as exemplars of human rights. And the burden of this incarceration rate falls heaviest on the most socially vulnerable populations. Columbia University sociologist Bruce Western has shown that at the peak of America's incarceration trend, among Black male high school dropouts in the US, something like 70 percent wound up spending time in prison by their mid-30s.[84] Many wind up exiting prison in poor health and having been violently victimized or otherwise traumatized by the experience.[85]

Nor has America's punitive turn been limited to its jails and prisons.

The US increasingly views juvenile offenders as bad people who can't change, treating juveniles accordingly like adults within the criminal-justice system.[86] In the 1990s, almost every state in the country passed a law making it easier for the courts to try juvenile arrestees in the adult criminal-justice system.[87]

Schools also increasingly sought to "set the wicked apart" through zero-tolerance policies that made it easier to kick out disruptive students. Between 1972 and 2006, suspension rates across the US increased by 67 percent for white students and fully 150 percent for Black students.[88]

And perhaps most irreversibly, Americans have also increasingly taken the job of protecting themselves against wicked people into their own hands by buying guns by the tens of millions. Between 1970 and 1990, the share of households owning handguns increased by nearly a third,[89] and owners increasingly cited protection against crime as the key reason for having a gun.

POLICIES AGING POORLY

So how do Wilson's intellectual ideas, so central to the emergence of an American concept of good and bad, look with the benefit of hindsight?

Wilson was *partly* right.

Let's start with his views about the potential of social policies to prevent crime. If we focus on "traditional" social policies like job training, subsidized jobs, individual counseling, group counseling, prison work experience, changes in the whole institutional environment of prison, intensive post-prison supervision, etc., Wilson's view holds up pretty well—especially if we focus on the determinants of the violent crimes that the public cares about most. For example, in 2004, the US Department of Justice commissioned a research center at the University of Colorado Boulder (Blueprints for Violence Prevention) to review what's known about social policies and violence prevention. The researchers identified roughly six hundred studies in total. Of those, only twenty-two—or about 4 percent—were found to work. This result is almost exactly what we'd expect to find purely by chance if nothing at all worked.[90] (I will return to this point in much greater detail in the next chapter.)

I say that Wilson was only "partly" right here because he seems to have overgeneralized a bit from these findings. The fact that what had been tried to date by the 1970s didn't work seems to have led him to conclude that "nothing *can* work." But as social science has advanced, including in psychology and behavioral economics, our understanding of human behavior has also advanced, including our understanding of violent behavior. As I will show in chapter 8, new data from large-scale randomized controlled trials reveals that the conclusion that "nothing *can* work," that "criminals" are inherently incorrigible, turns out to be wrong.

Similarly, with respect to the benefits and costs of prison, Wilson was again only partly right.

Wilson was right that, to a degree, prison *can* reduce violent crime. My University of Chicago colleague Steven Levitt proved this by studying the effects of prison overcrowding lawsuits. As prison growth produced a steady stream of lawsuits against states for overcrowding, Levitt saw an opportunity to compare crime trends in two kinds of states: those that were forced by lawsuits to slow their packing of prisons versus those that weren't. The data suggest that at least through the early 1990s (when Levitt's data ended), every 10 percent increase in prison population reduced property crime by 3 percent and violent crime by 4 percent.[91]

I say Wilson was only *partly* right because there are limits to the degree to which changing the incentives for crime changes criminal behavior. Ideally, if deterrence effects are strong enough, prison penalties might be increased in a way that not only reduces crime but also reduces imprisonment itself (if enough people are deterred). Unfortunately, deterrent effects don't seem to be *quite* that powerful.[92]

Economists think of deterrence as "whatever you wouldn't do while standing next to a cop." Taking that definition literally, I've seen the limits of deterrence firsthand. I was out on a ride-along with the police in Chicago one night when there was a report of the stabbing of a woman outside a liquor store. There was blood everywhere, a large crowd of people gathered, so in response half the police officers in the district showed up. While the police were trying to sort things out and get an ambulance, a second woman walked into the store, got into an argument with someone inside, and punched him in the face. Their fight spilled outside onto the sidewalk. Then as an older lady in a motorized wheelchair tried to mediate, a person standing on the sidewalk turned to her and said, "Why don't you take your ass home?" The 70-something would-be peacemaker turned in her wheelchair, looked up at him through her glasses, and said, in front of literally dozens of police officers, "Wait right here—I'm going to go home, get my piece"—her gun—"and come back and fuck you up."

You might argue that this story doesn't really tell us anything usefully representative about the limits of deterrence, since the woman in the wheelchair must be some sort of extreme outlier. But remember she started off in the role of *attempted mediator*. She went from "Can't we all get along?" to "I will fuck you up" in zero seconds flat. It also illustrates, as I will discuss in later chapters, how behavioral economics can help us make sense of why the deterrent effect of punishment is something less than perfect.

Given the limits of deterrence, an important reason why prison reduces crime is simply by mechanically keeping people off the streets (what criminologists call "incapacitation effects"). The problem is that incapacitation has diminishing marginal returns. If the criminal-justice system is even halfway good at its job, it should prioritize the relatively more dangerous people first for prison at whatever scale the prison system is built. That implies that as the scale of the prison population expands, the incapacitative benefits of detaining new people (who would not have been detained at all under the previous sentencing policies that gave us smaller prison populations) decline. That is, the first person put in prison generates more crime prevention than the two millionth person. Wilson might have been right that there were real crime benefits to incrementally increasing prison populations from 1970s levels. But it's less clear what the crime prevention effects on the margin are now, after prison populations have increased across most of the country by a factor of fully three or four.[93]

A third reason Wilson was only partly right about prison is because in hindsight, he (and for that matter, the whole social-science community) wasn't quite able to measure the full social harms of imprisonment itself.[94] Early assessments of the costs of incarceration tended to focus on the tangible dollar cost of building and running jails and prisons—staff salaries, building maintenance, food, medical care, clothing. Crime, especially violent crimes like gun violence, imposes extreme harms on society. Comparing the benefits of avoiding the full range of social harms from crime with the narrow dollar cost of imprisonment gave us a skewed picture of how reasonable prison is as a violence-prevention tool.

But over time the other, fuller human costs of imprisonment itself have become clearer. For starters, there's the trauma of families and loved ones being separated. Plus the very real risk to that loved one's health and safety behind bars: the risk of contracting a serious disease like AIDS, or a potentially serious one like COVID, along with the shockingly high risk that incarcerated individuals will be physically or even sexually assaulted.[95] The long-term consequences for your loved one's lives when they eventually get out: For young people in particular these consequences include a greatly elevated risk of high school dropout and future re-incarceration.[96]

In sum, the main problem with Wilson's argument is *not* that prison doesn't or hasn't or can't reduce crime and violence. The main problem is that prison achieves these goals at such a high cost to society.

INCONSISTENCY WITH BASIC FACTS

Wilson's solutions to the problem of violence in America didn't fully have their desired net effects because the underlying idea that violence is driven by incorrigibly wicked people is wrong. I don't mean here

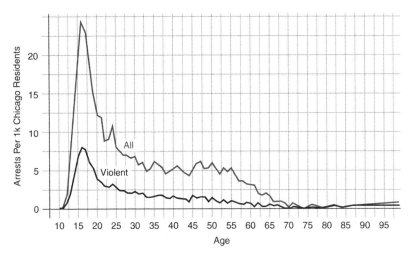

FIGURE 3.2: Age-crime curve for all arrests and arrests for violent crimes, Chicago, 2018

"wrong" in a moral or political or ideological sense (that's a subjective judgment that each reader can decide for themselves); rather, I mean "wrong" in a factual sense. Wilson's argument doesn't quite fit the data.

The idea that gun violence and other crimes are caused by immutable features of people's characters simply doesn't fit with facts like the steady decline in criminal offending starting in late adolescence (the so-called age-crime curve as in figure 3.2)[97] or the remarkable variation of gun violence by time (in Chicago, for instance, shootings are about twice as common on the weekends as they are during the week, and twice as common in June as in January). Nor can it explain why gun violence varies so dramatically by place, including across very short distances—such as across Dorchester Avenue, separating Greater Grand Crossing from South Shore, since surely people's morality cannot be so sharply different literally right across the street.

I saw the limits of the "wicked people" hypothesis firsthand during a visit to the JTDC a few years ago with two University of Chicago colleagues, Sendhil Mullainathan and Anuj Shah. We all wear glasses. None of us weighs even 150 pounds soaking wet. No one's taller than five foot ten unless it's one of those days Sendhil happens to be wearing those shoes with the thick soles that make him look a little taller.

A fearsome group we are not. We were standing along the back wall of one of the residential pods, observing some of the programming that the JTDC was doing for the residents. One of the kids—some giant teenager—kept looking back at us, scowling. Over and over. Then he stood up and walked over to us. I don't know how Sendhil and Anuj remember it—I think they closed their eyes—but this *very* large kid walked up to us, got *very* close, then asked, "Hey, do you guys want to sit down? You can't be comfortable just standing there like that." He pulled up three chairs. He even went to the front of the room and got us program booklets so we could follow along. After being at the University of Chicago for sixteen years now I can tell you firsthand: There are a lot of people on the faculty here, including more than a few Nobel Prize winners, who would *never* be this kind. To anyone. Ever.

Now, you might be skeptical that three economists can judge someone's character on the spot. Fair enough. But consider the attitudes of a more skeptical group: cops. I was on a ride-along once when a radio call came out: An undercover tactical team had been tailing a car when a hand holding a gun came out of the window of that car and fired at some people on the sidewalk. (In cop-speak, they "on-viewed a shooting.") There was a high-speed chase. A call came out on the radio by some skittish supervisor to terminate the chase. The police officer I was with at the time disagreed with the decision: "Pussies."

But then a police helicopter spotted the car. Someone over the radio announced that the chase was back on. Police cars were flying around. The cop and I were actually the ones who found the car, ditched in a parking lot, guns left in the back seat. But no sign of the passengers. Cops were sprinting around with AR-15s trying to find where the shooters were hiding. The manhunt eventually ended in an arrest.

I made it back to the police station before the suspects were brought in. As everyone sat there writing up the paperwork about the chase and the arrest, I was seated at a desk blending in (I think) wearing the unofficial "uniform" of the Chicago tactical team officer: baseball cap, sweatshirt, Kevlar vest, jeans, and sneakers. (I left my glasses and pocket protector at home.) That's just to say, when the two suspects were led into the room in handcuffs, both of them teenagers, I'm rea-

THE ORIGINS OF WICKED PEOPLE

sonably sure that what I happened next was not a sort of Hawthorne effect, in which the people being studied change their behavior out of awareness of the study. One of the tactical team guys turned, saw who the suspects were, and then yelled out: "Hey Romeo! Romeo! Was that *you?!?* How'd you learn to drive like that, man? You had that four-cylinder spinning up pretty good out there!"

This was not Supreme Court Justice Robert Jackson confronting the evil of Nazi leadership at Nuremberg. It wasn't DA Vincent Bugliosi confronting Charles Manson. It was more like Road Runner and Wile E. Coyote walking off the set together after the clock struck five.

But perhaps the strongest evidence against the argument that crime and violence are driven by incorrigible, immutably wicked people comes from an accumulating body of evidence—much of it from behavioral economics—that, with the right policy levers, people's propensity to engage in violence can change. As I show in chapter 8, it can sometimes even change dramatically.

It's hard to make progress on a problem that's been misunderstood.

4

IN SEARCH OF THE
ROOTS OF VIOLENCE

Barack Obama is the most famous politician to come out of Hyde Park, but the most locally beloved is surely Harold Washington.[1]

Washington, Chicago's first Black mayor, held the office from 1983 to 1987. Before that, he was a US congressman who had to be talked into running for the city's top job. As one staff member who served in Chicago's Department of Economic Development described it, the experience of working for Washington was "magical . . . like what it must have been to work for Kennedy."[2] Similarly, the *Chicago Reporter* called Washington's mayoralty "a kind of 'Camelot' . . . a shining moment when so much seemed possible."[3] Obama himself said that he "originally moved to Chicago in part because of the inspiration of Mayor Washington's campaign."[4]

Washington's election in 1983 was a surprise not only because of Chicago's race relations at the time—Dr. Martin Luther King Jr. had called it "the North's most racist city"[5]—but also because of the city's tradition of politics-as-contact sport. As a *New York Times* headline put it, "In the world of Chicago politics, the main rule is there are no rules." Corollaries include "Clout makes right"; "There can be only one winner"; and "Do unto others before they do unto you."[6] Carol Moseley Braun, who worked for Washington before eventually becoming a US senator herself, recalled that Harold was once in a fiercely contested race. To split the vote, his opponent recruited additional candidates to enter the race, "*all* with the name Washington . . . so there was a Fred Washington, an Ethel Washington, and a George Washington . . . running against Harold Washington. So he was *really* worried about losing." After he won by a slim margin of two hundred votes, Harold gave himself a new nickname: "Landslide Washington."[7]

As mayor, Washington inherited a level of gun violence unequaled in Chicago history. Chicago's murder rate per capita in the early 1980s was even higher than it had been during the Prohibition era of the 1920s. Washington could clearly see the correlation between the city's gun violence and the city's social problems: Shootings were concentrated in the city's poorest, most racially and economically segregated and socially isolated neighborhoods. This correlation seems to suggest an obvious solution: To stop violent crime, fix its root causes. That's the approach taken not just by his administration but by many others over the years, not just in Chicago but all across the country.

Yet Washington found, as have so many other mayors, that these root causes can run deep—they're hard to change. And even when they can be uprooted, doing so is often not the fix to violence that we'd expect.

THE DEEP ROOTS OF MODERN CHICAGO

Washington's life and political career illustrate not only the origins of Chicago's challenging social conditions but also why they've been so hard to change.

Washington was born in 1922 into a city of unlimited promise. Chicago had exploded from a village of 4,500 people in 1837 to a city of 2.7 million people less than a century later. The city's growth was so fast that the master plan in effect around the time Harold was born expressed concerns about *too* much success and growth: "Chicago is now facing the momentous fact that fifty years hence, when the children of to-day are at the height of their power and influence, this city will be larger than London: that is, larger than any existing city."[8]

Chicago developed at a time when most economic goods moved around by boat; the city had the great advantage of sitting at the intersection of the Great Lakes with the Mississippi River system. When trains were invented, Chicago's main Midwestern rival—St. Louis—committed a historic own-goal when, partly worried that this new technology would cannibalize their then-lucrative shipping business, the city did not significantly invest in railroads. Chicago capitalized on St. Louis's blunder and became the center of the nation's "iron spiderweb" of rails that connected 4,000 miles of track.[9]

Chicago's location in the center of the nation's transportation system fueled the city's industrial development. Chicago was home to (among others) McCormick reapers, Pullman railcars, Sears, US Steel, and the Union Stockyards, where Harold Washington's father Roy started his working life at $15 a week.[10] As one local historian put it, "Chicago was the Cupertino of the 19th century. . . . This is where people came with ideas and tried technology out."[11]

The Midwestern Cupertino of the time was a magnet for people looking for work,[12] including a flood of poor European immigrants eager to get one of the many factory jobs in Chicago that didn't require much schooling.[13] These immigrants clustered in neighborhoods near others who looked like them, spoke like them, ate the same things, and went to the same religious services.[14] The result was neighborhoods of ethnic enclaves, including Little Italy on the Near Southwest Side, the Polish neighborhood along Milwaukee Avenue to the north, the Czechs and other Eastern Europeans in Little Pilsen, and the Irish neighborhoods of Canaryville and Bridgeport on the South Side.[15] That's all to say that Chicago's status as one of America's most segregated cities goes back a long way.

One thing these different European immigrant groups had in common: They didn't want people like Harold Washington—that is to say, Black people—anywhere near them. The Washingtons moved houses frequently during Harold's childhood, but every address was always located within a fairly narrow strip of the South Side that ran from 12th Street down to 79th Street, one of only two neighborhoods at the time where Blacks were allowed to live—the so-called Black Belt.[16] Because landlords had a captive market, they could charge high rents for terrible, overcrowded housing. In the 1940s, the *Chicago Defender* reported that the housing stock in the Black Belt neighborhood, designed for 110,000 people, was home to 375,000.[17]

Such appalling conditions led progressive reformers at the Chicago Housing Authority (CHA) to push for new integrated public housing, including in the mostly white areas of the city's periphery. But as historian Bradford Hunt has documented in his book *Blueprint for Disaster*, these reformers came up short in achieving their goals. Instead, Chicago's city council forced CHA to build public housing for Black families in the city's predominantly Black areas.

As Hunt notes, Chicago's approach to public housing also suffered from good intentions that wound up having unintended consequences. For example, CHA's decision to build bigger apartments for bigger families had the noble goal of helping those who had the hardest time finding apartments in the private-housing market. But that decision inadvertently led to communities with an unusually high ratio of young people to adults, which in turn made it hard for public-housing residents to keep an eye on things and maintain order (what social scientists call "informal social control"). Another example is CHA's well-intentioned decision to prioritize the poorest families for public-housing units, since those are the families who need financial help the most. But that decision wound up exacerbating residential income segregation—creating communities where the overwhelming share of residents were poor. And because building upkeep came from tenant rent contributions that were (per federal law) set at a fixed share of tenant income, that decision also led to poorly maintained and run-down buildings. Projects like the Robert Taylor Homes and Cabrini-Green became known around the world for danger and destitution.

Harold Washington attended DuSable High School, which—since it was in the middle of the Black Belt—was one of the city's "Black schools." An 1863 ordinance had declared that it "shall not be lawful for such [colored] pupils to attend any public schools in the city of Chicago, at which white children are taught."[18] Even with many white schools at half capacity, crowding in the Black schools led Black students to attend school for just a half-day, so each school could run two shifts. In spite of these less-than-ideal circumstances, Washington became a voracious reader, to an extent that his brother "frequently accused him of eating a dictionary for lunch."[19]

Washington dropped out of high school in 1939 to join FDR's Civilian Conservation Corps (CCC).[20] This was the middle of the Great Depression; the US unemployment rate was 17 percent at the time.[21] The CCC and the Works Progress Administration together hired millions of jobless men in the 1930s, although both are defunct today. Since then, economic conditions have reverted back to their usual range (the US unemployment rate as I write this is 3.9 percent) and American social policy has as a result mostly focused on helping women, children, and the elderly.[22] The assumption behind the US social safety net in modern times has basically been that working-age men will be working in jobs that the market, not the government, provides for them.

When Harold Washington came back to Chicago in 1946 from the army, he had the GI Bill to help pay for college tuition but not a lot of college options available to him. He went to one of the first non-HBCU colleges to openly enroll Black students, Chicago's Roosevelt University.[23] There Washington got his start in politics as president of student government, which in turn gave him occasion for lots of practice with public speaking. He wound up giving one particularly pivotal speech in 1955 at Roosevelt in front of, among others, the then–newly elected mayor whose name would go on to become synonymous with corruption and bare-knuckled politics: Richard J. Daley.[24]

Since the late nineteenth century, Irish politicians in Chicago had sought to build a Democratic-political machine that would deal in, and be sustained by, favors (patronage jobs, welfare, city contracts, etc.) in exchange for votes. For much of this period, that approach didn't work because Chicago's electorate was too balanced between Republicans and Democrats.[25] There were attempts to convince people to cross party lines based on a purely ethnic-identity appeal ("Vote for Irish candidates"), but that didn't work because there weren't nearly enough Irish people living in the city. The political dynamic changed in 1931, when Czech Anton Cermak had the idea of putting together an ethnically balanced political slate to pull from other immigrant groups; one historian called him "the Democratic machine's George Washington."[26] The city hasn't had a Republican mayor since.

This was the state of Chicago politics when Washington started working for Alderman Ralph Metcalfe, famous for—among other things—coming in second to Jesse Owens in the 100-meter dash at the 1936 Berlin Olympics.[27] Metcalfe was part of the "Black sub-machine" that had developed in Chicago in the late 1930s, when the promise of patronage jobs and other benefits led William L. Dawson (a prominent politician of the time who'd become a US congressman) to switch his allegiance from the Republicans to the Democrats.[28] The Machine was at its peak. The Irish, only around 5 percent of the city's population, held over 40 percent of city and Cook County government jobs.[29]

Meanwhile, Chicago as a city was also at its peak. The city's population (3.62 million) was as large as it would ever be. Midway was the busiest airport in the world.[30] Chicago was producing more steel than all of Great Britain.[31] This would change. As one historian put it, "Chicago ended the twentieth century in a state that no one could have imagined in 1950."[32]

One set of unexpected changes stemmed from the Great Migration. Between 1940 and 1970, four million Black migrants left the South for the North. (By way of benchmark, there were about twelve million Black Americans left in the South by 1970.)[33] Chicago was a natural destination for many of those fleeing the South at the time in part because the Illinois Central Railroad connected the city to one of the states that Black Americans were most eager to leave: Mississippi, which had the most lynchings of any state between 1877 and 1950 (a total of 654)[34] and was the last state in the union to ratify the Thirteenth Amendment ending slavery (in 1995).[35]

White residents responded by fleeing in droves. Across US cities as a whole, data show that for every new Black resident who moved in, 2.7 whites moved out.[36] Between 1950 and 1989, the number of white residents in Chicago dropped by nearly one-half.[37] The number of white children in the Chicago Public Schools declined by three-quarters.[38] Since those whites who left were disproportionately drawn

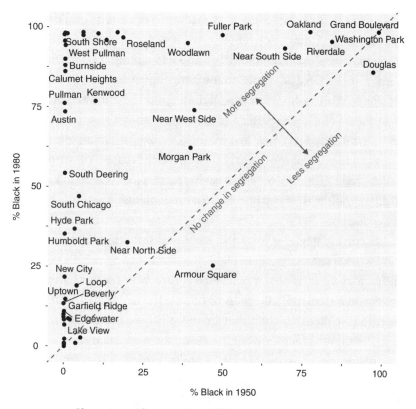

FIGURE 4.1: Change in racial composition of Chicago community areas, 1950–1980

from those who could afford to leave, white flight led to resource flight as well. Many neighborhoods in Chicago that were almost all white in 1950 had become almost all Black by 1980 (top left, figure 4.1).[39]

Macroeconomic forces were also changing in a way that undermined some of Chicago's biggest historical advantages.[40] Trucks made it easier for factories to be in suburban office parks or inland cities, rather than right next to key ports and railway nodes. As the economy shifted from manufacturing to the service sector, more jobs could be done anywhere. The telephone, fax machine, and Internet let economic value get transmitted electronically rather than physically. Economic success for cities started to depend more on their ability to attract highly educated workers looking for a high quality of life. Harvard economist Edward Glaeser has noted that one of the single best predictors of a city's growth is now its average January temperature.[41] That does not exactly play to Chicago's strengths.

Deindustrialization hit Chicago and its working class particularly hard. For the US as a whole, manufacturing peaked at 38 percent of all jobs in World War II but was all the way down to just 20 percent by 1983,[42] part of a larger pattern seen in most other high-income countries, too.[43] The Rust Belt lost manufacturing jobs at an even faster rate than the rest of the country.[44] In effect, the masses of people who had moved to Chicago for good-paying factory jobs that didn't require much schooling woke up one day to a fundamentally new and punishing economy.

Wisconsin Steel, for instance, employed something like five thousand workers at its 200-acre plant down at 106th Street. But in 1977, the factory's owner sold it to a small company in California that had never run a steel mill, allegedly to offload the pension obligations of its aging workers. In 1980 that small California company promised workers that the factory wouldn't close; the next day it closed. As the wife of one laid-off worker put it, "Families broke up. The men couldn't handle the loss [of their job], and the women couldn't handle what happened to the men." Another described the fallout: "These guys lost their wives, cars, homes, they lost everything. The wife, she said 'Get out, you aren't bringing in any money.'"[45]

Chicago also has the fiscal misfortune of being a city located within the state of Illinois. Set aside for the moment the state's unrivaled track record of corruption (four of its last seven governors have gone to jail). State policy decisions have led Cook County to be a net exporter of tax dollars to the state—the last time I checked the data, for every $1 in taxes sent to the state capital in Springfield, the county was getting just 90 cents of state services back.[46] In terms of state support for Chicago Public Schools, the Education Law Center gives Illinois an "F."[47] The state government in Springfield even limits how much Chicago can tax its own residents.[48]

This was the city Harold Washington inherited when he took the oath of office in 1983 at Navy Pier: shedding people and jobs; serving a disproportionately poor city population as affluent white people fled to the suburbs; segregated; struggling with budget problems; burdened by corruption; and suffering from a surge in gun violence. He recognized the scale of the problems in his inaugural address: "The only greater challenge in our history in Chicago was 110 years ago when Mayor Joseph Medill looked over a city burned to the ground and called for an enormous outpouring of civic spirit and resources to make the city new."[49]

ROOT CAUSES

At the time of Washington's inauguration as mayor, Chicago's murder rate was multiple times what it had been just a few decades earlier when he discharged from the army. To anyone who had been paying attention, the reason appeared tied to the decline in social conditions the city had experienced in the decades in between. In the proliferation of so many root causes, the city was seemingly manufacturing its own crime problem. As the nineteenth-century social scientist Adolphe Quetelet put it, "Society prepares the crime and the guilty is only the instrument by which it is accomplished."[50]

Washington—the Kennedy of "Chicago's Camelot"—sought to address and finally tackle the roots of these problems. His results and those of his successors tell us a lot about violence and its relationship to things we think we know about it.

Segregation and Social Isolation

The idea that neighborhood social and economic composition might affect crime and violence dates back at least to the Chicago school of sociology at the University of Chicago in the 1920s.[51] Many of the explanations for why segregation might affect crime are intrinsically related to the sociodemographic composition of a neighborhood per se—that is, there would seem to be no other way to undo the cause-and-effect link other than to reduce segregation. For example, many people believe that growing up in a segregated neighborhood shapes people's perceptions of their chances of success in mainstream society.[52] Those perceptions can lead to disillusionment that in turn leads people to turn to gangs and crime as alternative ways of achieving social status.[53] Segregated neighborhoods are also often depleted of middle-class residents who can role-model economic success and who might also help people get work through job referrals.[54]

Perhaps remarkable in hindsight is that there does not seem to be a single mention of segregation in Harold Washington's first or second inaugural addresses. Nor is the city's segregation really mentioned in the inaugural addresses of his successors, all Democrats.[55] Perhaps they were scared off by the prospect of white backlash. Or perhaps they were scared off by other NIMBY objections to building the sort of multi-family housing in the middle of single-family-home neighborhoods that's a key part of promoting economic and racial integration.

The net result has been remarkably little desegregation in practice (figure 4.2).[56] Looking at the racial composition of each of Chicago's seventy-seven community areas in 1980 and 2020, only two neighborhoods really desegregated: the Near South Side and the Near West Side, both next door to the downtown Loop. Each of these neighborhoods was predominantly Black in 1980 and then mostly non-Black by 2020 (to the bottom and right in figure 4.2). But almost every other neighborhood has almost the same racial composition in 1980 and 2020 (that is, located along the 45-degree line in figure 4.2). The result is that today, nearly three-quarters of Chicago's Black population lives in around one-quarter of the city's neighborhoods.

The same pattern holds in the other big cities of the Northeast and Midwest with large populations of Black Americans, what some experts on American inequality call the "Ghetto Belt."[57] To the extent to which there's been desegregation it seems to be largely limited to those metropolitan areas that have the fewest Black residents, and even the conclusion of progress in those areas is somewhat sensitive to the specific measure of segregation that one focuses on.[58]

The pattern of segregation by income is perhaps even more dispiriting. Rich people are increasingly living near other rich people, while the poor increasingly live near other poor people.[59] Given the correlation

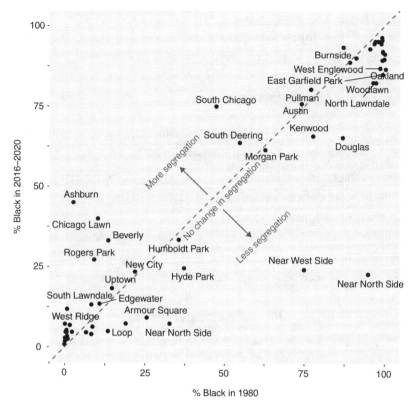

FIGURE 4.2: Change in racial composition of Chicago community areas, 1980 to 2016–2020

between race and income in America (and particularly within America's cities), this finding means that the rising economic segregation of neighborhoods helps reinforce the persistence of racial segregation as well.

The good news is there are other causal pathways through which segregation might affect crime and violence that could potentially be solved through policies that don't necessarily require widespread desegregation. Behavioral economics gives us ideas about what those key modifiable neighborhood features might be. For example, the absence of middle-class residents in segregated neighborhoods[60] may reduce the resources available to support local public goods—including local institutions like the churches, mosques, stores, and child care centers that can shape the level of social connection and informal social control in a place.[61] Therefore, policy could potentially ameliorate some of the harms of segregation in the near term while society continues the long-term effort to desegregate.

I return to this important point again in later chapters.

Racism and Discrimination

Racial bias and discrimination are arguably another root cause that sits upstream of every other root cause: They deny people access not just to integrated neighborhoods but to schools, jobs, government resources, nonprofit help, and everything else. In the late 1960s, President Lyndon Johnson commissioned the National Advisory Commission on Civil Disorders (the so-called Kerner Commission, after its chair, Illinois governor Otto Kerner) to investigate and explain the riots and violence wracking American cities at the time. The Kerner Commission wrote then, "Our Nation is moving toward two societies, one black, one white—separate and unequal. . . . Discrimination and segregation have long permeated much of American life; they now threaten the future of every American."[62] Johnson, in his foreword to the Kerner Commission's report, wrote: "The only genuine, long-range solution for what has happened lies in an attack—mounted at every level—upon the conditions that breed despair and violence. All of us know what those conditions are: ignorance, discrimination, slums, poverty, disease, not enough jobs."[63]

Harold Washington's administration made addressing discrimination a priority by building a "rainbow coalition" in Chicago—a formalized approach to bringing groups together to try to reduce intergroup tension. As one observer put it, "Harold, unquestionably, was committed to the welfare of Blacks, but not so much because they were Black, but because he saw this as a way of healing the divisions in our society that would make it possible for people to move forward." The same observer described Washington as one of the most skilled politicians of his generation, "the Joe Louis of politics."[64] Another observer talked about how he learned a new type of decency and openness from Harold Washington, that after seeing him Chicago residents "are more tolerant in an average, everyday sense."[65]

So how have racial attitudes changed over time? We don't have data to be able to track racial attitudes in Chicago specifically over a long period of time. But we can do that for the US as a whole by using data from the General Social Survey. This kind of analysis offers good news and bad news.

The good news is that compared to when Harold Washington was starting his political career in the 1970s, racial attitudes by whites (at least according to self-reported surveys) have gotten better. Back then, almost two-thirds of white Americans said they thought "most Blacks don't have the motivation or willpower to pull themselves out of poverty." Over half of whites would oppose a relative marrying a Black person, and nearly half said they wouldn't want to live in a neighborhood where half or more of residents are Black.[66] Figure 3.1 from the last chapter shows that those figures are all much lower today.

The bad news is how much bias remains: A remarkably large share of white Americans will admit to a survey interviewer that they hold quite discriminatory attitudes. Even today, around one in ten white Americans says they wouldn't want a relative to marry a Black person, one in four says they think it's okay to discriminate when selling a house, and one in three says the racial wealth gap is due to a lack of motivation among Black Americans (see figure 3.1).[67]

Stark as these numbers may seem in the twenty-first century, they surely understate how much racial bias actually remains in the US. One reason is that many other people who share these sentiments will be reluctant to say that to the survey interviewer, a phenomenon survey researchers call "social desirability bias." Another reason is that these surveys don't capture *implicit* bias, or discriminatory attitudes people have that operate below the level of consciousness; people might not even be aware they have these attitudes. How much implicit bias has changed over time, and how much remains today, is unclear.

Unfortunately, little is known about how to change racial attitudes through policy intervention. A review of 418 different randomized experiments in psychology by Betsy Levy Paluck of Princeton and her colleagues found that diversity training and implicit-bias training seem to have limited effects on people: "One of the sobering takeaways from this body of research is that while we find that the interventions often achieve some of their goals of reducing prejudice, their effects are often limited in size, scope or duration."[68] No wonder that in a 2019 survey, 56 percent of whites and 71 percent of Black Americans said that "race relations in the US are generally bad."[69]

City Fiscal Capacity

The city budget, like segregation, can be thought of as a sort of meta-root cause that sits upstream of so many other root causes. That is to say, the city can't help people with housing, childcare, food insecurity, schools, health care, transportation, or anything else without money. Fixing the city's budget situation was a top priority for Harold Washington. As one account of his administration put it, "His was the most fiscally responsible administration in decades. He inherited a huge deficit but balanced the budget and raised the city's credit rating."[70]

Yet the city's budget situation since Washington has for the most part been trending in the wrong direction. Politicians have learned that an easy way to buy peace with the city's public-sector unions is to buy them off with generous contracts. Local politicians have also learned how easy it is to paper over short-term budget problems by taking on more debt and underfunding current pension obligations.

The result: Chicago faces a budget deficit of $500 million for fiscal year 2024, which may grow to as much as $1.9 billion by 2026.[71] The city has the highest pension debt per person of any big city (nearly $19,000), which is about twice as much as the two next-worst places in the country (Puerto Rico and New York City).[72] People in Chicago got excited when Fitch Ratings upgraded Chicago's general obligation bond debt rating from BBB– to BBB in 2022.[73] You don't need to be a municipal finance expert to realize that BBB is farther from the top rating than one might wish.

Families

I wasn't living in Chicago when Washington was mayor, but since I moved here in 2007 I have observed a clear pattern in how mayors talk about addressing gun violence. Most new mayors come into office initially talking about solving poverty and other root causes. That goal usually doesn't go anywhere. Then they start talking about different "get tough on crime" policies. When those policies show limited progress, the mayor blames national gun laws. When people get sick of hearing about national gun laws, the mayor starts blaming the local prosecutor. When that eventually gets stale, we reach the endpoint of the cycle: The mayor starts blaming parents for not raising their kids properly. There have been a few administrations where I've had the thought, "Uh oh, the new mayor is talking about parents *already*."

In fairness, *lots* of Americans are worried about the state of families. In surveys about what causes crime, Americans seem to connect family to concerns about moral development. Survey respondents point to causes of crime like "lack of moral training in the home," "absence of fathers," or "breakdown of the family."[74] There's some data to support at least parts of this story; economist Melissa Kearney's book *The Two-Parent Privilege* documents all the ways in which having two parents shapes children's life outcomes.[75]

But public policy has not been able to shift trends in that direction. In fact, most trends have been going in the opposite direction. For example, from 1968 to 2020 the share of American children living with only one (or neither) parent doubled, from 15 to 30 percent.[76]

Corruption

Harold Washington saw up close how little the Chicago political machine had provided Black families in return for their votes. In his inaugural address, he noted that among his challenges, "in the waning days of the outgoing administration, hundreds of new city jobs were passed out and hundreds of other jobs reassigned." He noted, "My election was made possible by thousands and thousands of people who demanded that the burdens of mismanagement, unfairness and inequity be lifted so that the city could be saved."[77]

Corruption's links to gun violence take many forms: by draining resources from things that would help people and address their various needs (all the downstream root causes of gun violence); by granting underqualified people government jobs, including within the justice system and social-service agencies; by undermining the public's confidence in the government.

Here, for example, is longtime Chicago columnist Mike Royko's description of how police used to handle speeders "too shy or dense" to dispose of a traffic stop by folding a ten-dollar bill around their license: "On the Southwest Side, another policeman stopped a motorist and used a different approach when the motorist didn't gift wrap his license. He carried wooden pencils in his pocket, and he would announce: 'I have three kinds of pencils which I sell—a five-dollar pencil, a ten-dollar pencil, and a twenty-five-dollar pencil. I think you need a ten-dollar pencil, don't you?' The pencils were seldom sold for more than twenty-five dollars, because that would have meant somebody had been run over, and fixing that required the cooperation of prosecutors and even judges and was not something that could be arranged on the scene."[78]

As Royko noted, the problem ran up and down the justice system. "Vito Marzullo is a ward committeeman and an alderman. He was born in Italy and has an elementary school education, but for years when he arrived at political functions, a judge walked a few steps behind him, moving ahead when there was a door to be opened. Marzullo had put him on the bench."[79]

How has the drive for good government in Chicago turned out? If one wanted to start with the glass-half-full perspective, one might note that several of the state's last ten governors have *not* wound up in prison.[80] Similarly, only thirty city council members have been convicted of crimes since 1973.[81]

Perhaps less encouraging is that the year Washington was inaugurated as a reformer, Illinois started a forty-year stretch of being run through what one witness described as a system of "intimidation and fear" by Michael Madigan as Illinois House Speaker, who was recently hit with a federal indictment for racketeering, bribery, and conspiracy.[82] That's just the cherry on top of a slew of garden-variety corruption cases: the school official charged with overstating her salary to fraudulently get more pandemic relief aid than she was entitled to;[83] the city treasurer who asked her city employees to plan a birthday party for her daughter;[84] the police commander who ordered officers to babysit his son then tried to claim it was "really a secret study."[85]

Federal corruption convictions provide an objective measure of the problem. Looking at data for the period 1976–2020, Illinois comes in as the third-most-corrupt state in the US.[86] Chicago proudly picks up the slack—despite being notably smaller than other metropolitan areas like Los Angeles and New York, we're number one in total corruption convictions.[87]

I could go on. But the larger point is that some of the root causes that are plausibly most important for gun violence have proven enormously difficult to change. They were hard to change not just by Mayor Washington, an exceptionally talented politician (the "Joe Louis of politics," the Kennedy of Chicago's Camelot), but by subsequent mayors too. And that's a story we see not just in Chicago, but all around the country as well.

FROM JOBS TO "JOBS AREN'T ENOUGH"

If there is one root cause that the government *has* been able to substantially change, it is poverty: lack of income and lack of work. Harold Washington and many others (including me) long maintained that poverty, if anything, should be the most important root cause for gun violence—that giving someone a job or more social-program benefits would by itself be enough to reduce their risk of violence involvement. But it turns out that is not the case.

Jobs and income loomed large in Washington's own thinking about how to improve everything in the city, including crime and violence. In his second inaugural address, in 1987, he argued: "Our most urgent need is for jobs. Give us jobs and we'll take care of the rest. Jobs will rebuild self-esteem; jobs will restore community pride; jobs will cut down the dropout rate; jobs will slow down the cycles of crime, youth gangs, drugs, child abuse and abuse of women; jobs will reaffirm the justice of our economic system; jobs will reduce teenage pregnancy; jobs will ultimately end the human tragedy of welfare dependency."[88]

Washington was not alone in this focus. To address gun violence in LA, Father Greg Boyle founded Homeboy Industries with the motto, "Nothing stops a bullet like a job."[89] Former US secretary of education Arne Duncan returned to Chicago from the Obama administration to address gun violence here by founding Chicago CRED, for "Create Real Economic Destiny." When he was starting CRED, as he put it, "I always say we're trying to solve an economic problem, not a crime problem. We have to continue to employ and create jobs."[90]

Having been trained as an economist, for many years I myself focused on jobs as a key strategy for reducing crime and violence. The late University of Chicago economist Gary Becker argued that people's decisions to commit crime are "rational," involving a careful weighing of benefits and costs, the same way that all sorts of other behaviors are as well.[91] Under this perspective, poverty and joblessness will make the benefits of crime loom large, and—since jobless, low-income people might feel like they've got little to lose—the costs of crime from getting caught loom too modest.

Focus groups suggest that lots of normal Americans think the same thing: People "commit crimes because they have weighed the costs, benefits and risks associated with an act and then made a conscious choice or decision to break the law." Researchers who carry out focus groups about what Americans think about crime report that economic motivation for crime was "a dominant cultural model throughout our interviews in both its frequency and its power in crowding out other ways of thinking."[92] People recognize the role of "ecological factors" and tend to focus on poverty and joblessness.[93] Even professionals who see the criminal-justice system up close every day—judges—believe this, as revealed by their actions: They tend to give relatively more lenient sentences to unemployed defendants.[94]

No wonder. Just look at who's most likely to be involved in crime (as victims or offenders): those who are much closer to the bottom of the income distribution than to the top.[95]

But notice that the overrepresentation of low-income people as violence victims and offenders by itself isn't sufficient evidence that income or employment status causally affects risk of crime and violence. The reason is because there are different dimensions of disadvantage in America, and they tend to cluster together. People who are unemployed or otherwise have low income are also likely to have *other disadvantages*, too: They live in under-resourced neighborhoods; they have access to inadequate public schools or health care or housing; they live in cities where local government doesn't always work well.

The key factual question is whether a policy narrowly focused on changing someone's level of material deprivation—a policy that gives someone a job or food stamps or cash or a subsidized apartment—is enough to independently cause a reduction in gun violence.

The Good News

The good news is that there is one root cause the government does know how to solve: poverty, defined in the literal sense of having too little income. The government turns out to be really good at writing checks.

The idea that the government is capable of addressing jobs and poverty might be surprising, since the *official* poverty rate hasn't changed much over the past half-century. But in recent years, many economists have been taking another look at how the US measures poverty and have come to the conclusion that poverty has actually become *much* less common.[96]

For starters, the data indicate that over time, fewer Americans seem to be suffering from different types of material hardship. For example, from the 1970s to today, a much lower share of people live somewhere that's unheated or overcrowded or has a leaky roof.[97] The share of people with air conditioning has gone up by quite a bit.[98] The share of people without a car, which in a country like the US (with such limited public transportation) is critical for accessing jobs and educational opportunities and health care and grocery stores, has dropped by half.[99]

A similar conclusion comes from looking directly at poverty itself after addressing some subtle measurement issues like how one accounts for inflation, or whether one looks just at what people earn versus also considering what they get from government social programs.[100] While some academic debate still remains, it seems like a bipartisan consensus is developing: The right-of-center American Enterprise Institute and left-of-center Center for Budget Policies and Priorities seem to agree that over the past fifty years, poverty has been cut by nearly 50 percent.[101]

People struggling without jobs, without money, is one social problem that the country does seem to know how to solve. How useful is that knowledge for ending gun violence?

Relearning Old Lessons

While James Q. Wilson and Marvin Wolfgang were two of the most important criminologists of the twentieth century's second half, one of the most important in the first half of the twentieth century was Edwin Sutherland. He's gone down in history as the person who coined the term "white-collar crime," but he was also a leading expert on other crime topics, too. Sutherland noticed that while there was more crime in poor neighborhoods than in rich ones, when economic conditions *improved* within a neighborhood, crime rates didn't decline. Sutherland's conclusion: "Poverty as such is not an important cause of crime."[102]

With the benefit of decades more data I would amend Sutherland's conclusion slightly: Poverty and joblessness *do* seem to be associated with overall crime rates, particularly property crime, but by themselves they don't seem to be key causes of *gun violence* specifically.

Consider the New Deal, which gave Harold Washington his CCC job and helped lift millions of people out of poverty as well. The New Deal increased social relief spending in cities from $1.54 per person in 1930 up to $21.75 by 1940 (the equivalent of $8,000 per year in 2023 dollars for a family of four).[103] But that New Deal money wasn't spread evenly; more wound up going to places where people tended to be more reliable voters for Democrats. All that extra New Deal spending reduced property crime but had no detectable effects on homicides (the crime most frequently involving guns, and the crime that dominates the social harms of crime).[104]

We see the same pattern from looking at different natural experiments in modern-day America. For example, cities and states differ in whether they pay out welfare benefits weekly versus monthly. When they pay out monthly, people tend to wind up more economically desperate toward the end of each month because they wind up spending their monthly benefits faster. Comparing monthly to weekly cities, property crime increases toward the end of the month—but violent crime doesn't.[105] When people lose eligibility for Supplemental Security Income benefits at age 18, they're more likely to commit property crimes but not violence.[106]

You see the same pattern when you look at programs to help the people at statistically highest risk for crime and violence involvement: those who are already justice-system-involved. For example, back in the 1970s the US Department of Labor enrolled four thousand people exiting prison in Texas and Georgia and randomly offered half of them to get six months of cash payments worth about half of what this group could earn if they were working.[107] There were no detectable impacts on recidivism rates for any sort of crime.[108] More recent data on what happens when reentering prisoners are given subsidized jobs show similar findings. At best, these temporary jobs reduce re-offending for less serious crimes but not for violence.[109]

There's a similar pattern if we look not just at the effects of short-term cash or subsidized jobs but at the effects of long-term access to more generous social-program benefits. The research suggests that reentering from prison into a state and time period with more generous benefits reduces property crime but has mixed effects on violent crime—one study suggests that violence does decline,[110] but another suggests that violence may actually increase.[111]

Policymakers are often worried about giving people cash: Maybe recipients will squander those dollars on luxuries rather than necessities? That's why so many social programs provide in-kind benefits (food stamps, health insurance, housing).

Relative to cash transfers, do in-kind transfer programs have bigger impacts on gun violence? That's not what we seem to see in the data.[112] Changing food-stamp (Supplemental Nutrition Assistance Program, or SNAP) eligibility of people convicted of drug crimes changes their likelihood of property offenses but not violence.[113] States that give out SNAP benefits monthly rather than weekly see a rise in property crimes toward the end of the month (as people start running out of food) but don't see a rise in violent crimes like assaults.[114] I was part of a research team myself with Brian Jacob and Max Kapustin that looked at what happened when Chicago held a randomized lottery to decide which families got housing vouchers. These vouchers represented enormously generous benefits by the standards of US social policy, equal to about two-thirds of the average family's annual income. Yet there were no detectable effects on any type of crime over the fourteen-year follow-up.[115]

There seem to be only a few exceptions to the rule.

One exception is transfer programs that help people who are about to wind up in particularly risky or dangerous situations—people who are about to become homeless or who are living in situations with heightened risk of domestic violence—get out of those situations.[116]

A second exception is social programs that help build "human capital," like public education or public health insurance that allows people with mental illnesses to get treatment.[117] Interestingly, youth summer-jobs programs may be another example of a human capital intervention that reduces violence.[118] Summer jobs for teens reduce violent-crime involvement, but apparently not through a Gary Becker–like process in which better legal labor-market opportunities raise the opportunity costs of crime. That conclusion stems from the observation that the teens who show the largest reductions in violence from having a summer job are *not* the ones who experience the largest economic benefits. The summer jobs seem to be working instead through some sort of "human capital" effect. I will return to this important point in chapter 9.

But these exceptions to the rule aren't frequent enough to overturn the rule, as we can see from looking at what happens on net to overall violent-crime rates when macroeconomic conditions change. What happens when the rising tide of an improving economy overall lifts all boats? We don't see reductions in violence when a casino opens on an Indian reservation and hands out large-scale cash payments to residents,[119] or when a place gets selected by the Department of Defense as the location for a big new military base,[120] or when the Department of Defense gives a big new defense contract to the place that's home to the defense contractor.[121]

When the US economy comes out of recession, income-motivated crimes like robbery decline but murder doesn't. As Harvard psychologist Steven Pinker put it, violent crime does not "closely track the economic indicators. The careenings of the American homicide rate in the twentieth century were largely uncorrelated with measures of prosperity; the murder rate plunged in the mist of the Great Depression, soared during the boom years of the 1960s, and hugged new lows during the Great Recession that began in 2007. The poor correlation could have been predicted by the police blotters, which show that homicides are driven by moralistic motives like payback for insults and infidelity rather than by material motives such as cash or food."[122]

The surprising conclusion that murder rates don't increase during economic downturns but if anything *decrease*[123] was captured by the title of one particularly influential paper: "Are recessions good for your health?"[124] The leading explanation is that when people have more money in their pocket, they go out more (trips to bars, restaurants, concerts, etc.) and so they have more social interactions; they're also drinking more. That leads to more social friction—that is, arguments. I'll come back to this important point in the next chapter.

The lesson seems to be that gun violence is related to something *correlated* with joblessness and poverty, but changing joblessness and poverty by itself isn't enough to change whatever this other thing is. To see that there's something more going on, just look at the pattern of gun violence across Chicago neighborhoods (figure 4.3).[125] All rich neighborhoods are safe. And every high-violence neighborhood is poor. But there's enormous variability across equally low-income neighborhoods in Chicago in their rates of gun violence.

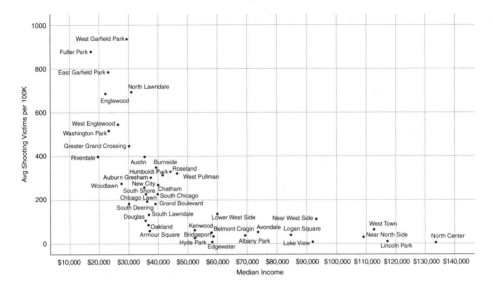

FIGURE 4.3: Median household income vs. shooting rates per 100,000 residents, Chicago community areas, 2016–2020

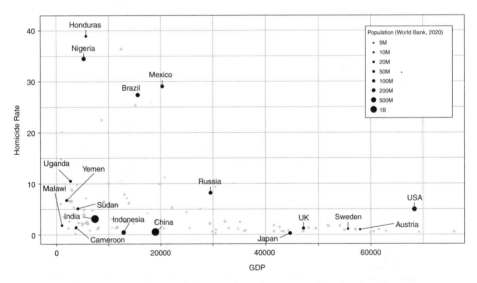

FIGURE 4.4: Homicides per 100,000 residents, by country, plotted against Gross Domestic Product (GDP) per capita (adjusted for purchasing power parity)

There's a similar pattern across countries: Almost every rich country (except the US) is safe, while all the most unsafe countries—Mexico, Brazil, Nigeria—are quite poor. But it's *not* true that every poor country is dangerous (figure 4.4).[126]

That would have been hard to figure out from news coverage. Reporters go to Greater Grand Crossing when there is a tragedy ("11-year-old girl shot in the cheek inside her bedroom from stray bullet"), but reporters (perhaps understandably) rarely write articles like "No one was shot in South Shore yesterday." Newspapers run headlines like "Drug gang kills 20 in town hall massacre in southern Mexico,"[127] not "Why does India have so few murders?"

CONCLUSION

Chicago mayors since at least the time of Harold Washington (if not long before) have been worrying about the root causes of gun violence. Segregation. Discrimination. Despair. Social isolation. Poverty. Joblessness. Broken families. Corruption. Empty city coffers. Those root causes didn't develop overnight, and they didn't develop by accident. They're the result of powerful forces. Out-group bias and discrimination. NIMBYism. Social isolation. Bitter city versus downstate politics. Deindustrialization. A limited federal social safety net.

No wonder so many of these root causes have proven so resistant to change, as the data unfortunately make amply clear. This isn't just a Chicago story. Look at Newark. Philadelphia. Baltimore. Washington, DC. Atlanta. Louisville. Cincinnati. Pittsburgh. Cleveland. Detroit. Milwaukee. Indianapolis. St. Louis. Memphis. New Orleans. Tulsa. Kansas City. Las Vegas. Oakland. This is to say nothing of the smaller satellite cities across the country like Camden, New Jersey; Gary, Indiana; and East St. Louis, Illinois. No wonder the public often feels like the problem of gun violence is simply "too big to fix."[128]

The good news is that there is one root cause that the government has been successful in fixing: poverty. Yet as the data accumulate, many of us who were sure that jobs and cash would be sufficient to reduce gun violence are realizing that's not the case. Father Greg Boyle of Homeboy Industries in LA, the one who came up with the slogan "Nothing stops a bullet like a job," has taken to saying, "It's not enough to just say 'here's a job.'"[129] Arne Duncan, the former US secretary of education who now runs the anti-violence organization CRED in Chicago, started off saying Chicago gun violence wasn't a crime problem but an economic problem. CRED is now saying, "You also need wraparound services."[130] That's a journey I've made, too. Jobs and cash by themselves don't seem to be enough to solve America's crisis of gun violence.

The lesson from the data seems to be that some of the root causes that potentially matter the most for gun violence are hard to change. The root causes that the government is best able to change are the ones that might matter the least for gun violence.

The conventional wisdom of the Left, in other words, provides an incomplete blueprint about how to make progress on this regressive public health crisis. *Of course* America should keep trying to solve root causes, even if doing so isn't sufficient to reduce gun violence, because root causes matter for people's lives in all sorts of other ways. Violence is one important policy goal but only one; lifting people out of poverty and segregation and social isolation is itself a key goal of policy as well. And just because many of these root causes are hard to solve doesn't mean we should give up. As Václav Havel put it, hope is the "ability to work for something because it is good, not just because it stands a chance to succeed."[131]

Yet from the perspective of solving gun violence, we can't *just* focus on trying to change these big, hard-to-change root causes. That's a recipe for subjecting millions of people living in the country's most distressed, disadvantaged, segregated communities to decades more of unrelenting gun violence. We need to try something new.

To do that, we need a new understanding of the problem.

5

Vital Statistics

Richard J. "R. J." Vanecko was named in honor of his grandfather, Richard J. Daley, who was mayor of Chicago from 1955 until his death in office in 1976. One of R. J.'s uncles served as commerce secretary, another was a Cook County commissioner, a third ran a big law firm that handles zoning appeals to city hall, and a fourth uncle, Richard M., ran city hall as mayor from 1989 to 2011. I'm not sure what it means to be a Windsor in London or a Kennedy in Boston, but I know what it means to be a Daley in Chicago.

It means growing up in one of the city's fanciest neighborhoods, Sauganash; going to one of the area's best high schools, Loyola Academy; having a father who is a surgeon at Northwestern University's glass-and-steel hospital complex downtown, near the park named in honor of your aunt Maggie Daley (Richard M.'s late wife); and working at an investment company run by someone who was, reportedly, a friend of the mayor's.[1] That same R. J. Vanecko, in one of the city's entertainment areas late one night in 2004, killed a 21-year-old named David Koschman.

The handling of this tragedy did not reflect local government at its finest. The detectives in charge of the case gave conflicting accounts about when they realized the suspect was the mayor's nephew. The same detectives never collected video evidence or took a statement from R. J. Vanecko. Their final report was six months late. They claimed their case files got lost. A few years later, a new police chief ordered a complete reinvestigation; only *after* the reinvestigation was finished were the lost files somehow "found" (the skeptical quotes here are not mine; they come from the official government investigation into the handling of the case).[2] The prosecutor's case files also somehow went missing—not just the hard copy, but the electronic version, too. As a *Chicago Sun-Times* headline put it: "No Charges in Fatal Fight Involving Daley's Nephew. Did Clout Play a Role? 'Of Course Not,' Police Chief Says."[3]

Vanecko was eventually convicted of involuntary manslaughter for delivering a punch to Koschman, who never regained consciousness after his head hit the sidewalk. While a lot of ink has been spilled about the government's handling of the case, most relevant for my purposes is the question: *Why* did Vanecko kill David Koschman?

Conventional wisdom can't explain it. Was Vanecko a psychopath? Was this killing part of a pattern of serial violence? There are no signs of either thing. Since being released from a sixty-day jail sentence, Vanecko does not appear to have gotten into any other major trouble. Was it a robbery gone bad or part of a turf battle over drug selling? Was it motivated by money? Considering Vanecko's status as a scion of Chicago royalty, it's clear that, whatever reason Koschman was killed, it was *not* because an economically desperate person was trying to put bread on the table.

Koschman was killed because, as one witness put it, he was being "mouthy."[4]

It's in this way that the incident, despite all the media attention, was indistinguishable from the vast majority of murders in America: It started with words. Most homicides are arguments that end in tragedy, usually because someone has a gun (or, in Vanecko's case, because they're such a physically large person they can kill without a gun).

If the mundane motivation behind this high-profile death comes as a surprise, it's because it doesn't fit with the countless news stories you've read over the years about violence in America. That's because the essential role of the free press in gathering and delivering the news of the day is complicated by financial realities: Media must tell a good story in order to make people pay attention, which is what in turn makes money. In the matter of gun violence, this kind of storytelling often means overemphasizing the stuff that sells—the scandalous, the salacious, the storybook. It also, unintentionally, often creates an understanding of the problem that is separate from the reality.

AN UNQUANTIFIED VIEW

In eighteenth-century London, only one-third of all children lived to see their fifth birthday.[5] It was a world, in the words of journalist Bill Bryson, of "tiny coffins."[6] Childhood deaths were viewed as inevitable, "a reflection of the natural order in which the strong outlived the weak."[7] The only solution, it was thought, was for parents to play the odds—to have lots of kids. This resignation and the negative outcomes that followed from it weren't unique to London. About half of children around the world never lived to see first grade.[8]

What has changed since then? An important first step was *quantification*.

Why were children dying? Most everyone could enumerate the same list of candidate reasons: Violence. Disease. Neglect. Malnutrition. Exposure. Birth defects. Complications at birth.

Even though everyone could list the same candidate causes of early death, there was nonetheless heated debate about what to do to prevent them. Many reformers were making impassioned pleas to end poverty.[9] Other people were making their own version of a wicked-person argument, calling for the government to get tough with parents and address their "defects in intelligence and moral character . . . [their] ignorance, laziness and substance abuse."[10]

The larger issue seems clear in hindsight. There were indeed *lots* of causes for childhood deaths and thus lots of different paths to the end state of childhood mortality. Child mortality was not a single problem with a single cause; it was a catchall term for a bundle of problems, each of which has different causes (and hence different solutions).

Different people came to different conclusions about what to do not because people had a different list of causes of child mortality, but because people had different assumptions about the *relative frequency* of each cause.

The solution, in hindsight, is also obvious: Collect careful data on individual deaths ("vital statistics"), count the relative frequency of each cause (as opposed to *assuming* the relative frequency of each cause), and then prioritize those policies that most effectively address the most common causes of childhood death.

What did the most common cause (by far) of childhood mortality turn out to be once vital statistics were collected? The answer turned out to be fairly mundane: *disease*, things like diarrhea and pneumonia.[11]

From there the solution was not to focus exclusively on achieving massive social change, like ending poverty. Nor was the solution to impose draconian punishments on parents. It was instead a series of targeted, pragmatic public health steps like pasteurizing milk and providing access to antimicrobial drugs. The result was a dramatic decline in child mortality, one of the key reasons why since 1900 life expectancy around the world has doubled.[12]

That technocratic approach wound up being enormously progressive in its impacts, helping the most disadvantaged the most, because child mortality imposed a much bigger burden on the poor than on the rich. Understanding the modifiable causal pathway between disadvantage and child mortality enabled society to make rapid progress reducing disparities in child mortality, greatly improving the lives of low-income families, without having to wait until the problem of poverty itself could be solved.

There's a similar sort of confusion or talking-past-each-other about candidate solutions—and a similar unrealized potential for progressive social gains—with the modern-day American problem of gun violence. What are the specific causes or motivations for gun violence? Everyone can give the same list of candidate explanations: Psychopaths. Robberies. Gang wars over drug-selling turf. Arguments.

But everyone has a harder time understanding the relative frequency of these causes, partly because the news headlines focus on a nonrepresentative set of cases. You can see this focus in surveys that ask Americans what they think of when they hear the term "gun violence."[13] Two of the three most common answers were "mental health" and "robbery" (the third was "assault"). No wonder so much of the policy discussion is about either locking up psychopaths or ending poverty. But those are not the most common motivations for shootings.

PSYCHOPATHS

If the business model of news and entertainment media is to give the people what they want, the people have been very clear on what that is: People want stories about psychopaths. We want serial killers and cults and premeditation.[14]

A media frenzy followed the killing of Sharon Tate in 1969 by Charles Manson's "family." In the 1970s, another media frenzy was set off by David Berkowitz, the Son of Sam killer. After Jeffrey Dahmer was arrested in Milwaukee for multiple murders involving sexual abuse and cannibalism, the *New York Times* ran a story at least a half-page long every day for eight straight days. Dahmer made the cover of *People* magazine—one of the "100 most intriguing people of the 20th century." Ted Bundy was the subject of over ten thousand news stories. After a well-received movie about him came out in 2020 (starring Zac Efron), *Women's Health* helpfully published a list of "best Bundy movies" for readers.[15]

In Chicago in January 2021, a 32-year-old named Jason Nightengale, who, as his family put it, was "fighting some demons,"[16] experienced some sort of mental break. After driving around Chicago for a few days in the new year flashing his gun on Facebook Live and talking about killing people ("I'm going to blow up the whole community, you all can start the fuck over over here"[17]), on Saturday, January 9, he snapped and shot seven people. Among the victims was a 30-year-old fourth-year PhD student in financial economics at the University of Chicago named Yiran Fan; Nightengale found him sitting in a car in the garage of a Hyde Park apartment building and shot him in the head.[18] This was not the only shooting in Chicago that weekend, to be sure. But it's the only Chicago shooting that made newspaper headlines all over the world.

Media directs readers and viewers to focus not only on the most violent, salacious crimes but on the most violent, salacious details. In the coverage of Dahmer's seventeen murders, the details offered included how "Mr. Dahmer drugged [the victim's] drinks, strangled them and cut up their bodies with an electric buzz saw . . . he discarded bones he did not want in a 57-gallon drum he had bought for just that purpose . . . he lined up three skulls on a shelf in his apartment. . . . Once, he told the police in Milwaukee, he fried a victim's bicep in vegetable shortening and ate it." This account is from not some trashy tabloid but the *New York Times*.[19]

You'll remember some of these vivid details forever. If you ever try to call to mind an example of a serial killer, it won't be hard to do.

But these exceptional cases have also seeded, unintentionally, a conventional wisdom that gun violence is due, pathologically, to bad people—people who are fundamentally different from the rest of us. The problem is not that this wisdom is always wrong but rather that it's only infrequently right. The question, in other words, is not *whether* there are psychopaths, or whether they harm people. The real question instead is: What share of gun violence do they account for?

Different ways of answering that question all point to the same answer: just a modest share.

One way to answer the question is to look at what share of people who commit murders meet clinical criteria for psychopathy. To do that, researchers interview convicted murderers in prison and assess them for psychopathy. This approach is imperfect, partly because diagnosis of psychopathy is itself imperfect[20] and partly because only around one in four murderers winds up in prison.[21] It's very possible that those murderers with the most extensive prior records—like psychopaths— are disproportionately likely to get caught and, if caught, to be sentenced to prison. So with the caveat that inmates aren't necessarily representative of all murderers,[22] the data suggest the share of those in prison who are psychopaths might be on the order of 15 to 25 percent.[23]

A different way to understand what share of all gun violence is due to psychopaths is to look at the *offenses* rather than the *offenders*. If a key characteristic of psychopaths is that they keep committing violent acts over and over, we could look, for instance, at what share of murders have multiple victims. The answer seems to be about 10 percent.[24]

Or one could look at serial killings, where a given offender has multiple victims over an extended time period. Here, the FBI's best guess is that the share of murders that are part of serial killings is less than 1 percent.[25]

Or one could look at how concentrated the predictable risk of gun violence is within the population. Suppose most gun violence *is* due to psychopaths. A defining characteristic of psychopaths is antisocial behavior over the life course—starting early in life and persisting throughout adulthood. So we'd expect most shooters would be people with long track records of prior criminal offenses, including violence. There would be a predictable pattern of who will be involved in most of the violence that will happen in the future—a small number of psychopaths with long, violent rap sheets.[26] This is, in fact, what many criminologists claim: that it's possible to walk into a Chicago community that's home to tens of thousands of people and spot the few dozen people who will be driving most of the gun violence.[27]

But this possibility is not what the data seem to suggest.

Some researchers who are alumni of my research center, the University of Chicago Crime Lab, predicted people's risk of gun violence involvement[28] using 12.7 million crime records from the Chicago Police Department over a twenty-year period (1999 to 2019). These researchers used data from someone's past criminal record to predict their likelihood of being involved in gun violence over the next year or two. It's true that a small group of people predictably account for an outsized share of shootings. For example, the highest-risk 0.1 percent of people in Chicago (3,381 people total) have a risk of gun violence involvement that's around eighteen times everyone else's. But this high-risk group accounts for "just" 9 percent of all the shootings. Most shootings involve people at much lower risk—those who are closer to "normal people" than they are to the highest-risk psychopaths.

Even this analysis may overstate the concentration of risk across a small number of people, because given the high levels of economic and racial segregation in Chicago and the concentration of community-level risk factors in those segregated neighborhoods, the characteristics of *people* are highly correlated with characteristics of their *situations*.[29] If gun violence is driven by a small number of high-risk people in each neighborhood, then most of the variation in predictable risk should be *within* neighborhoods: I should be able to walk into any neighborhood and pick out the high-risk shooters or victims based on their prior records. But if gun violence risk is driven more by high-risk *situations*, then most of the variation in risk should lie *between* neighborhoods—there will be big differences in average risk for every young man living in Greater Grand Crossing than in South Shore, but within each neighborhood, it's much harder to distinguish which specific people are at higher or lower risk from their neighbors. This analysis raises a number of subtle technical challenges, and it's possible that other researchers using other data or different methods might get a different answer. But as best I can tell from analyzing the Chicago data that I have access to myself, it seems like most of the predictable risk in gun violence involvement seems to be between rather than within neighborhoods; that is, risk of gun violence involvement seems to be more about the specific neighborhood than about the specific person.[30]

Consistent with that conclusion is evidence that when extra police get sent in to patrol some high-crime hot spot, displacement (the tendency of crime to pop up somewhere else) seems to be more likely with property crime than with violent crime.[31] This finding is what we would expect to see if violent crime (unlike property crime) is driven by fleeting rather than persistent motivations, and if situational factors are important in determining whether those fleeting motivations turn into violence. Similarly, we see in randomized experiments that moving people from distressed neighborhoods to less distressed ones reduces violent crime but not property crime, as I discuss more in chapter 8.

Ultimately, the strongest evidence about the importance of psychopaths for gun violence comes from the evidence on policy interventions, also discussed in much greater detail in chapter 8. A key component of the definition of psychopaths is that they're deeply resistant—maybe even immune—to rehabilitation. Indeed, as noted in chapter 3, the futility of most rehabilitation programs is one thing that led so many observers in the 1970s and 1980s to conclude that those who are involved with violence are incorrigible "super-predators." But it turns out that the people who are involved in violence can be remarkably responsive to intervention—if we deploy the *right* interventions. The conclusion of the 1970s that "nothing works" turns out to have been premature—people back then were just trying the wrong things. A little guidance from behavioral economics suggests that gun violence is more preventable than was long thought.

ROBBERY

On November 9, 2021, in Hyde Park, a graduate of the University of Chicago's statistics program, Zheng "Dennis" Shaoxiong, was walking near the university's main gym at two in the afternoon. The *Chicago Tribune* reported: "Zheng was walking on the sidewalk when the masked man approached him. The witnesses said there was a brief struggle before the gunman shot him in the chest."[32] *CBS News* reported: "The sounds of the gunman's car speeding away stood out after the deadly attempted robbery. Zheng was left bleeding on the sidewalk."[33]

A few days later after, after 18-year-old Alton Spann was arrested for the murder, *ABC News* ran a story noting that the killing of Zheng for his electronics netted Spann a total profit from a local pawnshop of just $100.[34] The *Chicago Sun-Times* ran an article talking about how the shooting had led to calls from the University of Chicago and other quarters to make the neighborhood safer.[35] *Block Club Chicago* wrote an article reassuring readers that there were no signs that the shooting had been racially or ethnically motivated.[36] The *Hyde Park Herald* covered the memorial service for Zheng on campus, where his advisor talked about how impressive his master's thesis on machine learning and gene regulation was and what a beloved teaching assistant he had been at the university.[37]

Robbery murders often get a lot of news coverage. Partly they get this level of attention because there's often a lot known about the circumstances with a robbery murder. In contrast, for a lot of shootings, nothing's taken, the motive is mysterious, and there's no arrest. The reporter often can't write much more than "Man, 27, dies after being shot in Humboldt Park."[38]

Robbery victims are also typically more representative of the general population than are murder victims in general. It's possible that reporters looking to write stories that lots of people will read think that robbery murders have greater news interest; who knows?[39]

Whatever the reason, the data confirm the phenomenon: When my research team looked at the media stories about every murder in Chicago in 2018, robbery-related murders were found to get almost 50 percent more news coverage than other types of murders.[40] No wonder robbery murders loom disproportionately large in the public's thinking about gun violence.

There's no question that some people *are* shot and killed as a result of robberies. The *real* question is instead: What share of gun violence do robberies account for?

The answer seems to be: a bit less than 10 percent of all murders.[41] While there are lots of gun robberies every year—perhaps something like 100,000 per year in the US as a whole[42]—luckily just a modest share result in the victim's death. That's true despite the fact that guns make interpersonal violence more deadly when violence does happen, because robbery victims tend to be very compliant when a gun is involved. So violence usually isn't necessary.[43] This point is not to minimize how terrifying and traumatizing gun robberies are, as I can attest from my own experience being robbed at gunpoint picking up my daughter from her piano lesson.

To the extent to which violence is used as part of robberies, it seems often to be a spontaneous in-the-moment decision rather than a premeditated part of the crime. I was talking once to a journalist who was out with a group of friends one night when two people held them up at gunpoint. Most of the people in his group did the smart thing and just complied. One of the journalist's friends for some reason got a little mouthy. The teenager holding the gun didn't like it and shot him. The other teenager took off running, then so did the one with the gun. The fact that they left behind a group of witnesses who could point them out in a lineup is a sign that the violence itself was spur-of-the-moment, not planned. This observation is consistent with research in criminology claiming that most muggers *don't* plan or want to kill their victims.[44]

I saw something similar going through data from Milwaukee, which has unusually good records on both fatal and nonfatal shootings because the city does a so-called social autopsy after every incident. Different government agencies come together and ask: What exactly happened, and how do we prevent more shootings like this one? A lot of the robbery-related shootings seem to be instances of something going wrong in the moment. Two people dead when a marijuana-and-Percocet deal goes wrong; whatever was changing hands in that deal surely couldn't have had enough street value to justify the risk of catching a murder case. A robbery suspect demands money from victim, gets a sarcastic response, then beats victim to death.[45] A man hires a sex worker, catches her stealing $300 from his wallet, strangles her to death, and puts her body in a rubber storage bin in his closet. During his interrogation by detectives, he said he hadn't really intended to kill her; he was initially just trying to keep her quiet. The whole thing was, as he put it, "a bad decision."[46]

GANG WARS

In terms of the media's need to tell a good story, one thing that's helpful for ratings is an extended plotline. Serial killers provide such a plotline, but so does organized crime: rational, premeditated violence motivated by the desire to grow some group's profits.

Organized crime is a staple of news coverage, too. Racketeering cases against entire gangs are regular headline fodder here in Chicago. The *Chicago Sun-Times*, for example, devoted countless stories to the "Goonie Gang's" trial: the ten murders the gang was charged with;

alleged Michigan-to-Chicago gun trafficking; the time they drove a stolen Jeep through the front of a downstate gun store and made off with twenty guns and hundreds of rounds of ammo; the code that gang members used to order a shooting of one of their own members ("Walk him to the backyard"); their leader's nickname on the streets of Englewood ("the Reaper").[47]

The *Chicago Tribune* gave a similar amount of coverage to the racketeering case against the West Side's Wicked Town faction of the Traveling Vice Lords: their nineteen murders, their nineteen attempted murders, the fifty guns police confiscated, and the detailed account of how one of their members handled two other gang members in the back of his car that he suspected of cooperating with police. He described how he shot them at point-blank range: "I say, 'Naw, man.' I get in the back seat . . . Pow! Pow! His bitch tried to bail out, I grabbed her by the back of her wig. I said 'Where you going?' Pow! Pow!"[48]

No wonder so many city leaders think gun violence is driven by economically motivated gang wars. The centerpiece of then-mayor Richard M. Daley's public-safety plan in the 1990s was to "fight gang-bangers and drug dealers."[49] Newspaper reporters hammered Daley's successor, Rahm Emanuel, for not getting the gang problem under control: "After leading the nation in murders every full year of Emanuel's mayoralty, Chicago has become more renowned for gangsterism than at any time since St. Valentine's Day 1929."[50] The next administration focused on taking away the "profit motive from them [the gangs] by seizing assets that they have been able to purchase because of their violent activity in our neighborhoods."[51] As the police superintendent told the press and city residents: "I just want to make sure we got the top line right: We're going after gangs."[52]

While there are lots of academic debates about how to define "gang,"[53] driving around Chicago makes one thing clear: There's no shortage of visible signs that young people feel affiliated with some group of some sort. Pitchforks, 7s, canes, crosses, crowns, Devil's Heads, diamonds, dice, dollar signs, eyes, pyramids, gloves, hearts, rabbits, or any of these turned upside down (a sign of disrespect by a rival gang). For every spray-painted GD (Gangster Disciples) you'll see a GDK ("Gangster Disciple killer") posted by a rival gang. The same is true for the Black Disciples, the Mickey Cobras, the Traveling Vice Lords, the Latin Maniac Disciples, the Sicko Mobb, the Trigger Happy Family, the Four Corner Hustlers, Lowe Life, the Goonie Boys, Brick City, Wuga World, Crazyville, Moe Town, No Love City, Hell Zone, La Raza, Terror Town, Death Row, the Latin Pachucos, the Insane Dragons, K Town, the New Breeds, the 4-6 Terror, etc. Police estimate that there are around a hundred thousand gang members in Chicago, which, if right, would mean that about 4 percent of the city's 2.7 million residents are in gangs.[54]

There's no question that there *are* gangs and that the organizational interests of these gangs *are* sometimes behind the gun violence we see play out on the streets of America's cities. The real question instead is: What *share* of America's gun violence is due to gang wars?

Gang wars are maybe the most deflating explanation for gun violence because they feel unsolvable. People have been worrying about Chicago gangs for literally a hundred years. Most of the gang wars over drug-selling turf nowadays happen on the West Side. What's officially called the Eisenhower Expressway, or Interstate 290—the road that connects downtown Chicago with the western suburbs—is nicknamed the "Heroin Highway." Unusually for an interstate highway, it has access roads that run parallel to the highway with lots of on-ramps and off-ramps. So it's easy to hop off the highway, buy drugs off the corner on the way home, and hop right back on. That's what the Wicked Town faction of the Traveling Vice Lords was fighting over: "Violently protect[ing] a drug-dealing operation on the West Side of Chicago."[55]

But the economics of drug selling seems to be changing over time. Crack has ebbed since the 1990s, thinning out one of the most lucrative street-drug markets. On the South Side, drug selling seems to be more often than not limited to the not-very-lucrative drug of marijuana. Buyers and sellers can now coordinate electronically, so drug turf in general is less important, and so less worth fighting over. And gangs seem to be finding other ways of making money over time, like stolen credit cards or stolen social security numbers (which are then used to apply for new credit cards under a fake name and date of birth).[56]

The gangs themselves seem to be changing as well, partly because the newer generation seems to be less enthusiastic about the idea of taking orders from other people or about hierarchy in general. Roberto Aspholm of the University of St. Thomas has documented these generational changes among gang members on the South Side of Chicago. And many of the older guys who were once in charge of the gangs are now in prison on racketeering and other charges, splintering the gangs.[57] Gangs are no longer hierarchical drug-selling corporations so much as loosely organized small crews or cliques, often just a bunch of teenagers who grew up together on the same block; they have a name and hang out but no one's clearly in charge.[58]

That's all to say that it seems like the nature of drug selling is changing over time, and the nature of the gangs themselves and their identity as "corporate entities" focused in large part on selling drugs might also be changing.

The result? A statistical report from the Chicago Police Department, detailing the city's murder problem, suggests that just 9 percent of the city's murders are related to gang wars over drug-selling turf, what the police call "gangland narcotics."[59] We might expect that rate to be even a bit lower in other US cities, since Chicago is one of the American cities that has one of the biggest gang scenes in the country, rivaled only perhaps by Los Angeles.[60]

You might be worried about the reliability of police statistics, but this conclusion doesn't come just from police data. For example, Roberto Aspholm interviewed and observed thirty-five gang members on the South Side, including from South Shore and Greater Grand Crossing.[61] His subjects described seeing or being part of a total of thirty-six different gang wars. How many of these were over drug-selling turf? Just two out of thirty-six (6 percent).

ARGUMENTS WITH GUNS

It *is* true that a lot of the people involved in shootings in Chicago are gang *members* (about half of all murder victims are members of gangs, according to police data).[62] But that doesn't mean the shooting was carried out to further some objective of the gang (like winning or defending some drug-selling turf). That is, a lot of shootings in Chicago are *gang-member involved* but they're not *gang motivated*. They're not driven by a gang member trying to further some instrumental goal of the gang (control of a drug corner, etc.).

These shootings are instead carried out by gang members who get into garden-variety arguments with other people, often people in other gangs, or else are retaliating for an argument-related shooting of someone's fellow gang member and friend. They're crimes of passion, not of profit.

Consider the 2020 murder of Dayvon Daquan Bennett, better known by the stage name he raps under: King Von. Because gun violence is referred to as shooting or "scoring," some people adopt NBA-inspired nicknames; "King Von" is a play on Lebron James's nickname, "King Bron." King Von was a member of the O-Block faction of the Black Disciples, based out of the Parkway Gardens housing development in Greater Grand Crossing.

King Von was killed outside a nightclub in Atlanta by a member of a rival gang, the Rollin' 60s Neighborhood Crips, associated with rapper Quando Rondo (a stage name that itself was an homage to NBA player Rajon Rondo). Because Rondo was in a rival gang, there was initial reporting that this killing was "gang related."[63] To a lot of people, that language was read as a synonym for "gang war over drug turf."

But the motive was actually far more mundane: King Von was apparently seen out with the ex-girlfriend of one of Quando Rondo's friends.[64] That they were in different gangs seems to have been largely incidental. This example highlights something that other criminologists have noticed, too: "Street fights are the major triggering events in gang-related homicides."[65]

Kenneth Davis Jr. described to a reporter his own experience in 1995 in the Englewood neighborhood just a few miles west of Greater Grand Crossing, when he shot a man who was after a friend of his with a machete. He said "This was not a matter of the Mickey Cobras and the Black P. Stones feuding—this had nothing to do with it. It was me coming to the defense of my friend. . . . It wasn't about the gangs. It was about the same thing these kids find themselves in today."[66]

You can see why the public assumes that people's gang affiliations must have some causal relation to a shooting when the news mentions it, *because* the news bothers to mention it. Imagine you saw a news story that said, "This morning by Buckingham Fountain, a financial analyst at Morningstar killed a mechanic for United Airlines." Naturally, you'd think the place of employment must be relevant to understanding the shooting, otherwise why mention it at all?

Similarly, a lot of retaliatory violence by people in gangs stems from some previous argument among people who happen to be gang members. Consider the series of shootings back and forth in the Englewood neighborhood a few years ago between the BrickSquad faction of the Gangster Disciples (known as "JoJo World") and the Black Disciples' Lamron set (which is their street name, Normal Avenue, spelled backward).[67] Their feud was set off after a Lamron named "Lil Durk" Banks released a video with lyrics like "BrickSquad, I say fuck 'em."[68] A BrickSquad member named Joseph "Lil JoJo" Coleman responded by putting out a video in which he rapped over another Lamron's song (Chief Keef's "Everyday") with lyrics like "Yeah bitch we BDK" (Black Disciples Killer) and "This not a diss song, this is just a message."[69] Not long after that, Coleman was biking through Englewood sending out live social media posts about his location. Coleman is now buried in Mount Hope Cemetery here on the South Side.

Or consider the ten murders and six attempted murders attributed to the so-called Goonie Boss gang in Englewood, a faction of the Gangster Disciples. As the *Chicago Tribune* put it in describing the federal case, "The Goonies allegedly engaged in a shockingly petty cycle of violence with rivals, where shooting at 'opps' was an almost daily routine and killings were bragged about on Facebook and other social media." The precipitating event for this violence? The 2008 death of 18-year-old Albert Vaughn Jr., killed as part of an altercation after someone said she was pushed at a 14-year-old's birthday party.[70]

As Cobe Williams, a street outreach worker who grew up Englewood, put it: "All that shit's that taking place right now ain't even gang related. It's personal stuff. . . . Say we at the bar, we drinking and all that, right? Me and him get into it, he looked at me crazy or I looked at his girl or something and we get into it. His background is BD [Black Disciples], my background [is] GD [Gangster Disciples]. . . . First thing they'll say is [it's] gang related. They ain't gang related, that's interpersonal shit."[71] Friends of victims then retaliate back and forth; what Roberto Aspholm calls "collective vendettas."[72]

Social media certainly doesn't mitigate the problem of interpersonal conflict. It used to be that people had to bump into each other in some public place to get into arguments or they had to be in a particular physical spot to see some other gang's graffiti insults ("BDK," etc.). Now the arguments can happen online, asynchronously, from anywhere.

The data on what share of murders stem from arguments (like trying to figure out the importance of other motivations, too) is complicated by the fact that in cities like Chicago the police never find out the motive for a large share of murders. The data are also complicated by the fact that police departments sometimes change how they classify motives over time, particularly for gang-related shootings, and it isn't always clear what sorts of instructions are given to detectives about how to classify motives.

With those caveats in mind, among the murders where police did figure out a motive, the share of them that the Chicago Police Department classified as stemming from an argument is typically 70 or 80 percent (figure 5.1).[73]

That finding is similar to what independent researchers (outside the police department) conclude when they look at the data. Two Chicago-area criminologists, Rebecca and Richard Block, painstakingly went through Chicago homicide records for a thirty-year period (1965–1995). They got a similar answer to the Chicago PD's. Some indication that unsolved murders aren't totally distorting the picture comes from the fact that the motive results are similar in years in which the murder arrest rate is much higher (like the early 1960s) or much lower (as it has been in recent years).

To make sure these results aren't an artifact of something weird in how the police collect the data in the first place, I had my own

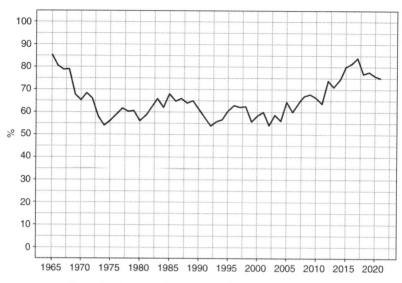

FIGURE 5.1: Share of Chicago murders that stem from arguments, 1965–2021

research team go through the *Chicago Sun-Times* public archive of every murder that happened in Chicago in 2018.[74] The news accounts alone (usually written immediately in the aftermath of the shooting, so the police haven't had lots of time to investigate further) let us figure out the motive for about a third of murders. Depending on how one makes some judgment calls about classifying some of the motives, the share of those murders that were due to arguments is between 57 percent and 68 percent.[75]

You see similar figures in other cities, too. In Philadelphia, the share of murders due to either an argument, domestic violence, or retaliation (usually for some previous act of violence, itself often instigated by an argument) has averaged in recent years 63 percent. The same is true in cities with higher clearance rates (that is, a higher share of murders results in arrest, which leaves a smaller share of murders where police have no idea what the motive was). Milwaukee in recent years has had a clearance rate far higher than the national average; the share of murders that stem from an altercation in that city is 61 percent.[76] As Charlie Beck, the former chief of the Los Angeles Police Department, put it:

"That first killing is often about some disrespect, some long-standing conflict, something that we may not have our hand on." As the *Economist* summarized it: "Most shootings start with trivial arguments, often between young men who know each other."[77]

While this fact has been known for a long time, somehow both the academic experts and the policymakers have forgotten it, or at least let it recede in importance. As early as the 1950s, criminologists like Albert K. Cohen saw that many crimes were *not* motivated by any sort of obvious financial consideration; he started calling them "nonutilitarian" crimes. Around then, Marvin Wolfgang was reading over the homicide case files of the Philadelphia PD and noticed how often murders stemmed from arguments that the person who would go on to become the victim either instigated or escalated. Franklin Zimring collected data on the 554 murders that happened in Chicago in 1967 and found that 82 percent stemmed from an argument.[78] Using data from Houston for the year 1969, Donald Black concluded that "only a little over one-tenth [of murders] occurred in the course of predatory behavior such as burglary or robbery." The rest? Often "a response to adultery or other matters relating to sex, love or loyalty, to disputes about domestic matters (financial affairs, drinking, housekeeping) or affronts to honor, to conflicts relating to debts, property, and child custody, and to other questions of right and wrong."[79]

Criminologists have come up with a classification system for violent crimes. "Instrumental violence" is committed in order to achieve some tangible or "instrumental" goal (getting someone's cash or phone or watch or drug turf), where violence is a means to some other, larger end. "Expressive violence" (or "reactive violence") has the primary goal not of acquiring something tangible but of hurting the victim—"often unplanned acts of anger, rage or frustration."[80] The violence is the end itself. A careful look at twenty years of US murder data collected by the FBI concluded that only 23 percent of all murders were instrumental; 77 percent of murders—nearly four of every five—were some form of expressive violence.[81]

PREVENTABLE

Returning to the case of childhood mortality, public health experts have lamented that policymakers have forgotten key lessons learned long ago. Government officials understandably find their attention drawn to the heartbreaking, highly salient causes of childhood death that are on the front pages of newspapers all the time. But that prior- itization mechanism has led to what some public health experts have come to call a "loss of focus"—vast resources poured into solving what- ever tragedy reporters decide to put on the front pages, rather than into making low-cost investments that could save millions of lives from the most common, but mundane, causes of death that don't make the news—things like diarrhea and pneumonia.[82]

Something similar has happened for gun violence.

For the past half-century, our policies have been designed as if most gun violence were due to super-predators or to income-motivated crimes like robberies or organized crime wars over drug-selling turf. In response to that assumption, public policy has focused on changing the rational incentives people have for engaging in violence—either more sticks or more carrots.

But most shootings in America don't appear to be committed by psychopathic super-predators or to result from some rational benefit- cost calculation about some profit motive. To be sure, the data aren't perfect; police never learn the motive in lots of murders. But with that caveat in mind, it looks like a large majority of murders in America seem to stem from arguments.

In hindsight, maybe this finding shouldn't be such a surprise. The overwhelming majority of all violent crimes in the US are assaults— arguments that escalated into some sort of physical confrontation. Surveys that ask American adults about their experiences with crime suggest there are *at least* eight times as many assaults as robberies each year.[83] If gun violence stems from introducing a gun into a violent situ- ation, then it makes sense that most of the violent crimes that are made more deadly by guns would be the type of violent crime that is far and away most common—assaults (arguments and fights).[84]

If this conclusion is indeed true, it changes our view of not just gun violence but also gun violence offenders. They're not necessarily different from the rest of us, since who gets into arguments? Everyone. Moreover, think about your own frame of mind in that argument; were you the instigator or the victim? You probably think of yourself as the aggrieved party in that argument—which, interestingly, the other person involved surely does as well. The vast majority of us are inclined to view ourselves in any conflict as the good guy, to construe the situation in a way that justifies the actions we go on to take, which helps illustrate why moral appeals so rarely work. As Steven Pinker put it, most violence is not "caused by a deficit of morality and justice. On the contrary, violence is often caused by a surfeit of morality and justice, at least as they are conceived in the minds of the perpetrators."[85]

It was spring in 2004 when R. J. Vanecko, the mayor's nephew, killed David Koschman with a single punch in one of Chicago's North Side bar areas. One witness said it was "like an explosion." Koschman must have blacked out immediately so that he couldn't break his fall. A witness later said that Koschman's head "actually bounced off the curb."[86] This particular argument happened to end in tragedy because Vanecko happened to be 6 feet, 3 inches tall and 230 pounds. But guns make *anyone* a potential Vanecko.

If gun violence = guns + violence, and if America's four hundred million guns aren't going anywhere anytime soon, then reducing gun violence is going to require doing a better job of preventing the violence part of the equation. Looking more closely at that violence and quantifying its causes suggests that the most common type of violence is expressive, driven by the emotional desire to hurt the other person rather than for some other instrumental gain like money. In other words, progress is going to require understanding why people get into a mental state that makes them so determined to hurt someone as part of interpersonal conflict. That's where behavioral economics comes in.

6

BEHAVIORAL ECONOMICS AND GUN VIOLENCE

When my oldest daughter was born, our family was living in Washington, DC. The day we brought her home from Sibley Hospital, I vowed to become a better person. I'd start eating better. I'd get more sleep. I'd be nicer to people, particularly behind the wheel. I'd swear less, and I'd especially never swear around my daughter.

By the time she was a toddler I was sure I'd made progress. Then one day when she was three, we were out on one of our favorite winter-weekend activities: visiting the Smithsonian's Museum of Natural History. Driving home, we stopped at a red light near the Tidal Basin. The light turned green. The car in front of us didn't go. That's when the trouble started.

Communicating frustration to another driver is the sort of interpersonal interaction that initially seems simple, because it's so common and familiar. But in terms of mental processes, it actually involves a fair bit of complicated cognition. The brain has to assess several things at once: What *situation* am I in? For example, what's this person's intention by not going—are they trying to provoke me specifically? Are they just generally inconsiderate? Do they happen to just be distracted in this particular instance? What is my *objective* for that interaction? I want to behave like a well-adjusted grown-up in front of my daughter, but I also want to get home as soon as possible; which of these goals is really essential, and which is secondary?[1] What are the *disadvantages* and *advantages* of different *solutions* that we might deploy? Behavioral scientists refer to this series of steps that our minds quickly go through—situation, objective, and the disadvantages and advantages of different candidate solutions—as SODAS. And while none of these assessments is usually made consciously, they collectively form the basis of our cognition and actions in a given setting.

How did my mind navigate these SODAS steps on the Tidal Basin? How did I construe the situation? My mental model of myself was "good dad getting kid home for lunch and nap"; my mental model of the other person was "jerk who clearly doesn't value other people's time and will lead my kid to miss her nap window." What's more, my mental model of *their* mental model of me was, "This guy must think I'm a sucker who won't stick up for himself." What was my objective? Get my daughter home for her nap with no delay. Every other goal (civility toward the other driver, role modeling for my daughter) seemed irrelevant in that moment. In terms of the disadvantages and advantages of different solutions, I'm not sure I considered the options "Wait patiently" or "Speed more on the drive home." All I could think was, "Literally nothing is worse than the catastrophe of any delay risking that my daughter misses her nap window."

So I did what any victim of injustice would do: I honked. Then, from the back seat, came a little 3-year-old voice: "Fucking people."

My first reaction was to be surprised at my own apparently appalling behavior—including that the behavior must have occurred so regularly that my darling 3-year-old knew the suitable context and setting for dropping an F-bomb on another driver. My second reaction was to be surprised that I was surprised; how was it possible to be surprised *by one's own behavior*? There's only one of me. Who exactly is doing the surprising, and who's being surprised?

These questions get at one of the major breakthroughs of modern behavioral economics: We are all aware of the deliberate, conscious type of thinking we do (what psychologists call System 2 cognition), but that's not the only kind of thinking there is. There's another type of thinking—subconscious, automatic—of which we're totally unaware

(System 1) that handles the vast majority of our routine day-to-day cognition and behavior.[2]

The data suggest that gun violence is much more a problem of System 1 than has been realized. In our conventional portrayals of conflict, two people or parties are at odds because their interests are unavoidably in opposition; they have thought about the matter rationally (that is, with their System 2 thinking) and remain at odds. But a lot of conflict actually stems from System 1—from making a mistake navigating the SODAS steps in a difficult situation.

These missteps are universal, common, and sometimes mundane. I misread situations, for example, by *catastrophizing*—making a negative event out to be even more negative than it is. That misreading leads me to honk and swear at other drivers ("Nothing's worse than getting home late and missing my daughter's nap window"); get into heated arguments with neighbors whose dogs attack my own ("Nothing's worse than having my dog get attacked"), which nearly led to violence but for the grace of God and a University of Chicago campus security guard who happened to be driving by; and, regrettably, even *actual* violence, in an unfortunate incident years ago in the parking lot of Meadowlands Stadium over an errant Nerf football. I was lucky myself that in each of these events, there was no gun around.

Less lucky were the participants in a summer 2023 argument at the Maxwell Street Express restaurant in the Pullman neighborhood on Chicago's South Side. Carlishia Hood was in line to order food. As her son, a 14-year-old honor student, waited in the car, Hood, a city employee, got into an argument with another restaurant patron, 32-year-old Jeremy Brown. After the disagreement escalated, Brown punched Hood in the face. Hood's son came inside, bringing Hood's registered handgun with him. As Hood's son looked on, he saw Brown prepare to punch Hood in the face for a second time. In that unenviable position, it's not hard to imagine System 1 catastrophizing: "Literally nothing is worse than letting my mom get beat up." The teenager, moments earlier just sitting in his mom's car looking at his phone while she ran in to pick up food, shot Brown in the back, killing him.[3]

Thinking about stories like Hood's, it does not require a big leap to understand why shootings happen over all sorts of interpersonal con-flict, large and small—especially when that conflict happens in less for-giving situations than the ones I encounter in my own day-to-day life in Hyde Park. When there is no security guard around to step in and de-escalate things. When the breakdown of an overwhelmed neigh-borhood's social control leads everyone to worry about self-protection, which in turn leads to a gun-saturated environment.

Thinking about shootings in terms of System 1 and System 2 has the effect of recasting most everyday gun violence in America. The princi-ples at play—albeit not the ones reported or discussed—are evident in countless tragedies across Chicago and elsewhere. When two groups of teens in South Shore were arguing about a used bike with a resale price perhaps not much more than $10 or $20, you wonder what 17-year-old Kalvin Carter might have been thinking to shoot 16-year-old Jamal Lockett over the dispute. But then you can perhaps imagine Carter's System 1 concluding, "Literally nothing is worse than letting this guy make me look like a coward in front of all my friends."

The realization that gun violence is due much more to System 1 than has been widely appreciated can explain why decades of public policy hasn't done more to reduce gun violence: It's been mostly focused on dealing with System 2, not System 1.

THINKING ABOUT THINKING

Why in the world was I driving around DC swearing in front of my kid when I had promised my wife—when I'd promised *myself*—I wouldn't do that? Did I think swearing in the car was better or different for kids than swearing at home? Did I think my daughter couldn't hear my foul mouth over the car stereo? What could I possibly have been thinking?

The problem is the word "think." That word conjures up what we normally think of as "thinking"—deliberate, conscious thought. All the ideas in your head that you're aware of. Psychology has different names for this kind of thought. Reason. Controlled. Higher-order. Explicit. Analytic. Systematic. Rule-based. Reflective. Rational.[4] In

Thinking, Fast and Slow, it's the mode of thought Daniel Kahneman calls "System 2."[5]

System 2 is our analytical and rational side. fMRI studies that track blood flow in the brain when doing analytical tasks show that System 2 thinking seems to be focused in certain identifiable parts of the brain: the lateral and medial prefrontal cortex and the medial temporal lobe.[6]

System 2 is how people solve complicated problems, deal with uncertainty, exercise self-control, develop and use language, think about the future, and conjure up alternative scenarios that could have happened but didn't (counterfactuals). System 2 thinking is unusually well developed in human beings compared to other animals. Our finely honed System 2 is what allowed a slow, weak, hairless creature to come to dominate life on Earth. System 2 is how humans designed modern societies, doubled life expectancy around the world since 1900, invented electricity, lifted a billion people out of poverty,[7] landed on the moon, and developed the Internet.

What was my System 2 thinking when it unleashed George Carlin's seven-words-you-can't-say-on-TV in front of my 3-year-old? Most likely System 2 wasn't thinking at all.

System 2 is amazing but slow. I can say the alphabet backward skipping every other letter, but I really have to deliberately think about it—I can't do it super quickly.

System 2 is amazing but can only do one thing at a time. I can say the alphabet backward skipping every other letter and I can multiply 456 times 7,192, but I can't do both at once.

System 2 is amazing but mentally taxing. The brain, along with a few other organs like the heart and kidneys, uses an outsized amount of energy. For the average person, the brain is about 2 percent of total body mass but is responsible for something like 20 percent of all calories burned.[8]

It's not just that the brain is such an energy-intensive organ, it's that the human brain specifically is gigantic (relatively speaking) compared to the rest of our bodies. Anthropologists have a formula that relates brain to body size. This formula fits the data pretty well for most mammals: As you go from a cat to a dog to a horse, body size gets bigger, and brains get bigger in a similar proportion—there's a reasonably consistent ratio that approximates the ratio of brain to body.[9] Compared to what you'd predict from that formula, the human brain is about five times as large.

One hypothesis for why humans developed such big brains is that we did so because, relative to other animals, humans are "ultra-social."[10] The cooperation and protection that come from living in groups are another part of our superpower as humans, which means we might need particularly big brains to navigate our unusually complicated social environments. When scientists compare the mental capacities of adult primates to 2-year-old human children, the overall levels of general intelligence are similar, but children have much higher levels of *social* intelligence.[11]

The fact that System 2 is slow, capacity-constrained, and mentally taxing led our brains to develop in a way that minimizes this type of thinking as much as possible—the brain is designed to be a "cognitive miser."[12]

I was struck by how little we all use System 2 a few years ago at a University of Chicago seminar in the research center of behavioral economist Richard Thaler. The speaker was presenting a paper in which some people were randomly assigned to be asked different versions of a question about what they thought of the Gap (the clothing store).[13] One group got asked what they thought about the Gap given its "Red" campaign, which gave 50 percent of profits to charity. People gave the Gap amazing ratings. A second group was asked the same question and told that the "Red" campaign gives 50 percent of profits to charity— but members of this group were then also told the Gap *keeps* the other 50 percent. Compared to the first group, their ratings of the Gap were much, much lower. A third group was told that the Gap gives away 50 percent of its profits and keeps the other 50 percent, but this group was also told that the Gap *could have* just kept *all* of its profits. This third group liked the Gap just as much as the first group did.

What's remarkable here is that the extra information the second and third groups got had such big effects on their attitudes toward the Gap, yet there was literally no new information in that information. When the second group is told not just that the Gap gives away half their profits (as the first group has been told) but *also* that the Gap keeps the other half, this extra piece of information was already logically implied by the first piece of information if only people had thought about it for even half a second. The same is true of the extra information the third group got, that the Gap could have just kept all their profits. People are not taking the briefest extra moment to reflect. People are not *thinking*.[14]

SYSTEM 1

So who, or what, made the decision to swear repeatedly in the car in front of my daughter?

The first clue comes from the fact that I was so *surprised* when my 3-year-old unleashed her profanity from the back seat. The fact that I didn't realize I was swearing in front of my daughter means that whatever my mind was doing, it was doing it *beneath* the level of conscious awareness.

A century ago, Freud thought our subconscious was where our minds pushed all the painful, embarrassing thoughts that our conscious selves were ashamed of and wanted to ignore.[15] The modern view of the subconscious is different: that it's not some sort of "shame closet" but rather an enormously useful way for the mind to conserve mental energy dealing with routine, low-stakes situations we see over and over. Timothy Wilson calls it the "adaptive unconscious." Other names for it are automatic, heuristic, associative, impulsive, intuitive, reflective, and stimulus bound.[16] Daniel Kahneman calls it System 1.

System 1, like System 2, is also amazing—it's adaptive, coherent, effortless, and fast.

But System 1, just like System 2, isn't perfect.

System 1: Adaptive

System 1's automatic responses usually work perfectly fine for situations we see over and over, where we can get feedback on what the right

TABLE 6.1: System 1 and System 2

SYSTEM 1	SYSTEM 2
Automatic	Deliberate
Below the level of consciousness	With conscious awareness
Quick	Slow
Effortless	Effortful and mentally taxing
Intuitive	Analytical
Deals with routine situations	Deals with uncertainty and novel situations

response is to that situation, and where making an occasional mistake is not the end of the world.[17] It's these System 1 responses that get you to read a word that's put in front of you without thinking about it, to say "Four" if you're asked a "What's two plus two?" and to automatically think "butter" when I say "bread."

If you live in Chicago, System 1 is what gets you to look left before crossing the street. If you live in London, System 1 gets you to look right.

How do we know that's System 1 at work? Partly from looking at amnesiacs, who have damage to some key System 2 parts of the brain so they can't deliberately retrieve things from memory. In one famous case, a French doctor named Edouard Claparede was treating a female amnesiac. Every meeting, she couldn't remember they'd met before and so would reintroduce herself. During one visit, Claparede hid a pin in his hand; when they were "introduced" and shook hands, she was surprised by a sharp pain. The next visit, she again had no memory of meeting him before—but she wouldn't shake his hand.[18]

System 1 had learned a useful if-then rule: The "triggering event" (handshake from the doctor), its association (pain), and its response (avoidance) were learned subconsciously by a different part of the brain from what System 2 relies on.[19] This example makes clear that our "triggers" often aren't things that System 2 is even aware of. If System 2 is the deliberate, rational part of the brain, the "fact checker," System 1 is the "pattern recognizer" or "coincidence detector."[20]

System 1 is what did most of the work driving my 3-year-old daughter and me from the Smithsonian Natural History Museum to the red light near the Tidal Basin. Since this was our regular weekend routine, I'd done it so many times by then that it had become automatic. If we're driving home, then I buckle my daughter into her faux-black-and-white-spotted-cowhide-cover car seat. If we're both buckled in and ready to go, then I put our little four-wheel-drive stick-shift station wagon into first gear. If traffic looks clear in the mirror, then I drive off. I was doing all these routine if-then steps basically on System 1 autopilot.

System 1 also includes some features that are there because they've been adaptive over the long arc of human evolution, what you might call "legacy components."[21]

For example, System 1 tends to interpret everything through the lens of "What does this have to do with *me*?"—a kind of interpretation that's known as "egocentric construal" or "personalization." You can see this phenomenon in studies that get two people to partner together on a project, then ask them afterward who did what. The average subject will say that they did most of their group's work (that is, they're much more focused on *themselves* and what *they* did than on everyone else and what these others did; everyone's view of the world tends toward that of a one-person play in which they're the star). We see the same pattern in studies of married couples, sports teams, etc.[22] If you spill soup on your shirt at lunch, you'll be sure everyone is staring at you when you are walking out of the restaurant, when in reality everyone is mostly focused on just one thing: themselves. Whenever my daughters feel self-conscious, I tell them, "You know what most people think of you? They don't." You can see how this tendency was helpful to our ancestors; if I overhear someone say "Let's get him," it maximizes my survival odds to assume the "him" might be me. It's often useful in modern life, too. When my daughter screams from the back seat, egocentric construal reduces the risk that her unhappiness really does have something to do with me and I don't fix it.

It's also been evolutionarily adaptive for System 1 to limit the set of options it chooses from in urgent situations—that is, to engage in *dichotomous thinking*. Imagine our ancestors out on the savanna: When everyone just takes off running, it's better to choose quickly between just two options (run or don't run) than to choose slowly from a wider range of choices (run full speed or seven-eighth speed or three-quarter speed or five-eighth speed . . .).

System 1 focuses more on *negative over positive information*. Our brains can't pay attention to everything. Negative information winds up being an "attention magnet" for System 1. This bias was surely helpful to our ancestors, for whom missing a negative signal could be the difference between life and death. All of us still share this tendency today, as we can see in data. One study gave infants a sweet (pleasant) liquid mixture, a sour (unpleasant) mixture, or distilled water (control), videotaped their reactions, then showed the videos to adult subjects and asked them to guess what the child was feeling. Subjects were much more confident classifying negative reactions than positive reactions.[23] It's no accident that for describing interpersonal interactions, there are more negative than positive nouns, verbs, and adjectives.[24] The same is even true for our understanding of our own feelings; as Schopenhauer noted in the nineteenth century, "We feel pain, but not painlessness."[25]

System 1: Fast

System 1 is thought to have developed in the human brain long before System 2. For most of human existence, physical danger was our main problem, so our ancestors needed a way to respond quickly. There you are out on the savanna, and everyone starts running. What do you do? You need *some* sort of rapid response. That's System 1.

System 1 helps us by quickly setting a default response—an "anchor"—that System 2 can always adjust later if it wants. Consider the problem of trying to form a *theory of mind* of someone else (what they're thinking, feeling, etc.). In one experiment, two subjects face each other with a set of rectangular boxes in the middle, each box containing an object. One subject (the "director") tells the other (the "addressee") to move some object from one box to another. The addressee can see what's in every box (for example, three boxes contained different candles of large, medium, and small sizes). But some boxes were shaded so that the director couldn't see into it (for example, the box with the smallest candle). Consider what happens when the director says, "Move the small candle to the top right box." The director *must* mean the medium candle, since they can't see the smallest candle. But eye tracking data shows that the addressee initially fixates on the smallest candle anyway.[26] Why does that happen? Because our default model or anchor of what's in the other person's head equals "what's in my head." That usually works fine with people we're close to and so share lots of information with. It saves a lot of time and mental energy when I'm coordinating with my wife about, for example, our young daughter's busy social calendar.

System 1 creates this anchor expeditiously by, among other things, focusing just on the information at hand. When our ancestors saw everyone running in one direction out on the savanna, System 1 didn't have time to scour through memory to come up with lots of candidate explanations. Kahneman calls it "what you see is all there is" (WYSIATI): a bunch of people all sprinting in one direction. In a time-constrained world, that's what System 1's working with. This tendency can lead to "omission neglect"—we ignore whatever's not right in front of us. That's why in the Gap Red study, a respondent who's told that the Gap gives away 50 percent of their profits has such different feelings about the Gap than does someone told that the Gap gives away 50 percent of their profits but keeps the other 50 percent. As Francis Bacon put it, "Contemplation usually ceases with seeing."[27]

Finally, if presented with a complicated question, System 1 often hurries things along by answering a simpler question instead (a *heuristic*). For example, when I'm trying to decide how best to get from the Smithsonian Natural History Museum back home to Foxhall Village in DC, there are two routes that are about equal in terms of distance (5 miles) and average travel time (twelve minutes). But with my young daughter near nap time, I'm particularly focused on reducing the risk of a really long delay. How System 2 would do that is to (a) recall all the trips I've taken on both possible routes, then (b) recall all the times I've gotten stuck in traffic on both routes, then (c) compare the ratio of delayed to total trips for each route (divide the number from [b] by the number from [a], or [b]/[a]). But that's time consuming. So

System 1 answers an easier question instead: *How easily can I call up a time stuck in traffic on either of these routes* (that is, *how easily I can recall an example from the number in [b], which is the numerator of the ratio of delayed trips to total trips*)? This technique uses what's known as the *availability heuristic*. That works okay here because I take a lot of trips on both routes usually, so a similar number of denominator instances (the number from [a] above) in the ratios ([b]/[a]) is being compared across routes.

System 1: Coherent

System 1 creates a picture of what's going on that's designed to be as coherent and complete as possible from whatever snippets of information are ready at hand.

Where there is ambiguity, System 1 automatically fills in the blanks—it "goes beyond the information given."[28] This automaticity is enormously helpful because, among other things, it helps us forecast what might happen next. Consider this short story: "John was feeling very hungry as he entered the restaurant. He settled himself at a table and noticed that the waiter was nearby. Suddenly, however, he realized that he'd forgotten his reading glasses."[29] What happens next? You probably guessed something like, "Oh no, John can't read the menu." But notice what specific word isn't mentioned anywhere in that short story: "menu." Your System 1 filled that word in by going beyond the data given and deploying a familiar script ("the restaurant script") to extrapolate to what's coming next.

Scripts help us interpolate details about events, not just extrapolate to what happens next. Ask someone to read a story about going to the dentist: They check in, get their teeth cleaned, get a fluoride treatment, then pay and leave. Afterward, show them a list of events and ask them to check off which ones happened in the story. People typically check off things that weren't actually mentioned in the story they read, but that are common elements of the usual "go to the dentist" script (like "They took an X-ray" or "They gave me a free toothbrush").[30]

This tendency is usually helpful in our day-to-day lives: When I'm driving and I see a ball bounce out onto the street, System 1 gets me to slam on the brakes because the "kid chasing ball" script tells me there's a reasonable chance the ball in the street will be quickly followed by a human.

But it also has a profound implication: System 1 does so much filling-in for us that our behavior is never truly responding just to objective reality. We're instead responding to some mix of objective reality *plus* everything that System 1 is subjectively construing and filling in.

System 1: Effortless

System 1 is *so* low effort that we confuse what System 1 is doing and filtering and interpreting and outputting below the level of consciousness with objective reality—"naïve realism." Because we assume we're seeing objective reality, we assume everyone else *must* see things exactly the same way we do. So if anyone disagrees with our assessment of what just happened, we conclude there must be something wrong with *them*—they must be acting in bad faith since our own rendition of events simply holds up a mirror to objective reality. This tendency is known as the "illusion of personal objectivity."[31]

System 1 is *so* low effort that it can handle lots of things at once; it winds up handling most of what our minds do, dealing with the eleven million (or so) pieces of information our senses gather each second and deciding what gets our "attentional spotlight."

System 1 is *so* low effort it does all of this work without you even realizing it—it's invisible. Psychologist Aaron Beck started working with patients back in the 1960s and realized they had lots of unhelpful automatic thoughts of which they weren't even aware. He'd tell his patients. They'd be skeptical. Beck came up with a clever idea: He'd give them a wrist-counter device and ask them to pay attention and count the number of times they'd have whatever negative thought they wanted to stop having. The patients were stunned at the results: They realized they were having these thoughts *one hundred to two hundred times a day.*[32]

System 1 is not only invisible, it's inaccessible. People might be able to access some of their mental *content* ("Michael Jordan won six championships") but not their underlying mental *process*.[33] In a classic study, subjects were shown four pairs of nylon stockings arrayed on a table and asked to pick the one of the highest quality.[34] People's choices revealed a clear "position effect"—the stocking in the right-most spot was chosen at a disproportionately high rate. When researchers asked subjects *why* they picked as they did, *no one mentioned position*. When researchers asked specifically whether the position of the stockings might have mattered, "virtually all subjects denied it, usually with a worried glance at the interviewer suggesting that they felt either that they had misunderstood the question or were dealing with a madman."[35]

Often, we don't even know *what* System 1 is doing.[36] In one study, a female interviewer asked male subjects to complete some task. The key was that some men were stopped and interviewed at ground level, while others were stopped and interviewed 230 feet above a river gorge on a rickety suspension bridge. At the end of the interview, the female interviewer tore off a corner of a sheet of paper, wrote down her name and phone number, and invited subjects to call her with any questions about the study. The male subjects were much more likely to call her (presumably to get a date) if they were interviewed on the rickety bridge rather than at ground level (50 percent versus 13 percent). What was going on? The men interviewed on the rickety bridge experienced a state of emotional arousal—fear and heightened alertness from being on the seemingly unsafe bridge—which they apparently confused for a feeling of attraction to the female interviewer. They could tell they were feeling something; they just had no idea what that something was—so System 1 looked around at the environment for clues. Evidence to support that interpretation of the study's findings comes from the fact that when the interviewers were men, rather than women, there was no difference in callback rates for those on the bridge versus ground level.

System 1, in other words, is amazing. It's adaptive, fast, coherent, and effortless. But nothing in life is perfect; everything involves some sort of trade-off. System 1's speed, coherence, and effortlessness can—sometimes—come at the cost of accuracy.

SYSTEM 1 AND SODAS

System 1, normally so helpful dealing with routine, low-stakes things we encounter over and over in daily life, can sometimes lead to mistakes. Those mistakes are more likely when we're trying to navigate a task that's nonroutine or has nontrivial stakes. A common novel, high-stakes task is navigating the key SODAS steps of social interactions: figuring out the situation, figuring out your objectives, and considering the disadvantages and advantages of different possible solutions. System 1 mistakes can happen at any of these steps.

Ideally, you'd want System 1 and System 2 to work together, since they have offsetting strengths and weaknesses: System 1 is the fast, low-effort "pattern detector," while System 2 is the more mentally costly "fact checker."[37] You'd want System 2 to check System 1's work in situations that are novel and high stakes. But sometimes we don't realize a situation is novel, or we don't realize a situation is high stakes, until it's too late. One implication is that every mistake of System 1 is also implicitly a mistake of System 2 as well.

It's also worth noting that a System 1 mistake at *any* SODAS step can lead to mistakes in all the cognition that sits downstream of that (a mix of System 1 and 2 thoughts). For example, a classic study asked Stanford undergraduates: "You drive up to San Francisco with friends in order to celebrate the end of the quarter. The plans include dinner and then some entertainment afterward. How much money will you personally spend on the dinner?"[38] The researchers show that people's answers depend on a series of System 1 assumptions they make without even being aware they're making them: who will be with them, what sorts of restaurants those other people like, what those people's budgets are, etc. All the rational System 2 calculations people make to answer the question—no matter how long System 2 takes to deliberate about its final number—wind up being shaped by the invisible assumptions that System 1 has made. If any of the upstream System 1 assumptions is wrong, all the System 2 deliberations that follow will be wrong. System 1 can trap us in a "prison of the mind"[39] that we don't even realize we're stuck in—because System 1 is invisible to us, we don't even realize which of its implicit assumptions are shaping our thoughts and behavior.

Or consider a different example: I'm a student with a test coming up. Suppose that System 1 assumes the test will be easy. Because of that assumption, I'll go on to make lots of downstream System 2 decisions (Instead of studying, should I play pool or go to dinner or see a movie? Which movie, and whom should I go with?) that will play out over days or weeks. Then, eventually, I'll do badly on the test because I got the upstream System 1 assumption wrong.

The key point is that System 1 mistakes made quickly can lead to problems that play out slowly. System 1 can be responsible for mistakes even if they don't *look* like "thinking fast" errors, since the negative outcome doesn't always immediately follow directly on the heels of the mistaken cognition. Anuj Shah coined a term for this: not thinking fast, but (given the implicit upstream System 1 assumptions that we often don't revisit) "thinking past."[40]

So what did System 1 get wrong, and System 2 fail to correct, when I was driving around DC with my 3-year-old daughter in the back seat, honking and swearing at other drivers? I can't know for sure since System 1 happens below the level of consciousness. But it's not hard to come up with some hypotheses for what could have gone wrong.

It's possible my System 1's if-then response was *triggered* by something I didn't even realize, like the pin hidden in Edouard Claparede's hand when he met his amnesiac patient. Every parent, for example, has developed an automatic response: "If there's a threat to my kid, then do whatever it takes to deal with the threat." Of course System 2 would realize that being delayed five seconds at a red light is not really a "threat to my kid." But it's possible that in the moment, the idea of experiencing any delay at all in going home (given my daughter's nap window) triggered that "threat to my kid" response for System 1 without my even realizing it.

In assessing the situation (the first S of SODAS), System 1's tendency toward an *egocentric perspective* might have led me to misconstrue the

*"There can be no peace until they renounce their
Rabbit God and accept our Duck God."*

FIGURE 6.1: "There can be no peace until they renounce their Rabbit God and accept our Duck God." *New Yorker*, December 21, 2014. Credit: Paul Noth / The New Yorker Collection / The Cartoon Bank

situation. Whatever led the driver in front of me to not go right away when the light turned green, it surely had nothing to do with *me*. I had never met that person before, I didn't talk to them in that moment, I'll never see them again in my life, I have no idea who they are, and they have no idea who I am. Yet System 1's tendency toward personalization makes it possible that I somehow wondered, "Why is this person intentionally trying to make me late?"

It's very possible that the other driver didn't go right away because of some situational factor: The glare of the sun made it hard to see the traffic light, or a family member was calling who had been waiting on some big news or was set to land at the airport. But the *fundamental attribution error* would have led me to conclude they didn't go not because of their situation but rather because of something about them as a person (incompetent, inconsiderate, etc.).

I might have misconstrued the situation because of *motivated reasoning*, a consequence of System 1 creating as coherent a picture as possible as quickly as possible. This sort of reasoning is what leads Princeton students to see far more Dartmouth football fouls against Princeton than Dartmouth students do. To overcome motivated reasoning, what I'd *ideally* like to do is what my friend Sendhil Mullainathan says he tries to do when faced with ambiguous information, like when he sees the famous rabbit-duck drawing: If he thinks he's seeing a rabbit, he asks himself, "Where might there be a duck here?" (Oliver Cromwell put it slightly differently a few hundred years earlier: "I beseech you, in the bowels of Christ, think it possible you may be mistaken."[41]) Unfortunately, at the Tidal Basin in DC all those years ago, System 2 was happy to take System 1's argument that it saw a rabbit without bothering to do any fact checking: "When the light turned green this guy sat there literally *forever!*"

Now imagine what happens when I pull up next to that driver at the next light. The *objectivity illusion* makes me confuse System 1's subjective beliefs with objective reality. So I assume the other person surely agrees on what just happened: that they took forever to go when the light turned green. So I am expecting an apology. But the objectivity illusion makes *them* sure that I will have seen the situation the same way they did: that I was *way* too impatient at that last light and honked before they even had a chance to get going. So *they* will be expecting an apology from *me*.[42] Both of us will wind up being disappointed—then infuriated.[43]

It's possible System 1 picked an objective for that social interaction (the O in SODAS) without my even knowing it. Studies show that subconscious System 1 goals can motivate people as much as consciously chosen System 2 goals. For example, in one study, workers in a call center were randomly assigned to a control condition (they got a regular script to use for their calls as normal) or to be subliminally "primed"[44] for achievement by having a photo of a runner winning a race put into the top corner of the call script. The primed workers raised 27 percent more money during the shift.[45] In my own case at the Tidal Basin traffic light, it's possible System 1 set a goal: "I *need* there to be no delays on the way home." That is, without even realizing it I may have subconsciously picked a goal and confused a want with a need.

Or System 1 might have gotten the disadvantages and advantages of different solutions (the DAS in SODAS) wrong. I'm driving home to get my 3-year-old daughter down for her nap. System 1's tendency toward dichotomous thinking, useful for quick responses, means there are only two ways to characterize the net benefits of waiting a few seconds for the car in front of me to get going: "no big deal" versus "end of the world." Since delay creates some small risk that my daughter will miss her nap window, the delay isn't exactly "no big deal." So that leaves only one other option—"end of the world." This kind of thinking, in other words, winds up leading me to interpret even minor negative events as being more negative than they really are— *catastrophizing.*

Or it could have been that System 1 didn't consider many candidate solutions. In one famous experiment, subjects are asked to place a candle at eye level. On the table in front of the subject is a box filled with tacks and matches. It turns out the solution is to empty the box and use it as a platform for the candle. A remarkably large share of subjects fail to see that. Their System 1s have made an assumption about the situation ("The box is holding stuff, so the box is a holder of stuff," a version of WYSIATI) that people fail to revisit. That causes them to miss a candidate solution to their problem. Placing the tacks and matches *next to* the box instead of *in* the box leads subjects to be more likely to—please forgive me for using this expression in this context—think outside the box.[46] At the Tidal Basin, there's the idiot driver in front of me just sitting there, and there's my horn right there in front of me as well. WYSIATI leads me to focus on the choice "Honk" versus "Don't honk." Here's a candidate solution to the delay that simply never occurred to me: Drive a little faster on the way home on the Whitehurst Freeway.

Or it could have been that System 1 just didn't think of the consequences of different solutions at all. For the problem of what to do when someone in front of me doesn't go when the light turns green, System 1 might have just skipped right over the whole task of thinking about the disadvantages and advantages of different possible solutions (D, A, and S)—like the effect on my young daughter of hearing me swear—the very definition of impulsive decision-making.[47]

BIGGER SYSTEM 1 MISTAKES

Whatever my System 1 did at the Tidal Basin (and what System 2 failed to step in and prevent), it wasn't *that* big of a deal. My 3-year-old just learned some cuss words that other American kids don't learn until, say, age four or five. But looking at my own life, I can see how System 1 has sometimes led me into bigger mistakes.

When I was walking my dog and my neighbor's dog was off leash and attacked mine, a rational System 2 benefit-cost calculation might have suggested that I either shield my dog from the other dog, drop the leash so my dog could run away, or just let my dog get attacked and then take her to the vet later. But System 2 was nowhere to be found in that situation, partly because I was on a stressful work call at the time. That stress depleted my mental bandwidth and, because System 2 is effortful, led me to rely even more than usual on System 1.

One way I know System 1 must have played a role is because I wound up doing what my rational, deliberate System 2 self realizes is truly the single dumbest thing possible to do in that circumstance: Start screaming profanity at the top of my lungs at someone who lives right near me. Neither he nor I is planning to move anytime soon, which means I have signed us both up for years, if not decades, of painful, awkward interactions. Great. And of course, it could have turned out even worse. There but for the grace of a University of Chicago security guard who happened to drive by, this *nearly* violent event might have turned into an *actual* violent event.

Nor was System 1 thinking of all the times I've intentionally or unintentionally had my own dog off her leash. That was not top of mind at all for me, given the "what you see is all there is" (WYSIATI) feature of System 1. So there was no preventive effect on my behavior exerted by the rank hypocrisy of screaming at someone else for doing something I've done myself.

I might have also *dehumanized* my neighbor as a result of System 1's desire for coherence, which can lead System 1 to confuse a thing's name for the essence of the thing itself.[48] One study put subjects in front of two containers of sugar, handed the subjects a label that said "sodium cyanide," asked the subjects to choose a sugar container and put the label on it, and then, label applied, asked if they'd be willing to eat the from the container they'd just labeled "sodium cyanide." A remarkable share of subjects said: "No way."[49] Once I've put a name on that container, it's hard for System 1 to believe the thing itself isn't that name. Similarly, when I call my neighbor an asshole, he's no longer a person; he's an asshole. He *is* the name I've called him. How do you treat a human being? With dignity and respect. How do you treat an asshole? Yell, swear . . . or worse. (This is why many people start to get nervous when politicians start calling their political opponents things like "vermin.")

I unfortunately got to experience firsthand what "or worse" means during my freshman year of college. Rutgers, the school I was attending, was playing a football game that fall up at Meadowlands Stadium. I'm pretty sure we were playing the University of Florida. I was tossing a Nerf football around in the parking lot with a friend when my inevitably errant throw hit some guy's pickup truck. I went to retrieve our football. That's when the trouble started.

The truck owner was *pissed*. Unsurprisingly. Having some object (whatever that object is) hit something you own (whatever that thing is) will, for most people, trigger an automatic angry response. He said, "You hit my fucking truck."

Then *I* got pissed. I was surrounded by all of his friends, who had gathered round to see what was going on. I was starting to feel very stressed out, which wound up draining a lot of my mental bandwidth. Since System 2 is effortful, I was relying even more than normal on System 1. I think my System 1 must have concluded: "This guy is overreacting to something that's really no big deal." A Nerf football weighs 8.6 ounces. I'm 150 pounds soaking wet with a rag arm; the Nerf football was most definitely not moving at supersonic speed. The basic laws of physics, together with my quick observations, made me sure my errant throw could not have done any damage whatsoever to the truck. So I concluded: "By overreacting like this, he's treating me unfairly." That interpretation triggered what was in hindsight an unhelpful, automatic System 1 response from me. Instead of just apologizing and lowering the temperature, I took things in the exact opposite direction. "Fuck off, it's just a fucking Nerf football."

Then he got *really* pissed. With his friends surrounding him, his System 1 might easily have begun catastrophizing: "There's nothing worse than looking like a coward in front of all my friends."

Trying to make sense of his anger over this nothing of an event, my System 1 must have set an implicit anchor for my theory of mind for him (that is, trying to figure out what is in this other guy's head)— namely, I assumed that what was in his head was exactly the same as what was in my head. I knew myself, full well, that this incident was an accident. So I concluded that *he* must have known it was an accident, too (yet another example of the curse of knowledge—assuming others know more of what you know than they actually do). System 2 can adjust that initial anchor, but—given my unfortunate state of high stress and depleted bandwidth in that situation—I under-adjusted. I wound up misconstruing the situation: I was sure he was acting in bad faith and knowingly, falsely accusing me of something he must have known I hadn't done on purpose. While the history books have no official record of what exactly I said in that moment, I am pretty sure it did not come out sounding like an apology.

I remember him taking another step toward me and then . . . nothing. I don't remember anything about what happened after that. I completely blacked out.

The next thing I remember, someone was picking me up off the asphalt. I said, "What happened?" The kind stranger helping me up said that the other guy had reached out and grabbed my shirt around the right shoulder—an old tactic that hockey players use in fights to wrap

up the other person's arm and prevent a right-handed person from being able to punch you. To the pickup-truck owner's surprise, it turns
out I'm left-handed.

What did this future University of Chicago professor do in that
blacked-out moment? Did I come to my senses and finally apologize?
Did I try to reason with this other fellow human being and see if we
could settle this misunderstanding peacefully? Apparently not. The
stranger said, "You were punching him in the head over and over as he
dragged you to the ground."

What would I have done if I'd had a gun? I think about that question every time I read a news story about road rage. The fact that I have
no conscious recollection of the fight itself, the fact that I was apparently on autopilot, makes me realize that I have no idea what I would
have done.

The larger point is this: As amazing as System 1 is in navigating daily
life, its normally helpful features can sometimes get us into trouble—
especially for complicated social interactions in stressful, difficult situations. It's true for all of us, and it's true for all sorts of settings and
behaviors. It's true for honking at other drivers. It's true for swearing at
other drivers. It's true for screaming at your neighbor. It's true for not
apologizing for hitting someone's truck with a Nerf football and then
doing your part to escalate that argument into a fistfight. And I believe
it's true for much more serious forms of violence as well.

MAXWELL STREET EXPRESS

Pullman is a neighborhood on Chicago's far South Side, 12 miles south
of downtown and located next to Lake Calumet, an inlet from Lake
Michigan not far from the Indiana border. If the name Pullman sounds
familiar, it's because you might have heard of the Pullman Palace Car
Company, which invented the luxury sleeper rail car—a "hotel on
wheels." In 1879, George Pullman bought 4,000 then-suburban acres
to build a company town—a place where his employees could enjoy living conditions far better than those found in Chicago at the time. The

Queen Anne–style architecture (the "first all-brick city," it was hailed)
is still striking to see today.[50] But it wasn't perfect. Pullman wouldn't
let residents own pigs or chickens, wouldn't let them buy their own
homes, and wouldn't lower their rents even during times when slumps
in the demand for sleeper cars reduced worker wages. So lots of workers lived in the neighborhood next door—West Pullman, where Jeremy
Brown was shot at Maxwell Street Express.

The decline of both rail travel and manufacturing in America hit
both Pullman and West Pullman hard during the twentieth century.

Maxwell Street Express, located at 116th and Halsted, is a twenty-
four-hour fast-food take-out spot. It's got a familiar Chicago layout: a
little lobby in front of the take-out counter. No tables, no chairs. Get
your food and go.

Brown seems to have had a history of violence. There's a video of
him on social media where he's talking about someone's unpaid $10
debt and threatens to "break legs." At his funeral, his relatives wore
T-shirts commemorating his nickname in the neighborhood: "The
Knock-out King."[51]

As Brown was waiting in line, the woman in front of him asked for
a special order. As a witness later said, Maxwell Street is a busy spot.
They're trying to get large numbers of people in and out quickly. Things
are pre-made and ready-to-go, not made-to-order. If you don't want
onions, you take the onions off. If you want extra ketchup, you grab
some ketchup packets.[52]

In Brown's view, by asking for a special order, the person in front of
him was holding up the line by asking for something the store isn't set
up to accommodate. Whether the woman knew the etiquette at Maxwell Street or not, who knows. But Brown knew it. And his System 1, in
formulating a theory of mind for the woman, set a default assumption
of what was in her head—the same thing that was in Brown's head, the
curse of knowledge: Since he knew the "no special orders" norm, he assumed that she also knew the norm. Given this System 1 assumption,
from there it's natural that Brown believed the person in front of him
was *deliberately* holding things up. She was being purposefully inconsiderate to everyone else in line.

The woman in front of Brown, 35-year-old Carlishia Hood, saw things differently. Hood was a 35-year-old mom who worked for the City of Chicago as a crossing guard, a steady job with an average salary of around $30,000 per year.[53] Carlishia Hood would later do an interview on social media and say her argument with Brown "was over nothing." Just as Brown believed Hood was willfully violating a Maxwell Street norm with her special order, Hood would have similarly expected Brown to know she didn't mean anything by asking for her special order. *Hood* knew she wasn't being disrespectful and deliberately trying to hold up everyone else in line, so the curse of knowledge led her System 1 to assume that Brown surely *also* knew that. So why was he getting so bent out of shape? She didn't mean to be inconsiderate to the people behind her in line; she just wanted the Maxwell Street Express people to change whatever it was that she wanted changed on the burger.

With Hood on the trip was her son, a 14-year-old honor student, waiting in the car.[54] In the glove box of the car was her legally-owned-and-carried handgun.

Who knows why Carlishia Hood had a gun? Lots of people get guns because they worry police won't come quickly enough when things go wrong. The relevant question for that decision is, *How often do police come too slowly to help, and would the presence of a gun help or hurt in that case?* That's a complicated question to think through. So System 1 answers an easier question instead: *How easily can I think of someone who didn't have a gun and got victimized by crime before the police could show up?* (This tendency to answer easier versions of hard questions is called heuristics, and this specific heuristic is the *availability bias*.) Because the answer is "pretty easily," that leads people to implicitly overestimate how useful a gun will be.

People also carry guns because they're worried lots of *other* people are carrying guns—a literal arms race.[55] The same availability bias leads people to overestimate the likelihood that other people are carrying a gun. Answering the question "What share of people are carrying a gun?" is too hard, so System 1 substitutes an easier one to answer instead: "How easily can I think of having seen someone carrying a gun?" Survey data among teens shows the effect of the availability bias at work for that population: In surveys, teens estimate that a third of their peers carry a gun, but the actual number is far lower, closer to one in twenty.[56]

As the disagreement in the lobby of Maxwell Street Express escalated, a bystander did what many bystanders today do: Rather than trying to defuse the situation or do something else helpful, the bystander instead pulled out their phone and started recording.

The video starts with Brown standing next to Hood at the take-out counter yelling at her, "GET YOUR FOOD." Brown is not a small guy. He's waving his arms for emphasis.

By that time Hood's son is no longer in the car. He can be seen from the store's security footage watching the argument unfold in the doorway of the restaurant.

Hood says to her son, who's standing behind Brown, "Get in the car."

Brown seems to think that comment is directed at him—another misreading of the situation. "WHO?!?" he says. "Get in the CAR?!?"

Hood says something that's hard to make out from the video.

Brown says, "Hey lady lady lady lady. GET YOUR FOOD. GET YOUR FOOD. If you say one more thing, I'm going to KNOCK YOU OUT." You can see his right fist, clenching and unclenching, over and over.

She says something that is again hard to make out on the video.

He says, "Oh my God I SAID if you say one more thing, I'm going to knock you out."

One surprising thing to me about violence is how much more violent it is than we imagine. The news reports said something like "Brown punched Hood in the face." But those words, flat on the page, don't do justice to the reality. "Punched in the face" sounds banal. But "punched in the face" *looks* like something else entirely. The video shows this grown man leaning back, loading up, and then throwing his entire body into striking a defenseless person in the head with his fist. Defenseless, she shrinks into the corner. He loads up and strikes her again as she cowers against the wall. I physically cringe every time I watch it.

And there, in the doorway, Carlishia Hood's 14-year-old son is watching all of this unfold. He has her handgun in the pocket of his sweatshirt.

What would *you* have done in that moment if you were Carlishia Hood's son?

You can imagine what System 2 might have done in thinking about how to construe the situation, figuring out what his most important objectives really are in the moment, and the disadvantages and advantages of different solution strategies (the SODAS steps). Maybe System 2 would have realized the most important objective was to prevent anything that would lead to lasting, irreparable damage to your mom's life or yours. Maybe you could have mobilized some of the others in the lobby to help stop Brown. Maybe you could have called 911 and hoped the cops came quickly. Maybe you could have just fired a warning shot to get Brown's attention. Maybe you would have realized that seeing your mom get beat up is truly terrible, but the downside of using the gun against Brown is much, much worse. There's no guarantee the police and prosecutor would necessarily view the shooting as justifiable. To shoot him would be to risk spending years or decades in prison— a much worse outcome even than your mom being beat up.

But for most of us in this situation, System 2 would be nowhere to be found. We'd feel the need to act quickly. That's System 1. Seeing this guy beat up our mom would create an adrenaline dump that would cost us whatever mental bandwidth we might have had, leading us to rely even more on System 1.

The System 1 of Carlishia Hood's son may well have catastrophized: *There's literally nothing worse than seeing my mom get beat up.* If System 1 has concluded that there's literally nothing worse than seeing your mom get beat up, what came next logically follows: He shot Brown in the back. On social media, lots of other people chimed in to say they would have done the same thing. Nicki Minaj, for example, posted on Instagram, "God knew [before] she [Carlishia Hood] knew that she'd be attacked that day [and] made sure they had protection on DECK. God is GOOD."[57] Some news accounts claimed Minaj offered to pay college tuition for Hood's son.

Brown, wounded, ran out of Maxwell Street.

Security cameras around the store captured mom and son running out of the Maxwell Street Express, continuing to shoot at Brown as he ran away, then leaving the scene. The decision to chase Brown down after the encounter inside the lobby was over was made in the shadow of the System 1 cognition that led to the initial shooting. If the System 1 of Hood's son thought, *There's nothing worse than this guy getting away with beating up my mom*, then everything after that was made in the shadow of that upstream System 1 assumption. It's not hard to imagine that running after a wounded Jeremy Brown in the parking lot would seem like a reasonable option—something akin to "not letting him get away with it." Hood's son might not have even been aware of the nature of his decision in the lobby, nor of the System 1 assumption behind that decision, so System 2 had no chance to revisit it—he was thinking past it.

What Carlishia Hood and her son saw as self-defense, the prosecutor initially saw as first-degree murder. Hood was held in jail on $3 million bail; her son was held in juvenile detention. Those charges got dropped once the video of what happened in the lobby was released.

But Brown's family continued to see Brown as the victim here because of the disproportionate response by Carlishia Hood and her son: Brown might have started it, but taking a life (what Carlishia Hood's son did) is much more serious than assault. Reports on social media suggested that Hood's friends even encouraged her to move out of Chicago altogether to avoid retaliation.[58]

The facts of the case, including the detail that Hood (a crossing guard) and her son (an honor student) continued to chase Brown after the initial shooting, tells us everything we need to know about the power of System 1. This incident was not a tragedy borne out of poverty or evil or desperation. It was a conflict that stemmed from a series of misunderstandings. When we look at the circumstances of gun violence in the real world of modern-day America, we find that it's driven by such misunderstandings far more often than we think. Most everyone's System 1 gets at least one SODAS step wrong all the time, every day. When and where that error happens is the major determinant of the consequences—of how big a problem that mistake turns out to be.

CONCLUSION

Conventional wisdom has conceived of gun violence in America as a "System 2 problem"—effortful, premeditated, deliberate, rational. The main political disagreement is whether the solution to the problem is more carrots (to encourage good behavior) or more sticks (to discourage bad behavior). In either case, everyone tends to agree and understand—even if only implicitly—that the problem of gun violence is largely one of incentives.

But gun violence in America may be much more a problem of System 1 than has been realized.

System 1 is our intuitive, automatic cognition. It happens below the level of consciousness—we don't even realize this thought process is happening within our minds. System 1 is amazing: It's fast, coherent, effortless, and adaptive to situations we see over and over again. None of us would be able to navigate daily life without System 1.

But those same features that make System 1 so useful for handling day-to-day routine situations (fast, coherent, effortless) can lead to mistakes in novel or high-stakes social interactions. System 1 can make mistakes in assessing what *situation* we've found ourselves in, figuring out what our *objectives* are for that interaction, or assessing the *disadvantages* and *advantages* of different candidate *solutions* (SODAS).

Why did Brian Willis shoot Alexander Clair and Jewel Washington in Greater Grand Crossing? Why did Carlishia Hood's son shoot Jeremy Brown in West Pullman? Why did I lose my mind over an off-leash dog and a car stopped at a green light and an errant Nerf football? Odds are they were all the same thing: human cognition in the wrong gear in a difficult situation.

Once System 1 has made a mistake, all of our cognitions and behaviors that sit downstream from that mistake can go sideways as well. If it never occurs to us to revisit the upstream System 1 mistake that is leading us astray—as it may well not, since System 1 operates below the level of consciousness and is invisible to us—we can spend endless time thinking about what to do and still not make a good decision because our upstream mistake has put us on the wrong mental track. That means System 1 can lead to mistakes that play out over an extended period, not just mistakes that look clearly rushed in the moment. Anuj Shah calls this phenomenon not "thinking fast" but "thinking past."

It's radical to think that even the most serious forms of violence could stem from cognition we're not even aware of, that happens below the level of consciousness. The idea, as Daniel Kahneman put it, "threatens our self-image as conscious and autonomous authors of our own judgments and our choices."[59] Much more than we realize, we are all, as the title of a pathbreaking book in psychology put it, *Strangers to Ourselves*.[60]

This radical idea helps explain many puzzles about gun violence that conventional wisdom can't. Among those puzzles is the question of how there can be so many more shootings in Greater Grand Crossing than right across Dorchester Avenue in the South Shore community.

7

UNFORGIVING PLACES

Jane Butzner was born in 1916 in Scranton, Pennsylvania. She had a contrarian streak from an early age. She got into trouble in elementary school for refusing to sign a pledge to brush her teeth every day. She explained that she wasn't against tooth-brushing, she was against coercion.[1]

At 18, she was laid off from her job as a reporter at the *Scranton Republican* and eventually made her way to Brooklyn to become a freelancer for *Vogue* and other magazines. She then became a propogandist for the Office of War Information during World War II and then the US State Department during the postwar period. She wrote for many years for *Amerika*, a US-produced publication for the people of the USSR set up by Joseph Stalin and Franklin D. Roosevelt at Yalta to promote cooperation across the countries.[2] After she wrote an article about America's wonderful modern-architecture scene, a Russian reader wrote in to criticize the article and complain about the sorry state of America's cities. That got her interested in urban issues.

Her ideas about cities were informed by some of the site visits she would go on to make as a writer for *Architectural Forum*. In Philadelphia she saw a neighborhood slated for impending "urban renewal" that was filled with street life, people hanging out on front steps and sidewalks. She also saw an area that had just gone through urban

renewal—a high-rise building with no one around. In East Harlem
she saw urban renewal drive small businesses out and erode any sense
of local community.[3]

The ideas that she became most famous for were in her 1961 book
The Death and Life of Great American Cities (she had by then taken the last
name of her husband, Robert Jacobs). Though she lacked any formal
training in urban planning or related fields, her book was a groundbreaking counter to the top-down model of city planning made famous
by Robert Moses. Emphasizing how a city could double as a community, not just a place, Jacobs focused on the relationship between a city's
social environment and its physical environment, and the structures of
the city itself—its buildings, its sidewalks, its stores. Most relevant for
present purposes, Jane Jacobs was also, as a *New Yorker* retrospective
put it, "*obsessed* with crime."[4] She noted how dramatically crime and
violence varied across sociodemographically similar neighborhoods:

> Some of the safest sidewalks in New York City, for example, at any
> time of day or night, are those along which poor people or minority
> groups live. And some of the most dangerous are in streets occupied
> by the same kinds of people. All this can also be said of other cities.[5]

What distinguishes the safe from the unsafe neighborhood? Jacobs
argued it was the willingness of residents to keep an eye out for one
another and intervene when something went wrong. Consider an example from her block, on Hudson Street in the West Village of New
York City:

> The incident that attracted my attention was a suppressed struggle go-
> ing on between a man and a little girl of eight or nine years old. The
> man seemed to be trying to get the girl to go with him. By turns he
> was directing a cajoling attention to her, and then assuming an air of
> nonchalance. The girl was making herself rigid, as children do when
> they resist, against the wall of one of the tenements across the street.
>
> As I watched from our second-floor window, making up my mind
> how to intervene if it seemed advisable, I saw it was not going to be

necessary. From the butcher shop beneath the tenement had emerged the woman who, with her husband, runs the shop; she was standing within earshot of the man, her arms folded and a look of determination on her face. Joe Cornacchia, who with his sons-in-law keeps the delicatessen, emerged about the same moment and stood solidly to the other side. Several heads poked out of the tenement windows above, one was withdrawn quickly and its owner reappeared a moment later in the doorway behind the man. Two men from the bar next to the butcher shop came to the doorway and waited. On my side of the street, I saw that the locksmith, the fruit man and the laundry proprietor had all come out of their shops and that the scene was also being surveyed from a number of windows besides ours. That man did not know it, but he was surrounded. Nobody was going to allow a little girl to be dragged off, even if nobody knew who she was.[6]

Jane Jacobs called this phenomenon "eyes on the street."[7] She argued that the presence of eyes on the street was at least as important for public safety as what police and the courts did. When one of those ten-minute windows that leads to violence starts up, local residents and shopkeepers are willing to step in and do something to break it up. Partly they were willing to do so because they trust everyone else around them to have their back.

(As a coda to the story above, Jacobs added: "I am sorry—sorry purely for dramatic purposes—to have to report that the little girl turned out to be the man's daughter.")

Different versions of that idea have come up in different forms in different fields over the past sixty years. In the mid-1990s, a team of leading sociologists surveyed people in different Chicago neighborhoods and showed that one of the strongest predictors of the neighborhood's level of violence was the trust residents had in one another, their cohesion around shared goals for the neighborhood, and their willingness to step in and intervene for the collective good—what they called "collective efficacy."[8] Economists try to understand the incentives that make anyone choose to get involved themselves rather than relying on others to do it instead—what they call a "free-rider problem" and what social psychologists call a "bystander effect." The catchall term in criminology for all the things local residents do to create safety is "informal social control."

Why informal social control varies so much from neighborhood to neighborhood remains something of an open question, since most of the research on that question is correlational rather than causal. Jane Jacobs pointed to the built environment. Others have pointed instead to things like the degree of residential turnover, levels of homeownership, or the racial, ethnic, linguistic, or cultural homogeneity of a place. Whatever the cause, most relevant for present purposes is that the available data suggest that social control seems to differ between Greater Grand Crossing and South Shore.

Behavioral economics gives us a way to understand *why* social control is so important in explaining differences in gun violence rates across neighborhoods.

Jane Jacobs claimed that informal social control contributed vitally to public safety by *interrupting* criminal and violent acts in the moment. Notice that this hypothesis makes no sense under conventional wisdom. If violent behavior is caused by rational System 2 benefit-cost calculation, the motivation for that behavior will be persistent. So long as the underlying moral poverty or actual poverty that drives the behavior is there, the motivation will be there. The man dragging off the girl might be interrupted by the locksmith or fruit man or laundry proprietor for that moment, but he will just wait until everyone eventually goes back inside to complete his plan. Under conventional wisdom, violence interrupted is merely violence delayed. But behavioral economics gives us a way to understand why violence interrupted can often be violence prevented: It is so often due to System 1 motivations that can be fleeting in the face of time or with a bit more System 2 reflection.

Moreover, behavioral economics explains why System 1 mistakes are more likely in the first place in neighborhoods with low social control, why such places are more difficult for System 1 to navigate. Such places are more unpredictable than routine, they're more stressful (and so deplete people's mental bandwidth), they engender policy responses like zero-tolerance policing that can make it harder to get the sort of feedback that helps train our System 1 responses about the right thing to do in any given situation, and they may also engender private responses like public gun carrying that make System 1 mistakes more likely to end in tragedy.

WHERE SOCIAL CONTROL EXISTS (AND DOESN'T)

Why do some neighborhoods have more versus less social control?

For starters, we can consider why Jane Jacobs was so focused on informal social control—what private neighborhood residents do—rather than on what the government does. The answer in part is because it's a numbers game. The average police district in Chicago has 170,000 residents spread out over about 10 square miles. In that average district at any point in time there are probably around fifty cops out on patrol—fifty official government eyes on the street.[9] By comparison, in this district with 170,000 residents there are 170,000 potential private eyes on the street. When a guy starts a fight after you've hit his truck with a Nerf football, sometimes it's a cop who steps in and stops it and pulls you up off the ground. But just as often—perhaps even more often—it's a private citizen instead.

Jane Jacobs thought it was the built environment that was crucial for determining the availability and willingness of neighborhood residents to step in and do something. She argued for the need for cities to preserve the sort of diversity—of residents, of how buildings are used, of economic activity—that preserves the ecology of local neighborhoods and keeps them "lively." Lively neighborhoods with lots of businesses interspersed with residential areas would have lots of people walking around, driving around, or just standing around, people like Joe Cornacchia and the locksmith and the fruit man and the laundry proprietor. These are people who are familiar with one another, who know each other, at least by sight ("That's Joe Cornacchia, and over there is the locksmith . . ."). This diverse, built environment that helps bring eyes out onto the street is what Jacobs thought was essential to the ability of local residents to informally maintain social control.[10]

From the available data, it looks like South Shore has more "live-liness" than Greater Grand Crossing. In the specific case of South Shore this liveliness seems to be due to an accident of geography. South Shore, unlike Greater Grand Crossing, is right alongside Lake Michigan, one of Chicago's most beloved (and genuinely wonderful) amenities. This desirable location led South Shore to become much more densely and diversely developed than Greater Grand Crossing, with more businesses per square mile (149 versus 123),[11] nearly 50 percent more of its land devoted to commercial uses (4.9 percent versus 3.4 percent), 50 percent more of its land area devoted to residential housing (44.5 percent versus 30.8 percent), and many more residents per square mile (18,000 versus 8,800). So while the neighborhoods are sociodemographically similar today, the legacy of their built environments creates different conditions for liveliness and eyes on the street.

A second potentially relevant feature of the built environment for informal social control, one emphasized by historian Bradford Hunt in his book *Blueprint for Disaster* (and also potentially related to location and local land value) is apartment size. Housing units wind up being notably larger in Greater Grand Crossing; relative to South Shore, the share of local apartments and houses with four or five bedrooms is 60 percent higher (13.9 percent versus 8.7 percent).[12] The result is that compared to South Shore, in Greater Grand Crossing there are fewer adults per young person (the group disproportionately involved in violence),[13] 1.8 versus 2.5.[14] That there are fewer potential adult eyes on the street, or what criminologists call "guardians," is potentially another contributor to differences in informal social control.

A third feature of the built environment that sociologists like Robert Sampson and Steve Raudenbush have implicated for informal social control is "public transportation nodes." Interspersing stores with residential areas leads to lively streets—streets filled with neighborhood residents who know one another, feel like other people around have their back, and have some ties to the neighborhood and care about its well-being. The potential downside of transportation nodes is that they might fill the streets with strangers in ways that make it harder for residents to monitor what's going on or disrupt community cohesion. As Sampson and Raudenbush put it, there is the risk that "large flows of population [might] overwhelm local services."[15]

If transportation nodes do indeed degrade informal social control, the consequences will be more pronounced in Greater Grand Crossing than South Shore. Greater Grand Crossing is where two of Chicago's largest highways intersect, routes 90 (the Chicago Skyway) and 94 (the Dan Ryan). The result is a fourteen-lane-wide interstate that's one of the widest roadways in the world. Greater Grand Crossing also has two high-volume Chicago Transit Authorities subway lines, with two red-line stops along the Dan Ryan at 69th and 79th streets that have 600,000 to 900,000 riders per year getting on and off, and a green-line stop at 63rd and Cottage Grove with another 100,000 or so.[16] South Shore by comparison is disconnected from the city's subway system—the only rail service is a sleepy electric commuter line—and the neighborhood's only highway is Lake Shore Drive, which by the time it reaches South Shore is a quiet country road compared to the 300,000 drivers who use 90/94 in Greater Grand Crossing every single day.

A final relevant feature of the built environment that shapes social life in Greater Grand Crossing and South Shore, although it involves buildings that aren't even located in either neighborhood, is the Illinois Department of Corrections. The fact that Greater Grand Crossing has an imprisonment rate that's around a third higher than South Shore's is another contributing factor to the higher rate of adults to young people in South Shore.[17] It might initially be counterintuitive to think of prison as serving the function of removing *pro-social* people from a neighborhood. But criminologists have shown that one of the key factors that shape whether someone gets sent to prison, and for how long, is the length of their rap sheet. Most people naturally desist from crime as they age. But the tendency of the system to assign longer prison sentences to those with longer prior records means that when older people do get arrested, they're disproportionately likely to wind up behind bars because these are the people who, all else equal, have had more time to accumulate longer rap sheets.[18] This sentencing practice, in other words, has the effect of disproportionately incarcerating older people who are already past their peak crime-offending ages.

Whether it ultimately is due to these differences in the built environment across neighborhoods or to some other explanation, what *is* clear is that informal social control seems to be higher in South Shore than in Greater Grand Crossing. We can see, for example, that adults in South Shore are more willing to step in and do something when there is trouble—collective efficacy. While this metric is usually measured by sociologists via survey questions that ask people about hypothetical behavior (what they would do if something happened), I can measure it by looking at data on people's *actual* behavior when something happens: Are people willing to call the police when there are shots fired? I measure this willingness as the ratio of 911 calls for shots fired in a neighborhood divided by the number of shooting victimizations. (One could also measure this denominator using alerts from Shotspotter, a network of directional acoustic microphones that detect the sound of gunshots; the two approaches produce similar results.) Based on this kind of approach, people in South Shore are 50 percent more likely to call the police than people in Greater Grand Crossing.[19]

A different measure of informal social control is the degree to which neighborhood residents have been able to work together to tamp down disorder.[20] Looking at some of the common indicators of physical disorder that sociologists tend to look at, relative to South Shore, Greater Grand Crossing has 50 percent more vacant land (6.6 percent of total land acres vacant versus 4.5 percent);[21] 100 percent more graffiti, judging from people's 311 calls to the city to request graffiti removal (2.35 versus 1.28 per 1,000 neighborhood residents in 2019);[22] and, from city business records, nearly three times as many liquor stores per capita (32 versus 11 per 100,000 neighborhood residents).[23]

Beyond just the mechanical effect of more eyes on the street to interrupt the ten-minute windows that lead to violence in South Shore, behavioral economics implies several additional reasons to expect fewer of those ten-minute windows to arise in South Shore in the first place.

WICKED LEARNING ENVIRONMENTS

System 1 works well when it sees the same situation over and over. You can usually count on System 1 in that case to develop a useful if-then response that makes your life easier. System 1 will learn a response that works well usually, then automatically deal with the situation over and over without you mentally taxing yourself and having to devote deliberate System 2 thought to it.

System 1 works much less well when the environment is more unpredictable—that is, when System 1 has to deal with more situational variability. What particularly trips System 1 up is when it faces a series of situations that look similar to one another but differ in the right adaptive or strategic response to the situation. Psychologists call this kind of scenario a "wicked learning environment."[24] Such an environment can lead normally useful System 1 responses to be over-generalized into wrong situations. Compared to South Shore, reduced social control in Greater Grand Crossing means more situational variability—it's more of a wicked learning environment.

To see the core idea, consider one of the most famous experiments in all of psychology, the *Stroop test*. It shows people a series of colored objects (squares, triangles, etc.) and asks them to call out the color of the object. Objects are then shown in quick succession. The final object is a typewritten word, specifically the name of a color. But the letters are printed in a different color from the word. For example, the word "green" might be the object, but it would be printed in red ink. People are supposed to say "red" (the object's color) but often can't help themselves from saying "green."

What is the Stroop test illustrating?

All of us have developed the same automatic System 1 response that's enormously helpful in navigating routine, day-to-day situations: "See text, read text." In normal life, that automatic response works perfectly for every situation where we encounter text: a restaurant menu, a note from our kid, a billboard on the street, our email inboxes, the *New York Times* headline as we walk past the newsstand, a flier advertising the latest musical at the local community center, the chyron scrolling across the bottom of our television screen. We deploy that response without consciously or deliberately thinking about it. We do that because System 1 has learned over time that that's a useful, adaptive response in this situation.

The Stroop test demonstrates how System 1 can get tripped up when it's faced with an unusual, novel situation—a seemingly familiar situation that calls for a different strategically correct automatic response. In routine daily life, "See text, read text" is the right response. In the Stroop test we again encounter text, but now the right automatic response that's required is different: "See text, say color." In situations where the right response to seeing text is no longer "Always read it" but rather "It depends," it's not hard to see how System 1 is at greater risk of getting tripped up—of deploying an automatic response that's great for routine situations but unhelpful for nonroutine situations.

The logic for the Stroop test is the same as for the classic kid's game Simon Says: The System 1 of kids gets trained to do what adults tell them to do. That normally adaptive response gets tripped up when kids encounter a nonroutine situation ("Only do what the adult says IF their command is preceded by Simon Says"). The CIA, reportedly, used the Stroop test in trying to screen out the Russian spies from among the pool of job applicants. The last word would be in Russian. After all, who besides a native Russian speaker would say "зеленый" and not "red"?[25]

In the case of gun violence, the lack of informal social control winds up creating wicked learning environments that can trip System 1 up, but with far greater consequences than in the Stroop test or Simon Says. The key issue is that the strategic System 1 response in a situation of low social control is different from that in a situation characterized by high social control. This phenomenon was nicely documented in the wonderful book *Code of the Street* by sociologist Elijah Anderson. In situations of low social control, in under-resourced communities where local formal and informal institutions are overwhelmed, when trouble starts up, no one intervenes. No one's around, or they're unwilling to intervene and interrupt potentially violent events, or even to just call the police. When the police are called, they may or may not come, or they might not stay very long or do anything helpful while they're there.

Under those conditions of limited social control, people quickly learn that in terms of their safety, they're on their own.[26] There's little deterrence from the threat of government or neighbor intervention, so people learn they've got to deter future victimization on their own. One way to do so is to establish a reputation that they're not an easy victim. If a kid walking to school is challenged for their lunch money today and hands it over, they quickly learn that tomorrow they'll be challenged for their winter coat, and the day after that it will be for their phone.

In these settings of low social control, System 1 learns an adaptive response: "When challenged, fight back hard." Dr. Chico Tillmon, who grew up on the West Side of Chicago, told me that in his neighborhood, not fighting back would be to "open the flood gates to victimization."[27] Psychologist Aaron Beck called it "retaliation as communication."[28] Elijah Anderson calls environments like this "people's law" or the "code of the street."[29] The sociologist Donald Black had a different term for the strategic use of violence in situations like this: "self-help."[30]

In other words, the purpose of System 1's violent response is not *backward looking* (punishment or retribution or revenge for what some other person just did) but rather *forward looking* (to strategically signal that no one in the future should try to do this again). Therefore, the severity of the response need not be proportional to the seriousness of the challenge. Anderson describes driving down Germantown Avenue in Philadelphia:

> A man opens his car door despite approaching traffic, seeming to dare someone to hit him. Farther down the block a woman simply stops her car in the middle of the street, waiting for her man to emerge from a barbershop. She waits for about ten minutes, holding up traffic. No one complains, no one honks a car horn; people simply go around her, for they know that to complain is to risk an altercation, or at least heated words. They prefer not to incur this woman's wrath, which could escalate into warfare.[31]

Compared to being in a neighborhood with high levels of social control, for life under "people's law" (low social control) things are from System 1's perspective more *unpredictable*. It's important to figure out what situation you're in, but that's harder to do because there are lots of situations that look similar in many ways to one another but differ in the strategic response that's needed, and the stakes of misconstruing the situation can be high.

Imagine a teenager living in a neighborhood with low social control. They learn that if they're challenged out on the street, if someone speaks to them with an unnecessarily sharp tone, the right response to deter future trouble is to fight back hard. Now imagine that teenager in school, standing around chatting with their friends before class is about to start. The teacher uses a sharp tone to get the student's attention to get them to sit down. It's not hard to imagine the student's System 1 getting confused about the situation and deploying the wrong automatic response. Yelling profanity and threats on the street might be helpful in deterring future aggression. But yelling profanity and threats at your teacher gets you suspended.

Notice how different this dynamic looks for people living in places with *high* levels of social control. When they're challenged out on the street, when someone speaks sharply to them and demands their lunch money or jacket or phone, the adaptive, useful response is to comply and then just go get help from some nearby adult, whether that's a cop or a coach or store owner or local neighbor. So when the teacher uses a sharp tone with them in order to get class started, even if the teen's System 1 confuses being spoken to sharply in school for the sort of challenge situation they encounter out of school, the automatic System 1 response they've learned still works: comply. The teenager in this setting doesn't have to worry in the same way about being sure they know exactly what situation they're in, because the right response on the street is the same as in school.

Or consider how System 1 makes sense of the situation in which someone tells you, "I don't have the money yet for the used car I bought from you." There's inevitably some ambiguity about what this statement means. It might literally mean "I don't have the money yet." Or it might be a euphemism for "You'll *never* get your money—eat shit." In a neighborhood with high social control, the right response is the same either way; just give them more time and if they eventually don't pay, ask someone for help (the police, the courts, a respected local community leader, etc.). In a neighborhood with low social control, in contrast, the adaptive response depends crucially on which of these two meanings the speaker intends with their statement. If the speaker means they'll never pay you back, and if you then just let that go, you risk making life in your community moving forward nearly unlivable, because of the future crime victimization you have inadvertently just invited.

As a final example, consider the stakes for System 1 in figuring out whether there's a gun present in this situation. It turns out that gun carrying seems to be at most an intermittent behavior, rather than an omnipresent one. One study of juvenile-justice-system-involved teens, for example, found that even the group that described themselves as "always carrying" say they had a gun with them only about once a week.[32] In a neighborhood of high social control, since the right System 1 response to being challenged on the street is always "Comply" or "Just let it go," it doesn't matter so much whether someone's got a gun or not. "Just let it go" works perfectly in that type of situation whether there's a gun around or not. But in a neighborhood of low social control, the normal System 1 response to being challenged of "Fight back hard" might be strategically optimal if there's no gun around—but can lead to a life-altering tragedy if there's a gun at hand.

The first S of SODAS—the first thing people typically figure out to navigate any social interaction—is what *situation* they're in. Everyone's System 1 will inevitably get that wrong sometimes. But that type of situational assessment is much harder in neighborhoods with less social control and more unpredictability about what situation you're in and what response is needed. If you're living in Greater Grand Crossing, the adaptive response to being challenged out on the street is to fight back hard. So System 1 learns "If challenged, then fight back hard"— which usually works, unless you happen to be in school or there's a gun at hand, in the same way that "See word, read word" usually works, unless you're doing the Stroop test. The unpredictability of such settings—the kind that intersperse unusual situations requiring a different response from the similar-looking usual ones people repeatedly see—is why they're called wicked learning environments.

FEEDBACK

The only way we as human beings can learn to navigate social interactions is through feedback. We see a situation over and over, try different responses, and then use feedback about whether things have gone well or badly to help us figure out which response is best to a given situation. There's no substitute for lots and lots of reps. We need multiple chances to try something, for which second chances are critical. That sort of feedback is even more important in neighborhoods with low social control, since those are the social environments that are most complicated to navigate. Yet unfortunately, far too often feedback is particularly hard to get where it is needed most.

In their groundbreaking book *Nudge*, behavioral economists Richard Thaler and Cass Sunstein illustrate the importance of feedback with the metaphor of learning how to putt.[33] Take a golf novice, put them on a putting green for a day. By the end of the day almost anyone will be much better. But now imagine a golf novice placed on a putting green *blindfolded*, so they have no idea which putts are too short, long, far left, etc. Without feedback, they'll get no better at all over the course of the day.

One place we all get feedback growing up is in school. In my own New Jersey public high school, I quickly figured out I was unlikely to be the captain of the football team or the prom king. I tried cigarettes once and made myself sick, so hanging out in the Lenape High School smoking section with the burnouts was not an option. But then one day in class I made a joke. People laughed. The teacher didn't do anything. So I assumed she must have thought this was as amusing as everyone else had. I ran with it. Then, as is the nature of such things, I eventually went too far. At some point one of my teachers kindly pulled me aside and said, "One day someone is going to slap the shit out of you, and it very well might turn out to be me."

This constructive feedback taught me that apparently not everyone sees things the same way. Because of the curse of knowledge, in my mind the teacher's perspective on my jokes was surely not that far from mine: hilarious. System 1 had set a default or anchor for what's in her head (equal to exactly what's in my head—*this is hilarious*), which System 2 can in principle adjust ("Remember that adults don't like goofing around as much as teenagers do"). But because System 2 thinking is effortful, we all under-adjust—as I apparently did in that case. Luckily, this experience turned out to be a fairly low-cost way to get feedback and learn this valuable lesson. After all, the teacher only *threatened* to slap the shit out of me; she didn't actually do it.

What happens when the cost of getting feedback goes up? Harvard economist David Deming and his colleagues studied the natural experiment of what happens when a school gets itself a new principal who has a much harsher attitude toward discipline than their predecessor. Students who go to schools that are quicker to kick them out when they make mistakes—schools that make feedback very costly for students to get—are 30 percent more likely to drop out of high school and 40 percent more likely to ever wind up in prison.[34]

We all get a lot of important feedback *outside* of school, too. When I was 16, I spent the summer in Germany visiting my cousin who lived in Steinbach, a quaint little village just outside of Frankfurt. For an American teenager it was heaven: unlimited pickup soccer games every day and (with basically no legal drinking age) unlimited beer. One day my cousin and I took the train into downtown Frankfurt with two of my cousin's friends. We wanted to go check out the latest Adidas soccer gear at the downtown department stores (this was long before Amazon, at a time when people still had to go to stores). One of my cousin's friends started bragging about what a good shoplifter he was and what a great chance this would be to get some free stuff. I had never done anything illegal in the US besides drink beer on summer evenings out on the Ramblewood Country Club golf course with my friends. But now, *shoplifting*?

My mind started working through the D, A, and S steps of SODAS (disadvantages and advantages of different candidate solutions). The advantage of going along with this scheme was that, at least according to my cousin's friend, the risks were low. He'd shoplifted from these downtown department stores a few times before and, he said, had never gotten caught. The disadvantage of *not* going along with the plan was to look like a coward.

I had plenty of time to reflect on my decision in the back of the police car that took us from the department store to the police station. One thing I learned was that I had miscalculated the risks. I learned from firsthand experience what psychologists Daniel Kahneman and Amos Tversky called the "belief in the law of small numbers": System 1's desire to quickly create as coherent a picture of the world as possible leads it to assume that whatever snippets of information it has available must be representative of the world as a whole.[35] Imagine that every time you shoplift there's, say, a one in five chance you'll get caught. With those odds, it's very possible that my cousin's friend could have shoplifted two or three times before and not gotten caught. From that, his System 1 leapt to the conclusion that the chances of getting caught were *literally* zero ("The zero percent of times I've been caught so far is the overall population-level arrest rate"). Which, as we learned, was not the case.

Luckily, the Frankfurt police just called everyone's parents and then let us go. So I got enormously valuable feedback about the mistaken belief in the law of small numbers at fairly low cost. Aside from speeding, I've never done anything illegal since. I now find it very easy to resist people who, when trying to coax me into doing something stupid, say, "Don't worry, I do this all the time."

But it's harder to learn through trial and error when feedback is much more costly, as would have been the case if the Frankfurt criminal-justice system had decided to press forward with our cases rather than just calling our parents. A study by economists Amanda Agan, Jennifer Doleac, and Anna Harvey show how much this issue of feedback cost can matter. They analyzed a natural experiment that arose from having misdemeanor cases (low-level arrests) randomly assigned to prosecutors. Not all the prosecutors treated these cases the same; depending on the assignment of prosecutor, the chances that they decided to prosecute versus drop a case varied enormously.[36] The stakes of such decisions turn out to be substantial. Having the case dropped reduced the chances someone would be rearrested over the ensuing two years by 53 percent, and it reduced their chances of getting rearrested for a violent crime specifically by 65 percent.[37] To return to the *Nudge* analogy about the importance of feedback for someone learning to putt, the involvement of the legal system in feedback is akin to getting charged $20 every time you pulled down your blindfold to peek at where a putt went. But of course the stakes are completely different than a meaningless game of golf: Feedback at high (legal) costs can change the arc of a person's life.

Unfortunately, the data show that in both Greater Grand Crossing and South Shore, feedback delivered in schools has been getting costlier. Starting in the 1970s, as the criminal-justice system got harsher in America, public schools got harsher too: From 1972 to 2006, suspension rates increased by 67 percent for white students and by 150 percent for Black students.[38] While it's hard to tell if that phenomenon is more pronounced in Greater Grand Crossing versus South Shore,[39] the larger national trends suggest it's almost surely different in the predominantly Black schools of Chicago's South and West sides compared to the predominantly white schools on the North Side or in the suburbs. That might be one explanation for widening safety inequality in Chicago: Over the past thirty years, we see widening disparities in homicide rates between predominantly Black and predominantly white neighborhoods.[40]

More costly feedback *outside* of school can also help explain why there is more gun violence in Greater Grand Crossing than in South Shore.

The data are much clearer in indicating that out-of-school feedback—corrective experiences outside the classroom—comes at greater cost in Greater Grand Crossing than South Shore because of the greater prevalence of zero-tolerance-style policing. This law enforcement pattern may itself be a downstream response to the relatively

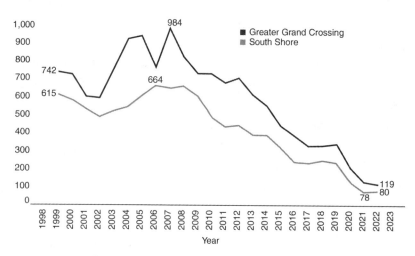

FIGURE 7.1: Misdemeanor arrests per 10,000 residents for South Shore and Greater Grand Crossing, 1998–2022

greater lack of informal social control in Greater Grand Crossing. Many scholars have hypothesized that with respect to misdemeanors, "arrest and prosecution patterns reflect police and prosecutors' judgments about which individuals and populations are so disorderly or dangerous as to require the state's coercive control."[41] For example, if neighbors are unwilling to help move kids along if they're selling drugs in front of an elderly person's house, then the police may step in and do that in a way that leads to misdemeanor arrests. If witnesses to violent crimes are unwilling to cooperate, police may, for better or worse, try to make more misdemeanor arrests to create leverage in the form of criminal liability to incentivize cooperation.

Whatever the cause, data show that the rate at which people are arrested for misdemeanors (on a per capita basis) is typically between 20 percent and 50 percent higher in Greater Grand Crossing than in South Shore (figure 7.1).[42]

This is all to say that another reason why shootings over things like a disputed used-car sale are more common in Greater Grand Crossing is that everyone's System 1 there gets less feedback about how to navigate the social environment, how to work through the SODAS steps for each social interaction. As they were arguing in Greater Grand

Crossing, both Brian Willis and Alexander Clair would have been more challenged to figure out what situation they were in ("Is this other person thinking I'm a chump?"), what their objective was ("It's just a stupid car" versus "Nothing is worse than being shown up in public like this"), and the disadvantages and advantages of different strategies than they would've been in South Shore.

BANDWIDTH

System 2 is what helps us navigate novel or high-stakes situations, leaving System 1 to deal with run-of-the-mill ordinary situations. But System 2 is effortful; it's tiring. When we have less mental energy—less mental bandwidth—we're less likely to draw on System 2 and more likely to rely on System 1, even in situations where we'd be better off using System 2. In *Scarcity*, Mullainathan and Shafir show how extra stress, trauma, and worry can shape people's behavior in all sorts of ways that's relevant for poverty. The same is true for gun violence.

Mullainathan and Shafir randomly told some people, but not others, to imagine something stressful before they took the Stroop test (something like, "Suppose your car broke down and it would cost $2,000 to fix it"). That sort of stress led to more System 1 automaticity, especially among poorer people, as revealed by more errors on the Stroop test. The size of the effect of this extra stress and depleted mental bandwidth on System 1 automaticity was enormous—about the same size effect as what we see when someone goes a whole night without any sleep.

Stress and anxiety tend to be more common in neighborhoods with less informal social control and collective efficacy.[43] So are elevated rates of morbidity (poor health) and even mortality. Those physical health differences across neighborhoods, bad as they are in their own right, surely exacerbate the disparities across places in stress and anxiety as more neighborhood residents worry about sick loved ones or grieve loved ones who have just passed. On top of all the other hardships of life, people living in neighborhoods with low social control and high rates of stress and trauma are further burdened with having to navigate daily life under the mental bandwidth equivalent of having pulled an all-nighter.

We see that same dynamic play out in Greater Grand Crossing and South Shore, as a result of the lower levels of social control in the former than the latter. One common measure in public health is years of potential life lost before age 65 or 75 per 100,000 residents. (Since we're trying to understand the determinants of gun violence and murder, we want to subtract premature deaths *via murder* for this calculation; we don't want Greater Grand Crossing's higher murder rate to tautologically be an explanation for more trauma that drives murders.) The figures for Greater Grand Crossing versus South Shore are 13,301 versus 12,505, respectively: Per 100,000 people, Greater Grand Crossing has 796 more years of premature death than South Shore, and in turn that much more carried trauma from the Greater Grand Crossing residents who've lost loved ones.[44] This difference was even more stark during the pandemic, when deaths per 100,000 from COVID-19 were over a third higher in Greater Grand Crossing than South Shore (143 versus 108).

This framework gives us another way of understanding the shooting at 69th and Calumet Avenue on the night before Halloween in 1996. The choice set facing Brian Willis was: Go ahead and kill Alexander Clair and Jewel Washington and run a 50 percent chance of getting arrested for double homicide, or just give back the $3,500 used car he bought if he didn't want to pay Clair the money he owed for the car. For System 2, making this call would have been easy.

But it's very possible Brian Willis had depleted mental bandwidth from being in Greater Grand Crossing and as a result relied too much on System 1 in the moment. Maybe egocentric construal led Willis to think all eyes in the neighborhood were watching Clair talk back to him—that is, he might have misconstrued the situation. System 1 might have set an implicit objective that Willis wasn't aware of—confusing the "want" of keeping the car with a real "need" (like avoiding life in prison). Or maybe Willis's System 1, in considering the disadvantages and advantages of different solutions to this encounter, concluded, "There's literally nothing worse than letting this guy get away with showing me up"—catastrophizing. The risk of any of these System 1 mistakes, of relying too much on System 1 in this fraught encounter because of depleted mental bandwidth, is much higher because Willis was in Greater Grand Crossing rather than in South Shore.

GUN CARRYING

If Greater Grand Crossing has less social control compared to South Shore, it means that people in Greater Grand Crossing are more ready for conflict as a means of deterring future conflict. And it might be one reason why more people seem to be carrying guns out in public (on their person or in their car) in Greater Grand Crossing.

This phenomenon of illegal gun carrying seems to be self-reinforcing or self-accelerating. Survey data show that a key reason people carry guns is for protection against other people, including other people whom you're worried might have guns themselves. As one commentator put it, "You only need one 12-year-old with a gun, then other 12-year-olds feel they need a gun."[45] In many areas of life we speak figuratively about an "arms race." But with gun carrying, it's *literally* an arms race. In my study of the Chicago underground gun market with Philip Cook, Anthony Braga, and Sudhir Venkatesh, Sudhir's interviews with young people on the South Side illustrated how this arms race plays out:[46]

> As one young gang member notes, in the absence of having a gun: "Who [is] going to fear me? Who [is] going to take me seriously? Nobody. I'm a pussy unless I got my gun." Just showing rather than actually firing guns is usually sufficient for the purposes of achieving the desired result. As one youth noted, "You have to let [other people] see it without letting them see it. See, it's all about them not messing with you." As another youth noted, "Like them slick flicks [pornographic movies], it's all about the bulge. It never even gets that far [explicitly showing other people the gun]." Another non-gang affiliated youth notes: "Thing is, see, it ain't really about fighting or nothing,

because even if you have a group of guys and you see a group of guys, lot of times, it's just you show 'em you got one, they show you they got one, and you just be on your way. It's just like signifying that you prepared."

Here again, the implications of gun carrying are not what they've been understood to be under the conventional wisdom about crime and violence. If violence were perpetrated by bad or psychotic people, or people who were under- or over-policed, or people who were acting out of desperate impoverished circumstances, then their motivations to engage in crime should be persistent. In other words, so long as those underlying causes are there, the person's System 2 benefit-cost-comparing motivation to engage in gun violence is there. And if someone persistently motivated in this way doesn't have a gun with them and the need arises, they'll just commit their intended crime whenever they can get their gun. Under conventional wisdom, reducing guns in public would merely delay, but not prevent, shootings.

But the hypothesis of more fleeting System 1–related motivations highlights why the behavioral-economics perspective implies that gun carrying is so central to gun violence. Because so many of those arguments happen in public places, gun carrying in public creates special dangers to public safety. A gun under someone's mattress or in a nightstand or closet or basement isn't nearly as dangerous as a gun on crowded 69th Street near the intersection with Calumet Avenue, where it's more likely to be available during one of the fleeting ten-minute windows that leads to violence.

While it's impossible to measure exactly how many people are carrying guns out in public at a point in time (that is, there are no databases for it nor even any means for collecting such data), I can construct a proxy: the share of people who are stopped by the Chicago Police Department who are found to have an illegal gun on them at the time of their stop.[47] These data are available, and they show that compared to South Shore, gun carrying is approximately 50 percent higher in Greater Grand Crossing.

The data imply, in other words, that when two people start arguing over a used-car sale, the chances that someone's System 1 mistake ends in tragedy is higher in Greater Grand Crossing than South Shore because the odds are higher a gun is ready at hand.

UNFORGIVING PLACES

Greater Grand Crossing is sociodemographically similar to South Shore, has the same criminal-justice system, and surely has the same basic morality among its residents; nothing less could be true of two neighborhoods that sit literally right across Dorchester Avenue from one another.

But Greater Grand Crossing is a much more complicated decision-making environment for residents. The more limited informal social control in Greater Grand Crossing means that neighborhood is more unpredictable, provides less feedback, depletes people's mental bandwidth due to higher levels of stress and trauma, and requires more reliance on self-help for protection that leads to higher levels of gun carrying—raising the stakes for System 1 errors.

The decision-making complexity of a neighborhood is correlated with neighborhood disadvantage, but they're not the same things. This point helps explain why similarly low-income neighborhoods can have such dramatically different rates of gun violence. This finding isn't just about Greater Grand Crossing and South Shore. As I showed in chapter 4, while all affluent neighborhoods in Chicago have low levels of gun violence, across the city's low-income communities there are *enormous* differences in murder rates.

From the perspective of solving gun violence, the wide variability in rates of shooting across poor neighborhoods is good news. It means that while society is trying to address the big, difficult root causes of the gun violence problem—income and racial segregation, social isolation, discrimination—there are other neighborhood factors that policy can productively target to reduce gun violence in the near term. Behavioral economics, in other words, expands the set of situational factors that we can target with public policy to prevent gun violence from happening in the first place, even in a place like the US where guns are widely available.

But like behavioral economics itself, this perspective on the problem of gun violence is relatively new. And the tragedy for the US is that for the past fifty years, the country's public policies aimed at reducing gun violence may have inadvertently made the neighborhood features that affect gun violence even worse.

These policies, many of them animated by a belief that gun violence is due to intrinsically characterologically bad people, have led to high rates of imprisonment that in too many places remove older adults who could have contributed to informal social control.[48] Spending on prisons and jails has also diverted money from the sort of local public goods that might otherwise strengthen local social control: economic development of the sort Jane Jacobs emphasized that creates lively areas with retail interspersed with residential or support for the sort of other local social institutions (religious organizations, colleges, childcare centers, etc.) that Columbia sociologist Mario Small has found create the sort of social capital that increases the willingness of local residents to work together to promote the public good, including safety.[49]

The presiding view of bad people as the root of violence has also motivated the rise of zero-tolerance policies, which have in turn disrupted the possibility of social feedback dynamics in so many neighborhoods. Meanwhile, the underinvestment in public goods in poor communities may itself be motivated by a cynical belief: that people's life outcomes reflect something about them rather than their situation (so why bother changing the situation?).[50] And—hovering over all the challenges specific to under-resourced low-income communities—one contributing factor to the frequency of illegal gun carrying in some areas like Greater Grand Crossing is that guns themselves are so common in America *everywhere*. Guns are ubiquitous in America because so many Americans believe in the need to protect themselves from incorrigible, characterologically bad "criminals."

While most of these policies enacted over the past fifty years have come from the Right, the view from the Left—that the only solution to the gun violence problem is to fix every other big social problem (that is, to attack its root causes)—has left many Americans feeling like gun violence is too big to fix. That there is, in other words, no realistic alternative approach to get-tough policies. This perspective is its own form of cynicism.

Often with the best of intentions, our policies have, in other words, created far too many unforgiving places.

8

WEIGHT OF EVIDENCE

This book's central claim is that American gun violence is driven to a large extent by System 1 thinking—the automatic, below-the-level-of-consciousness type of cognition that is useful for navigating the routine parts of life but gets us into trouble when we're navigating fraught interpersonal interactions. That's especially true in neighborhoods where the decision-making environment is particularly demanding— places and settings where social signals are unclear and the consequences of mistakes can be severe.

Maybe you're not buying that argument. Or maybe you're buying it to an extent, but you still think the lion's share of the gun violence problem in the US can be traced to the old reliable narratives. According to those old stories, the ones that you and I and everyone else have been hearing for fifty years or more, gun violence is due to premeditated, deliberate, rational benefit-cost calculation. That people with either compromised morality or compromised economic conditions go through that calculus and decide to engage in gun violence because powerful forces lead the benefits to outweigh the costs. That story, in other words, is a story about System 2—deliberate, calculated malevolence or desperation.[1]

Here it is crucial to be clear that these explanations of how and why violence occurs are not mutually exclusive. The role of System 1 as a driver of violence is remarkable partly because it is relatively unexplored. But it is not a wholesale alternative to the System 2 story. It's a complement, not a substitute.

The relevant question is really one of relative importance: In terms of the drivers of gun violence, is System 1 a sideshow, or is it more like the main act? To resolve the issue, one might ask: Which answer best fits the data? That's the sort of reasoning skeptical people used to change their minds on major issues in the past. Five hundred years ago, for instance, everyone believed the sun revolved around the Earth. Copernicus noted that the alternative explanation of the Earth revolving around the sun yields a set of predictions for what we should see in nature that fit the available data much better.

In that spirit, we've already seen a number of examples of basic facts about gun violence that System 2 can't explain very well, like why gun violence varies so much by age, time of day, day of week, season, or geography—including right across Dorchester Avenue. These facts just don't easily fit the narratives of conventional wisdom, narratives of bad guys and troubled circumstances.

This chapter is going to go beyond showing System 2 *can't* explain lots of things, to show that a behavioral economics, System 1–focused perspective *can* explain things. To do that I look at a set of randomized controlled trials (RCTs), the sort of data that provide gold-standard evidence in medicine, that test a series of policies that can *only* work on gun violence events that are driven by people's System 1 thinking. These policies may stimulate more eyes on the street to interrupt ten-minute windows when fleeting System 1 motivations lead people to do something in the moment that their System 2s would not endorse, or these policies may subtly improve people's ability to navigate difficult social situations. They don't do anything else to change the incentives for or root causes of violence; they don't change poverty or morality or punishments or the other "carrots" and "sticks" we typically associate with our usual policy responses. Behavioral economics predicts these policies should work; conventional wisdom predicts they shouldn't.

One interesting feature of these examples is that they were dreamed up not by some professor in a lab but rather by people living and working in the places most affected by gun violence. As a professor myself examining their interventions and testing whether the policies actually work, I am astounded at both the brilliance of their design and the reproducibility of so many of these results. There would without question be much more work needed to map out a full blueprint for ending gun violence on a truly nationwide scale. But the evidence that we already have in hand taken together provides clear *proof of concept*: Policies that address System 1 mistakes *can* reduce violence—often by remarkable amounts. That finding has radical implications for our understanding of the gun violence problem itself.

DOROTHY

Altgeld Gardens was built in 1945 on the far South Side of Chicago. Other, more famous housing projects, like the Robert Taylor Homes or Cabrini-Green, were massive mega-complexes of ten- or sixteen-story-tall high-rise buildings arrayed one after the other on super-blocks (created by closing streets to create big contiguous parcels of land) surrounded by oceans of concrete. But Altgeld Gardens and its sister project, Phillip Murray Homes, consist of around two thousand row houses in their own little subdevelopment of winding streets and open green space.

One thing all these Chicago public-housing developments had in common—Altgeld Gardens, Murray Homes, Robert Taylor, Cabrini-Green—is that almost everyone who lived there was Black. That was not an accident.

The president of the local Altgeld Gardens PTA was a dynamic 30-something-year-old named Dorothy Gautreaux, whom one friend remembered as "a builder of community, a breaker of barriers, an inspiration and organizer to her fellows, a visionary."[2] Before moving into Altgeld, Gautreaux, her husband, and their five kids lived crammed into one bedroom in a relative's house.

Gautreaux applied to the Chicago Housing Authority (CHA) for a public-housing unit and was told that yes, sure, technically she *could* apply for an apartment located in a predominantly white, affluent part of the city. But, she was told, the waiting list for one of *those* units was *really* long. Did she *actually* want to put up with that wait, given her overcrowded conditions? Didn't she want something as soon as possible? If so, her best bet, the CHA said, was to say on the housing application form that she preferred something in a mostly Black neighborhood. The CHA would then go on to say that the concentration of Black families in public-housing buildings on the mostly Black South and West sides wasn't due to discrimination by city government. It was due instead, the CHA claimed, to the agency simply giving people what they themselves wanted.

Moving into Altgeld Gardens, Dorothy quickly realized that the nearby schools (George Washington Carver elementary and high schools) were of substandard quality. Her community organizing began when she joined the PTA to try to make both schools better. From there, she organized local Girl Scout and Boy Scout groups and eventually joined the citywide Chicago Freedom Movement, where she represented the interests of CHA tenants; she later helped bring Dr. Martin Luther King Jr. to Altgeld Gardens for a protest. When the ACLU filed class-action lawsuits in 1966 against both the CHA and the US Department of Housing and Urban Development (HUD) for racial discrimination—first for building so much of the city's public-housing stock in predominantly Black neighborhoods, then for steering Black families into those projects—Gautreaux was a natural choice for lead plaintiff.

One of the animating beliefs behind the Gautreaux lawsuits was that where people live shapes who people are. Our behavior isn't due to just things about us as *people*, it's also about our *situations*.

While Dorothy Gautreaux wouldn't live to see the final results of this litigation herself—she died in 1968, only 41 years old—her lawsuits culminated in a unanimous ruling by the US Supreme Court in 1976, requiring that HUD move 7,100 Black public-housing families into either low-poverty, racially integrated suburbs or to other parts of the city of Chicago itself that might be still poor and racially segregated in that moment but that showed signs of trending in the direction of becoming more economically and racially diverse.[3]

In the late 1980s, a Northwestern University sociologist named James Rosenbaum began tracking families to see how these moves coincided with different life outcomes. His research offered suggestive evidence that moving to the low-poverty, mostly white suburbs (as opposed to the other option provided by the Supreme Court ruling, that of moving to other parts of Chicago) led to better jobs for moms and better schooling outcomes for kids.[4]

Rosenbaum's findings captured people's imaginations. It was an optimistic story at a time when many were in despair about American cities. Crack cocaine and the gun violence that came with it were sweeping the country. Social-policy experts were worrying about a so-called underclass of people that were not only poor but increasingly being left behind and isolated from the key institutions of mainstream society.[5] Journalists were writing moving accounts of the difficult circumstances so many families had to navigate, including Nicolas Lemann's *The Promised Land* and Alex Kotlowitz's *There Are No Children Here*.

It was also around this time that the lead ACLU lawyer in the Gautreaux case, Alexander Polikoff, pitched an idea to HUD during President George H. W. Bush's administration: What about doing a national version of the Gautreaux mobility program that was focused on desegregation not by race but by poverty instead?[6] Money for the policy experiment was appropriated in 1992. After President Bill Clinton took office in early 1993, his new HUD secretary—Henry Cisneros, previously the mayor of San Antonio—launched the Moving to Opportunity (MTO) for Fair Housing Demonstration.

One unusual feature of MTO was that it was intentionally structured like a randomized controlled trial. The Gautreaux study decades earlier had posed a sobering hypothesis to HUD: Did the billions of dollars that HUD invested over decades to build high-rise public-housing developments actually *harm*, rather than help, people's life chances? To answer such a high-stakes question, researchers and policymakers at HUD designed a policy demonstration to get as close as possible to learning the truth.

Beginning in 1994, MTO families were recruited from public-housing developments in Baltimore, Boston, Los Angeles, New York City, and Chicago. (The site in Chicago was the Robert Taylor Homes, which until they were torn down were just a few miles west of the University of Chicago along Garfield Boulevard, the main surface road that runs east-west from Hyde Park to Midway Airport.)

By 1998 a total of 4,600 families had signed up across the five cities, making MTO one of the largest social experiments in modern times. Given the heavy racial segregation of the housing projects from which families were drawn—the whole reason Dorothy Gautreaux helped file a lawsuit against the Chicago Housing Authority and HUD in the first place—it is perhaps not surprising that two-thirds of MTO families were Black, and most of the remainder Hispanic.

As part of MTO's RCT design, HUD randomly assigned some families the chance to use a Section 8 housing voucher to rent an apartment in a lower-poverty area.[7] The families that were randomly selected to not be offered a housing voucher kept the same public-housing apartment they were living in originally; that is, no one lost any services to which they were otherwise entitled as a result of MTO. So the random assignment created two groups of families that were on average comparable in all of the other ways that people differ and that shape their life outcomes, except for the fact that one group got the chance to move to a new neighborhood and the other group didn't. That means any difference in follow-up outcomes *must* be due to the causal effects of the different neighborhoods. The scientific evidence would be as close to unassailable as anything in public policy ever gets.

At the time families enrolled in MTO, they were asked as part of a baseline survey about the most important reason they signed up to move. On the survey, nearly two out of every five families said someone in their household had been victimized by a crime in the prior six months; the most common reason families said they signed up for MTO was for safety.

That finding made a big impression on me.

Discussions about poverty in America often tend to focus, for better or worse, on the aspects of living in poverty that middle-class people most easily understand. Most college-educated people have gone through a period (if only during college itself) where they had to live on very little money, struggled to varying degrees with food insecurity or inadequate housing or not having a car or worrying about the status of their health insurance, dealing with irregular work schedules at whatever part-time job they worked to help pay their way through school. Comparatively few middle-class people have ever spent time in a community where the risk of gun violence is anything like what it is in many South Side or West Side Chicago neighborhoods. So the awfulness of the experience is, for those living outside such circumstances, literally unimaginable. But as the MTO baseline surveys illustrated, the topics of the public conversation about poverty often miss one of the most important concerns of low-income families themselves: safety.

I first heard about MTO myself in fall 1993, as it was just ramping up. My last year of graduate school I went to Washington, DC, to give a talk at the annual public policy conference. My talk was a shambles; the content was bad, and the delivery was, if anything, even worse, with my nerves leading me to sweat profusely from the start of the talk all the way through the end. But afterward, someone from HUD emailed to ask if I wanted to help review proposals from outside research teams that wanted to help study MTO. I asked instead if I could apply myself rather than review proposals; they said yes. So my friend Helen (Sunny) Ladd from Duke and I applied, then started work on MTO in fall 1994, as I began my first professor job at Georgetown.

As the MTO demonstration started up, one of the first things that became clear was that MTO was indeed getting families into very different types of neighborhoods. One year in, the MTO families who *weren't* offered housing vouchers lived in neighborhoods where around 50 percent of all residents were poor. For families that *did* move via MTO, that figure was around 15 percent (a number not all that different from the nationwide average poverty rate).[8]

Other aspects of these neighborhoods were different, too. Of the families in the MTO control group, 42 percent said they felt like their local police don't respond when called, versus 28 percent for MTO movers. In terms of collective efficacy, 59 percent of MTO control group families said neighbors would do something if local kids were spraying graffiti, versus 75 percent of MTO movers. The families who moved through MTO also reported less physical disorder (litter, trash, graffiti, abandoned buildings) and social disorder (like public drinking). In other words, informal and formal social controls were stronger in the new MTO neighborhoods, which meant that ten-minute windows of trouble were more likely to get interrupted and the new neighborhoods were less like wicked learning environments.[9] That's to say: Based on all these features, the behavioral-economics view would predict that MTO moves should reduce violence.

Here, it is also worth noting what MTO did *not* change. Moral character does not change just from moving a few miles. Nor did criminal-justice sanctions change, since most people stayed within the jurisdiction of the same Cook County court system. Nor did the economic desperation of families change; it turned out the incomes of MTO families didn't change much as a result of these MTO moves. That is, conventional wisdom predicts that MTO shouldn't really reduce violence.

What do the data show actually happened? In a study I carried out with economists Larry Katz and Jeff Kling, we found that among the teens whose families moved through MTO, arrests for violent crime declined by nearly 40 percent.[10]

The study showed that what matters most is not so much the neighborhood in which a person grows up but rather their contemporaneous neighborhood environment; that is, for MTO teenagers, the neighborhoods they were in as teens (what criminologists would call *situational* neighborhood effects) mattered more than the neighborhoods they experienced as younger children (so-called *developmental* neighborhood effects).[11] These MTO findings don't seem to be a fluke; they're consistent with other natural experiments that study what happen when teens randomly wind up in juvenile correctional facilities with more crime-prone teens (teens become more crime prone when surrounded by more crime-prone peers),[12] or when someone's class at school happens to contain relatively more students who are more crime prone.[13]

Behavioral economics 1, conventional wisdom 0.

JANE

In her groundbreaking 1961 book *The Death and Life of Great American Cities*, Jane Jacobs argued for the need for cities to preserve the sort of diversity—of residents, of how buildings are used, of economic activity—that preserves the ecology of local neighborhoods and keeps them "lively." She believed in the need for intellectual humility and argued for incremental rather than sudden, transformative changes.[14] She hated cars and Robert Moses. These were all radical ideas at the time. One urban-planning expert compared her book to the "paperwork [Martin] Luther nailed to the Schlosskirche Wittenberg four centuries earlier," which "sparked a reformation—this time within planning."[15]

She thought lively neighborhoods with lots of businesses interspersed with residential areas would have lots of people around, which she thought was essential to the ability of local residents to informally maintain social control—the "eyes-on-the-street" principle this book references often.[16] As I've noted, this tenet is close in spirit to some important ideas in modern sociology around collective efficacy.[17] Collective efficacy, eyes on the street, informal social control, or whatever you'd prefer to call it is about the "public goods" in a neighborhood. As Jacobs noted, solving the "private-goods" problem in disadvantaged neighborhoods doesn't necessarily solve this public-goods problem: Giving people more money (say, through a larger Earned Income Tax Credit or a child tax credit) will make people less poor, but that's neither a necessary nor sufficient condition for improving the neighborhood public good of collective efficacy or informal social control. We know that Jacobs was right about this point, because we see that informal social control varies enormously even between similarly poor places.

But conventional wisdom predicts that informal social control shouldn't really matter for gun violence. So long as the underlying root causes that lead people to engage in crime or violence are there (moral poverty, economic poverty), the motivation to offend will still be there. Simply having someone around to interrupt them for ten minutes won't do anything—they'll just wait until the interrupter is gone, then commit their crime at the eleventh minute. Under the conventional wisdom of Left and Right, violence interrupted is merely violence delayed.

Behavioral economics narrates the role of eyes on the street differently. If gun violence is motivated by System 1 rather than System 2, then the motivation to shoot someone should often be fleeting rather than persistent. Time, in other words, gives System 2 a chance to reassess a situation, and a chance for strong emotions to ebb. Interrupting someone during one of the ten-minute windows that lead to violence has a real chance to prevent, not just delay, violence. And, moreover, a neighborhood where people are regularly willing to do that sort of interruption is one in which daily life becomes much more predictable for people to navigate. From System 1's perspective these neighborhoods become kind learning environments rather than wicked learning environments.

What does the FDA-standard evidence say?

One way that economists study questions like Jacobs's is to look at the opening or closing of local businesses—the sort of event that, Jacobs argued, is an important determinant of eyes on the street. In a natural experiment that was studied in Los Angeles in 2010, 417 of the city's 597 marijuana dispensaries were closed all at once due to a local regulatory change.[18] In the vacuum created by these suddenly shuttered businesses, crime rose by 20 percent in the areas immediately surrounding dispensaries that were forced to close (and which experienced reduced foot traffic in the areas). It's not just property crimes that rose as eyes on the street declined; violent crimes did as well.[19] The results were qualitatively similar (although a bit noisier) in another study of local restaurant closings.[20]

Another thing that creates more eyes on the street is better street lighting. In 2016, New York City identified eighty public-housing communities with high crime rates to prioritize for additional lighting (out of the city's 340 total housing developments), then randomly selected forty of them to get more outdoor lights. The other forty were the control group. Because of randomization, any difference in later crime rates between the two groups of housing developments could confidently be attributed to the extra lighting that went to one group but not the other. The result of more lights? A 35 percent reduction in serious offenses.[21]

The presence or absence of vacant lots also seems to matter for eyes on the street. As one study noted, American cities altogether have something like 7 million acres of vacant land (15 percent of total land area), the equivalent of the surface area of Switzerland.[22] Researchers from the University of Pennsylvania partnered with local government in Philadelphia to identify 541 vacant lots in that city and randomly assign some but not others to be cleaned up and restored to green spaces ("pocket parks")—to "de-blight" them. These lots were made more inviting: Trash and other debris was carted off, uneven ground was made even, grass and trees planted, nice wooden fences were put up. The RCT showed that compared to untouched lots, people living near cleaned-up lots were 75 percent more likely to use the outdoor space for hanging out, perceptions of crime declined by 37 percent, and actual gun assaults declined by 5 percent. In lower-income neighborhoods, the changes were even more pronounced; gun violence declined by 29 percent, and actual gun assaults declined by 10 percent.[23]

Another determinant of people's willingness to spend time in public (thereby providing Jacobs's eyes on the street) is the presence or absence of abandoned houses. In 2011, Philadelphia stepped up enforcement of a city ordinance that required owners of abandoned homes to have "well-maintained" windows and doors on the house, as opposed to, for example, having them boarded over with plywood, as well as requiring yards be well-kept and free of litter. Another University of Pennsylvania team worked with the city to study the effects of fixing up these houses. A total of 258 abandoned houses were identified and randomly assigned to have the house fixed up, the yard fixed up, or neither. Cleaning up trash in the yard reduced perceived disorder; fixing up the house itself not only reduced perceived disorder but also reduced shootings in that area by 9 percent.[24]

Behavioral economics 2, conventional wisdom 0.

DR. CHICO

Informal social control on Jane Jacobs's West Village block came from neighbors running out to help and interrupt trouble when it happens. But Jacobs also noted that society sometimes also *pays* people to act as eyes on the street—*formal social control*. Her New York example was Park Avenue: doormen on the sidewalk, maintenance workers and building superintendents and delivery people and service workers running around. Most of these people create eyes on the street as a secondary benefit of the work they do. But there are also people whose day jobs are to create social control more directly: teachers, police, security guards, and, increasingly, the sort of violence interrupters and street outreach workers who work for local nonprofit community violence intervention (CVI) organizations.

That's how I had the privilege of getting to know Dr. Chico Tillmon, one of the leading violence-prevention experts in the country. Tillmon grew up in the Austin neighborhood out on Chicago's West Side. It's sandwiched between the Chicago neighborhood of Garfield Park to the east (one of the city's most violent) and the affluent suburb of Oak Park to the west, which native son Ernest Hemingway was famously reported to have called "a neighborhood of wide lawns and narrow minds."[25]

To drive around Austin on the West Side is to see the same type of diversity you see driving down Dorchester Avenue here on the South Side. In the north part of Austin, between Lake and Erie streets, is Austin Village. Here you can find some of the most beautiful houses in the city, a mix of Victorian and Prairie-style architecture, sitting on giant, beautifully landscaped lots.[26] (These homes always make me feel a little sheepish about the tiny patch of grass and dirt in front of my own house in Hyde Park.)

The southern part of Austin is bisected by the Eisenhower Expressway (Interstate 290) that connects downtown to the western suburbs. If you get off the Eisenhower on Central Avenue you'll pass one of the grand public parks Chicago is famous for, 140-acre Columbus Park, the crowning achievement of the "dean of Prairie-style landscape architecture," Jens Jensen.[27] Driving over to Central from Hyde Park on the Eisenhower you'll notice there are surface streets running parallel to the highway on both sides, with lots of on- and off-ramps. These are perfect spots to sell drugs to suburban commuters driving to and from work downtown, hence the Eisenhower's nickname: "the Heroin Highway."

Tillmon was a very smart kid growing up, at a time when the Chicago Public Schools were not at their very best. The US secretary of education at the time, Bill Bennett, called Chicago public schools "the worst in the nation."[28] This wasn't a great time for the local schools to be struggling, since manufacturing in America was declining and education was becoming ever-more important for reaching a middle-class life. The West Side once had factories turning out Schwinn bikes, Brach's candies, Hasbro toys, and Zenith electronics. Today most of those factories are either abandoned buildings or vacant lots.[29]

In the part of Austin where Chico grew up, gangs were everywhere. I've talked to people who wonder why someone would *choose* to join a gang. As Tillmon points out, it's not always a real choice. If you grow up in Austin and someone asks where you're from, and you say block X, they'll just *assume* you're part of block X's gang, whether you are or not. So *not* joining the gang gets you all the costs of being in the gang (getting targeted for violence by other rival gangs) without any of the benefits (protection plus any money-making opportunities they offer).

Being in a gang got Chico caught up in the drug trade, shot at, arrested, and ultimately sent to federal prison for sixteen years, three months.

The world came precariously close to squandering Tillmon's enormous potential. America's prison system makes it much harder than it should be for inmates to get an education and overcome the less-than-great schools so many people had access to growing up. Nonetheless Tillmon wound up getting his college degree and eventually a PhD from the University of Illinois Chicago. Chico Tillmon is now Dr. Chico Tillmon.

One of Chico's first jobs was with the Chicago nonprofit Cure Violence (called Ceasefire at the time), founded by Dr. Gary Slutkin and described in the wonderful movie *The Interrupters*. While Jane Jacobs got to the idea of "eyes on the street" through the lens of urban planning, Slutkin and Tillmon got there through the lens of public health.

A key part of what Cure Violence and other CVI organizations do is hire people with extensive experience, credibility, and contacts out on the street ("credible messengers"). They find conflicts that are at risk of escalating—new conflicts or potential retaliation stemming from past conflicts—and then try to defuse them. They interrupt the ten-minute windows that lead to violence.

I'd long been interested in what violence interrupters say to change someone's mind. Would it be an appeal to morality ("The church or mosque you grew up attending, what would they say about this")? Would it be an appeal to ethics ("Violence is always wrong")? An appeal to empathy ("Remember that this person you've targeted is someone's son or brother or father")?

I was surprised at how often their tactic of choice doesn't seem to be any of those. It's often instead an attempt to get System 2 to reflect a bit more on the situation, consider what the person's objectives actually are, and think a bit more deliberately about the disadvantages and advantages of different candidate solution strategies. That is, often it's an appeal to *self-interest*.

Talking to Tillmon is to realize all the clever ways to make this sort of appeal that smart, talented people can come up with. For example, Tillmon told me about a time he was talking to a guy who had said something sexually explicit to a girl in the neighborhood. The girl's brother said a sharp word back. Now word was out that the guy who had said the sexually explicit thing had a gun and was out for the brother. Tillmon started by asking a question he often starts off with, even if Tillmon already knows exactly what happened: "What happened?" Tillmon told me, "I want them to *think* about what they're saying." The guy said the brother had disrespected him—the sharp word was apparently triggering an automatic, subconscious response. Tillmon asked, "If someone said that same thing to *your* sister, and *you* said something to *them*, would you mean that as disrespect?"

What Tillmon is essentially doing here with this question was illustrated in a canonical study in psychology, in which researchers asked Stanford undergraduates to answer a hypothetical question: "You drive up to San Francisco with friends in order to celebrate the end of the [academic] quarter. The plans include dinner and then some entertainment afterward. How much money will you personally spend on the dinner?"[30] Study responders come up with a dollar amount answer, not realizing that their answers had hinged on a set of assumptions that System 1 made below the level of consciousness but weren't actually specified (which specific friends would go with them, what they would be willing to spend, etc.). In the study, the researchers randomly assigned half the Stanford students to be encouraged to reflect on what assumptions they're making—the details that hadn't been specified in the framing of the question. That reflection-intervention got the students to realize not only what assumptions were behind their initial forecast but how those assumptions might have been wrong—that the world (or at least their planned trip to the city) might be different from how they had assumed. These students wind up (appropriately) updating their forecasts for how much they'd spend on dinner to be less confident, more uncertain. People on their own had not adequately considered all the possible alternative ways the world might be different from their implicit assumptions.

Tillmon, through role reversal, similarly got the agitated guy he was working with to reflect on a key assumption that *he* had made about the situation (effectively, the first S of SODAS): "This guy is intentionally being a jerk to me" (egocentric construal). Once this assumption is pointed out to System 2, from there it's a small leap to realize that alternative interpretations are possible ("Maybe it's not about *me*, maybe the guy's just sticking up for his sister as anyone would"). Tillmon got the guy to ask himself: *Is it really in my own self-interest to go shoot the brother, with all the risks that brings of ruining my own life, if I'm not even sure the brother had any bad intent?*

There was another time Tillmon was talking to a guy who was owed $40 by someone who seemed reluctant to pay it back. The guy said, "I'm being punked. I'm going over there and am going to shoot up the whole block." Tillmon asked, "What is this *really* about?" The guy said: "He owes me forty bucks!" Tillmon pulled $40 out of his wallet, handed it to the guy, then asked, "Okay, *now* what are you going to do?" Tillmon is getting the guy's System 2 to reflect on whether the $40 is really a *need* or is instead a *want*; that is, to revisit an implicit objective System 1 might have made without the guy's conscious realization. Tillmon is also cleverly getting the guy to realize that in going through the disadvantages and advantages of different strategies (the D, A, and S of SODAS), he might be catastrophizing: It's not really about the $40, it's about System 1 concluding, "Literally nothing's worse than this guy showing me up."

Tillmon told me about a different time when some gang was systematically shooting one person after another in some other gang. After a handful of deaths, Tillmon got called in to intervene. It turned out the gang doing the shooting had had something of theirs stolen; that by itself wasn't so bad until the other gang then publicly bragged about it. Tillmon met with the leader of the gang doing the shooting and asked: "What do you *want*?" Tillmon is prompting the leader of this gang to consider the possibility that System 1 might be catastrophizing— "Nothing's worse than letting these guys get away with this." Surely System 2 doesn't think the proportional response to some shit talk on social media is to kill literally everyone else in the other gang? Tillmon also asked, "If *I* found out you're doing this myself, don't you think the *cops* know too?" (Hey, System 2, is it possible System 1 skipped over thinking through the disadvantages and advantages of the candidate solution "Kill everyone in the other gang"?)

Tillmon never tells people what to do. He's not teaching or preaching any particular type of morality. He's just recognizing that everyone relies on System 1 to deal with low-stakes, routine situations; he's helping their System 2s realize when people are in either high-stakes or nonroutine situations, and then teaching them to use System 2 to reflect more deliberately on what's happening and what choices *they* think are in their own best interest, as they define it. Do you *really* want to beat up your girlfriend because she *didn't unload the dishwasher*? If someone spit in your face, sure that would be gross, but would that really be bad enough to make it worth doing what you just said you'd do to someone who did that—"blow their fucking brains out"?

It's been hard to get good evidence on the effects of CVI organizations specifically, the sort of work done by paid violence interrupters or street outreach workers, because they usually work at the level of the neighborhood and sometimes run out to other nearby neighborhoods if trouble is brewing there. So it's hard to figure out which neighborhoods should be compared to one another to measure the impacts of CVI.

Luckily, there are many other forms of formal social control that have been rigorously studied that often use the same sort of behavioral-economics logic that Chico uses, and which suggest very encouraging impacts on violence.

The most obvious example is cops. The conventional wisdom of the Left suggests police shouldn't matter because they don't directly end poverty or other root causes. Conventional wisdom of the Right implies police should only matter to the extent to which they arrest people (that is, incapacitate or deter criminals). But that's not how police seem to spend most of their time. The data suggest that even in a fairly high-crime city environment like Chicago, the average Chicago cop makes about one arrest every three months.[31]

So what *do* police do with their time? One thing they do with at least part of their time is help problem solve—including, sometimes, stepping in and interrupting conflict before it escalates.

I was riding around with a police sergeant one night when we turned the corner and came across a middle-aged guy who had a woman pinned against a fence. The guy was right in her face, screaming at her and physically preventing her from getting away. He looked furious. She looked petrified. The sergeant stopped the car, got out, and said, "Hey buddy why don't you take a walk." The guy turned to the sergeant and said, "Everything's fine." The sergeant replied, "I said TAKE A WALK." (He was good at making his point clear when he wanted to.) We gave her a ride home. What made this particularly heartbreaking was that as she was being screamed at by this guy in her face, pinned against the fence, standing right next to her holding her hand the whole time was her little kid.

Another night I was in the back of a police car in Englewood, a neighborhood just a few miles west of Hyde Park that usually has one of the city's highest murder rates. It was like 2:00 or 3:00 a.m. on a warm summer night, so the police car's windows were all down. As we drove by the CTA train stop, we saw a crowd of people standing there; everyone spontaneously started shouting all at once, "He's over there!" and pointing to the McDonald's. On the drive to McDonald's someone else on the sidewalk saw the police car and also yelled out: "Hey, he's right there!" Everyone in the police car wondered: What is everyone talking about? What in the world was going on? We got to the McDonald's, and there was a young white guy sitting on the curb, glassy eyed, with a golf ball–sized lump on his head. Chicago's segregation is so extreme, *this* turned out to be the unusual event that got everyone's attention. One of the cops got out and asked, "How did YOU get here?" The guy looked up, held up his fists, and said, "With THESE bad boys." I don't know if he was drunk or high or what, but he was definitely belligerent. If the cops hadn't picked him up and taken him to St. Bernard's hospital for a psychiatric evaluation, there's a real chance that him sitting around for a few more hours itching to use his "bad boys" would have escalated into something unhelpful or even tragic.

The best cops, like the best teachers, are clever at figuring out strategies not so dissimilar to ones that Chico Tillmon uses. One police officer told me what he does when someone starts yelling at him: He gets quieter. By the time the other person is shouting, the cop is literally whispering. The other person starts off thinking this is a familiar script that System 1 has seen a million times before—a heated argument that's going to get more heated. But when the cop breaks the script and starts whispering, the other person stops in their tracks, startled—it's a novel situation, which engages System 2. From there, System 2 has a chance to step in and reconstrue things.

The best available evidence suggests that police prevent violence, and that they might not do this *only* through deterrence. Teasing out the independent causal effect of police on crime is not easy; many cities intentionally increase spending on police *because* of higher crime levels. Honolulu has fewer than half the number of cops per capita as Chicago; Honolulu also has less crime. Does that mean that fewer cops lead to fewer crimes? Or does it mean Honolulu feels like it doesn't need to hire so many cops *because* it has lower crime?[32] To reflexively conclude that *more cops = more crime* from this pattern would be like looking at the waiting room of a doctor's office, noting that everyone there's in poor health, and concluding that going to the doctor makes you sick.

Social scientists have gotten better at figuring out how to isolate the effects of police on crime. Sometimes this isolation takes the form of randomized experiments, where some crime hot-spot areas get assigned extra police resources and others don't. Sometimes it takes the form of studying natural experiments where some policy changes and creates as-good-as-random increases or decreases in police resources. For example, in the Clinton administration, the US Department of Justice gave out police hiring grants through its COPS program to some departments and not others based on factors unrelated to each city's crime trend.[33]

The best available data suggest that when cities hire more cops, violent crimes go down.[34] In the average city, when the number of police goes up by 10 percent, the murder rate (most of which involve guns) goes down by around 10 percent.[35] Arrests for serious crimes also decline,[36] while the clearance rate (ratio of charges filed to crimes reported) doesn't increase.[37] People sometimes say "We can't arrest our way out of this crime problem," which they usually intend as a skeptical take on police being a useful part of the solution. What that skepticism misses is that when policing is done right, it seems to be doing something to *prevent* violence in the first place—as behavioral economics (unlike conventional wisdom) would predict.

It is unfortunately true that some cities, when they hire more cops, wind up asking those cops to go out and make lots more arrests for minor crimes like misdemeanors—a version of zero-tolerance policing. But those minor arrests don't help reduce serious violent crimes. That is, departments that use their extra officers to carry out zero-tolerance policing could cut out a lot of those extra misdemeanor arrests and reduce the harm of enforcement without losing the beneficial effects police can have in preventing crime and violence.[38]

A second example of formal social control is security guards, which in the US are even more common than police (1.1 million[39] versus 800,000).[40] Security guards are hired by K–12 schools, businesses, nonprofits, even universities, as you see walking around Hyde Park with unarmed University of Chicago security guards wearing distinctive neon-blue or -yellow clothes on every other corner. Conventional wisdom suggests that security guards shouldn't matter for crime and violence. If someone is persistently motivated to commit crime because of psychopathy or economic desperation, a security guard doesn't fix those problems. But if the behavioral-science perspective is right in asserting that violence stems from conflict in key ten-minute windows, then security guards have a chance to help by, among other things, intervening and interrupting.

One of the best available studies looks at what happens when business improvement districts (BIDs) do things like hire more security guards. The data suggest that the result of having a BID do things like hire more private security is for serious crime to decline by 11 percent. Moreover, the evidence shows that having more security guards around reduces the number of arrests police make and may even reduce the rate at which crimes result in arrest (the so-called clearance rate).[41] In other words, as with police, the reduction in violence we see might be about more than just deterrence.

Another way to see that both cops and security guards may be preventing violence through something like interruption, not just deterrence, is by looking at the effects of a policy that *only* deters and *can't* interrupt: security cameras.

One study looked at what happened in Stockholm's subway system when security cameras were installed: "Planned crimes," that is, income-motivated property crimes like pick-pocketing and robbery, declined. That's deterrence at work, which makes sense: Property crimes have a rational, instrumental goal that's plausibly driven by System 2. But, interestingly, security cameras—unlike cops and security guards—did *not* generate detectable reductions in *violent* crimes like assaults, which, I've argued, are more likely to be in-the-moment System 1 offenses.[42] This finding is at least suggestive evidence that for in-the-moment, System 1 crimes of passion rather than profit, having human beings around to step in and *do* something (de-escalate and interrupt and intervene, as with Jane Jacobs's neighbors in Greenwich Village) might be important for reducing violence.

A final example of a source of formal social control is teachers. I have a friend who was a middle-school math teacher in Indianapolis. Here's what he and his teacher friends would do when a student got *really* out of control in class: Ask the student to step into the hallway for a chat. The kid's System 1 is sure they know this familiar script: "I'm getting pulled out of class to get yelled at by an adult." In the hallway, the teacher turns to the kid. The kid steels themselves for what's coming. But the teacher then says: "Hey, did you watch the Bulls game last night? Can you believe Michael Jordan only took two shots the entire second half, even though no Pacer could guard him?" The kid, on System 1 autopilot, ready to deploy a "scream at teacher" response to a "yelled at by teacher" situation, stops in their tracks. They're surprised. It's not a routine interaction, it's weird—*novel*. Novelty engages System 2. System 2, once engaged, then reconstrues the situation (the first S of SODAS)—What in the world is actually happening here?

We can see signs that this type of thing works in the data. One study used data on ten million student-by-year observations from North Carolina public schools over a period of seventeen years, involving over forty thousand different teachers, to look at how teachers influence student outcomes.[43] Students aren't randomly assigned to teachers, so we need some sort of natural experiment to control for other things that vary across families and neighborhoods that might affect student outcomes besides teachers. Researchers solve that problem by comparing siblings who come from the same family and neighborhood but wind up with different teachers. The data shows that there are indeed teachers who have figured out how to be unusually good at helping kids learn to control themselves (less acting up, fewer suspensions, and fewer arrests—including for serious crimes).

This reduction in serious offending shouldn't be happening, according to conventional wisdom. The right-of-center view is that the main way teachers could possibly reduce misbehavior is through harsher punishment. Yet we see in the data that the teachers who are best at reducing future crime involvement are the ones who have to discipline their students *less* often in school—something *preventive* is happening. Meanwhile the left-of-center view that gun violence is due to economic desperation would suggest the teachers who are best at preventing student violence must be the ones who are best at boosting academic outcomes and hence future lifetime earnings. But that's also not the case; the teachers who are best at improving student behavior *aren't* the ones who are best at teaching math or reading. In the final chapter I'll discuss the implications for making school even more useful for violence prevention.

Teachers, security guards, cops. They don't magically make immoral people moral, or end poverty, or merely reduce crime by locking lots more people up. At least part of what they seem to be doing is interrupting System 1 when it's about to make a mistake—about to do something System 2 would regret. And the result seems to be, fairly consistently: less violence.

Behavioral economics 3, conventional wisdom 0.

TONY

Anthony Ramirez-DiVittorio—"Tony"—grew up on the Southwest Side of Chicago, near Midway Airport. He's built like the martial artist that he used to be. Like me, he didn't cut his hair during the pandemic. Unlike me, Tony didn't get a haircut when the pandemic ended. He looks a lot like the actor Jason Momoa without the beard. A tattoo of two crossed flags on his arm, of Mexico and Italy, is a nod to the countries his parents came from.

With a master's degree in psychology, Ramirez-DiVittorio worked as a counselor in a mostly Puerto Rican neighborhood in Chicago. He was, as an observer of his work put it, "surrounded by kids who were younger versions of himself."[44] Ramirez-DiVittorio became known for developing a program for the Chicago nonprofit organization Youth Guidance called Becoming a Man (BAM), which sought to instill the same principles behind the work of Chico Tillmon and other CVI workers. The difference was Ramirez-DiVittorio's program wanted to help young people intervene on themselves *before* the challenging ten-minute windows ever happened, so they'd be better prepared to navigate those windows on their own.

To do that, Ramirez-DiVittorio teaches students that the first step of every social interaction (the S in SODAS) is construing the situation— What's going on, and what's the other person's intention here? In the first exercise teens do in the BAM program, called "The Fist," they're divided into pairs. One teen is given a ball; the other has thirty seconds to get it. Almost all of them rely on force to try to complete the assignment; they try to pry the other person's hand open, or wrestle or even pummel the other person. During the debrief that follows, a BAM counselor asks why no one *asked* for the ball. Most youth respond by saying their partner would have thought they were a punk (or something worse—you can imagine). The counselor then asks the partner what he would have done if asked. The usual answer: "I would have given it, it's just a stupid ball."

This exercise is, first and foremost, engaging—it's "show," not "tell." Lots of participants walk into the first BAM session suspecting it's going to be corny, yet many of them will inevitably find themselves drawn in by the fist exercise. That's important because the hardest thing with most social programs is getting people to buy in and show up.

The other thing this exercise does is get participants to see how, from the very beginning, their System 1 had made an assumption about what situation they were in. Whereas Chico Tillmon helps people see alternative construals of situations by getting them to try things like role reversal, in the fist exercise, Ramirez-DiVittorio takes advantage of the fact that there's a program participant in the other role who can help the partner see they misconstrued the situation by directly telling them what they were thinking. This BAM exercise gives participants a low-cost way to get feedback that System 1 made a mistake—to show that their automatic assumptions are often wrong. It helps participants recognize that when there's a high-stakes situation, it's worth engaging System 2 to ask, "Hey, what's really going on here? Is it possible I think I'm seeing a duck but there's really a rabbit here somewhere?"

In a different BAM session, participants do a role-playing exercise: They discuss a conflict (real or hypothetical) and are asked to explain why the conflict came about. Participants will describe the setting, the interaction with the other person, and their explanation for why things went sideways: "He challenged me" or "He treated me like a punk." The BAM counselor gets the participants, as they're describing the event, to answer the question: "What would a *camera* have seen?" This question helps show participants how System 1's often-useful tendency to "go beyond the information given" and fill in all sorts of things about what's happening in an event can sometimes lead to trouble, especially when they're about to escalate a conflict based on some subjective interpretation. "You *say* he challenged you, but all the camera would have seen is that he furrowed his brow. How do you *know* that's a challenge? What *else* might it be?"

Here's a third BAM exercise: Participants pair up and play out an exchange where one student has borrowed $10 from the other but then not paid it back. It's not hard to see how, for many teens in this role-playing exercise, things can escalate quickly. This escalation gives the BAM counselor a chance to ask questions of the kids like: "Is it *really* about the $10? Or is it about something else instead?" (Echoes of one of Dr. Chico's prompts.) Did System 1 set an objective that System 2 isn't even aware of? Is System 1, in thinking through the disadvantages and advantages of different candidate solutions, potentially—for example—catastrophizing?

Because System 1 is effortless and invisible, its output is easy to not notice, and even when System 1's output *is* noticed, it's easy to confuse the subjective construals System 1 is offering up with objective reality. So BAM spends a lot of time just helping people better *notice* what's going on *within* their own minds. Every BAM session starts with a check-in at the beginning where everyone reports on how they're feeling—physically, intellectually, emotionally, spiritually (PIES)—to be more aware of their System 1–generated inner states.

One of the biggest mistakes System 1 can make is to skip over key SODAS steps in navigating a social interaction, which is the very definition of impulsive behavior. So BAM helps participants learn to recognize high-stakes and/or novel situations and adopt some strategies to slow down and "stop, look, and listen" (engage the System 2 fact checker) in these difficult situations. Programs like BAM also encourage participants to avoid name-calling, since, as we've seen, someone who is called an asshole *becomes* an asshole—dehumanization—which in turn makes violence easier.

The program's overall goal, in other words, is to help young people better understand how their own minds work as they're navigating difficult, fraught situations out in the real world.

Notice what BAM does *not* do. BAM does not teach morality. BAM doesn't lecture kids or tell them what the right thing to do is. BAM never tells kids that fighting is wrong. Ramirez-DiVittorio acknowledges that, unfortunately, to grow up on the South or West side of Chicago is to sometimes *have* to fight. His goal instead is to help kids make sure that when they fight it's only in situations where they really have to. Nor does BAM give families lots of cash or in-kind help to solve their money woes, nor does it desegregate Chicago neighborhoods by race or income or solve any of the city's other glaring root causes. So conventional wisdom says BAM shouldn't prevent violence.

Yet the FDA-standard data say something extraordinarily different about BAM's effects in practice.

A large-scale RCT run out of my research center studied the effects of BAM on several thousand teens from middle schools and high schools on Chicago's South and West sides. The program was delivered during the school day once a week (with something like fifteen to twenty sessions total per student) in groups of about a dozen kids for every one BAM counselor. We measured crime involvement using official arrest records, so the study findings weren't just an artifact of BAM participants telling us what we wanted to hear on surveys. We also collected official school records, too. We found that BAM participation not only increased high school graduation rates by 20 percent; it led to a drop in violent-crime arrests of *nearly 50 percent*.[45]

We anticipated some effect, but we were very surprised by the *magnitude* of the effects. Many of us on the research team were economists who were used to thinking that System 2's response to incentives was the key to understanding all human behavior. We were shocked that a policy focused on System 1—which we'd never seen before—could have such big impacts. We were so shocked, in fact, that we did another large-scale RCT of BAM to see if the first result was just a fluke. In our second RCT, again with several thousand kids across the South and West sides, we *again* saw nearly 50 percent reductions in violent-crime arrests.

These are *big* effects, akin in size to the nationwide drop in violence of the 1990s that criminologists have come to call the "Great Crime Decline."[46]

While it's a little harder to measure impacts on shootings specifically,[47] we see that BAM reduced both assaults (arguments that escalate into fights) and weapons offenses (like illegal gun carrying) each by around 33 percent.[48] If gun violence = guns + violence, BAM reduces the chances that kids will engage in violence, and it reduces the chances that they'll have a gun on them when violence does happen. If BAM is affecting both guns and violence, it seems reasonable to extrapolate from the RCT results to conclude that it is likely reducing violence committed with guns, too.

BAM may also prevent the economically motivated crime of robbery, too, by as much as 50 percent.[49] This result is surprising since BAM doesn't directly alleviate poverty. So why the potentially big effect on robbery? When I was in high school in Frankfurt listening to my cousin's friends outline their shoplifting scheme, I wish in hindsight that my System 2—in thinking through the disadvantages and advantages of the solution of just going along with the scheme (the D, A, and S of SODAS)—had more deliberately considered the question, "Is this *really* worth it?" Maybe BAM is helping kids avoid the mistake I made, albeit in situations now where the stakes are much higher.

This evidence shows BAM *can* have amazing results. There's a separate question about whether BAM can still be this effective if we increase its scale by a factor of ten or a thousand or a hundred thousand. The data we've collected in Chicago so far suggest that scale-up could be a challenge. The program may have lost some of its amazing effectiveness during its initial scaling-up period, although the data on that point are a bit noisier than we'd like.[50] In any case, before we start thinking about at-scale solutions, we need to first understand the problem we're trying to solve. The BAM results provide proof of concept that System 1 may very well be strongly implicated in a lot of the most serious violence.

And, importantly, the evidence for that conclusion doesn't come just from BAM.

Over the past fifteen years at the University of Chicago Crime Lab, we've now looked at a growing number of programs that rely on the same basic behavioral-economics logic of BAM: helping young people recognize when they're in high-stakes or novel situations, when System 1 might be misconstruing a situation or confusing a want with a need or catastrophizing or just skipping over any consideration of pros and cons. The emphasis can differ across programs; some spend more time helping people think of different solutions to avoid conflict ("Just walk away" or "Count to ten backward," which requires engaging System 2). Other programs spend relatively more time helping people recognize what triggers unhelpful System 1 responses (for example, "He called me dumb"); some programs even have participants write out "thinking reports" to reconstruct events that ended badly to see System 1 assumptions for which they could have considered alternatives. But all these programs share the core underlying logic of behavioral economics.

For example, the Chicago Public Schools partnered with Children's Home + Aid (now Brightpoint) and Youth Advocates Program on a behavioral economics–informed program, Choose 2 Change (C2C), that combines BAM-like programming with mentorship.[51] Two University of Chicago researchers—Nour Abdul-Razzak and Kelly Hallberg—did an RCT of C2C. Through the first six post-program months, violent-crime arrests declined by about 50 percent; through thirty-six months, the researchers still found signs of a large effect.[52] The impact was larger for the most serious violent crimes, consistent with the idea that C2C helps kids recognize that they most need System 2 to step in when the stakes are highest.[53]

I realize that even encouraging RCT results like these can be a little abstract. A different way to see the impacts of the program is to look at what the participants themselves say. As one put it: "If I was rich . . . [I would] put some money to the program. It's a good program."[54]

We see similar types of results with even *higher*-risk teens, testing a BAM-like, C2C-like behavioral-economics program carried out as an RCT inside the Cook County Juvenile Temporary Detention Center (JTDC).[55] The JTDC is where the teenagers whom the juvenile justice system deems to be at highest risk are taken as their cases make their way through court. The program was delivered by the detention center's staff in the afternoons, when residents weren't in school and otherwise would have just sat around watching TV. This intervention was remarkably cheap (the cost was mostly a little staff training and printing up some program booklets), yet data from 5,278 youth in total show a decline in recidivism of about 20 percent.[56]

When murders spiked by 60 percent in the city of Chicago in 2016, Chicago nonprofit Heartland Alliance helped implement a program called READI (Rapid Employment and Development Initiative) that combined BAM-like behavioral-economics programming with an $11 an hour job for thirty hours a week over eighteen months. The target population here was 20- and 30-something-year-old men in Chicago at highest risk for gun violence involvement. I've shown in chapter 4 that giving people jobs alone doesn't seem to be enough to prevent violence involvement. The new ingredient here is the behavioral-economics component, which the participants themselves nicknamed "CAD" (for "control-alt-delete"). What does the FDA-standard evidence say? While the data here are a bit noisier than we'd like, the estimated impact on shooting arrests, taken at face value, implies something like a 65 percent reduction.[57]

Some evidence that it's the behavioral-economics component that helps in READI comes from interviews of participants by Megan Kang, Kathy Edin, and Tim Nelson. Participants can now recognize their own egocentric construals when assessing situations. As one said, "I used to fight any and everybody. . . . Now I know, I'll just sit back and watch because sometimes people don't even be talking to me." As another put it, "Somebody walk past you and call you a bitch, what do you do in that situation? I say, shit. Some situations ain't take a minute. They might be having a bad day. They might have just got into it with their people." People recognize that System 1 can often skip key SODAS steps, so they need to stop, look, and listen ("It takes only 3 seconds to ruin your life. . . . You just got to think to yourself. Sometimes somebody make you frustrated, count to 10 backward or something. Take a walk."). It's no accident that READI participants are counting to ten *backward*; counting forward is routine enough for System 1 to do, but counting backward is novel enough for most people to require engaging System 2.[58]

Moreover, these sorts of results aren't coming exclusively from "name-brand" behavioral-economics programs; we see encouraging results from all sorts of other interventions that rely on some of the same underlying logic, too.

"Restorative justice" has gotten a lot of attention as an alternative to punishment for dealing with antisocial behavior. The idea is to get the offender to accept responsibility for their actions and help repair the harm inflicted on the victim, in a process that is typically less adversarial than a normal court proceeding. You can see behavioral-economics insights at play in things like asking offenders to write apology letters to other people that include some discussion about what they would do differently if they could do it all over again—that is, getting System 2 to reflect on an event and alternative interpretations or candidate solutions the person might have tried. Nearly a dozen different RCTs suggest that restorative justice reduces crime involvement. In one recent study of a San Francisco program for teens, recidivism rates dropped by 44 percent.[59] A similar type of program in the Chicago Public Schools led to an 18 percent reduction in violent-crime arrests.[60]

Other studies suggest that the "writing down and reflecting" part of restorative justice may be a key part of its active ingredient. We can see the importance of this step from looking at the data on a local jail program in Ashville, North Carolina, where the main thing the jail did with inmates was just to ask them to write down their reflections about how their choices landed them in jail ("reflective journaling"). An RCT that was carried out with 183 inmates showed a 22 percent drop in recidivism.[61]

A Midwestern juvenile-detention center offered teen residents a program that combined a number of different approaches to stimulating System 2 reflection at every step of SODAS: mentoring, reflective journaling, and reading and reflecting on the "Great Books" (Aristotle, Thomas Aquinas, etc.). An evaluation by the Lab for Economic Opportunity at the University of Notre Dame found that the program reduced overall recidivism, with particularly large reductions (on the order of 60 percent or more) for the most serious crimes.[62]

Notice what all these policies have in common. Aside from the subsidized employment component of READI, none of the other policies does anything to directly address poverty, much less any of the other, larger root causes like segregation or social isolation. None of the policies tries to teach morality; nor even, for that matter, do they ever tell people directly what to do. And none of the policies tries to deter people with harsher punishments. "All" these policies do is try to get people to make fewer System 1 mistakes in high-stakes, difficult situations. And "all" they do is show enormous promise for reducing violence.

Behavioral economics 4, conventional wisdom 0.

MAYOR LIGHTFOOT

Lori Elaine Lightfoot was born in Ohio, played point guard in high school, went to the University of Michigan, graduated from the University of Chicago Law School, clerked for a Michigan Supreme Court justice, worked as an assistant US attorney for the federal prosecutor in Chicago, then as a lawyer for the Chicago Police Department's Office of Professional Standards, then for one of the big fancy "white-shoe" law firms in downtown Chicago, Mayer Brown.[63] I got to know her when she was head of the Chicago Police Board and then chair of the Police Accountability Task Force, organized by then-mayor Rahm Emanuel, when my research center did some data work in support of the Task Force's efforts.[64]

In 2019 she ran for mayor after Rahm Emanuel announced he wouldn't run again. This announcement came on the heels of the release of a video showing Chicago PD officer Jason Van Dyke repeatedly shooting teenager Laquan MacDonald in late 2015, followed in 2016 by a massive surge in gun violence. Police reform and criminal-justice issues were top of mind for lots of voters at the time.

Voters were also feeling sick of the so-called Chicago way. Lightfoot's opponent was Toni Preckwinkle, for many years the city council representative for Hyde Park, later the president of the Cook County board and then chair of the Cook County Democratic Party. Preckwinkle started off as a good-government reformer before basically taking over the Democratic machine. Preckwinkle had the bad luck of having accepted political fundraising help from City Council member Ed Burke, who in 2019 was under indictment for corruption after having been caught on a federal wire asking a colleague, "So did we land the, uh, tuna?" Since this is Chicago, Burke's wife was naturally the chief justice of the Illinois Supreme Court. Preckwinkle had also just fired her chief of security after he crashed a government SUV with campaign materials in the back seat (government resources not being allowed to be used for campaigning), fired her chief of staff for covering up a sexual harassment scandal in her office, and fired her campaign manager for comparing Lightfoot to the Nazis at Nuremberg.[65] The significance of Lightfoot's campaign slogan—"Let the Light In"—was not lost on anyone.

As the 56th mayor of Chicago, one of Lightfoot's priorities was to get illegal guns off the streets. Part of her strategy was moral suasion: She'd say things at press conferences like, "No amount of policing, no superior crime strategy can address these private moments where adults allowed children and teens access to deadly weapons. Adults, we have to be better. . . . And for teens and young adults, my plea is put the guns down. You're not a punk or weak if you don't carry a gun."[66] Part of her strategy was also to crowdsource information that community members often have about who is selling, carrying, or using illegal guns—including via a tip line offering $1,000 rewards for information.[67] A third part of her strategy was continuing the Chicago PD's emphasis on getting illegal guns off the street. In 2022, her last full year in office, the police confiscated fully ten thousand guns,[68] far more than either LA or New York.[69]

Lightfoot's focus on reducing gun carrying was behavioral economics in practice. As I've noted, conventional wisdom implies that whether someone has a gun with them at any given moment shouldn't matter much for gun violence, since System 2–driven motivation for gun carrying is persistent. The offender will just wait and commit the crime next time they have their gun handy. Behavioral economics, in contrast, implies that to prevent someone from having a gun at hand in a difficult ten-minute window is to help prevent a shooting.

What does the data say?

The best evidence on this question comes from analysis of Chicago crime data by Priyanka Goonetilleke, Hanming Fang, and David S. Abrams at the University of Pennsylvania.[70] Using data from Chicago, they construct a proxy for illegal gun carrying similar to the one I used in the previous chapter, equal to the share of citizen stops that police make that result in confiscation of a gun. They compared what happened to gun violence across police districts when gun carrying goes up by larger or small amounts, holding the number of stops the police make constant. Their estimates imply that a 50 percent increase in gun carrying would roughly double the number of shootings in Chicago.[71]

That conclusion is consistent with studies of the effects of changing state laws that make it easier to carry guns legally. Back in the 1990s, two economists, John Lott and David Mustard, looked at what happened when states enacted laws that made it easier for people to get government permits to legally carry guns around in public.[72] While the University of Pennsylvania team is looking at what happens when *illegal* gun carrying goes up,[73] the Lott-Mustard study looks at a slightly different question: the effects of more *legal* gun carrying. While Lott and Mustard claimed that more legal gun carrying reduces crime, over time better data and evidence have reversed that conclusion: More people walking around with guns—and with permits to carry them legally—seems, on net, to lead to more crime.[74]

Behavioral economics 5, conventional wisdom 0.

CONCLUSION

I have presented data on the effects of five different types of policies that behavioral economics predicts should reduce gun violence: changing people's social environments without changing their moral character or their own income level; changing the level of *informal* social control specifically within someone's social environment (that is, increasing the odds that a neighbor or passerby interrupts a ten-minute window that might lead to violence); changing the level of *formal* social control within someone's social environment; working with people in advance to anticipate and better navigate those difficult ten-minute windows; and keeping illegal guns off the street so they're not ready at hand during those ten-minute windows when they happen.

One thing each of these policies has in common is that conventional wisdom suggests it shouldn't work. None of these policies changes morality or threatens people with harsher punishments. Outside of the temporary job that READI provides participants, none of these policies does anything directly to address poverty or other big root causes.

A second thing these policies have in common is that they've been subject to rigorous empirical testing with data, of the sort that the FDA requires for new drugs or medical devices.

A third thing these policies have in common is they seem to *work*. They prevent violence.

Of course, many open questions remain with each of these policies. Who benefits the most? For how long do these behavioral impacts persist?[75] What is the ratio of benefits to costs for these programs? How does that ratio compare to those of alternative policies? Can these impacts persist when the policies are scaled up? How do we scale these policies in ways that ensure they don't experience diminishing marginal returns?[76] These are obviously critically important scientific and policy questions that will need to be answered.

But the key point for now is that *proof of concept has been established*— the FDA-level evidence is more consistent with the predictions of behavioral economics than of conventional wisdom. The Enlightenment led people to start viewing the world through reason and science. We have seen here that policies that could only reduce gun violence that is driven by System 1 wind up reducing gun violence substantially in practice. A post-Enlightenment view of the world suggests that we need to update our understanding of the underlying causes of gun violence and recognize that System 1–driven shootings—that is, shootings driven by System 1's universal frailties in high-stakes, difficult situations—are far more important than we've thought.

9

The Case for Hope

To drive down Dorchester Avenue on the South Side of Chicago is to be reminded, over and over, of the heartbreaking puzzles—the seeming inexplicability—of gun violence.

Not far from the northern end of Dorchester Avenue is Vivian G. Harsh Park, named after Chicago's first Black librarian. It was there, on January 29, 2013, that Hadiya Pendleton, a 15-year-old attending King College Prep High School, was hanging out with her friends after school. Into the park walked Micheail Ward,[1] age 18, and Kenneth Williams, age 20. Confusing Pendleton's group with a rival gang, Ward opened fire, hitting two of Pendleton's friends—and killing Pendleton. It was just a week after Pendleton had performed in Washington, DC, as part of the celebration of President Obama's second inauguration.

The call Pendleton's parents received was the call every parent in America lives in terror of getting one day. As Pendleton's mother, Cleopatra, put it in court, "Hadiya is serving a death sentence handed down by Micheail Ward, and all of the family is doing life as a result of her death."

Why did this happen?

Micheail Ward had been administered a psychological evaluation at school a few years earlier and was diagnosed with depression and anxiety—but not psychopathy. Growing up, Ward had a friend with no place to live; he begged his family to take the friend in. As Ward put it in court: "I'm not a sociopath, I'm not none of that. I'm not retarded, I'm not fucked up, I'm not insane. . . . I'm just a normal person like everybody else is."[2]

Ward's mother worked for the City of Chicago, an employer that pays its workers an average salary of $49,000 per year. That's far above the poverty line, about equal to the median salary for all US workers.[3] Ward was apparently surrounded by relatives and role models. His mom got him into karate classes with his grandfather. As the judge put it, "He did have opportunity." According to the police, Ward's gang (SUWU, named after a Lil Wayne song) was not really an "economic" gang focused on making money from drug selling or trafficking in stolen credit cards; it seemed to be more of what the police called a "lifestyle gang."[4]

Drive a few blocks further south on Dorchester, away from the heartbreaking tragedy that happened in Harsh Park, and one reaches 53rd Street, the main commercial thoroughfare of Hyde Park and one of the most densely developed stretches on the entire South Side. On November 9, 2021, the leader of a local gang had finished lunch at a restaurant on 53rd just east of Dorchester and was leaving when a gray Honda drove past, followed by—as a witness put it—"machine-gun shots." The target of the drive-by had hoped to have lunch safe from the rival gangs near his house, but word apparently got out. The front window of the local ice cream shop, Kilwin's, was shot up; by the end of the day, every employee had requested a transfer.[5]

That wasn't even the first shooting of the day near the University of Chicago's Hyde Park campus. Just a few hours earlier a 24-year-old recent graduate of the statistics department was shot dead on the sidewalk during a robbery that yielded the offender $100 from a pawn shop for the victim's phone and laptop.[6]

Even the most liberal Hyde Parkers must have looked at the news and wondered, even if fleetingly, what these events implied about the capacities for evil in human nature.

Others, especially those inclined to see gun violence as the byproduct of an unfair society, could just look southbound down Dorchester to see the inequality that so many are convinced is implicated in the gun violence problem. 53rd has been the focus of much of the University of Chicago's community development efforts, animated at least in part by the necessity of recruiting faculty and students away from places like Berkeley, Palo Alto, Princeton, and Cambridge. The view down Dorchester from 53rd is stark. At the Sophy Hotel's Mesler Kitchen, located on that corner, you can get a $34 blue crab cake appetizer and a $58 twelve-ounce New York strip with seasonal garnish and red wine sauce, which you can wash down with a $40 flight of apricot, pear, and blood orange margaritas. Just a few blocks south, crossing over the Midway Plaisance and 60th Street, you see an increasing number of vacant lots and abandoned homes in the Woodlawn neighborhood, home to over eighty thousand people in 1950 (two-thirds white) and just twenty-four thousand today (four-fifths Black), with a per capita income half the Chicago average.[7]

At 67th Street is the most racially and economically integrated place in all of Chicago: Oak Woods Cemetery. The cemetery is the final home to, among others: Bishop Arthur Brazier, who for many years ran the Apostolic Church of God at 63rd and Dorchester and helped organize MLK's visit to Chicago in 1966; Jesse Owens, the man who at the 1936 Berlin Olympics "single-handedly crushed Hitler's myth of Aryan supremacy"[8]; J. Young Scammon, businessman, newspaper publisher, and co-founder of the Chicago Humane Society and the original University of Chicago[9]; William Hale "Big Bill" Thompson, the last Republican mayor of Chicago back in 1931; Fred Rice, the first Black superintendent of the Chicago Police Department; physicist Enrico Fermi, who created the first sustained nuclear reaction under the bleachers of the University of Chicago's Stagg Field during World War II; University of Chicago economist and Nobel laureate Gary Becker, who pioneered the study of crime by economists; and civil rights icon Ida B. Wells.

Finally, at 71st Street, the starkest part of the puzzle. It is here that Dorchester serves as the boundary between the South Shore and Greater Grand Crossing neighborhoods. Both neighborhoods are filled with earnest Midwestern folks trying to hold down jobs and raise their kids and desperately hope for the Bears to win another Super Bowl someday. Both places are served by the same city, county, state, and federal governments, including the same criminal-justice system (with all its flaws) and the same gun laws. The two neighborhoods are even quite similar sociodemographically. Hence the puzzle: Why are shootings, on a per capita basis, twice as common in Greater Grand Crossing?

This is one of the many puzzles about gun violence that conventional wisdom can't explain. The idea that gun violence is due to immoral people unafraid of the justice system doesn't fit the facts of these two neighborhoods. Nor does economic desperation. How can gun violence differ so dramatically across such nearby places?

Gun violence makes for easy, tidy storytelling—stories about bad people, about the economy and society, about tragic situations. As a closer look at the details of these different tragedies shows, sometimes stories are just that: stories. Accounts of each murder contain what might initially appear to be unspeakable degrees of human malevolence or desperation. But looking closer, many of these shootings can also be understood as momentary misjudgments in extraordinarily difficult situations—choices that were made in these instances that might not be made again.

Amid puzzle after puzzle, behavioral economics is the missing piece to bring the larger picture together: to see and understand the problem of American gun violence in a new way and, potentially, to even start solving it.

THE BEHAVIORAL ECONOMICS OF GUN VIOLENCE

The conventional wisdoms of both the Left and Right assume that gun violence stems from rational, deliberate, conscious benefit-cost calculations (System 2). The main difference between the Left and Right is often just whether to focus on bigger sticks or on more carrots.

Behavioral economics, in contrast, recognizes that actual human beings out in the real world are *not* always perfect System 2 rational benefit-cost calculators. We're often *boundedly* rational, especially during the heated arguments that lead to most shootings. Navigating these social interactions requires working through a series of cognitive steps: figuring out what situation we're in, our objectives, and the disadvantages and advantages of different strategies (SODAS). Things can go wrong at each step, especially when people are behaving automatically.

Gun violence, in other words, is much more a problem of System 1 than has been appreciated to date.

System 1 is the effortless, quick, automatic, below-the-level of consciousness type of thinking we use for low-stakes, routine things we encounter in daily life. Relying on System 1 for nonroutine, high-stakes situations—especially fraught, ten-minute social interactions when a gun is present—can lead to tragedy. Thinking, as one decision-making expert put it, should be "thorough in proportion to the importance of the question."[10] For most of us that is often not the case. For some of us the consequences of such an error during a key ten-minute window can be particularly severe if our ZIP code of residence is an unforgiving place.

This perspective on gun violence helps us understand why shootings can vary so much across neighborhoods: Some places are much less forgiving of System 1's frailties than others. Even though South Shore and Greater Grand Crossing are so similar sociodemographically, Greater Grand Crossing seems to have less informal social control, so daily life out on the street is more unpredictable—the sort of "wicked learning environment" likely to trip up System 1. Zero-tolerance policing is more common in Greater Grand Crossing, which makes feedback to System 1 more costly. Stress and trauma are also more common in Greater Grand Crossing, which depletes people's mental bandwidth and leads to greater reliance on System 1. And even though the number of guns may be the same across neighborhoods, more people carry them illegally in public in Greater Grand Crossing, increasing the chances that System 1 mistakes will end in tragedy.

The behavioral-economics perspective explains a number of other puzzles as well.

Why does gun violence vary so much with age? Violence peaks around the late teens or early twenties,[11] then declines steadily. This trend doesn't fit with the conventional wisdom of the Right, which assumes that characterologically bad people can't change. Nor does this age pattern fit with the conventional wisdom of the Left, since for most people economic stress doesn't decline with age, it increases. But behavioral economics tells us: As people get older, they get wiser.[12]

Why are rates of gun violence so much higher in the evenings, particularly late at night, than during the day? Conventional wisdom can't explain it. Do people's moral characters change with their diurnal rhythms? Are people poorer at different times of day? Or why is there more gun violence on weekends than weekdays, or over the summer versus in the winter? Behavioral economics emphasizes how fleeting the motivations of System 1 can be during the arguments that give rise to most shootings, and hence the great value of having "eyes on the street" to interrupt conflicts before they escalate. Late at night, on the weekends, and over the summer the ratio of young people to adult eyes on the street goes up.

Why did Micheail Ward shoot Hadiya Pendleton that January afternoon in Harsh Park? It turns out his friend Kenny Williams had recently been shot by a rival gang (the 4-6 Terror) and was looking for revenge. Kenny gave the gun to Micheail and asked him to do the shooting. System 2 would have concluded that that was a bad idea (middle of the day, crowded, lots of security cameras around). But Ward was living in an area with at least as much stress and trauma as in Greater Grand Crossing—Washington Park, where the average life expectancy is fully a decade below Chicago's average.[13] That ongoing stress and trauma likely depleted his mental bandwidth and led Ward to rely even more on System 1. It's not hard to imagine System 1 concluding, "There's literally nothing worse than looking like a coward in front of my friend"[14]—the sort of *catastrophizing* that our System 1s are prone to do.

It might be surprising that System 1, operating below the level of consciousness, can generate feelings and emotions strong enough to get people to do the seemingly unimaginable. But I can report from firsthand experience—experience I never really wanted to have—that the *intensity* of the feelings System 1 can generate is difficult to fathom.

A few years ago, I was out driving around with a police sergeant in a big American city. We were in the parking lot in front of the police station putting on what the lawyers now, for liability reasons, have come to call "bullet-*resistant* vests." Just a week before, one of the local gangs, confusing undercover cops doing a stakeout in an unmarked van for rival gang members, drove by and shot up the van with an AR-15 assault rifle. Standard bullet-resistant vests turn out to not do much good against AR-15 rounds. The sergeant, as he was velcroing his vest on, sighed and said, "Not sure why we bother."

A call crackled over the radio: A drive-by shooting had occurred a couple miles east of where we were. The car involved, one of the bigger Jeep SUV models—I think it was something like a Grand Cherokee— was heading west, right toward us, on the street we were on. We jumped into the sergeant's little covert car, a four-cylinder Chevy Equinox, and headed east. There was the Jeep, flying in our direction. And there we were, flying in *their* direction. The sergeant pulled into the left lane— the same one the Jeep was in. Our 3,500-pound Equinox was on a high-speed collision course with the 5,000-pound Jeep. They showed no signs of slowing down. Neither did we. At the last second the sergeant swerved into the right lane. The Jeep passed. The sergeant turned to me and said dryly, "That would have hurt."

According to an episode of *Mythbusters* I watched years later, what would have happened in a head-on collision at those speeds is that both cars would have basically disintegrated: A collision at that speed and with those weights would have destroyed them. I have a wife and two kids at home. A good job. A lot to lose. Moreover, it's possible, too, that that might not have even been the Jeep from the shooting. And, even if it had been, the people in the car were surely not more than teens or young adults; maybe they might still have turned their lives around.

But I remember very vividly the *intense* feeling in the moment generated by System 1, which System 2 was in hindsight horrified by: "Damn, nothing's worse than them getting away."

THE BEHAVIORAL ECONOMICS OF GUN SUICIDES

The powerful but short-lived thoughts and feelings implicated by behavioral economics for gun homicides are relevant for gun suicides, as well. Self-inflicted gunshot wounds claim more lives every year than gun homicides and have nearly tripled in number over the past fifty years.[15] The demographics of gun suicide are also starkly different than those of gun homicides: They're concentrated among white and disproportionately middle-aged men, unlike homicides, which are more concentrated among younger Black men.[16]

Why do people commit suicide? Common hypotheses implicate powerful root causes: declining religiosity,[17] fewer good jobs for working-class Americans,[18] or fewer marriages or social connections more generally.[19] These explanations tend to imply that suicide stems from conscious System 2 deliberation, a weighing of benefits and costs: *I just don't have much to live for.* Princeton economists Anne Case and Angus Deaton coined the term "deaths of despair" in part as a nod to this growing phenomenon and its deadly effects.[20] But these explanations also imply that the motivation to commit suicide should be *persistent* so long as the powerful root cause—the underlying motivation for self-harm—is still there.

Yet the data don't support that view. The vast majority of people who attempt suicide (well over 90 percent) will not die as a result of suicide.[21] Survivors of past attempts don't keep trying again and again until a suicide attempt is completed. Suicide instead results from, as one doctor put it, "a temporary state of the mind"[22]—a state of mind that a recent study estimated as lasting roughly one to three hours.[23]

We can see this phenomenon in a study of people who attempted suicide by jumping off the Golden Gate Bridge but survived. One of them, Ken Baldwin, described his thoughts as he was falling toward the water: "I instantly realized that everything in my life that I'd thought was unfixable was totally fixable—except for having just jumped."[24]

Kevin Hines, another Golden Gate survivor, described his own feelings as he cleared the handrail of the bridge: "Instant regret, powerful, overwhelming. As I fell, all I wanted to do was reach back to the rail, but it was gone. The thoughts in those four seconds [until striking the water], it was 'What have I just done? I don't want to die. God please save me.' Boom."[25]

How do we know that suicide really is often the result of fleeting System 1 motivation? Because we have RCTs of interventions that don't address religiosity or jobs or marriage. "All" they do is help people use System 2 to reflect more on what System 1 is doing. For example, given System 1's inclination to attend more to negative than positive information—negativity is an "attention magnet"—one thing these types of interventions do is try to get people to evaluate in a more even-handed way all the information that is available about how someone's life is going, the positive things and not just the negative ones.[26] The RCTs suggest that these interventions can reduce suicide attempts by up to 50 percent.[27]

Behavioral economics can, in other words, explain not just gun homicides but suicides, too. And the explanations are very different than what we thought we knew.

THE BEHAVIORAL ECONOMICS OF POLICE VIOLENCE

The situational misconstruals and miscalculations of the disadvantages and advantages of different solution strategies implicated by behavioral economics aren't just relevant for gun homicides, they're also relevant for police use of force as well. Some police uses of force will of course be justified under the law, but there is growing concern about those that might not be. Something like 250,000 Americans are injured by police each year, and six hundred are killed.[28]

The data also show evidence of the role of race in the likelihood of being injured by police. Black and white officers use force at roughly similar rates in predominantly white neighborhoods, but white officers are much more likely to use force than Black officers are in predominantly Black neighborhoods.[29]

Why do adverse policing outcomes happen? One type of explanation is that police departments employ some "bad apples"—characterologically bad people who aren't afraid of whatever their supervisor might do to them. A second type of explanation is that police policies are broken—that rules around when police are legally allowed to use force might be too lenient, and that accountability for out-of-policy use of force is inadequate. That is, the organizational incentives are wrong. Both explanations have the flavor of implicitly assuming that misconduct is due in large part to System 2 rational benefit-cost calculation. Both explanations also suggest hard-to-implement solutions, such as dramatically changing who gets hired as a police officer (in an environment in which most departments are already struggling to hire any officers at all) or changing police policies in our current climate of hyperpolarized American politics.

Behavioral economics suggests a third explanation for some adverse police outcomes: Officers are making System 1 mistakes in extraordinarily difficult ten-minute windows.

I was talking to a Chicago cop a few years ago who told me about a time he was out on patrol when a "man with a gun" call came in over the radio. He turned on his lights and sirens and raced over to the address. As he pulled up to the home there was a teenager on the front porch. When the kid saw the cop pull up, he sprinted into the house. The cop jumped out of his car and chased the kid into the house. He described to me racing up the stairs after the kid, tackling him from behind, and screaming, "Drop it! Drop it! Hands! Hands! Let me see your fucking hands!" The kid wasn't complying, the cop had his gun drawn when, at the last second, the cop looked over and saw it was actually a plastic toy gun on which someone had unfortunately removed the orange safety tip (indicating it was a toy). The cop said, "IT'S A FUCKING TOY?! SO WHY THE FUCK DID YOU RUN?!" The kid said, "I don't know—I got nervous."

What's the behavioral-economics explanation?

A 911 call about a man with a gun. Lights and sirens blaring. The racing engine of the SUV. The high rate of speed—60, 70, 80 miles an hour over surface streets. The terror of speeding through red lights, not knowing if some other driver who ignored the siren will T-bone the police car in the intersection. Anyone in this situation experiences an adrenaline surge; it's unavoidable—exactly the sort of thing that helps deplete mental bandwidth and gets any of us to rely even more on System 1 than normal.

The radio call over the police channel from the dispatcher: "Man with a gun." That sets a System 1 anchor: *There's a gun.* In principle, System 2 can adjust that anchor as new information becomes available. But because System 2 is mentally taxing, all of us wind up underadjusting, particularly when our bandwidth is depleted.

In this case everyone involved got lucky—the cop's System 2 stepped in at the last second and considered an alternative interpretation: "That's not a real gun." But, tragically, 12-year-old Tamir Rice wasn't so lucky in Cleveland in 2014 in roughly similar circumstances.

How do we know there's something to this behavioral-economics explanation? Two of my University of Chicago colleagues, Oeindrila Dube and Anuj Shah, worked with Sandy Jo MacArthur, a former assistant chief for LAPD, to develop a behavioral-science training for police. The idea is to help cops recognize when they're in nonroutine, high-stakes situations and be a little less System 1, a little more System 2. They then worked with the Chicago PD to implement the training. Because they had limited capacity for how many officers they could train at once, they randomly assigned the order in which officers would get trained—an RCT to evaluate the impacts. The results? Data from over two thousand Chicago police officers showed that the training reduced non-lethal uses of force by 23 percent, reduced low-level discretionary arrests by a similar amount, and reduced Black-white disparities in arrest rates.[30]

People shooting one another. People shooting themselves. Police shooting other people. That there's a common connection that helps explain each of these behaviors perhaps shouldn't be surprising since at the end of the day people are people. Challenges with high-stakes decision-making in extraordinarily difficult situations aren't unique to any one of us.

A DECISION-MAKING EXPLANATION, NOT A PSYCHOLOGICAL ONE

It might be tempting to label behavioral-economics theories about gun violence a "psychological explanation" for the problem. I don't love that label. "Psychological" makes it seem like gun violence is due to something "wrong" with someone's mind. That the perpetrator is somehow different from everyone else.

To me, the issue is instead more about common features of human decision-making being overwhelmed by difficult situations.

We've already seen that the most extreme psychological explanation—psychopathy—doesn't fit the data. Of course, there are psychopaths in the world. But as I showed in chapter 5, most shootings don't seem to be committed by psychopaths.

There is no shortage of other, less extreme psychological explanations for gun violence. For example, one of the most influential criminology books of the twentieth century argued that violence is due to low self-control, which, it claimed, is hard to remediate (Michael Gottfredson and Travis Hirschi's *A General Theory of Crime*). But this self-control explanation doesn't seem to fit with the real world, either.

For starters, just look around. Consider the teenagers living in the Parkway Gardens apartment complex in Greater Grand Crossing, which the *Chicago Sun-Times* at one point called the most dangerous block in Chicago. Some of those kids go to school 2 miles east over at Hyde Park Academy. Chicago doesn't do school buses. So they have to walk, bike, or take the city bus. Their home is Black Disciple territory. They have to go through the turf of at least two different rival Gangster Disciple sets, plus the Mickey Cobras, plus the Black P. Stones.[31] For a lot of the school year they're doing that in the dark and freezing cold (this past December we had several days in a row where the daily high was minus 1 degree Fahrenheit—that was the *high!*). Whatever you might say about a teen who does that over and over, "low self-control" isn't it.

The data confirm that. Self-control is modestly correlated with property offending but not really correlated with violence.[32] People in prison don't seem to have noticeably different levels of measured self-control than people outside of prison.[33] The fact that programs like BAM, Choose 2 Change, and READI generate large reductions in violence suggests that the problem is *not* driven primarily by self-control deficits that are hard to change.[34]

Unfortunately, a lot of the social programs that draw on behavioral-economics insights fuel the unhelpful psychological-explanation frame by labeling themselves with unfortunate jargony names like "cognitive behavioral therapy" (CBT).[35] I hate those terms because of the word "therapy." That feels like "fix."

I think of those programs instead as being more like giving people a *user's manual for their minds*—to help everyone understand the decision-making infrastructure that we all share, the strengths and weaknesses of both System 1 and System 2, and how those can trip all of us up in difficult situations.

The behavioral-economics explanation for gun violence, in other words, does not view those involved with gun violence through the lens of "Here's what's wrong with *them*." It views gun violence instead through the lens of "There but for the grace of God go I"—any of us, put in the same extraordinarily difficult situation, might well do the same ourselves. All of us are imperfect; the difference is that some of us find ourselves in situations that are especially cognitively demanding.

CONSILIENCE

Others over the years have also recognized the limits of conventional wisdom. Other explanations for gun violence have been offered. But somehow nothing's taken hold to rival conventional wisdom in the public's imagination. "Bad people" is a clear, intuitive idea. So is "a bad economy" or "bad social conditions." Alongside that conventional wisdom there's been a mishmash of different ideas. They imply a set of policies that can often feel like a random laundry list of things to try.

I argue that behavioral economics is a meta-explanation—that all these other ideas, and the policies they imply, might actually flow from the same underlying wellspring. This linking together of facts derived from different methods is what the nineteenth-century philosopher William Whewell (and later Harvard's Edward O. Wilson) called "consilience."[36]

For example, the field of public health has been talking for a long time about the value of using data and levers beyond the justice system to solve gun violence. But to say that gun violence is a public health problem, while true, doesn't shed light on *why* gun violence happens. Behavioral economics does.

Steven Pinker notes that another limitation of the common public health view that "violence is a kind of disease" is that it "flouts the basic definition of a disease, namely a malfunction that causes suffering to the individual. Most violent people insist there is nothing wrong with them; it's the victim and bystanders who think there's a problem."[37] Why do so many gun violence offenders think *they're* the ones on the side of the angels? Why is so much of the violence moralistic violence? Behavioral economics tells us that people's behavior is in reaction not to objective reality but to the person's own subjective—and often self-serving—construal of reality.[38]

Urban planners and architects have long believed that the built environment can matter for crime. Jane Jacobs argued that a mix of residential and retail contributes to more eyes on the street. Architects emphasize "defensible space" for buildings so residents can monitor what's going on (as opposed to hidden hallways, stairwells, etc.).[39] None of this emphasis on the physical features of a place makes any sense under conventional wisdom, since it doesn't have anything to do with the underlying causes that conventional wisdom implicates—immorality or inadequate punishments or economic desperation. But it does make sense if violence is due to fleeting System 1 motivations in difficult ten-minute situations, so that violence interruption is preventive—as behavioral economics suggests.

The growing field of community violence intervention (CVI) emphasizes the value of deploying "credible messengers" with street credibility who know what conflicts are brewing and can interrupt and defuse them, people like Dr. Chico Tillmon. This approach echoes what sociologists and criminologists have been talking about for years under names like "collective efficacy" (the willingness of local residents to step in and do something for the public good) or "informal social control" (all the things local residents do to keep peace) or "situational crime prevention" (having "guardians" around in the times and places where crime happens).[40] Conventional wisdom implies that violence interrupted is merely violence delayed. Behavioral economics, in contrast, implies that violence interrupted can be violence prevented.

These ideas taken together give us a way to understand why changing people's neighborhood environments seems to be more important
for preventing violence than changing someone's specific personal financial condition. Some neighborhoods are much easier for System 1
to navigate than are others. Giving someone more cash doesn't change
neighborhood factors because it turns out that most people, when they
get more income, don't move as a result, and when they do, they usually
don't move to a substantially different type of neighborhood.[41]

Some CVI groups focus not just on interrupting ten-minute windows but also on helping people learn in advance to anticipate and de-
escalate those windows themselves (BAM, READI, Choose 2 Change,
etc.). These programs make no sense under conventional wisdom. They
don't do anything to solve root causes. Nor do they teach morality; they
never try to tell people what to do, like "Don't fight," since they realize
that unfortunately, in many distressed areas, "Don't fight" is not a realistic strategy. They say, "Only fight when you really need to," and help
people figure out how to better use System 2 to figure out when they
really need to versus not. Behavioral economics explains why these
programs can be as effective as they often are.

Restorative justice is about having the victim and offender meet in
a non-adversarial setting to try to repair the damage that some violent
act or other crime has created. Here again this approach makes no
sense under conventional wisdom. But behavioral economics gives us
a way to understand why restorative justice works: It gets the System 2s
of offenders to reflect on their own thinking and see the different ways
that System 1 can make mistakes.

Even gun control itself only makes sense if the behavioral-economics
lens on gun violence is right. Conventional wisdom, after all, implies
that people who are motivated by moral poverty or actual poverty will
be people who are persistently motivated. Making it a little bit more of
a hassle to get a gun shouldn't do much to the ultimate risk of a shooting. But the behavioral-economics perspective about System 1–driven
violence, for which motivation is much more fleeting, provides a way to
understand why some gun regulations can help save lives.

As I noted in chapter 1, the best available data suggest that for long
stretches of recorded human history, violence was declining. Steven

Pinker shows for example that in England, the country for which we have some of the earliest records, homicides were somewhere between 10 and 100 murders per 100,000 people in 1200; by 1900 that figure had declined to a rate of around 1 or 2 per 100,000. Then that progress seems to have stalled.[42] In the US we see that same stalled progress as in England, but, unfortunately, violence is stalled out here at a much higher base rate. The current murder rate in America of around 5 or 6 per 100,000 is four or five times what we see in the UK today and about the same as what the US had back in 1900.

Pinker argues that one of the reasons for the long-term decline in interpersonal violence was essentially an inadvertent consequence of steady social change and specifically of growing societal sophistication. The development of a state with a monopoly on violence (that is, one with increasing formal social control) meant that people's System 1s learned to rely less and less on self-help and private violence to deter future victimization. The development of a modern economy and its emphasis on positive-sum (rather than zero-sum) exchange meant people's System 1s were increasingly rewarded for considering other people's alternative perspectives, to recognize, even if only implicitly, that there isn't just one way to see a situation.

That this long-term progress toward declining violence seems to have stalled since 1900 suggests that relying on the inadvertent, indirect violence-reducing effects of larger social changes may have run its course. It may now be time to consider paying more explicit, deliberate, direct attention to solving the challenge of System 1–driven violence.

Environmental design. Violence interruption. Collective efficacy and informal social control. Neighborhood effects and desegregation and residential mobility and community development. BAM, READI, Choose 2 Change. Restorative justice. Gun control. We already have the start of some promising policy levers on hand. But without some underlying idea about what drives gun violence, this set of policy responses can feel like a random grab-bag of things. No wonder this approach hasn't captured the public imagination and mobilized a national response. Since these different policy ideas have all percolated up independently in an environment in which there is no clear, intuitive explanation for why they all work, we have been doing these things sporadically, half-heartedly. It would be like trying to explain how to prevent COVID ("Wear a mask, wash your hands, stay six feet away from other people, and get a shot") without the benefit of knowledge of the germ theory of disease.

Behavioral economics provides the equivalent of the underlying explanatory theory of gun violence—a unifying explanation that makes everything else make sense.

IMPROVING THE CRIMINAL-JUSTICE SYSTEM

Behavioral economics doesn't just steer us toward new things to try—everything listed above—but it can also help make the things we've already been trying work much better. For example, behavioral economics can make the key pillar of the conventional wisdom of the Right, the criminal-justice system, more effective and humane. Behavioral economics and the criminal-justice system are, in other words, complements, not substitutes.

Notice for starters how many pathologies of the criminal-justice system arise because it is overwhelmed. In California, the prison system at its peak operated at 180 percent of designed capacity, harming the physical and mental health of inmates.[43] In Chicago, only one in ten nonfatal shootings leads to arrest; even mass shootings rarely lead to arrests.[44] This impunity for committing gun violence stems partly from the fact that detectives have too many cases.[45] The behavioral-economics measures outlined above could prevent many cases, letting the justice system deal much better with the cases that remain.

Behavioral economics can enhance deterrence. The justice system often threatens people with severe punishment with the hope that the "stick" will never have to be used; that people will be deterred instead. But people acting on System 1 autopilot are not very deterrable. I think of the elderly woman in a wheelchair I saw a few years ago outside of a liquor store; when someone said something mouthy to her, she threatened to go get her gun and take care of him despite the fact that she was surrounded at the time by half the district's police officers. Behavioral-economics programs, by helping people be at least a little bit more System 2 in high-stakes situations, are essentially making them more deterrable. To the extent to which people do become more deterrable, the result is less violence *and* less imprisonment simultaneously.

Behavioral economics can make policing more *preventive—* simultaneously fewer shootings *and* fewer arrests. I argued in chapter 8 that police already do lots of things besides make arrests; the average Chicago cop makes only one arrest every three months. What do police do with all their time? They sometimes mediate conflict and solve problems before they even turn into conflicts:[46] They take a drunk kid looking for a fight to the hospital for a psych evaluation; they tell a guy screaming at a woman and her little kid to take a walk; they realize after there are several shootings of people waiting in line at the same liquor store that maybe the store should get a security camera. Many decades ago one observer of day-to-day police work described the role of police officers as that of "street corner politicians."[47]

RCTs confirm that this aspect of policing is enormously valuable. The data show that compared to simply sending more cops to high-crime hot spots and having them just stand there ("create presence") or try to arrest and deter people, having officers engage in problem solving types of activities, things that can anticipate and help defuse situations that lead to conflict or its escalation, can increase the amount of crime prevented by up to 60 percent.[48]

Police do this kind of problem solving now but could probably do much, much more.[49] A guy I know rose nearly to the very top of one of America's biggest, best-regarded police departments. After a bad weekend of shootings, his team within the police department did some after-action reports. In many shootings there was first a 311 or 911 call for something else beforehand that might lead to conflict—a noisy neighbor, an argument, an unauthorized block party on the street. He concluded that if his officers had only done just a little more mediation, a little more problem solving, many more shootings might have been prevented.

I saw the limits of current practice myself a few years ago from the back seat of a police car here in Chicago. A radio call came in: Two groups of people standing in the middle of the street, lots of yelling and shoving. It turned out that a teenage boy on one side of the street had been dating the girl across the street. They broke up. Someone from the girl's family thought it would be a good idea to cross the street, walk into the boyfriend's house, and punch him in the face. His family didn't appreciate that. The police showed up, separated the two groups, and tried an improvised attempt at mediation: "EVERYBODY SHUT THE FUCK UP! Go inside. If we need to come back, ALL y'all are going to jail." As we got in the car and drove off, I asked the supervising sergeant, "Think that'll settle things down?" He said, "Definitely not."

It's not just that behavioral economics can complement the criminal-justice system; the reverse is true, too. As I've noted, behaviorally informed policies often don't try to appeal to empathy or morality so much as to self-interest. I think of Dr. Chico Tillmon saying to the leader of a gang that was killing every member of a rival gang over a social media slight: "If *I* know that you're the one going around shooting everyone in this other gang, don't you think the *cops* know by now, too?" The less credible that formal criminal-justice accountability seems, the less useful it is to engage System 2 to think through what's really in the person's self-interest.

America spends something like $300 billion per year on its criminal-justice system.[50] Given the enormous toll that gun violence imposes on society, and our lack of progress, why *not* start making it as effective as possible in preventing shootings in the first place?

IMPROVING CRIME PREVENTION AND REHABILITATION

Historically, a common focus of crime prevention and rehabilitation programs has been on improving people's incomes (jobs, job training, cash or in-kind transfers, etc.). That focus is obviously incredibly important for lifting people out of poverty, which, it goes without saying, is a vital societal goal. But as I showed in chapter 4, jobs or higher

incomes by themselves aren't enough to also solve a different problem—to not just solve poverty but create a "double dividend" and keep
low-income communities safe from violence.

The good news is that there are lots of ways to optimize existing
social programs to more intentionally and explicitly incorporate
behavioral-economics insights, thereby making them more likely to
prevent gun violence. We for sure need to learn more about how to
scale these programs. That's a common challenge in social policy. But
in principle that's a problem that might be solved. By contrast, we've
learned from the past hundred years of experience the clear limitations
of the usual approach: No long-term decline in murder rates per capita. Rather than keep trying the same old things that aren't leading to
progress, why not try something different?

For example, every subsidized jobs program could easily fit in a few
hours per week of behavioral-economics programming, as did READI
Chicago. Every mentoring program for teens could easily do the same,
like Choose 2 Change in Chicago. The result can be very large reductions in violence involvement, sometimes on the order of 50 percent
or even more.

Every detention facility in the country—every jail, every prison, every juvenile-detention center—already has incurred most of the fixed
costs associated with social programming: They've paid for space,
they've paid for staff. Moreover, those facilities have already implicitly
solved one of the hardest problems for most social programs to solve,
which is to recruit and retain participants (especially those at highest
risk for gun violence involvement, who are often not showing up at the
front of the line to voluntarily sign up for social programs). And those
facilities almost always have lots of underutilized time that could be op-
timized to have existing staff provide behavioral-economics programming to residents at very low marginal cost. That's what was done at
the Cook County, Illinois, Juvenile Temporary Detention Center in the
afternoons, instead of having the kids watch TV, which at astonishingly
low cost reduced recidivism by 20 percent.[51]

Behavioral economics can even increase the violence prevention achieved by our biggest and most important social program: public education. The way to do this is to be more intentional and active in having schools do something they already do implicitly, which is develop System 2 reflection about what System 1 is doing. That is, education is not *just* about the 3 R's; it's also *implicitly* about learning how to solve problems and how your own mind works—to learn "metacognition," or how to think about your own thinking.

You get your math homework back and see you made a stupid mistake (2 + 2 = 5). That's teaching you math, sure. But it's also teaching you something deeper than that: You've just learned that your own cognition can be faulty. School doesn't explicitly teach you about the dual-system model of cognition ("Here's System 1 and now here's System 2 . . ."). But the mistake you made as you were flying through this math exercise has, implicitly, taught your deliberate, conscious System 2 to become a little bit more skeptical of what System 1 does on autopilot. Next time you do a math problem you anticipate System 1's potential for mistakes and preempt that by redoing the problem in the margin to check your work.[52] That's metacognition.

After years of math, you develop a heuristic: "Multiplication makes bigger, division makes smaller."[53] This heuristic usually works well for you in most of the situations you see over and over. Then one day the teacher asks you to multiply (or divide) by 0.5. There's an "aha" moment: You can see that your automatic System 1 response that *usually* works can lead you astray when it's overgeneralized into the wrong situation. That's metacognition.

When you're studying for your next math test, you experiment with different strategies to figure out when your understanding is good enough. Your System 2 learns to test System 1's answer ("Of course I'm ready") with strategies like empirical testing—quizzing yourself on the material. That's metacognition.

In English class you're assigned a novel. Of course, you're learning something about the key ideas in *War and Peace* or *Catcher in the Rye* or *Tom Sawyer*. But you're also learning something else that's arguably much more important. As you discuss the book in class, you realize:

You've got one take on what the book means. You were *sure* that was the right take. But in class you hear other people offer up *different* takes on exactly the same book. The teacher encourages everyone to take everyone else's takes seriously. You learn that different people can see the same thing differently. You start to ask yourself questions like "How do I know that my beliefs are more correct than hers? Where do accurate beliefs come from?"[54] You learn you can be too confident in your original ideas. You learn to be more open to alternative ideas. That's metacognition.

What all these examples illustrate is how schooling implicitly teaches thinking about metacognition, or what University of Pennsylvania psychologist Jonathan Baron calls "actively open-minded thinking," and about problem solving more generally. The data show that among the problems people get better at solving from schooling is how to get along with others.[55]

This finding explains why more schooling doesn't just reduce property offending (which makes sense under conventional wisdom, since education increases earnings and property crimes are economically motivated) but also reduces violent crimes (which doesn't make sense under conventional wisdom since higher income by itself doesn't reduce violence). The effect is not small, either. Social scientists have isolated the causal effect of schooling on violent crime by looking at the "natural experiment" created by state changes in minimum compulsory schooling ages. Social scientists compare how crime changes in states that do versus do not change compulsory school ages in a given year. The results show metacognition at work: Every 10-percentage-point increase in high school graduation rates—roughly the amount by which graduation has increased over the last fifty years in the US[56]—reduces murders by fully 20 percent.[57]

There is no shortage of ways we could make education even *more* helpful in preventing gun violence.[58] The easiest initial step in this direction would be to simply repurpose part of every high school's health curriculum. At least based on my own personal experiences in New Jersey public schools, health classes currently mostly cover things teens either already know (where babies come from) or will mostly ignore (eat broccoli; don't drink; make sure to get eight hours of sleep a night). Why not use this already-scheduled time in a much more socially productive way, to help prevent one of the leading causes of death to US teens—gun violence?[59]

More ambitious still would be to intentionally infuse into the academic curriculum itself more efforts to develop thinking and reflection and the skill of generalizing those skills to new settings, including outside of school. This is not a new goal; it dates back at least to the Ancient Greeks.[60] And this goal, if achieved, wouldn't only make K–12 schooling much more useful for preventing violence. Given that more and more jobs require decision-making and interacting with other people, as the Harvard economist David Deming has noted, this educational shift would also have tremendous benefits for economic growth and upward economic mobility.[61]

To maximize the impacts of any educational changes of this kind, we will also need to ensure that there's enough money to carry them out in those school systems that serve the places where gun violence is disproportionately concentrated: big cities.[62] The state of Illinois admits, for example, that it owes the Chicago Public Schools (CPS) an extra $1 billion in funding help per year. There's no principled reason for this shortfall. Cook County, which contains Chicago, is a net exporter of tax dollars to the state (we send out more tax dollars to Springfield than we get back).[63] Yet with respect to the owed CPS funding, the state says it simply doesn't have (which is to say, it won't figure out a way to come up with) the money.[64]

This is all to say, behavioral economics gives us a plausible new answer for why public education has such substantial violence-reducing benefits: Education seems to help System 2 learn to check System 1. We already spend $800 billion every year on public K–12 education.[65] Given the enormous importance of the gun violence problem and our lack of long-term progress, why *not* make education as helpful as possible in addressing one of the nation's biggest public health crises?

IGNORING ROOT CAUSES, OR UPROOTING THEM?

It might initially seem that the behavioral-economics approach to gun violence ignores or sidesteps root causes. But one of the best ways to solve root causes is to solve gun violence.

Too many American cities are currently stuck in a vicious cycle. An accumulating body of data show that gun violence makes it hard for kids to succeed in school,[66] makes it hard for traumatized parents to be their best selves as parents,[67] and drives people and businesses out of impacted cities—seventy people on net for each murder.[68] A rise in gun violence drives more people out, which begets even more gun violence, which prompts even more population flight, etc. That's fewer taxpayers to help support government efforts to reduce gun violence (or to carry out any other government function, for that matter), fewer customers for local businesses, and sometimes even population loss so severe as to make the functioning of basic community institutions no longer viable.

This dynamic undermines even the best-intentioned efforts at local community development. In 2016, for example, Chicago subsidized Whole Foods to open a store at 63rd and Halsted Street in the heart of Englewood, one of the city's most violent neighborhoods.[69] Six years later Whole Foods closed,[70] as customers either moved out of Englewood or went elsewhere to shop.[71] Or consider that Chicago has at least twenty high schools operating at less than one-quarter capacity. Douglass High School, built to serve nine hundred students, in 2022 enrolled just forty-four students.[72] Who wants to move into or start a new business in a neighborhood with ever-more abandoned buildings, boarded-up houses, and struggling schools? That's to say, gun violence creates a massive headwind for every policy that seeks to improve local economic conditions.

One of the starkest examples of this dynamic is in Detroit (figure 9.1).[73] A few years ago I gave a talk at Wayne State and was moved by the deep commitment to the city of so many local residents and leaders. Yet the city—consistently one of the nation's most violent (figure 9.2)[74]—has been caught for many decades in this vicious cycle. Local

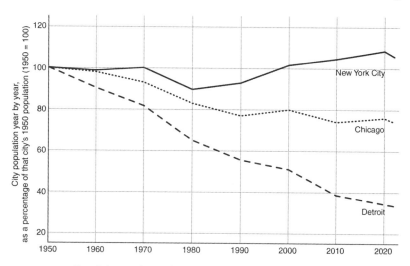

FIGURE 9.1: Trends in population for New York City, Chicago, and Detroit, 1950–2018, expressed each year as a share of the city's 1950 population

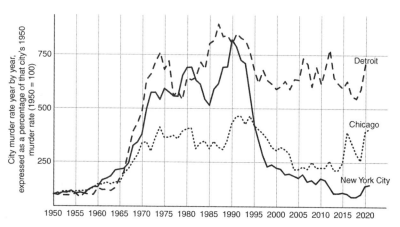

FIGURE 9.2: Murder rates per capita for New York City, Chicago, and Detroit, 1950–2020, expressed as a percentage of each city's own 1950 murder rate

newspapers celebrated when the 2023 murder rate dropped down to 40 per 100,000,[75] about seven times the nationwide rate. Not coincidentally, Detroit has also lost fully two-thirds of its population since 1950, has about one-third of its surface area (40 square miles) sitting vacant, struggles to deliver basic city services, and in 2013 declared bankruptcy.[76]

The good news is that these cycles can be reversed: Controlling gun violence can turn vicious cycles into virtuous cycles. Just look, for example, at New York City. Violent crime surged in the 1970s. The city's fiscal problems became national news; President Ford was unwilling to help bail the city out (or as the *Daily News* put it: "FORD TO CITY: DROP DEAD").[77] By 1980, New York City's population was down fully 10 percent compared to what it was in 1950. But as public safety improved in New York, people and businesses moved in. The city is even larger now than it was in 1950, full of economic activity that strengthens the city's fiscal capacity to address all sorts of problems.

If the murder rate in Chicago had plummeted like New York's over the past few decades, we'd have six hundred thousand more people today; we'd be a city of 3.3 million rather than 2.7 million.[78]

If gun violence, uncontrolled, is a challenging headwind for economic development, safety is a massive tailwind. The failure to control gun violence creates the biggest economic burden on the same economically and socially disadvantaged people and communities most directly affected by gun violence itself.

I was in the back of a police car a few years ago when a call came in over the radio about a double shooting. We showed up and saw the aftermath: streams of blood all over the street and sidewalk. It looked like someone had taken a hose and sprayed blood everywhere. The sergeant, who leads one of his city's gang homicide teams, has been to dozens if not hundreds of crime scenes. But even he was affected; he turned to me and said, "What a mess." We went over to the emergency room to talk to the victims. It was a dad and his teenage son who had been confused for members of a rival gang and got ambushed in the middle of the street walking home from the community center. The kid was in surgery, so we talked to the dad. The sergeant said, "If you hadn't had the presence of mind to use your belt as a tourniquet for your son's leg, he would have died. You saved his life." The dad looked up from his hospital bed, sighed, and said, "Man, I got to go to work tomorrow."

A MORE FORGIVING COUNTRY

The tragedy is that over the past fifty years, many of the policies America has implemented to try to reduce gun violence may have made the problem of gun violence worse. Incarceration rates with no historical or international precedent, motivated by the view that crime and violence are due to inherently bad people, surely helped weaken informal social control in our country's most distressed communities. Zero-tolerance policies in schools and by the police. People arming themselves against "super-predators" by buying guns by the tens or hundreds of millions. As a country, our policies have created far too many unforgiving places.

What now?

There's an old Will Rogers saying, "If you find yourself in a hole, stop digging."

The second step is to realize the problem is not hopeless. Despair comes easily to anyone living in almost any American city. But despair is the enemy of progress.

I think back to 1991, my first year of graduate school. The crack-cocaine epidemic had murder rates at 30 per 100,000 in Chicago, Los Angeles, and New York. The sense of despair was palpable. The *Chicago Tribune*: "Remedies are elusive. All evidence suggests that the killing of children is the result of a web of social ills, each filament lending strength to its neighbors, each so strong that it is overwhelming just to contemplate doing something to cut it."[79] The *New York Times*: "New Yorkers rang in the New Year last week by committing seven homicides in five hours. . . . Are authorities helpless against the mounting violence?"[80] A letter to the *LA Times*: "In the past five years I have had a car stolen, two car stereos stolen, my wallet stolen and most recently my home was burglarized. Rarely a weekend passes that innocent people aren't killed in some gang-related activity. We hardly dare go to Westwood, Hollywood, or even local beaches anymore. We've alarmed our cars. We've alarmed our houses. What else can we do?"[81]

Every city in the country made what are in hindsight countless mistakes in responding to this problem. Zero-tolerance policing was widely adopted across the US, leading to large numbers of misdemeanor arrests that the data show often have low public-safety value for the type of crime the public cares most about: violence. Not In My Back Yard (NIMBY) policies made it hard to build affordable housing, particularly in the sorts of neighborhoods that would contribute to the economic and racial desegregation of our cities. Almost no American city made public education enough of a priority to achieve world-class schools. The result are high school graduation rates 10 to 20 percentage points lower in big cities than in the suburbs.[82] The burden of each of these problems falls heaviest on communities of color.

The result? Look around the world at other major cities—they have murder rates per 100,000 residents on the order of 3 in Zurich and Toronto, 2 in Istanbul and Amsterdam and Montreal, 1 in London, and 0.3 in Hong Kong. By contrast, the murder rate per 100,000 is about 30 in Chicago, 40 in Cleveland, nearly 50 in Trenton and Memphis, nearly 60 in Baltimore, 70 in Flint, and 90 in St. Louis.

And yet, despite these difficulties, progress at large scale *is* possible.

While the words "behavioral economics" don't show up *explicitly* in the policy planning documents of cities like Los Angeles and New York, many of their specific policy responses *implicitly* build on behavioral-economics insights. For example, both cities were early and rapid adopters of community violence intervention (CVI) efforts. In 2002 Erica Ford started LIFE Camp in the Jamaica neighborhood of New York, which eventually led to the city-funded Crisis Management System implemented citywide by the de Blasio administration. In the late 1990s, Los Angeles started funding initiatives like LA Bridges and the Gang Reduction Program, which by 2007 had led to a citywide Mayor's Office of Gang Reduction and Youth Development and to stepped-up CVI efforts.[83] Bill Bratton, the police commissioner who worked in both cities over this period, was arguing for a shift away from the usual reactive, investigative approach in policing toward more data-driven prevention and problem solving. Police would, for instance, keep track of the anniversary dates of major gangs, a key gathering time when other gangs would often try to attack, and focus extra police presence to try to defuse and head off conflict.[84]

The result in those two cities? While no one would say that things are perfect in either city—not by a long shot—incarceration rates have gone down in both LA and New York, opinion polls suggest that public approval of police surged in LA,[85] and murder rates didn't just drop from 1991 to 2019 (the last pre-pandemic year), they *plummeted*: in LA by nearly 80 percent and in New York City by nearly 90 percent.

The even better news is not just that progress is possible but that behavioral economics suggests there may be multiple paths to success. Many cities might want LA and New York–style results but, because of different local political preferences, might not want to make exactly the same specific policy choices.

So if you live in a city where "police" is a four-letter word, great— invest instead in neighborhood infrastructure that helps build more informal social control. Get the public schools to do more work for you in preventing gun violence. Invest more in behaviorally informed programs like BAM, Choose 2 Change, and READI. Infuse behavioral-economics programming into your jails and prisons. Make your city's distressed areas more forgiving places.

If you live in a city where "social program" is a four-letter word, great—focus on getting your local police to be as focused as possible on mediating conflicts and on problem solving to prevent conflicts in the first place, rather than making lots of low-public-safety-value misdemeanor arrests. For that matter, ask your police department to redirect some officers from its narcotics team to worry instead about underground gun markets and getting illegal guns off the streets.

One appealing feature of preventing gun violence with behavioral economics is that it should appeal to both sides of the political aisle. A lot of our political fights over crime and criminal justice are about what the right punishment is for someone *after* they've committed a crime. That's a genuinely difficult question about which reasonable people will inevitably disagree. But preventing gun violence in the first place sidesteps that issue entirely and is something that everyone should be able to get behind.

The problem of gun violence is not one of characterologically bad people or a bad economy or, more accurately, not *just* a problem of those things. It's a problem of fallible human beings making automatic System 1 mistakes in key ten-minute windows. Progress is possible by changing the decision-making environments that people have to navigate, and by directly helping them to better navigate those difficult situations. To make, in other words, more of our unforgiving places into forgiving ones.

This idea has unfortunately been largely absent from the policy conversation.

Who's marching on the White House *demanding* someone do something about human fallibility in trying situations? Despite the lack of long-term progress on gun violence, we are having literally the same debates over and over and over. Almost a century ago, in the 1930s, the Republican presidential platform argued for "the enactment of rigid penal laws that will aid the States in stamping out the activities of gangsters, racketeers and kidnappers."[86] President Franklin D. Roosevelt, a Democrat, was arguing that "crime cannot be held in check by a good police system alone . . . through a broad program of social welfare, we struck at the very roots of crime itself."[87] The political conversation of the 1930s is remarkably similar to that of the 1960s and 1990s and 2020s and, at the rate things are going, probably also the 2050s and 2080s . . .

It is time—or perhaps long past time—for some new ideas.

ACKNOWLEDGMENTS

This book wouldn't exist if University of Chicago trustee Emmanuel Roman had not encouraged (told?) me to write it.

This book also wouldn't exist were it not for an amazing collection of people who believe that data can make the world better, and who have contributed to the University of Chicago Crime Lab in countless ways, large and small. At the University of Chicago this group includes Roseanna Ander first and foremost, as well as the late Robert Zimmer, Harold Pollack, Thomas Rosenbaum, Katherine Baicker, Nour Abdul-Razzak, Anjali Adukia, Ashna Arora, Martin Baron, Marianne Bertrand, Monica Bhatt, Chris Blattman, Ethan Bueno de Mesquita, Abbie Castiglione, Aaron Chalfin, Kerwin Charles, Ken Corey, Jonathan Davis, Derek Douglas, Oeindrila Dube, Ellen Dunn, Nick Epley, Sadie Stockdale Jefferson, Dylan Fitzpatrick, Nicole Gillespie, Hays Golden, Michael Greenstone, Jeffrey Grogger, Jonathan Guryan, Bernard Harcourt, Sara Heller, Russ Herron, Nathan Hess, Katie Hill, Maggi Ibis, Zubin Jelveh, Ariel Kalil, Max Kapustin, Salman Khan, Erin Kuller, David Leitson, Steven Levitt, Stacy Tessler Lindau, John List, Sandy Jo MacArthur, Matteo Magnaricotte, Kirsten Mahoney, Sean Malinowski, Jeanne Marsh, Susan Mayer, David Meltzer, Bruce Meyer, Thomas Miles, Christian Mitchell, Fatemeh Momeni, Derek Neal, Ed O'Brien, Michelle Ochoa, Aurelie Ouss, LuAnn Pennell, Julia

Quinn, Sarah Rand, Steve Raudenbush, Evan Rose, Dan Rosenbaum, Michael Rosenbaum, Mark Saint, Kimberly Smith, Greg Stoddard, Meredith Stricker, Dana Suskind, Kim Taylor, Richard Thaler, Bec Weeks, Michael Weiss, Brian Williams, John Wolf, and George Wu.

Key supporters and friends outside the university who have made the Crime Lab and its work possible include Ellen Alberding, Andy Alper, John and Laura Arnold, Anthony Braga, Carol Brown, Val Chang, Jadine Chou, Don Cook, the Hon. Richard M. Daley, Brendan Deenihan, Caroline Delaney, Evelyn Diaz, Arne Duncan, Tom and Susan Dunn, the Hon. Rahm Emanuel, Wendy Fine, Elizabeth Glazer, Brent and Katie Gledhill, Mary Lou Gorno, Ken Griffin, Ira Handler, David Hiller, Craig Howard, Ray Iwanowski, Valerie Jarrett, Eddie Johnson, Diane Latiker, Anna LauBach, Susan Lee, Adam Levine, the Hon. Lori Lightfoot, Gary MacDougal, Michael Masters, Garry McCarthy, Al McNally, Anne Milgram, Joe Neubauer, the Hon. Michael Nutter, Tom and Margot Pritzker, the Reinsdorf family, Janey Rountree, Michael Sacks, Michael Small, Julia Stasch, Robert Tracy, Craig Turk, Asheley Van Ness, Julie Wilen, Dave Williams, and Matt and Marny Zimmer.

I am grateful to everyone who was willing to talk about the ideas behind this book: David Abrams, Philip Alpers, Charlie Beck, Shawn Bushway, Jillian Carr, Corey Ciorciari, Kathy Edin, Dan Godsel, Priyanka Gooletilleke, Cornelia Grumman, Derrick and Cragg Hardaway, Randi Hjalmarrson, David Hureau, Elena Kempf, Helen Kim, Alex Kotlowitz, Jill Loevy, Tom McBride, Sam Mormon, Tim Nelson, Mallory O'Brien, Steven Raphael, David Robinson, Robert Sampson, Jeff Severts, Patrick Sharkey, Leo Smith, and Gerard Torrats-Espinosa.

Having never written a book quite like this before, I had no idea exactly what would be involved. I'm thankful to the incredible team that was willing to take this journey with me: Saul Arnow, Tom Ballard, Megan Cordes, Kate Daugherty, Geneva Kirk Drayson, Jordyn Flaherty, Rory Gates, Rowan Gledhill, Megan Kang, Javier Lopez, Melissa McNeill, Jacob Miller, Khoa Nguyen, Elizabeth Rasich, Alejandro Roemer, Gwenyth Ross, Arjun Subramanian, Divya Subramanian, Gargi Sundaram, Matt Triano, Jeffrey Wang, and Daria Zelinina.

I'm grateful to my agents, Rebecca Nagel and Sarah Chalfant at the Wylie Agency, and my editor, Chad Zimmerman, for their help turning some vague ideas about what this might be into a hopefully coherent book. My deepest thanks to Joel Wallman and the Harry Frank Guggenheim Foundation for hosting an author's conference that generated useful feedback on an early draft.

I feel especially lucky for a set of friends who have helped shape my thinking about the world. Were it not for my good fortune to work with Philip Cook, the world's leading expert on gun policy, there would not only be no Crime Lab, but I never would have learned to think even semi-clearly or string two words together. Everything I learned about running big research projects came from working with Jeffrey Kling on the Moving to Opportunity demonstration. Everything I know about the city of Chicago and its challenges I learned from Jose "Pepe" Lopez, Anthony Ramirez-DiVittorio, and Dr. Chico Tillmon. The ideas behind this book stem from countless conversations over the years, often occurring on the drive to either Los Comales #3 in Pilsen or Margie's Candies, with two of the most wonderful, talented people one could ever be lucky enough to have as colleagues and friends, Sendhil Mullainathan and Anuj Shah.

And too many thanks to mention to my parents, Almuth and Gunter, my daughters, Annika and Willa, and my wonderful wife, Liz.

NOTES

PREFACE

1. Lescaze, "Reagan Blames Crime on 'Human Predator.'"
2. DiIulio, "The Coming of the Super-Predators."

CHAPTER ONE

1. Sulski, "Riding High."
2. Grossman, "Dubbed a 'Toll Bridge' to Sidestep a Legal Hurdle, Chicago Sky-way Soon Became a White Elephant.'"
3. Main, "'O Block.'"
4. According to the appellate court's decision, some witnesses put the length of the argument at something like five to ten minutes; others said it unfolded over a long period of time, as much as twenty minutes.
5. Taken from the court transcript of the appeal, available at "People v. Willis," *Casetext*, June 1, 2004, https://casetext.com/case/people-v-willis-200.
6. Willis was convicted in 1996, appealed, and was then granted a new trial. He was convicted again and then appealed again. In 2013 the court upheld the conviction. See "People v. Willis," *Casetext*, June 14, 2013, https://casetext.com /case/people-v-willis-294.
7. Chalfin and McCrary, "Are U.S. Cities Underpoliced?," 168. Table 1 of their study shows that murders (most of which are committed with firearms in the US) are just a small share of all crimes in US cities but account for most of the social costs of crime.
8. Dionne, "Milwaukee Mayor Tom Barrett's Battle against 'Slow-Motion Mass Murders.'"
9. This figure was created by the University of Chicago Crime Lab using data from

Gunpolicy.org; our thanks to Philip Alpers for sharing additional information following the closure of the website. Data for each country are for 2019 except for the UK (2015), Canada (2018), France (2016), Germany (2015), Ireland (2014), Turkey (2015), Poland (2018), New Zealand (2018), Denmark (2018), Italy (2017), Portugal (2014), Netherlands (2018), and Hungary (2016). A figure that uses data for the same year for each country (2015) is qualitatively similar. Thanks to Kate Daugherty for creating this figure.

10. See, for example, Zimring and Hawkins, *Crime Is Not the Problem*.
11. Fitzsimmons and Rubinstein, "Mayor Eric Adams Grapples with Two Shocking Acts of Violence."
12. Holmes, "Chicago Holds Neighborhood Town Halls about Community Safety, Efforts to Reduce Violence."
13. Bunten, Kendall-Taylor, and Lindland, *Caning, Context, and Class*, 17.
14. Becker, "Crime and Punishment."
15. See Moffitt, "Adolescence-Limited and Life-Course Persistent Anti-Social Behavior," and Kiehl and Hoffman, "The Criminal Psychopath."
16. See table 5 in Drago, Galbiati, and Vertova, "The Deterrent Effects of Prison."
17. Wohl, "Racism and Anti-Irish Prejudice in Victorian England."
18. A version of this saying is often attributed to Napoleon; see "Poland's Double-Edged Vodka Tradition."
19. Falco, "When Italian Immigrants Were 'the Other.'"
20. Thrasher, *The Gang*, 191–92.
21. This figure comes from University of Chicago Crime Lab calculations of the cumulative distribution function of murders over the period 2016–2022 by community area. Austin had 9.6 percent of all Chicago murders over this period, North Lawndale had 5 percent, South Shore had 5 percent, Englewood had 4 percent, and East and West Garfield Park together had 7 percent. South Shore has a larger share of Chicago murders than does Greater Grand Crossing because South Shore has so many more people; on a per-capita rate basis, shootings are far more common in Greater Grand Crossing.
22. For population and arrest figures, see Beck, *Race and Ethnicity of Violent Crime Offenders and Arrestees, 2018*; data on police shootings taken from "Washington Post Fatal Force Tracker"; data on incarceration from Ghandnoosh, "One in Five"; and for data on murder victims, see Federal Bureau of Investigation, "Expanded Homicide Data Table 1—Murder Victims by Race, Ethnicity, and Sex, 2019."
23. Western, "Inside the Box."
24. Levitt, "Understanding Why Crime Fell in the 1990s."
25. For example, in the last mayoral election here in Chicago, one candidate's plan to address the root causes of violence added up to something like $5 billion a year; by way of comparison, the city's entire budget is only around $17 billion. See Spielman, "Mayoral Challenger Ja'Mal Green Unveils $5 Billion Public Safety Plan"; and Chicago Mayor's Press Office, "Whole Foods Market and Mayor Emanuel Announce New Store in Chicago's Englewood Neighborhood."
26. Hulse, "As Shootings Continue, Prospects for Gun Control Action in Congress Remain Dim."

27. Sources: Homicide rate (1900–1932): Eckberg, "Estimates of Early Twentieth-Century U.S. Homicide Rates"; Homicide rate (1933–2002): Bastian et al., "Mortality Trends in the United States, 1900–2018"; Homicide rate (2003–2020): CDC WISQARS database, accessed July 2, 2024, https://wisqars.cdc .gov. Thanks to Thomas Ballard for creating this figure.

28. Bastian et al., "Mortality Trends in the United States, 1900–2018."

29. In 2006–2010, median annual household incomes were $34,149 and $35,257 for the two neighborhoods, at a time when median annual household income in the US as a whole was around $50,000. In 2016–2020, median household incomes for South Shore and Greater Grand Crossing equal $35,887 and $30,110, respectively, while median household income for the US as a whole is around $68,000. Note that the slight divergence in median household incomes in recent years (equal to about 5 percent of median household income in the US as a whole) could be due in part to the growing divergence in rates of gun violence that started around 2002 (see graph in text), which based on existing data would have been expected to drive relatively more families of means and businesses out of GGC than out of South Shore. Data taken from Chicago Metropolitan Agency for Planning, *Greater Grand Crossing*.

30. Figure created using public data from the Chicago Police Department; see City of Chicago, "public safety" dataset search results, Chicago Data Portal, accessed July 2, 2024, https://data.cityofchicago.org/browse?category= Public+Safety&limitTo=datasets. Thanks to Javier Lopez for creating this graph.

31. Casanova, "'They Are Somebody.'"

32. The 1996 Kelley's Blue Book lists somewhat lower resale prices for four-door 1986 LTD models, which were mostly six-cylinder vehicles; the two-door LTDs from 1986 were all eight-cylinder Crown Victoria models. The listed price above of $3,500 is for a vehicle in good condition; that would be $6,974 in today's dollars. The price would obviously have been less if the vehicle was not in good condition; that fact is difficult to determine from the transcripts of the appeal court's ruling.

33. There are multiple ways to calculate the so-called clearance rate, the chances that a murder results in arrest, but most of the common definitions put Chicago's clearance rate in recent years somewhere between 30 percent and 50 percent. Since this shooting happened not too late at night (10:00 p.m.) when lots of other people were still around, we might reasonably expect the odds of arrest here to be toward the upper end of this range.

34. A natural objection might be that it's implausible that Willis would have done this calculation in his head of the used car value amortized over the expected prison sentence. That is precisely my point.

35. For example, one recent survey found that the share of people who suffer psychologically because of stress over finances is higher among those 26–41 years old (48 percent) and 42–57 years old (46 percent) compared to those in the age range where murder rates are highest, 18–25 (40 percent). The same survey finds that a larger share of women than men suffer psychologically as a result of financial concerns, 46 percent versus 38 percent (Gailey, "More Than Half of Americans Say Money Negatively Impacts Their Mental Health,

up Sharply from a Year Ago"). Other surveys find the middle-aged about as stressed as young people over finances (Bennett, "Most Americans Are Significantly Stressed about Money"), but I have not seen data myself to suggest that young people are substantially *more* concerned about money than middle-aged people, and certainly not that the concern among the young is *so much* higher as to explain their much higher rate of crime and violence involvement.

36. "October 1996 Weather History at Chicago/Rockford International Airport."
37. Churchill, "My New York Misadventure."
38. Kahneman, *Thinking, Fast and Slow.*
39. Darley and Batson, "'From Jerusalem to Jericho.'"
40. Pinker, *The Better Angels of Our Nature*, 84.
41. Jacobs, *The Death and Life of Great American Cities*, 35.
42. Baron, "A Brief History of Evidence-Based Policy."
43. Hastorf and Cantril, "They Saw a Game," 133.
44. Hastorf and Cantril, "They Saw a Game," 132.
45. Coy, "Goodhart's Law Rules the Modern World."
46. Beck, *Prisoners of Hate*, xiii.
47. Black, "Crime as Social Control," 36.
48. Whether there is any progress beyond 1900 depends a bit on the country being examined and the exact data source being used; see Pinker, *Better Angels*, 60–64.
49. See, for example, Thaler, *Misbehaving*, and Thaler, "Prize Lecture." Other excellent discussions of some of the core ideas of behavioral economics and behavioral science (with varying degrees of accessibility to non-economists) can be found in Camerer, Loewenstein, and Rabin, *Advances in Behavioral Economics*; Cialdini, *Influence*; Thaler and Sunstein, *Nudge*; Congdon, Kling, and Mullainathan, *Policy and Choice*; Gneezy and List, *The Why Axis*; Sunstein, *How Change Happens*; Shiller, *Irrational Exuberance*; and Frank, *Microeconomics and Behavior.*
50. Personal communication, Darrien McKinney to Jens Ludwig, Sendhil Mullainathan, and Anuj Shah, October 18, 2012.

CHAPTER TWO

1. Cordery, "UK PM May Holds Knife-Crime Summit with Teachers Ordered to Identify Violent Youths."
2. WGN News, "55 Shot, 11 Fatally over Labor Day Weekend in Chicago."
3. Masterson, "68 People Shot, 8 Killed in Shootings across Chicago over July 4th Weekend."
4. "A Brief History of the NRA" and Elving, "The NRA Wasn't Always against Gun Restrictions."
5. In what follows I describe the laws in effect in England, Wales, and Scotland; firearm regulations are slightly different in Northern Ireland.
6. Malcolm, *Guns and Violence*, 176, describing the explanation for the 1903 Firearms Act several years later by the undersecretary of the Home Office.
7. Malcolm, *Guns and Violence*, 136, and United Kingdom, Firearms Act, 1920, https://www.legislation.gov.uk/ukpga/1920/43/pdfs/ukpga_19200043_en .pdf.

8. Cook, Molliconi, and Cole, "Regulating Gun Markets," 59.

9. The government language was even the same as with the Boer War: "After any great war, there is a certain callousness with regard to life that needs to be dealt with." Malcolm, *To Keep and Bear Arms*, 173.

10. Malcolm, *To Keep and Bear Arms*, 172, 171.

11. The 1937 modification banned anyone outside the armed forces from having automatic firearms. (United Kingdom, Firearms Act, 1937, https://www .legislation.gov.uk/ukpga/1937/12/enacted). In addition, in 1937 the home secretary announced that self-defense would no longer be considered an acceptable reason to request a firearm certificate. There is some debate about when that stipulation was codified into law, in 1937 or in 1946, although Malcolm (*Guns and Violence*, 157) cites 1937 as the key year.

12. See United Kingdom, Firearms Act, 1920, https://www.legislation.gov.uk /ukpga/Geo5/10-11/43/contents/enacted. The Prevention of Crime Act 1953 would go on to prohibit the carrying of *any* weapon or other object for purposes of self-defense (https://www.legislation.gov.uk/ukpga/Geo5/10-11/43 /contents/enacted).

13. Malcolm, *To Keep and Bear Arms*, 175.

14. Malcolm, *Guns and Violence*, 201.

15. "Thatcher and Atlee Top PM List."

16. The 1988 law banned semiautomatic center-fire rifles, that is, those where the charge for the ammunition is in the middle of the round, which tends to be the standard for rifles of caliber above 0.22. Put differently, exempt from the ban were semiautomatic rifles using smaller rim-fire ammunition, such as 0.17, 0.20, and 0.22 caliber. See United Kingdom, Firearms (Amendment) Act, 1988, https://www.legislation.gov.uk/ukpga/1988/45/contents.

17. Malcolm, *Guns and Violence*, 205. See also United Kingdom, Firearms (Amendment) Act, 1997, https://www.legislation.gov.uk/ukpga/1997/5/contents; and United Kingdom, Firearms (Amendment) (No. 2) Act, https://www.legislation .gov.uk/ukpga/1997/64/contents. The main exceptions to the handgun ban were muzzle-loading handguns and starting pistols.

18. Barbash, "Britain Votes to Ban Handguns."

19. "British Lawmakers Vote for Total Handgun Ban."

20. The requirements are a bit different for shotguns than rifles; I focus on rifle requirements here.

21. "Referees are asked if they have any knowledge of the applicant having any medical or emotional problems, alcohol or drug abuse, or significant relationship difficulties which may give cause for concern given that a firearm or ammunition may be available in the household, as well as commenting upon the applicant's experience with and attitude towards firearms" (Haw et al., "Suicide by Gunshot in the United Kingdom").

22. Home Office, "Statistics on Firearm and Shotgun Certificates, England and Wales: April 2022 to March 2023."

23. "John Dillinger (1903–1934)."

24. Leff and Leff, "The Politics of Ineffectiveness," 53.

25. "Assassination Attempt."

26. The tax was $200 in dollars denominated at the time when average annual income was $1,780, so the tax is equal to one-eighth of the average annual

income, or about 1.5 months' worth of income. See Shafer, "They Were Killers with Powerful Guns."

27. Ryan, "History of Gun Law and the Second Amendment in the United States," 128.

28. Leff and Leff, "Politics of Ineffectiveness," 53.

29. Leff and Leff, "Politics of Ineffectiveness," 62, citing a 1938 Gallup poll.

30. Madonna, "The National Firearms Act of 1934."

31. Leff and Leff, "Politics of Ineffectiveness," 55.

32. Zimring, "Firearms and Federal Law."

33. Lund, "The Second Amendment and the War on Guns," 107.

34. "Where'd They Get Their Guns?"

35. "The Reagan Presidency."

36. Holmes, "Gun Control Bill Backed by Reagan in Appeal to Bush."

37. Reagan, "Why I'm for the Brady Bill."

38. Holmes, "Gun Control Bill Backed by Reagan."

39. The peak murder rate per capita in the twentieth century has been around 10 per 100,000, achieved in the 1920s and 1930s (the Prohibition era), and then again in the early 1970s, the early 1980s, and the early 1990s.

40. Aborn, "The Battle over the Brady Bill and the Future of Gun Control Advocacy," 419.

41. Bunting, "Feinstein Faces Fight for Diluted Gun Bill."

42. Biden, "Remarks by President Biden at Signing of S.2938, the Bipartisan Safer Communities Act."

43. Alvazzi del Frate et al., *Small Arms Survey Annual Report 2018*.

44. The Small Arms Survey 2018 annual report (Alvazzi del Frate et al.) estimates that the US had 393 million guns in civilian hands at the end of 2017, with a total of 857 million guns in civilian hands worldwide.

45. Cohn and Farrington, "Who Are the Most Influential Criminologists in the English-Speaking World?"

46. In 1968, Franklin Zimring showed that most gun offenders had a chance to administer an additional gunshot wound that would guarantee the victim's death, but that they didn't do so (Zimring, "Is Gun Control Likely to Reduce Violent Killings?," 721). Most gunshot victims are instead shot only once; lots of those victims wind up surviving. That's not what we'd expect if gun assailants had a sustained, single-minded, "do-whatever-it-takes" intent to kill. The characteristics of gun and non-gun attacks in terms of circumstances, offender, and victim all wind up looking quite similar with one important exception: The victim is much more likely to die if a gun is involved. A few years later Philip Cook at Duke showed that robbery murders increased much more in a city when gun robberies went up than when non-gun robberies increased, also consistent with the idea that while guns don't kill people, guns make it lots easier for people to kill other people (Cook, "The Technology of Personal Violence").

47. "Sunday, June 28, 1998: Questions For; Ozzy Osbourne."

48. Part of the issue is that many defensive gun uses may never get reported to the police; that is, government records may do a better job recording crimes than prevented crimes. In an influential study, Kleck and Gertz ("Armed Resistance to Crime") carried out a population survey and asked people whether they had ever used a gun in self-defense, the results of which imply 2.5 million defensive

gun uses per year, more than the number of gun crimes per year at that time (around 1.3 million). Cook, Ludwig, and Hemenway ("Gun Debate's New Mythical Number") note that these survey estimates have some implications that do not line up with other known facts (for example, the number of criminal attackers whom survey respondents claim to have wounded with their gun is equal to the total number of people who show up in emergency rooms every year with gunshot wounds), and suggest the survey estimates may be biased due to false positives. Even if the 2.5 million number were true, in a country of 330 million people, most Americans will not have had a defensive gun use. So in a survey, the only misreporting possible by the vast majority of respondents will be to falsely indicate they have had a defensive gun use (false positives). In any case, regardless of the true number of times guns are used in self-defense every year, from a public-policy perspective the real question is what happens on net to public safety when gun laws change, which requires a different measurement approach to figure out beyond point-in-time surveys like this one. See also Ludwig, "Gun Self-Defense and Deterrence."

49. As recently as 1978, 71 percent of gun owners said they owned their guns (usually a rifle or shotgun) for leisure purposes like hunting, sport shooting, or collecting (Wright, Rossi, and Daly, *Under the Gun*, 60). See also Yamane, "The Sociology of U.S. Gun Culture." By 2015, 63 percent of gun owners said they had a gun for protection against other people (Azrael et al., "The Stock and Flow of U.S. Firearms," 38.)

50. For example, the FBI collects data from local police departments across the country as part of the Uniform Crime Reporting (UCR) System, with common definitions issued to departments for key crime categories. The UCR isn't perfect because not all departments report (it's a voluntary system) and some departments report in weird ways that make it hard to figure out what the numbers are exactly (for example, they might forget to report in one month so those numbers are all zeros; if the next month has a higher-than-average number of crimes, that leaves open the question of whether there was an actual crime surge or whether the department just added the missing numbers from the previous month to that month's figure). A different source of crime information is the Vital Statistics census of death certificates, which lets us measure murders and gun murders specifically. The FBI has a newer crime reporting system, the National Incident-Based Reporting System (NIBRS), that is used in just a subset of all places, historically mostly less-populated places.

51. This result is from the second edition of Lott's book, published in 2000.

52. Cook and Ludwig, "The Social Costs of Gun Ownership."

53. See Zimring, "Firearms and Federal Law"; Kleck and McElrath, "The Effects of Weaponry on Human Violence," and Cook, "Great American Gun War."

54. Ludwig and Miller, "We Are Seeing a Lethal Shift in America's Gun Violence Crisis."

55. To test the law's effects, criminologist Franklin Zimring looked at trends in handgun murders in Boston and New York City, the two places with some of the strictest handgun laws in the country. Those were the two cities where the largest share of crime guns were coming in from out of state. If the GCA was successful in preventing guns from moving from places with loose gun laws into those with stricter gun laws, we should have seen after the GCA larger declines in handgun crime in Boston and New York relative to other cities that have more lax gun laws themselves (so more of the gun supply is local and hence unaffected by the GCA). Zimring found that if anything, handgun murders increased *more* in Boston and New York than in other cities—the *opposite* of what we'd expect if the GCA were achieving its goals. Zimring, "Firearms and Federal Law," 177.

56. Ludwig and Cook, "Homicide and Suicide Rates Associated with Implementation of the Brady Handgun Violence Prevention Act."
57. Title IX, Subtitle A of the Violent Crime Control and Law Enforcement Act of 1994, Pub L. 103–322, 108 Stat. 1796 (1994).
58. A comparison of data before versus after the national Crime Bill suggests mixed results: The share of shootings involving banned assault weapons seems to have declined but the share of shootings involving high-capacity magazines may have increased. The problem with this sort of before-versus-after comparison is that it risks confounding the effects of the law with all of the other things that are changing within the US over the same time period. See Koper, "Assessing the Potential to Reduce Deaths and Injuries from Mass Shootings through Restrictions on Assault Weapons and Other High-Capacity Semiautomatic Firearms."
59. Klarevas, Conner, and Hemenway, "The Effect of Large-Capacity Magazine Bans on High-Fatality Mass Shootings, 1990–2017"; Webster et al., "Evidence Concerning the Regulation of Firearms Design, Sale, and Carrying on Fatal Mass Shootings in the United States"; Koper, "Assessing the Potential to Reduce Deaths and Injuries from Mass Shootings."
60. Vigdor and Mercy, "Do Laws Restricting Access to Firearms by Domestic Violence Offenders Prevent Intimate Partner Homicide?"
61. Cooper and Smith, *Homicide Trends in the United States, 1980–2008.*
62. Loftin et al., "Effects of Restrictive Licensing of Handguns on Homicide and Suicide in the District of Columbia."
63. Several years later there was a lively debate about the DC findings in the journal *Law and Society Review.* Britt, Kleck, and Bordua ("A Reassessment of the D.C. Gun Law" and "Avoidance and Misunderstanding") noted the decline in Baltimore, while McDowall, Loftin, and Wiersema ("Using Quasi-Experiments") noted that on its face the change observed in Baltimore seems to follow a slightly different pattern than in DC; where in DC the decline in murders was only statistically significant for gun murders, in Baltimore there was a statistically significant decline in both gun murders and non-gun murders. But looking at the data more closely, my own take on this issue is that the changes in Baltimore and DC look qualitatively similar to my eye. Whether non-gun homicides show a statistically significant decline or not in DC turns out to be sensitive to which data source is used to measure murder: The FBI's UCR system shows a statistically significant decline, while the Vital Statistics death certificate data does not. Moreover, the 95 percent confidence interval around the DC Vital Statistics point estimate for non-gun homicides allows for a reasonably sized decline—or put differently, there's a lot of overlap between the confidence intervals for the DC and Baltimore effects for non-gun homicides, while the point estimates for gun homicides are quite similar.

While Chicago's handgun ban, enacted in 1982, has never been formally evaluated, Philip Cook and I showed ("Aiming for Evidence-Based") that trends in gun ownership rates for Chicago over this time period tracked what we see in the Chicago suburbs, and the rest of Illinois, quite closely.

64. Among the most common are state-level background check requirements (which may be easily circumventable by across-state gun trafficking) or efforts to restrict gun access to domestic-violence offenders or ban assault weapons (helpful, but which have, as noted above, very small overall effects). See Cherney et al., "Development of the RAND State Firearm Law Database and Supporting Materials."

65. The term was coined by Cook, Molliconi, and Cole ("Regulating Gun Markets").

66. Kovaleski and Thrush, "A Craigslist for Guns, with No Background Checks."

67. These calculations come from the city of Chicago's *Gun Trace Report 2017*, which my research center (the University of Chicago Crime Lab) helped carry out with the Mayor's Office and the Chicago Police Department.

68. Cook et al., "Underground Gun Markets."

69. "The NRA Is in Disarray."

70. Mittendorf, "Wayne LaPierre Leaves a Financial Mess Behind at the NRA."

71. The Second Amendment historically was not interpreted by the Supreme Court as guaranteeing an individual right to bear arms, which changed in 2008 with *District of Columbia v. Heller* (554 U.S. 570), when the Court struck down the handgun ban in Washington, DC, because, Justice Antonin Scalia argued in his majority opinion, at the time the Second Amendment was ratified it was understood to "enable individuals to defend themselves." Reconciling this point with the first clause of the amendment, Scalia argued that "the debate with respect to the right to keep and bear arms . . . was not whether it was desirable (all agreed that it was) but over whether it needed to be codified in the Constitution." The mention of the militia, it was argued, was an explanation of why the right was codified in the Second Amendment, not the setting of a boundary or limit of the right. See Moore, "Developments in Constitutional Law."

72. Denning and Reynolds, "Retconning Heller," 3.

73. The courts apply a two-step process, the first step of which involves determining to what degree any law burdens a constitutionally protected right. The level of scrutiny the court applies in its second step depends on "the nature of the conduct being regulated and the degree to which the challenged law burdens the right." If a law burdens a "core" element of what the Second Amendment protects, the courts are to apply the "strict scrutiny standard" (the law must be "narrowly tailored to achieve a compelling governmental interest"); otherwise, the courts apply an "intermediate scrutiny" test ("reasonably adapted to a substantial governmental interest"). See Congressional Research Service, *Legal Sidebar: The Future of the Second Amendment*.

74. Aborn, "Battle over the Brady Bill," 423.

75. The initial research on this question by Lott and Mustard ("Crime, Deterrence, and Right-to-Carry Concealed Handguns") and Lott (*More Guns, Less Crime*) seemed to show that permissive gun-carry laws reduced crime. But as more states have enacted such laws and more data are available, and more advanced statistical methods have been developed to help isolate the effects of these gun

laws from other confounding factors, that conclusion has—in my view—been overturned. Donohue, Aneja, and Weber ("Right-to-Carry Laws and Violent Crime") suggest that the net effect is in the direction of more violent crime, while Donohue et al. ("Why Does Right-to-Carry Cause Violent Crime to Increase?") explore the mechanisms of action behind that adverse effect.

76. Bailey, "In Bodycam Footage, Nashville Police Seen Confronting School Shooter."

77. Sotomayor and Goodwin, "In Congress, Little Urgency to Address Gun Violence with Legislation."

78. Karni, "Shooting Prompts a Shrug in Washington, as G.O.P. Rejects Pleas to Act."

79. The National Firearms Act of 1934 banned machine guns. The Federal Firearms Act of 1938 required gun dealers to get a federal license. In 1968 we banned gun sales to those under 21, to felons, and to the mentally ill. The Brady Act in 1993 required dealers to carry out background checks; there was also the 1994 assault weapons ban.

CHAPTER THREE

1. Gramlich, "The Gap between the Number of Blacks and Whites in Prison Is Shrinking."

2. This chapter was inspired by and draws heavily from the fascinating discussion of the influence of Wilson and his ideas on criminal-justice policy over this period in Crimmins, "Incarceration as Incapacitation."

3. Jones and Harris, "The Attribution of Attitudes."

4. In principle, it is possible that subjects thought the essay authors might have had their own personal attitudes swayed by the act of having written an essay arguing a particular position. While this outcome is a logical possibility, it does not seem to fit the data. Note that there was actually a second condition in the experiment, in which subjects were asked to assess the essay author's attitudes after being told that the author got to pick their topic themselves. The association between writing a pro-Communist (versus anti-communist) essay in the "no-choice" condition (where the essay author was assigned their topic) on the author's pro-Communist attitudes was about half the size of what we see in the condition in which authors were able to select their own topic. Put differently, the study subjects would need to believe that the influence of being assigned to write a pro-Communist essay on someone's attitudes is about half the influence on someone's attitudes of all of their cumulative life experiences and thinking, which to me seems unlikely.

5. As John Dewey put it over a hundred years ago, even a young child "soon distinguishes persons as the most important and interesting of all the objects with which he has to do. . . . It is a commonplace that what is moving attracts notice when that which is at rest escapes it" (Dewey, *How We Think*, 159, 194).

6. Ross and Nisbett, *Person and the Situation*.

7. See Crimmins, "Incarceration as Incapacitation," and Wilson, *Thinking about Crime*.

8. Sandel, Verba, and Mansfield, "James Q. Wilson."
9. Weber, "James Q. Wilson Dies at 80."
10. Zimring, "Will Success Spoil James Q. Wilson?"
11. See Wilson, *Thinking about Crime*, as well as Vold and Bernard, *Theoretical Criminology*.
12. As Bowman and Marsico ("The Public's Verdict on the War on Poverty") note, surveys showed great enthusiasm for the War on Poverty in the 1960s, an enthusiasm that seems to have waned—even among low-income Americans—by the 1980s. There weren't many relevant survey questions in the 1970s, but we might take some signal from the outcome of the 1972 presidential race, in which Republican Richard Nixon beat liberal Democrat George McGovern with 61 percent of the popular vote, carrying forty-nine states total in the electoral college.
13. For example, Alesina, Stantcheva, and Teso ("Intergenerational Mobility") find that Americans, much more than Europeans, believe in the possibility of social mobility, which reduces support for social policies. Wingrove et al. ("Tying the Value of Goals to Social Class"), in a different study, find that American respondents tend to believe the poor value the goal of achievement less than do more affluent people.
14. Haney, *Criminality in Context*.
15. Vold and Bernard, *Theoretical Criminology*, 37, 51; Haney, *Criminality in Context*, 25.
16. Wilson and Herrnstein, *Crime and Human Nature*.
17. Wilson, *Thinking about Crime*, 260.
18. Wilson, *Thinking about Crime*, 117.
19. Wilson, *Thinking about Crime*, 121.
20. Gibbs, "Review Essay."
21. Wilson, *Thinking about Crime*, 118.
22. Wilson, "Lock 'Em Up and Other Thoughts on Crime."
23. Wilson, "Lock 'Em Up."
24. Johnson, "Special Message to the Congress on Crime and Law Enforcement."
25. Wilson, *Thinking about Crime*, 25.
26. Crimmins, "Incarceration as Incapacitation," 144–66.
27. "Robert Martinson and Nothing Works."
28. In the second edition of *Thinking about Crime*, Wilson summarizes a number of other literature reviews of that era that came to conclusions similar to Martinson's.
29. Messinger and Berk, "Review Essay," 773.
30. "Recidivism and Reentry."
31. Recent research has pointed out a subtle logical problem with those sorts of calculations: If I take (say) ten years' worth of data from a state prison system and calculate what share of people released from prison over that decade wind up rearrested or re-imprisoned, I will indeed see that something like two-thirds will be rearrested and half re-imprisoned. But notice something with that calculation: A disproportionately large share of prison spells over that ten-year period will be accounted for by high-risk people who get released, re-imprisoned, released again, re-imprisoned again, released yet again, and re-imprisoned yet again, etc. The high-risk person, in other words, contributes multiple prison-

release "events" to the data. In contrast, the person who gets released from prison just once and never gets rearrested or re-imprisoned will only contribute a single prison-release "event" in that type of dataset. If we asked, instead, what share of all people who ever spend time in prison ever get re-imprisoned, the answer is only about one-third. In other words, the way everyone has been looking at recidivism data for decades has created, inadvertently, an overly pessimistic picture of the degree to which "criminals" are incorrigible versus are capable of changing their ways. (See Rhodes et al., "Following Incarceration, Most Released Offenders Never Return to Prison.") My thanks to Aaron Chalfin for pointing me to this study.

32. This calculation comes from the 1977 National Crime Victimization Survey data and the 1977 FBI UCR data. My calculation is close to what Wilson reported in *Thinking about Crime*: "On the average, no more than three felonies out of one hundred result in the imprisonment of the offender" (118).

33. About 52 percent of robberies are reported to the police, according to data from the 2000 National Crime Victimization Survey. According to data from the FBI's Uniform Crime Reporting system for official police statistics, about 26 percent of robberies reported to the police result in arrest in 2000. And data from Neal and Rick shows that about 20 percent of robbery arrests resulted in prison time in 2000. The implication is that the odds that the average robber winds up in prison for a robbery equals (52 percent x 26 percent x 20 percent) = 2.7 percent ("The Prison Boom and Sentencing Policy," table 2).

34. Crimmins, "Incarceration as Incapacitation," quoting Arendt, *On Violence*.

35. Blumstein et al., *Deterrence and Incapacitation*.

36. Wilson, *Thinking about Crime*.

37. Crimmins, "Incarceration as Incapacitation."

38. Crimmins, "Incarceration as Incapacitation."

39. Crimmins, "Incarceration as Incapacitation."

40. Haney, *Criminality in Context*, 34.

41. Klein, "'Headless Body in Topless Bar.'"

42. "Mr. Dahmer drugged [the victim's] drinks, strangled them and cut up their bodies with an electric buzz saw . . . he discarded bones he did not want in a 57-gallon drum he had bought for just that purpose . . . he lined up three skulls on a shelf in his apartment . . . Once, he told the police in Milwaukee, he fried a victim's bicep in vegetable shortening and ate it" (Barron and Tabor, "17 Killed, and a Life Is Searched for Clues").

43. DiIulio, "What Happens in Real Bureaucracies."

44. DiIulio, "Coming of the Super-Predators."

45. Haney and Greene, "Capital Constructions."

46. Haney and Greene, "Capital Constructions." 145.

47. The World Values Survey (https://www.worldvaluessurvey.org/wvs.jsp) asked people in 120 countries to report which statement is closest to their view: "There are absolutely clear guidelines about what is good and evil, these always apply to everyone, whatever the circumstances," or "there can never be absolutely clear guidelines about what is good and evil. What is good and evil depends entirely upon the circumstances."

48. Kossowska et al., "Religious Fundamentalism Modulates Neural Responses to Error-Related Words," 285.
49. Evans, "U.S. Adults Are More Religious than Western Europeans."
50. Grasmick and McGill, "Religion, Attribution Style, and Punitiveness toward Juvenile Offenders."
51. Seto and Said, "Religious Perceptions of Crime and Implications for Punitiveness." See also Tonry, "Explanations of American Punishment Policies."
52. Curry, "Conservative Protestantism and the Perceived Wrongfulness of Crimes"; Tonry, "Explanations of American Punishment Policies." The US Supreme Court, in a 1951 decision, offered a different hypothesis: "Crime, as a compound concept, generally constituted only from concurrence of an evil-meaning mind with an evil-doing hand, was congenial to an intense individualism and took deep and early root in American soil." See also Haney, *Criminality in Context*.
53. See Enns, *Incarceration Nation*, figure 2.3.
54. See for example Bunten, Kendall-Taylor, and Lindland, *Caning, Context and Class*, 25. I view what that report describes as a "rational-actor" model (people decide to commit crime by comparing benefits and costs) as being related to two other models of the causes of crime that focus group respondents report: the "moral development" model (people never learned right from wrong during childhood, a formative period during which that moral sense is developed) and the "ecological model" that emphasizes the role of economic hardship. I exclude cultural explanations, such as that people engage in crime because their peers encourage them, since such explanations just push back one level the question of why some peer groups are more or less encouraging of criminal behavior in the first place.
55. See for example Erskine, "The Polls"; Thompson and Bobo, "Thinking about Crime"; and Mizell, *An Overview of Public Opinion and Discourse on Criminal Justice Issues*. Americans tend to have a similar view about drug users as well: The common thread is that "criminals" are different from "the rest of us" (see also Haney, *Criminality in Context*).
56. The 1994 Gallup poll asking Americans why crime was rising yielded the following distribution of responses: 30 percent said "crisis of personal values"; 20 percent said "drugs," which many Americans seem to attribute to personal failings; 20 percent said "failure of the criminal justice system"; and only 8 percent said "unemployment and social distress." See Mizell, *Overview of Public Opinion*. In terms of the public's attitude toward those who use drugs, as one study of public opinion put it, "the feeling [among the public] is that the addict is a bad or weak person, especially because much drug use is illegal." In surveys, only 22 percent say they would be willing to work closely on the job with someone struggling with drug addiction. Fully 64 percent said employers should be able to deny employment to people who have a drug addiction (Salmassi, "Survey: People Have More Negative Opinions about Drug Addiction Than Mental Illness").
57. For example, Blumstein and Cohen ("A Theory of the Stability of Punishment," 200) argued that "in a given society, during a relatively stable period, there is a

balance of forces that maintains [a rate of punishment that is] fairly constant. The rationale for this argument is fundamentally that the level of punishment in a society is homeostatic."

58. Gottschalk, "The Folly of Neoliberal Prison Reform."

59. For example, Spelman ("Crime, Cash, and Limited Options") argues that among the most important explanations for rising incarceration in America was simply increased state revenues, claiming that prison expenditures increased similarly to state spending on other functions. Many others point to the importance of changes in sentencing policies. See, for example, Raphael, "Explaining the Rise in U.S. Incarceration Rates"; and Neal and Rick, "Prison Boom." Pfaff, *Locked In,* emphasizes the role played by prosecutors.

60. It's possible that people attribute too much of the rise in imprisonment to the War on Drugs because the federal prison system often gets so much news attention, and in the federal system it is true that a large share of the growth in imprisonment was due to drug cases. But the federal system is small relative to state prisons and local jails.

61. Sawyer and Wagner, "Mass Incarceration."

62. Gottschalk, "Folly of Neoliberal Prison Reform."

63. Gotsch and Basti, "Capitalizing on Mass Incarceration."

64. Widely prevalent out-group bias, or at least white bias against Blacks, is a necessary part of the New Jim Crow story but by itself not sufficient. A different concern one might have is how a constant (bias) could explain a change (in imprisonment rates). One candidate answer is that a constant (bias) combined with one change (constraints on how that bias is expressed as a result of civil rights legislation of the 1960s) leads to another change (rising imprisonment starting in the 1970s).

65. Sherif et al., *Intergroup Conflict and Cooperation.*

66. Calculated using data from the General Social Survey's Data Explorer, accessed July 3, 2024, https://gssdataexplorer.norc.org/home. Thanks to Kate Daugherty for creating this figure.

67. Wihbey, "White Racial Attitudes over Time." This out-group bias seems to occur more generally, not just by whites toward Black Americans. The famous study by Clark and Clark, "Racial Identification and Racial Preference in Negro Children," in which young Black American children preferred a white doll over a Black doll, seems to reflect a preference for the high-status group among young children in particular that may change as people reach adolescence and adulthood (see for example Phinney, Ferguson, and Tate, "Intergroup Attitudes among Ethnic Minority Adolescents"; and Allen, "African Americans' and European Americans' Mutual Attributions").

68. Hoekstra and Sloan, "Does Race Matter for Police Use of Force?"

69. Arnold, Dobbie, and Hull, "Measuring Racial Discrimination in Bail Decisions."

70. Anwar and Fang, "Testing for Racial Prejudice in the Parole Board Release Process"; and Mechoulan and Sahuguet, "Assessing Racial Disparities in Parole Release."

71. Sahgal and Mohamed, "In the U.S. and Western Europe, People Say They Accept Muslims, but Opinions Are Divided on Islam."

72. Silver, Fetterolf, and Connaughton, "Diversity and Division in Advanced Economies."
73. For state-by-state patterns in imprisonment rates, see Travis, Western, and Redburn, *The Growth of Incarceration in the United States*. For data on regional differences in white racial attitudes, see Valentino and Sears, "Old Times There Are Not Forgotten."
74. Travis, Western, and Redburn, *Growth of Incarceration*.
75. Enns, *Incarceration Nation*.
76. Young, "Analysis: Black Leaders Supported Clinton's Crime Bill."
77. "Jackson Calls Himself 'General' in Drug War."
78. Duke, "Summit Brings Together Gang Members, Black Elders."
79. See, for example, Cullen et al. "Attribution, Salience, and Attitudes toward Criminal Sanctioning"; Grasmick and McGill, "Religion, Attribution Style, and Punitiveness"; Heider, *Psychology of Interpersonal Relations*; Yelderman and Miller, "Religious Fundamentalism and Attitudes toward the Insanity Defense"; Cochran, Boots, and Heide, "Attribution Styles and Attitudes toward Capital Punishment for Juveniles, the Mentally Incompetent, and the Mentally Retarded"; Sims and Johnston, "Examining Public Opinion about Crime and Justice"; Maruna and King, "Once a Criminal, Always a Criminal?"; and Enns, *Incarceration Nation*.
80. Carroll, "The Effect of Imagining an Event on Expectations for the Event."
81. The definition of "fundamentalist" is a complex issue; see Smith, *Classifying Protestant Denominations*. One question is on what basis to classify people, a process that could rely for example on questions about how people self-classify, questions about what national umbrella organization their particular church belongs to, or questions about their specific beliefs. Another part of the issue is that while everyone can recognize the continuum of different religious denominations from fundamentalist on one end (or what we could instead call orthodox, conservative, or Evangelical) to liberal on the other (secular, modern, humanistic), where to draw the "cut point" in this continuum in defining someone as fundamentalist is not clear. As Smith (*Classifying Protestant Denominations*) puts it: "In addition to their opposition to the growth of secular influence in society, the Fundamentalists are distinguished by belief in (1) the inerrancy of the Bible (or more technically in the verbal, plenary inspiration of the Bible), (2) personal salvation by accepting Christ as their saviour in what is often called the born-again experience, (3) the personal, pre-millennial imminent return of Christ (4) an evangelical or revivalist desire to reach out to save and convert others and (5) acceptance of most traditional Protestant beliefs such as in Trinity, the Virgin birth, and the existence of angels and devils." The general suggestion of the General Social Survey report is that different classification schemes tend to yield generally similar results.
82. These figures come from averaging together self-reports from respondents to the General Social Survey over the period 1972–2000. I use the average share over this time period because it turns out that the share of people who hold fundamentalist religious views is fairly stable over time within regions.
83. Figure E.1. Relationship between religious fundamentalism and changes in imprisonment by region of the US, 1972–2000

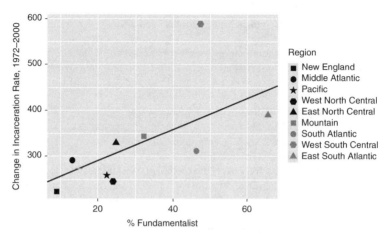

Source: University of Chicago Crime Lab calculations.

Notes: Religious fundamentalist measure is the average percentage of respondents who report having fundamentalist views, pooled over the period 1972–2000 from the General Social Survey; change in imprisonment rate by region is taken from Travis, Western, and Redburn, *Growth of Incarceration*.

84. See Western, *Punishment and Inequality in America*; and Western, "Inside the Box."

85. Western, "Inside the Box."

86. As Roberts put it: There "seems to be near unanimity among English-language scholars that public pressure has been responsible, in whole or part, for many juvenile justice reforms in recent years" ("Public Opinion and Youth Justice," 521).

87. Hansen, *Kids in Prison*.

88. Pandolfo, "School Discipline Records Show Racial Disparities."

89. Kang and Rasich, "Extending the Firearm Suicide Proxy for Household Gun Ownership."

90. The usual threshold for statistical significance in social scientists is that there's not more than a 5 percent chance that the result seen in the data is due to random chance. So if only 5 percent of programs reviewed are found to be "successful," that would be consistent with 0 percent of the programs truly being effective and just 5 percent being "false positive" results.

91. Levitt, "The Effect of Prison Population Size on Crime Rates: Evidence from Prison Overcrowding Litigation."

92. Kessler and Levitt ("Using Sentence Enhancements to Distinguish between Deterrence and Incapacitation") note that increased prison penalties do seem to deter crime, but not by quite enough to also reduce imprisonment at the same time.

93. See, for example, Donohue, "Assessing the Relative Benefits of Incarceration."

94. If deterrence effects were big enough, we could in principle increase prison sentences and reduce crime and imprisonment rates at the same time, but deterrence isn't that powerful. Longer sentences reduce crime but wind up

leading to more incarceration. See Kessler and Levitt, "Using Sentence Enhancements."

95. Evidence on the effects of prison on AIDS infection rates is from Johnson and Raphael, "The Effect of Male Incarceration Dynamics on AIDS Infection Rates among African-American Women and Men." There is no question also that rates of COVID infection, assault victimization, and sexual assault victimization are much higher in prison than in the general population (see, for example, Kim et al., "The Health Impacts of the COVID-19 Pandemic on Adults Who Experience Imprisonment Globally"; and Western, "Inside the Box"). What has not been established yet in the research, as far as I know, is exactly how much lower those rates would be for incarcerated people if they were not incarcerated.

96. See Aizer and Doyle, "Juvenile Incarceration, Human Capital, and Future Crime," for the effects of incarceration on teenagers. For a review of the more complicated pattern of results for adults, see Norris, Pecenco, and Weaver, "The Effects of Parental and Sibling Incarceration"; and Garin et al., "The Impact of Incarceration on Employment, Earnings, and Tax Filing."

97. "All crimes" refers to arrests for all serious (so-called Part 1) crime classifications in the FBI's Uniform Crime Report; "violent crimes" refers to Part 1 violent offenses. Calculated using 2019 Chicago PD arrest records and 2019 census population estimates. Thanks to Thomas Ballard and Alejandro Roemer for creating this figure.

CHAPTER FOUR

1. This chapter draws on Ludwig and Schnepel, "Does Nothing Stop a Bullet Like a Job?"
2. Private conversation, Jens Ludwig with David Robinson, July 19, 2023.
3. Black, "Harold Washington's Legacy Provided Touchstones for Progressive Politics."
4. Trussell, "Building Leaders for Today's World."
5. "The Harold Washington Story."
6. Malcolm, "In the World of Chicago Politics, the Main Rule Is There Are No Rules."
7. "Achieving the Dream."
8. Quoted in McDonald, *Chicago: An Economic History*, 65.
9. See McDonald, *Chicago: An Economic History*; and Duis, "Chicago in History."
10. This section draws on Travis, *Harold, the People's Mayor*; and McDonald, *Chicago: An Economic History*.
11. Dukes, "'Poland Elsewhere.'"
12. Much of the discussion here borrows from the wonderful book by McDonald, *Chicago: An Economic History*.
13. See McDonald, *Chicago: An Economic History*, 61.
14. See, for example, the discussion in Eriksson and Ward, "The Ethnic Segregation of Immigrants in the United States from 1850 to 1940."

15. For early trends in immigration segregation, see Eriksson and Ward, "Ethnic Segregation of Immigrants in the United States." For evidence on the conditions under which segregation may yield positive vs. negative effects, see Cutler, Glaeser, and Vigdor, "When Are Ghettos Bad?" For a discussion of patterns of economic mobility among immigrants over time, see Collins and Zimran, "Working Their Way Up."

16. These figures come from the 1930 census.

17. McDonald, *Chicago: An Economic History*, 115.

18. "Early Chicago, 1833–1871."

19. Travis, *Harold, the People's Mayor*, 17.

20. Travis, *Harold, the People's Mayor*, 19.

21. Gordon, "Back to the Future."

22. It's true that today there are state unemployment insurance systems and state and federal earned income tax credits, but those really only help men connected to the labor market to some degree.

23. Travis, *Harold, the People's Mayor*, 35: "In 1946, Roosevelt College was an island unto itself, a bold experiment in democracy in education. An open enrollment for Blacks had never been attempted at any non-Black college or university in America. The daring experiment occurred during a period when Blacks were not allowed to eat or sleep in a downtown hotel or any other place outside of the defined Black Belt. All Chicago restaurants outside of the ghetto were off-limits to Blacks, even the greasiest of the greasy-spoon variety. The one exception in downtown Chicago was a lunch counter in a Woolworth store located on the southwest corner of State and Washington. Even there, I learned later, they had special drinking glasses for Blacks. At an earlier period, this store had painted the 'for blacks only' drinking glasses red at the bottom in order to avoid serving whites with glasses that had been used by Blacks."

24. Travis, *Harold, the People's Mayor*, 47.

25. Biles, "Machine Politics."

26. Biles, "Machine Politics." See also Inglot and Pelissero, "Ethnic Political Power in a Machine City."

27. Hautzinger, "The Olympic Athlete Who Became a Powerful Chicago Politician."

28. Travis, *Harold, the People's Mayor*, 20.

29. Inglot and Pelissero, "Ethnic Political Power in a Machine City," 530, figure 1.

30. McDonald, *Chicago: An Economic History*, 100.

31. Duffy, "Manor Tool & Manufacturing Co."

32. McDonald, *Chicago: An Economic History*.

33. *1970 Census of Population Supplementary Report*.

34. "Lynching in America."

35. Nuwer, "Mississippi Officially Ratifies Amendment to Ban Slavery, 148 Years Late." In 2013, the movie *Lincoln* prompted two academics to discover that Mississippi had not actually completed the final step necessary to ratify the Thirteenth Amendment—sending a copy to the federal government. The state has since done so.

36. Boustan, "Was Postwar Suburbanization 'White Flight'?"

37. The white population in 1980 was somewhere between 1.3 and 1.7 million. The

range here comes from the fact that the census before 1980 did not distinguish between Hispanic white and non-Hispanic white, while the 1980 census did, so counting "white" comparably requires some uncertainty about how many Hispanics in later years would have been counted as white in earlier years.

38. Rury, "School Desegregation."

39. This figure reproduces a version of a wonderful graph from Robert Sampson's book *Great American City* using data from Paral, "Chicago Community Area Data." Thanks to Arjun Subramanian and Alejandro Roemer for creating this figure.

40. See Glaeser and Ponzetto, "Did the Death of Distance Hurt Detroit and Help New York?"

41. The invention of air conditioning also helped accelerate the country's long-term trend of people moving to the South and West regions of the country. Glaeser and Tobio ("The Rise of the Sunbelt") also argue that right-to-work laws in the South have made that region more appealing for economic activity.

42. Hunkar, "Manufacturing Jobs as a Percentage of Total U.S. Workforce since 1939."

43. See, for example, Bernard, Smeets, and Warzynski, "Rethinking Deindustrialization."

44. The Rust Belt had 50 percent of all American manufacturing jobs in 1950 but just 33 percent by 1983.

   The Rust Belt in this analysis is defined as Illinois, Indiana, Michigan, New York, Ohio, Pennsylvania, West Virginia, and Wisconsin. See Alder, Lagakos and Ohanian ("Competitive Pressure and the Decline of the Rust Belt"), who attribute the decline to noncompetitive markets for the goods produced in the Rust Belt up through 1980 (lots of monopolies and oligopolies that were subject to limited price or quality competition from other companies) and in the "input" or labor markets due to, they argue, overly generous labor union contracts. They note that manufacturing worker wages were higher in the Rust Belt than in other parts of the country, while productivity growth there was slower.

45. "Forged in Steel, Soon Forgotten."

46. Jackson and Foster, "The Politics of Public Budgeting in Illinois (Second Edition)."

47. Smylie and Vevea, "Chicago Will Get Smaller Share of State's Increased K-12 Education Budget for Second Year in a Row."

48. Chicago mayor Richard J. Daley only agreed to the introduction of a statewide income tax because the governor at the time agreed to pass 10 percent along to Chicago. Cook County, which is Chicago plus its suburbs, accounts for about 45 percent of the state's total GDP—so even the Daley agreement is probably a sweetheart deal for the state. In exchange, the 1970 Illinois constitution prevents Chicago and other cities and towns from imposing their own income taxes. But the state's been steadily walking away from that deal, and Chicago's been getting only around 6 percent of state income taxes (Schmidt, "Illinois Should Restore the 10% Local Share of State Income Tax to Chicago, Other Municipalities").

49. Washington, inaugural address, April 29, 1983.

50. See Vold and Bernard, *Theoretical Criminology*, 132.

51. See, for example, Shaw and McKay, *Juvenile Delinquency in Urban Areas*; and Sampson, Wilson, and Katz, "Reassessing 'Toward a Theory of Race, Crime, and Urban Inequality.'" Part of the key hypothesis advanced by sociologists Robert Sampson and William Julius Wilson in recent years is the idea that aspects of the social environment that matter for violence matter the same way for Black and white Americans, so that the elevated rates of violence we see in predominantly Black neighborhoods are due mostly to the greater concentration of neighborhood social disadvantage present in those communities. There is a large literature about different aspects of neighborhood environments that might matter for crime and violence, from socioeconomic disadvantage to strengths of social bonds (Hirschi, *Causes of Delinquency*) to the willingness of neighbors to work together to uphold shared local social norms, or "collective efficacy" (Sampson, Raudenbush, and Earls, "Neighborhoods and Violent Crime").

52. See, for example, Mickelson and Saatcioglu, "Structure and Agency in Resistance to Schooling."

53. See Cloward and Ohlin, *Delinquency and Opportunity*; and also Merton, *Social Theory and Social Structure*; Agnew, "Foundation for a General Strain Theory of Crime and Delinquency"; and Messner and Rosenfeld, *Crime and the American Dream*.

54. Wilson, *The Truly Disadvantaged*.

55. Mayor Lori Lightfoot ("We Are Each Other's Business") did mention it, but not regarding Chicago—rather, she referenced segregation in the context of her growing up in a segregated Ohio steel town. ("My mother and my late father, Elijah, gave us the best they could in the segregated Ohio steel town where we grew up, even when they had almost nothing left to give.") Even Mayor Brandon Johnson, the most progressive in the city's history (a former teacher's union organizer), mentioned it only once in his own inaugural address—in the context of how the civil rights movement of the 1960s ended legal racial segregation: "How many decades of slow grinding progress—think about the labor movement, which produced luminaries like my mentor and dear sister Karen Lewis, who modeled true social justice unionism, and helped lead the multiracial, multicultural, working class movement that organized its way to this moment. The same labor movement that raised wages, established the 40-hour workweek, and built the middle class in this city. From the Civil Rights Movement, embodied by our very own brother, Rev. Jesse Jackson Sr., which abolished racial segregation in our laws and gave us the Voting Rights Act."

56. This figure is a variant of a graph published in Sampson, *Great American City*, created using data from Paral, "Chicago Community Area Data." Thanks to Arjun Subramanian and Alejandro Roemer for creating this figure. Summary statistics of the level of racial segregation in a city have changed only modestly in Chicago. One way that social scientists measure segregation is via the so-called dissimilarity index, which asks, if we wanted the share of Black residents in every neighborhood to equal the share of Black residents in the city as a whole, how many Black residents in the city would need to wind up in a different neighborhood to make that happen? For the city of Chicago that number was 91 in 1980—that is, 91 of every 100 Black city residents would have had

to live in a different neighborhood in order to reach perfect integration. That number is about as close to perfect segregation as you can get. By 2020 that number had barely declined: The segregation index was still at 80.

57. Logan and Stults, *The Persistence of Segregation in the Metropolis*. See also, for example, Logan and Parman ("The National Rise in Residential Segregation"), who document the sizable rise in racial segregation in the early part of the twentieth century (1880 to 1940). Frey ("Neighborhood Segregation Persists for Black, Latino or Hispanic, and Asian Americans") shows that Black-white residential segregation has declined somewhat since its peak in the 1960s, but that substantial segregation remains today. See Boustan ("Was Postwar Suburbanization 'White Flight'?") for a discussion of the role that white flight from cities to suburbs played in contributing to changes in segregation. See also Sander, Kucheva, and Zasloff, *Moving toward Integration*.

58. Looking at the largest metropolitan areas in the country, the dissimilarity index peaked at 79 in 1970 and had declined to 59 by 2010, according to Brown University research, but most of that progress occurred in the metro areas that contain the fewest Black residents. Progress has been much slower in the big cities of the Northeast and Midwest. Progress is even more limited if we look instead at the so-called exposure index, which captures the share of people who are white in the neighborhood of the average Black American. In 1940, long before the civil rights movement, that figure was 40 percent. By 2010, that figure had actually *declined* to 35 percent. The reason why the dissimilarity index suggests segregation is declining (modestly) while the exposure index says segregation is getting worse is because of the influx of Hispanics into US cities. Black Americans are more likely to live near Hispanic neighbors (so the dissimilarity index goes down) but are no more likely to be living near white neighbors (so the exposure index doesn't change much or even gets worse). See Logan and Stults, *Persistence of Segregation in the Metropolis*.

59. See, for example, research by the Pew Foundation showing this for 1980 to 2010 (Fry and Taylor, "The Rise of Residential Segregation by Income"), as well as Reardon et al., "Has Income Segregation Really Increased?"; Logan et al., "Income Segregation"; and Watson, "Inequality and the Measurement of Residential Segregation by Income in American Neighborhoods."

For example, looking at data for the 117 medium- and large-sized metropolitan areas (with populations above five hundred thousand), which together capture about two-thirds of the total US population, the share of families living in neighborhoods with lots of other poor families (defined as those with a median income less than two-thirds of the metropolitan-area-wide median) doubled from 1970 to 2007, from 8.4 percent to 17 percent. We see the same growing segregation of the rich at the other end of the income distribution; the share of people living in neighborhoods with lots of rich people (median income above 1.5 times the metropolitan-area-wide median) more than doubled, from 6.6 percent to 14.1 percent. See Logan and Stults, *Persistence of Segregation in the Metropolis*.

Fry and Taylor ("Rise of Residential Segregation by Income") find a similar pattern from 1980 to 2010 using data on the 942 metropolitan and micropolitan statistical areas in the US.

60. Wilson, *Truly Disadvantaged.*

61. See Shaw and McKay, *Juvenile Delinquency in Urban Areas*; and also Small, *Unexpected Gains.*

62. National Advisory Commission on Civil Disorders, *Report of the National Advisory Commission on Civil Disorders*, i.

63. National Advisory Commission on Civil Disorders, *Report of the National Advisory Commission on Civil Disorders*, iii.

64. Travis, *Harold, the People's Mayor*, 114.

65. Maragos, "Who Was Harold Washington?"

66. "The Views of White Americans."

67. These attitudes seem to diffuse even more widely throughout society beyond whites. See, for example, Clark and Clark, "Racial Identification and Racial Preference in Negro Children," which shows that young Black American children also preferred a white doll over a Black doll, which seems to reflect a preference for the high-status group among young children in particular that may change as people reach adolescence and adulthood. See also Phinney, Ferguson, and Tate, "Intergroup Attitudes among Ethnic Minority Adolescents."

68. Paluck et al., "Prejudice Reduction," 553. The types of interventions they examine include out-group contact; modal studies (these involve secondhand or imagined contact with out-groups); cognitive/emotional training to help people "fight off their personal prejudices"; information provision intended to break down negative stereotypes; social categorization (people are asked to redefine in-group/out-group boundaries to prioritize shared identities—for example rather than focus on race we might be asked to focus on the fact that in a mixed-race group, "we're all Sixers fans"); and efforts to remind people of their own or their group's egalitarian views. They found little impact from the sorts of politics that organizations most often implement in the real world: diversity training and implicit bias training. For other interventions, they find evidence of "publication bias," the unfortunate practice wherein positive results are more likely to be published in peer-reviewed journals than null or negative results. And the results tend to be much larger for those done with college students than for those done in real-world settings.

69. Horowitz, Brown, and Cox, "Race in America 2019."

70. Black, "Harold Washington's Legacy Provided Touchstones for Progressive Politics."

71. Spielman, "Worst-Case Scenario."

72. Ballantine, "Chicago's Per-Capita Pension Debt, Visualized (Gulp!)."

73. "Chicago's Recent Rating Upgrades."

74. The following surveys can be found through Cornell's Roper Center (https://ropercenter.cornell.edu): Gallup 1993 (Roper study no. 31088208); Hart-Teeter 1994 (no. 31094745); *Los Angeles Times* 1994 (no. 31093021); America's Research Group 1994 (no. 31094167); *Los Angeles Times* 1995 (no. 31093049); *CBS/NYT* 1996 (no. 31091428); Public Policy Research Institute/Texas A&M 1996 (no. 31106757); Gallup 2000 (no. 31108409); Princeton Survey Research Associates 2006 (no. 31096871); *CBS/NYT* 2016 (no. 31113964); and Beacon Research 2021 (no. 31119092) and 2022 (no. 31120044).

75. Kearney, *The Two-Parent Privilege.*

76. Hemez and Washington, "Percentage and Number of Children Living with Two Parents Has Dropped since 1968."

77. Washington, inaugural address, April 29, 1983.

78. Royko, *Boss,* 104–5.

79. Royko, *Boss,* 61.

80. Schmid, "4 of Illinois' Past 10 Governors Went to Prison."

81. "A List of Chicago Aldermen Indicted, Raided or Implicated by the Feds, Criminally Charged or Convicted since 2019."

82. US Attorney's Office, Northern District of Illinois, "Superseding Federal Indictment against Former Illinois Speaker of the House Adds Charge for Alleged Corruption Scheme Related to AT&T Illinois."

83. FitzPatrick, "PPP Fraud Investigation in Chicago Public Schools Results in a Top CPS Official, 13 Others Losing Their Jobs."

84. Aoraha, "Democrat Chicago Treasurer Melissa Conyears-Ervin Is Accused of Forcing Taxpayer-Funded Staff to Plan Her Daughter's Birthday and Act as Her Personal Bodyguard."

85. Gorner, "Accused of Having His Officers Baby-Sit His Son, Chicago Police Commander Said It Was Really a Secret Study."

86. "Corruption Convictions Decline Nationally but Chicago and Illinois Remain at, near Top."

87. Simpson, Rossi, and Gradel, *Corruption Continues through the COVID-19 Pandemic.*

88. Washington, inaugural address, May 4, 1987.

89. For an extended discussion, see, for example, Dickerson, "'Nothing Stops a Bullet Like a Job.'"

90. "Arne Duncan."

91. Becker, "Crime and Punishment."

92. Bunten, Kendall-Taylor, and Lindland, *Caning, Context and Class,* 25.

93. Bunten, Kendall-Taylor, and Lindland, *Caning, Context and Class,* 26; and Mizell, *Overview of Public Opinion.*

94. See Stevenson and Doleac, "Algorithmic Risk Assessment in the Hands of Humans."

95. Many students of crime are often nervous about relying on official crime statistics, since such statistics may tell us at least as much about who is willing to report crimes to the police as they do about to whom crime happens. There's also always a concern about whether the likelihood that police arrest a suspect could be affected by the suspect's sociodemographic characteristics. Luckily, the US collects data from crime victimization surveys as well (the National Crime Victimization Survey), so one can look instead at people's self-reports of crime involvement. Those data suggest that the chances of being the victim of a violent crime are twice as high among the poorest households (earning under $25,000 per year) than among the richest (above $200,000).

96. This section draws in large part on Han, Meyer, and Sullivan, "Who Is Poor, How Poverty Has Changed, and Why It Matters."

97. In 1973, the share of people who said their apartment's heating unit had broken down at some point in the winter was 8.3 percent; by 2019 that figure was

down to 2.5 percent. The share of people who reported a leaky roof went from 7.6 percent to 4.4 percent, and the share of people in overcrowded apartments (more than one person per room) went from nearly 6 percent to under 2 percent. See Eggers and Thackeray, *32 Years of Housing Data*. See also Moura, Smith, and Belzer, "120 Years of U.S. Residential Housing Stock and Floor Space"; and "American Housing Survey."

98. Beall and McNary, "Nearly 90% of U.S. Households Used Air Conditioning in 2020."

99. In 1960, 22 percent of Americans had no cars, a figure that had declined to around 8.3 percent by 2020. See "Percentage of Households by Number of Vehicles, 1960–2020."

100. The official poverty measure also ignores the ability of at least some people to draw on savings to tide them over during bad times, which is important because most people who experience poverty are temporarily poor rather than permanently poor. See, for example, the analysis of longitudinal tax data by Larrimore, Mortenson, and Splinter ("Presence and Persistence of Poverty in U.S. Tax Data"). They find that over a twelve-year period, one in ten people is poor at a given point in time, but one in four will be in poverty at some point over that period. Among those who were poor at any point in the twelve years, on average they will spend three of these years in poverty. The other problem with the official poverty measure is how it accounts for inflation and overstates how the cost of buying a minimum bundle of stuff to live on has grown over time. It turns out that even small differences in how year-to-year inflation is measured lead to major differences when aggregated over several decades. The original poverty measure was defined as the cost of buying some given bundle of basic goods. Several blue-ribbon commissions have argued that the price adjustment baked into the official poverty rate overstates the increase in cost of buying some given bundle of goods, because holding the bundle of goods constant ignores the fact that in the real world, people adjust to rising prices by shifting from goods whose prices are increasing relatively more quickly to those whose prices are increasing relatively more slowly. The regular poverty rate also gets its price data just from "regular" stores and ignores the rise of big-box discount stores.

101. See for example Han, Meyer, and Sullivan, "Who Is Poor"; and Trisi and Saenz, "Economic Security Programs Reduce Overall Poverty, Racial and Ethnic Inequities." Bergant, Medici, and Weber ("Winning the War?") argue that prices have actually risen differently for the poor vs. the rich, and so argue that the price adjustments made in the different studies by Bruce Meyer and Jim Sullivan overstate declines in poverty over time. That argument depends on studies that use retail-scanner data to look at what people actually buy, a literature that seems to have somewhat mixed results across different studies. In a recent review, Fitzgerald and Moffitt ("The Supplemental Poverty Measure") argue that poverty has not declined very much over time, but that review seems to largely sidestep the question of the right price deflator to use.

102. Sutherland and Cressy, *Principles of Criminology*.

103. Fishback, Johnson, and Kantor, "Striking at the Roots of Crime."

104. In fairness, the elasticity of murder with respect to relief spending is not that

different in size overall compared to the estimated elasticities for property crime (Fishback, Johnson, and Kantor, "Striking at the Roots of Crime," table 2), the main difference being that the murder elasticity is estimated less precisely. But if we look at things not in elasticity terms but in standard-deviation units (focusing on the point estimates themselves, not the standard errors here), a one-standard deviation increase in relief spending reduces property crimes by 0.275 standard deviations but by only 0.076 standard deviations for murder.

105. Foley, "Welfare Payments and Crime."

106. Deshpande and Mueller-Smith, "Does Welfare Prevent Crime?" The international data seems to show a more mixed pattern. Meloni ("Does Poverty Relief Spending Reduce Crime?") looks at the effects of a change in welfare spending in Argentina and finds no detectable impacts on murders. (One might worry that in this study the main estimating equation on page 32 does not seem to include either time or jurisdiction fixed effects, but appendix table 3A controls for lagged explanatory variables, which intuitively is in the same spirit as controlling for jurisdiction fixed effects.) Giulietti and McConnell ("Kicking You When You're Already Down") look at the effect of a broader set of austerity reforms in the UK in 2012, which affected welfare spending but also seems to have affected all sorts of other types of government spending as well; they do find changes in violent crime. But D'Este and Harvey ("The Unintended Consequences of Welfare Reform"), who look at a more narrowly targeted 2019 welfare reform in the UK, find changes in burglaries but not violent crimes. Chioda, De Mello, and Soares ("Spillovers from Conditional Cash Transfer Programs") look at the effects of a conditional cash transfer program in Brazil and find a reduction in violent crimes, although it might be noted that the result is statistically significant at just the 10 percent cutoff, with no apparent correction made for the fact that this result is presented alongside (in their table 4) six other types of crime. It is possible that the importance of income motivation for serious violence is different across different countries; for example, it could be that more murders are motivated by wars between drug-selling gangs in some countries, or that robberies (an income-motivated crime that is usually classified as a violent crime) account for a relatively larger share of all violent crimes in some countries than others.

107. Rossi, Berk, and Lenihan, *Money, Work, and Crime*. The average weekly wages for those working in the study were $148 in Texas and $110 in Georgia. The average financial support under the Transitional Aid Research Project (TARP) equaled $63 per week in Texas and $70 in Georgia (Rossi, Berk, and Lenihan, *Money, Work, and Crime*, 9, 3).

108. The researchers applied some structural modeling to try to separate out impacts on those who were versus were not disincentivized to work by the cash payments, and they claimed to find some impact on those who weren't disincentivized, but this analysis is nonexperimental and so it's hard to know what to exactly make of it. See also Berk, Lenihan, and Rossi, "Crime and Poverty." Mallar and Thornton ("Transitional Aid for Released Prisoners") examine a smaller-scale experiment of around four hundred ex-inmates in Baltimore called LIFE. The inmates were selected to be at elevated risk for property

(theft) crimes specifically, and the analysis focuses on recidivism for income-motivated crimes (robbery, burglary, auto theft, and larceny). They do find a reduction in these income-motivated crimes in their study.

109. Redcross et al. (*More Than a Job*, table ES.1) report "hints" of a reduction in misdemeanor convictions (relatively more minor crimes) in the New York City CEO demonstration. I say "hints" because the estimated decline in misdemeanor convictions is statistically significant at the 10 percent level if we treat that as the only test carried out in the study. But they actually examined at least thirteen different recidivism-related outcomes in the study. A follow-up transitional jobs study, the Transitional Jobs Re-Entry Demonstration (Jacobs, "Returning to Work after Prison"), found no statistically impacts on any sort of crime, which might mean that the initial CEO results were false positives (spurious results from looking at lots of different outcomes). In any case, neither study found detectable impacts on the type of crime that gun violence would be classified as: felonies.

Bollinger and Yelowitz ("Targeting Intensive Job Assistance to Ex-Offenders by the Nature of Offense") show that intensive job-placement assistance reduces recidivism for ex-offenders who were imprisoned for a non-violent crime, but not for those who had been imprisoned for a violent crime, although it is worth noting that the sample size is modest so the risk of false negative results for the violent-crime-offender subsample is nontrivial. Cook et al. ("An Experimental Evaluation of a Comprehensive Employment-Oriented Prisoner Re-Entry Program") look at an intensive re-entry program in Milwaukee and find hints of a decline in rearrest rates, but do not look at rearrests for different types of crime. Some studies (like Rossman et al., *Confronting Relapse and Recidivism*) look at the combined effects of employment with other services, and also find no detectable effects on recidivism, although the sample size is modest so the risk of a false negative is nontrivial. Other studies look at job training programs for ex-offenders, which do not directly increase income but could in principle wind up increasing income if the training were able to improve employment rates and earnings. Unfortunately, these studies are often plagued by some combination of small sample sizes (creating a high risk of false negative) and weak research design; see, for example, Anderson and Schumacker, "Assessment of Job Training Programs"; and Costopoulos et al., "The Impact of US Government Assistance on Recidivism." Uggen ("Work as a Turning Point in the Life Course of Criminals") looks at data from the National Supported Work Demonstration program and finds a reduction in recidivism for offenders 27 and older but not for younger ones; however, he does not seem to examine recidivism separately by type of crime, so we cannot tell if there is any impact on violence specifically.

110. See Yang, "Local Labor Markets and Criminal Recidivism"; and Yang, "Does Public Assistance Reduce Recidivism?" Results by separate crime type from personal communication, Jens Ludwig and Crystal Yang, October 4, 2021.

111. Agan and Makowsky, "The Minimum Wage, EITC, and Criminal Recidivism."

112. The degree to which an in-kind benefit gets people to consume more of that thing will depend in part on how much the person is spending on that thing initially. Imagine, for instance, that someone gets $500 in food-stamp benefits

per month, and set aside for the moment the possibility that someone could potentially "sell" their food stamps to someone else for cash. If the person is spending more than $500 per month on food initially, they could in principle just take the cash they would have spent on food absent the food stamps and devote that money to something else entirely—that is, they could in principle take the whole food stamp subsidy in the form of something else other than food. If the person was spending only $200 per month on food initially, the person would be able to take part of the subsidy in the form of higher consumption of something other than food, and part of the subsidy would necessarily come in the form of increased food consumption.

113. Tuttle, "Snapping Back." Similarly, Luallen, Edgerton and Rabideau ("A Quasi-Experimental Evaluation of the Impact of Public Assistance on Prisoner Recidivism") look at the same eligibility elimination but find no effect on recidivism.

114. Carr and Packham ("SNAP Benefits and Crime") focus on overall crime and property crimes; in private correspondence, Jillian Carr tells me that there is some effect on robbery (not surprising given the income motivation for that crime, which happens to be classified as violence) but not on assault (which accounts for most violent crimes). Personal communication, Jens Ludwig and Jillian Carr, November 1, 2022.

115. Jacob, Kapustin, and Ludwig, "The Impact of Housing Assistance on Child Outcomes"; and Carr and Koppa, "Housing Vouchers, Income Shocks and Crime."

116. Palmer, Phillips, and Sullivan, "Does Emergency Financial Assistance Reduce Crime?" Carr and Packham ("SNAP Benefits and Crime") use the timing of food-stamp delivery across the month to show that these benefits reduce domestic violence and child maltreatment. Aizer ("The Gender Wage Gap and Domestic Violence") found declines in domestic violence from improvements in labor-market opportunities for females in the US. Rose ("The Effects of Job Loss on Crime") links administrative earnings records to arrests for a population of 340,000 criminal offenders in Washington State and finds an increase in domestic-violence offenses following job loss, as well as a protective effect of unemployment insurance.

117. Elisa Jácome at Northwestern looked at what happens when people lose access to Medicaid, the government health-insurance program for low-income Americans. She collected data from a state that makes Medicaid available to children (under 19) but not adults, and then compares what happens to arrests to people who are on Medicaid as children and then lose Medicaid as they turn 19, to the arrest patterns she sees in the data for people who were also low-income in the same state but not on Medicaid as children, and so for whom turning 19 doesn't change Medicaid receipt status. Losing Medicaid causes involvement in every type of crime to rise—including violent crimes (Jácome, "Mental Health and Criminal Involvement"). That effect seems to be concentrated among people with a recent history of mental illness. A different study found that an 8 percent increase in mental-health providers reduced violent crime by 2.3 percent (Deza, Maclean, and Solomon, "Local Access to Mental Healthcare and Crime").

118. See Heller, "Summer Jobs Reduce Violence among Disadvantaged Youth,"

for Chicago results; and Modestino, "How Do Summer Youth Employment Programs Improve Criminal Justice Outcomes, and for Whom?," for results from Boston. Gelber, Isen, and Kessler ("The Effects of Youth Employment") find that the youth summer jobs program in New York reduces likelihood of incarceration as well as reducing mortality rates from external causes, such as homicide. Kessler et al. ("The Effects of Youth Employment on Crime") find a reduction in the New York summer jobs program for teens in felony crime arrests; the estimated effect on violent-crime arrests is negative but not quite statistically significant, while there is a large (75 percent), statistically significant reduction in convictions for violent-crime arrests.

119. Akee et al., "Parents' Incomes and Children's Outcomes."
120. Freedman and Owens, "Your Friends and Neighbors."
121. Raphael and Winter-Ebmer, "Identifying the Effect of Unemployment on Crime."
122. Pinker, *Better Angels*, 675–76.
123. See the discussion in Ruhm, "Recessions, Healthy No More?"
124. Ruhm, "Are Recessions Good for Your Health?"
125. The figure presents the results for only forty-two of Chicago's seventy-seven community areas, to increase readability of the graph; the pattern with all seventy-seven neighborhoods is qualitatively similar. Data sources: Chicago Data Portal Victims of Homicides and Non-Fatal Shootings (2016–2020) (https://data.cityofchicago.org/browse?category=Public+Safety&limitTo=datasets); Chicago Metropolitan Agency for Planning (2016–2020 five-year American Community Survey data) (https://www.cmap.illinois.gov/data/community-snapshots#Chicago_neighborhood_data_2017). Each community area's median household income was taken from the individual community area reports. My thanks to Javier Lopez for creating this graph.
126. Sources: Population data: World Bank, "Population Estimates and Projections"; GDP data: International Monetary Fund, "GDP Based on PPP, Share of World"; Country-level homicide data: FBI (USA); Anuario Brasileiro de Segurança Publica (Brazil); Respective National Statistical Office (Yemen and Mexico); Respective National Police (China, Uganda, Malawi); Respective Ministry of Interior (India, Japan); National Criminal Justice Data as Collected through the United Nations Surveys on Crime Trends and the Operations of Criminal Justice Systems (UN-CTS) (Cameroon, Indonesia, Sweden, Austria, Russia, Honduras, Sudan); Data based on a statistical modification of an original value by UNODC (UK and Nigeria). Thanks to Alejandro Roemer for creating this figure.
127. Verdugo, "Drug Gang Kills 20 in Town Hall Massacre in Southern Mexico."
128. See the results presented in Bunten, Kendall-Taylor, and Lindland, *Caning, Context and Class*, 7. A different angle on this sentiment was expressed in an op-ed by a city resident in the *Chicago Tribune*: "Public safety is essential to a functioning society—on this, we all agree. Yet we find ourselves in crisis . . . Many of our local representatives have simply echoed a common theme—a focus on fighting the root causes of crime. We all agree that this must be done and are supportive of those efforts. However, what we desperately need are clear actions, not a discussion of old thoughts and ideas that at best will take years, if not decades,

to make any difference" (Reinhardt, "An Uptick in Robberies Has Made Chicagoans Feel Unsafe").

129. Boyle, "On Being with Krista Tippett."
130. Ahmad, "Arne Duncan on Violence Prevention in Chicago."
131. Havel, *Disturbing the Peace*.

CHAPTER FIVE

1. Novak, "Vanecko's Life after the Punch, Moved to Hollywood."
2. Webb, *Death of David Koschman*, 109.
3. Cited in Webb, *Death of David Koschman*.
4. Webb, *Death of David Koschman*, 131.
5. Razzell and Spence, "The History of Infant, Child and Adult Mortality in London, 1550–1850."
6. Bryson, *At Home*.
7. Brosco, "The Early History of the Infant Mortality Rate in America."
8. This point is hard to determine exactly because the UK is one of the few places for which we have life expectancy data going all the way back (to the mid-sixteenth century in the case of the UK). But for the other places where we do start to see life expectancy data available, starting around 1800, the UK almost always has a higher life expectancy at that point in time. See Dattani et al., "Life Expectancy."
9. Brosco, "Early History of the Infant Mortality Rate."
10. Brosco, "Early History of the Infant Mortality Rate," 481.
11. Pozzi and Farinas, "Infant and Child Mortality in the Past," 56.
12. See Centers for Disease Control and Prevention, "Achievements in Public Health, 1900–1999," on the importance of pasteurized milk and antimicrobials. For data on the doubling of life expectancy around the world since around 1900, see Dattani et al., "Life Expectancy."
13. Skelley and Fuong, "How Democrats and Republicans Think Differently about Crime and Gun Violence."
14. There really are people who in brain scans seem to have different frontal lobes (the part of the brain that controls higher-order cognitive tasks like executive functioning) due to a combination of genetic factors and traumatic events during early childhood. The result is a constant need for stimulation, parasitic social relationships, lack of empathy, a grandiose sense of themselves, pathological lying, failure to feel remorse or guilt, refusal to take responsibility for anything, signs of problem behavior early in life (including cruelty to animals), and engagement in antisocial or violent behavior for most of their lives. Estimates suggest that around 1 percent of US males fit this definition of psychopath, though most psychopaths are of course not serial killers (Kiehl and Hoffman, "Criminal Psychopath").
15. Girdwain, "11 Movies and TV Shows about Ted Bundy to Watch after 'Falling for a Killer."
16. Main, "Gun Used in Hyde Park-to-Evanston Killing Spree Likely Used in Prior South Side Shootings."

17. CWB Chicago, "Chicago Spree Killer Jason Nightengale Police Stop."
18. Villagomez, "University of Chicago Scholar Killed in Shooting Spree Remembered as 'a Kind Individual and an Extraordinary Student.'"
19. Barron and Tabor, "17 Killed, and a Life Is Searched for Clues."
20. See, for example, Martens, "The Problem with Robert Hare's Psychopathy Checklist." See also Blais, Forth, and Hare ("Examining the Interrater Reliability of the Hare Psychopathy Checklist"), who note that the degree to which measures of psychopathy have different predictive power than measures of antisocial personality disorder winds up depending a lot on what specific outcome is being predicted. They also note that the level of agreement of raters in carrying out psychopathy measurement, the so-called intra-class correlation, can be low for many of the items in the most widely used psychopathy checklist.
21. Police only arrest a suspect in about half of all murders in the US, and for nonfatal shootings, in cities like Chicago the figure can be as low as one in ten or even one in twenty. And then only about half of all murder arrests lead to any prison time at all, with a far lower rate for nonfatal shootings—perhaps as low as one in twenty-five (Neal and Rick, "Prison Boom and Sentencing Policy").
22. On the one hand, to the extent to which psychopaths select their victims randomly, their cases might be particularly hard for the police to solve (with the same logic for why domestic violence homicides are among the easiest for police to solve). On the other hand, psychopaths could be overrepresented among the murderers who wind up in prison if their repeat offending leads to long criminal histories, since prior record is a key determinant of whether and how long someone is sentenced to prison. See Shen et al., "Locking Up My Generation."
23. See Kiehl and Hoffman, "Criminal Psychopath." This figure is not specific to people in prison for violent offenses; across all state prisons in the US, about half of inmates at a point in time are incarcerated for violent crimes, and there is some suggestion that psychopaths seem to be overrepresented in violent crime relative to nonviolent crimes (Cornell et al., "Psychopathy in Instrumental and Reactive Violent Offenders"). On the other hand, as noted below, the share of violent crimes that result in the arrest of a suspect is low (as is the likelihood that an arrest results in prison time, especially for violent crimes that are less serious than murder), and criminologists believe that many criminal offenders engage in what is called "cafeteria-style offending"—they commit a little bit of multiple types of crime, rather than specializing in just a single type of crime. That means that even people in prison for a nonviolent offense may have some history of involvement in violence, whether that history shows up on their prior criminal record or not. Consistent with this hypothesis, Kuziemko and Levitt ("An Empirical Analysis of Imprisoning Drug Offenders") find that the likelihood of committing a new violent-crime arrest after release from prison is similar for people who are incarcerated for either violent crimes or property crimes or drug offenses.
24. Data from the National Violent Death Reporting System, a collection of vital-statistics data from around the country, suggests that 82,463 people in the US were killed at the hands of others from 2003 through 2017. Of those, 74,623, or 90 percent, died as part of single-victim homicides. See Fowler et al., "Ex-

amining Differences between Mass, Multiple, and Single-Victim Homicides to Inform Prevention."

25. Morton, *Serial Murder*.

26. Note that the key question here is *not* "What share of the population accounts for what share of the gun violence that happened last year?" If the murder rate is, say, 1 in 1,000, at the end of the year when we look back on that year's crimes of course just 0.1 percent of the population will have accounted for all the murders. The question instead is whether the ex-ante risk of being involved in gun violence in the future is highly concentrated. Is this murder rate of 1 in 1,000 due to one person having a 100 percent chance of committing a murder in the next year and the other 999 people having a 0 percent chance? But if gun violence is committed often by "normal people" in difficult situations, the ex-ante risk should be more diffuse; is the 1-in-1,000 murder rate due to a thousand people all having an equal 0.1 percent risk of committing murder?

27. For example, as Northwestern sociologist Andrew Papachristos put it, "a small proportion of individuals are at the center of gun violence within any given community—and by small I mean a couple of hundred people in a community of tens of thousands" (quoted in Berman, "Violence Is Contagious").

28. The problem with the data on offenders is that the police make arrests in just a small share of all shootings in Chicago, so whom we have arrest data on is not necessarily representative. The researchers (Heller et al., "Machine Learning Can Predict Shooting Victimization Well Enough to Help Prevent It") look at victims instead, capitalizing on the fact that risk of offending and victimization seem highly correlated.

29. This observation isn't a criticism of their study, since they were trying to answer a slightly different one from the one I'm trying to answer here.

30. To carry out this analysis, we combine two different sources of data. We start with the dataset assembled by Heller et al. ("Machine Learning)." This dataset uses demographic information and prior-criminal-record data to predict gunshot victimization risk over an eighteen-month period for everyone in Chicago who has a prior record. The analysis focuses on predicting gunshot victimization, rather than offending, because the rate at which shooters are arrested in Chicago is not very high (as low as 5 percent or 10 percent for nonfatal shootings), while it is widely believed that law enforcement finds out about most shooting victimizations. In practice it is widely believed that offending and victimization risk overlap strongly. In this dataset we have not only who is shot and the person's prior characteristics, but a machine-learning-based prediction of risk of shooting victimization. (We use a version of that prediction that excludes geographic information—the predictions in Heller et al. include beat information as predictors, but our version used here does not.) To that data we append information on shooting victimizations for the general public in Chicago within each of the city's seventy-seven community areas ("neighborhoods"), for demographic groups defined by age, race/ethnicity, and gender. We create victimization counts for those without criminal records by subtracting out shooting victimizations for those in the Heller et al. dataset within each neighborhood and demographic group (recognizing there is some noise in the data about which community area people live in). When we use data on people

of all ages and genders and regress shooting victimization against demographics, prior predicted risk based on criminal histories (using the machine learning
predictions from Heller et al. for those with prior records, and using zero for
everyone else), and community area, the R^2 is .231; community-area fixed effects alone yield an R^2 of .117. If we redo the analysis but now focus on the age
and gender group at highest risk for gun violence involvement, men 15–34, the
R^2 values are .491 and .384, respectively—that is, most of the risk for this group
is between and not within neighborhoods. This last calculation to me feels like
the answer to the question of whether it's possible to walk into a neighborhood
and pick out the few dozen people at highest risk for gun violence involvement.
We know from the citywide data that those people will likely be young men.
But this analysis suggests that most of the information about who is likely to be
shot comes simply from knowing what neighborhood you are in. (My thanks to
Alejandro Roemer for his amazing work on these calculations.)

31. See Blattman et al., "Place-Based Interventions at Scale."
32. Rosenberg-Douglas and Goodman, "'I Arrived a Few Minutes Too Late,' Says
Doctor Who Tried to Save International Student Killed in Hyde Park."
33. "University of Chicago Graduate Who Was Shot and Killed in Robbery Is Identified as Dennis Shaoxiong Zheng."
34. Horng, "Man Charged with Murder of University of Chicago Graduate Killed
in Hyde Park Shooting."
35. Struett and Kenney, "Violent Death of Chinese Student in Hyde Park Sparks
Calls for Action."
36. "Man Charged with Murder in Killing of UChicago Graduate in Hyde Park."
37. Belanger, "Shaoxiong 'Dennis' Zheng Remembered as 'Not Only a Promising
Scholar, but a Wonderful Person' at Memorial Service."
38. Issa, "Man, 27, Dies after Being Shot in Humboldt Park."
39. See, for example, Harlow, *Robbery Victims*.
40. Compared to the average non-robbery murder in Chicago, which on average
gets between four and five articles and 1,336 words of total coverage, the average robbery-murder gets between seven and eight articles and 1,972 words of
total coverage—or nearly 50 percent more. The sample frame comes from the
Chicago Sun-Times archive of 2018 Chicago murders. Our research team took
the first and last robbery-related murder of every month, and the first and last
non-robbery murder of every month, so twenty-four murders total of each
type. We then did an Internet search for each of these murders to count the
total number of news articles and words published for each, and then averaged
over the two murder-motive categories.
41. In Chicago, the figure is 9 percent for the most recent year for which data are
available (2021) and 10 percent if we look at the average over the 2010–2021
period (among murders where some cause is known). The FBI UCR puts this
number closer to 6 percent for 2019, the last year before the pandemic. In the
Supplemental Homicide Reports for the US as a whole, the share is 7.4 percent
for 2018 and 9.7 percent for the period 2010–2018. The figure was closer to 6
percent as reported by Cook ("Robbery"), but that figure may be calculated
among all murders, not just those for which the police believe they have some
idea of the motive or circumstance.

42. Data from 2018 from the National Crime Victimization Survey (NCVS) suggests that 17 percent of robberies involve a gun; the average figure for the 1993–2018 period is 23 percent. See Kena and Truman, *Trends and Patterns in Firearm Violence, 1993–2018*. On the other hand, data from the FBI's Uniform Crime Report system, of robberies reported to the police, suggest that something like 30 percent of robberies are committed with a gun (about eighty thousand); see FBI, "Table 19—Rate: Number of Crimes per 100,000 Inhabitants."

43. We can see the victim compliance in the robbery success rates. Of all robberies, 66 percent are successful from the perspective of the offender (the victim complies); of robberies with guns, the figure is 79 percent. These figures are for the period 1993–2001 from the NCVS; see Perkins, *Weapon Use and Violent Crime*.

44. See Maxfield, "Circumstances in Supplementary Homicide Reports."

45. Cornell et al., "Psychopathy in Instrumental and Reactive Violent Offenders," 788.

46. Sanchez, "I Wasn't Trying to Kill Her.'"

47. Main, "Goonie Gang Terrorized Englewood, Bragged on Facebook, Made Goonie Gang T-Shirts, Feds Say."

48. Sweeney and Meisner, "Federal Authorities Announce Sweeping Conspiracy Case against Chicago Street Gang Involving 19 Slayings."

49. "Daley Pursuing Anti-Gang Law."

50. McClelland, "Rahm Emanuel Has Not Been Good for Chicago."

51. Laurence, "Lightfoot's Plan to Sue Gang Members for Assets Clears Key Committee Hurdle, but Could Face a Tight Vote at City Council."

52. Gorner, "'We're Going After Gangs.'"

53. Some of the questions that come up in this debate include: Is a gang just any group of young people who have a name and sometimes engage in crime? Or do they have to be brought together explicitly for the purposes of carrying out some sort of organized crime activities? How organized does the group need to be exactly to count as a gang? See, for example, the excellent review of these debates in Decker, Pyrooz, and Densley, *On Gangs*.

54. Drug Enforcement Agency and Chicago Police Department, *Cartels and Gangs in Chicago*.

55. US Attorney's Office, Northern District of Illinois, "Leader of Violent Chicago Street Gang Convicted on Federal Racketeering Charge."

56. See, for example, Police Executive Research Forum, *New National Commitment Required*; and "Synthetic Identity Theft."

57. Beyond the federal indictments of key gang leaders, also relevant may have been ongoing wars between rival gangs, as well as changing attitudes by young people toward the economic deal (or, in some people's view, exploitation) that the leaders of drug-selling gangs offered younger members, as well as all the rules and hierarchical control that came with that deal; see Levitt and Venkatesh, "An Economic Analysis of a Drug-Selling Gang's Finances"; Drug Enforcement Agency and Chicago Police Department, *Cartels and Gangs in Chicago*; and Aspholm, *Views from the Streets*.

58. See, for example, Aspholm, *Views from the Streets*; Chavis, "Problems with Chicago's Gang-Centric Narrative of Gun Violence"; and Drug Enforcement Agency and Chicago Police Department, *Cartels and Gangs in Chicago*.

59. From Chicago Police Department, *2011 Chicago Murder Analysis*, corresponding to either gangland narcotics (26) or narcotics-territorial (3). The police department has changed their classification system in subsequent years in a way that makes it harder to tease out what the motivation is exactly for violence that involves gang members.

60. Cook et al., "Underground Gun Markets."

61. Aspholm, *Views from the Streets*.

62. Kapustin et al., *Gun Violence in Chicago, 2016*.

63. Main, "Rapper King Von's Killing Puts a Spotlight on Chicago Gang Ties to Atlanta."

64. Or, in the words of one reporter, "the kind of petty discrepancy that could have easily been talked through" (Gee, "Lil Durk vs. NBA YoungBoy Is More Than Rap Beef")

65. See Miethe, Regoeczi, and Drass, *Rethinking Homicide*, 103; and Block and Christakos, "Intimate Partner Homicide in Chicago over 29 Years."

66. Chavis, "Problems with Chicago's Gang-Centric Narrative."

67. See McVeigh, "Chicago Hip-Hop Feud Deepens after Death of Joseph 'Lil Jojo' Coleman" for details of the murder; for the hypothesis that he was killed by Lamron, see *Chicago Gang Index Wiki*, s.v. "Deceased Gang Members," last edited April 25, 2024, https://chicago-gang-index.fandom.com/wiki/Deceased _Gang_Members.

68. This type of naming of a specific rival gang was relatively new in Chicago's drill rap scene ("drill" being a slang term for gun violence). As Lil JoJo's younger brother John "Swagg Dinero" Coleman later said in an interview, "He [Lil JoJo] didn't really wanna rap until he heard Lil Dirk's song L's anthem. This on the radio fool, know what I'm saying? You driving around, you hearing about fuck us on the radio, man he went crazy." See Djvlad, "Swagg Dinero on Lil Jojo's 'BDK' Starting War in Chicago."

69. Maybe surprisingly, one of the most detailed documentaries of the back-and-forth here is from a London-based YouTuber named Trap Lore Ross; see Ross, *Trap Lore Ross on "Gangs of Chicago – 300 vs JoJo World."*

70. Meisner, "Founder of Chicago's 'Goonie Gang' Tells Federal Jury How It Morphed into Violent Faction Responsible for at Least 10 Slayings."

71. Cobe Williams, interview by Megan Kang, March 6, 2020, interview transcript shared privately with author.

72. Aspholm, *Views from the Streets*.

73. Data sources: University of Chicago Crime Lab analysis of confidential Chicago Police Department crime data, as well as Homicides in Chicago Dataset 1965–1995, assembled by Carolyn Block and Richard Block (ICPSR 6399). See Block, Block, and Illinois Criminal Justice Information Authority, "Homicides in Chicago, 1965–1995." The Chicago PD data have changed their classification systems over time; in the 2011 Chicago PD data, for example, "street gang altercation" accounted for 38 percent of the murders where police could determine a motive, separate from gangland narcotics (Chicago Police Department, *2011 Chicago Murder Analysis*). In the 2021 Chicago PD report on crime overall, which provides less rich detail about murder motives compared to previous murder reports (and does not break out gangland narcotics–related murders separately), 49 percent of murders where a motive is known were attributed to

what the department is now calling "gang-related altercation" (Chicago Police Department, *2021 Annual Report*). Thanks to Alejandro Roemer, Biz Rasich, and Kate Daugherty for creating this figure.

74. The *Sun-Times* includes links to articles written at the time of the murder itself; my research team then also did Internet searches to see if we could learn anything about the motive over time as suspects may have been arrested and brought to trial, etc.

75. There are some cases where, for instance, there might be a hint in the news story about motive; that some of the people involved, say, were in gangs. But we don't actually know what role the gang affiliation played in the shooting, if any. I return to this point below.

76. These data come from the Milwaukee Homicide Review Commission, which brings together the police, the prosecutor, and social-services providers to carry out after every shooting what you might call a "social autopsy"—to go back and figure out what happened and at what points along the sequence leading up to the event the city or local nonprofits could have intervened to prevent it. See "Milwaukee Homicide Review Commission."

77. "An Anatomy of Hard Times in the City."

78. Zimring, "Is Gun Control Likely to Reduce Violent Killings?"

79. Black, "Crime as Social Control," 36.

80. The original categorization is often attributed to Feshbach, "The Function of Aggression and the Regulation of Aggressive Drive." A useful current discussion of these issues is in Miethe, Regoeczi, and Drass, *Rethinking Homicide*. Carolyn Block, Richard Block, and the Illinois Criminal Justice Information Authority, as part of their classification of the motives of Chicago murders from 1965 to 1995, offer their own definition: *Expressive* murders include fights, brawls, or other murders where the offender's goal is not money but to "hurt, kill, or maim either the actual victim or someone else," while *instrumental* murders are defined as murders where the "offender's immediate and primary goal was to obtain money or property (e.g., robbery, burglary, attempted theft, blackmail, deceptive practice, insurance fraud, arson for profit, contract killing, random, drug business, organized crime)" ("Homicides in Chicago, 1965–1995").

81. See Miethe, Regoeczi, and Drass, *Rethinking Homicide*.

82. See Jones et al., "How Many Child Deaths Can We Prevent This Year?," 68.

83. Morgan and Thompson, *Criminal Victimization, 2020*.

84. The FBI in 2019 recorded 15,586 murders, 90,178 rapes, 408,016 robberies, and 911,706 aggravated assaults. (There are many, many more simple assaults that do not involve either injury to the victim or use of a weapon.)

85. Pinker, *Better Angels*, 83.

86. Webb, *Death of David Koschman*, 34.

CHAPTER SIX

1. Duncker, "On Problem-Solving," 23.

2. Chaiken and Trope, *Dual-Process Theories in Social Psychology*; Gawronski and Creighton, "Dual Process Theories;" and Kahneman, *Thinking, Fast and Slow*

provide excellent reviews of the history and state of so-called dual process theories in psychology. See also Nisbett and Wilson, "Telling More Than We Can Know;" Gilbert, "How Mental Systems Believe;" Haidt, "The Emotional Dog and Its Rational Tail;" Jacoby, "A Process Dissociation Framework"; Bargh, "The Four Horsemen of Automaticity"; and Kahneman and Frederick, "A Model of Heuristic Judgment." The two systems are also sometimes referred to as implicit versus explicit, or fast or automatic or intuitive versus deliberate. Wilson (*Strangers to Ourselves*) calls automatic or System 1 thought the "adaptive unconscious."

3. Some uncertainty and debate remain about the exact sequence of events. It was the Cook County prosecutor's office that claimed Hood texted her son and instructed him to come into the store (see, for example, Alund, "Chicago Mom Accused of Telling Son to Shoot Man Sues Police after Murder Charges Dropped"). Initial reports claim she also ordered her son to shoot Jeremy Brown. But later a video was released, taken by another customer on their cellphone, showing that she seems to say "Get in the car" (presumably speaking to her son, who was standing behind Brown in the doorway of Maxwell Street Express) before Brown punches her again; the video ends just at the sound of what appears to be a gunshot ("Video Shows Moments before Mom Allegedly Encouraged Teen Son to Shoot Man in Chicago Restaurant"). The police also later released a compilation of video excerpts from surveillance video at the store ("Mother Allegedly Orders 14-Year-Old Son to Shoot Man at Fast Food Restaurant"). For the purposes of understanding why shootings like this one happen, whether she texted her son to come into the store or not is less essential than the decision her son faced in that difficult situation, and how he might have navigated it.

4. See Evans, "Dual-Processing Accounts of Reasoning, Judgment, and Social Cognition," table 1.

5. Kahneman credits the term to Keith Stanovich and Richard West.

6. This kind of thinking is sometimes called the C-system; see Lieberman, "Social Cognitive Neuroscience."

7. Hasell et al., "Poverty."

8. Dunbar, "The Social Brain Hypothesis"; Aiello and Wheeler, "The Expensive-Tissue Hypothesis."

9. Aiello and Wheeler, "Expensive-Tissue Hypothesis."

10. See, for example, Tomasello, "The Ultra-Social Animal."

11. In these studies, general intelligence about the physical world is measured by asking the primates (chimpanzees and orangutangs) and children to distinguish larger from smaller quantities of food or small toys. To measure social intelligence, the experimenter puts a treat (food or a toy) under one of two different plastic cups; the experimenter looks at the cup that has the treat and then sees if the study subject takes the social cue and picks that cup. See Herrmann et al., "Humans Have Evolved Specialized Skills of Social Cognition."

12. See, for example, Stanovich, "The Cognitive Miser."

13. Newman and Cain, "Tainted Altruism."

14. As I will discuss below, this case is an example of System 1 only considering whatever information is present in the moment—or what Kahneman (*Thinking, Fast and Slow*) calls "what you see is all there is" (WYSIATI).

15. This paragraph draws on Timothy Wilson's wonderful book *Strangers to Ourselves*.
16. See, for example, Evans, "Dual-Processing Accounts."
17. Kahneman, *Thinking, Fast and Slow*, 79–80.
18. Wilson, *Strangers to Ourselves*, 25.
19. System 1 relies on parts of the brain including the amygdala (which handles emotion), the basal ganglia (motor control), ventromedial prefrontal cortex (processing of things like risk and fear), lateral temporal cortex (hearing, visual processing), and dorsal anterior cingulate cortex (which helps regulate attention, motivation, error detection and performance monitoring, novelty detection, and reward assessment). See Lieberman, "Social Cognitive Neuroscience"; as well as Bush et al., "Dorsal Anterior Cingulate Cortex."
20. See Newell, "Duncker on Thinking."
21. As Beck, *Prisoners of Hate*, 29, put it: "Since each person is the vehicle for transferring his or her genes to the next generation, evolution has placed a priority on self-serving bias, acquisitiveness and self-defense."
22. Ross and Sicoly, "Egocentric Biases in Availability and Attribution."
23. Steiner, "Human Facial Expressions in Response to Taste and Smell Stimulation."
24. Beck, *Prisoners of Hate*, 61.
25. Rozin and Royzman, "Negativity Bias, Negativity Dominance, and Contagion."
26. Keysar et al., "Taking Perspective in Conversation." See also Lin, Keysar, and Epley, "Reflexively Mindblind"; and Epley et al., "Perspective Taking as Egocentric Anchoring and Adjustment."
27. Thanks to Ed O'Brien for steering me toward this quote and the next several examples in the next paragraph.
28. Bruner, "Going Beyond the Information Given."
29. This story is taken from Abelson, "Psychological Status of the Script Concept."
30. See Abelson, "Psychological Status," 717.
31. Ross, "From the Fundamental Attribution Error to the Truly Fundamental Attribution Error and Beyond."
32. Beck, *Prisoners of Hate*, 256.
33. Wilson, *Strangers to Ourselves*, 105.
34. See the discussion in Nisbett and Wilson, "Telling More Than We Can Know."
35. Nisbett and Wilson, "Telling More Than We Can Know," 244.
36. Dutton and Aron, "Some Evidence for Heightened Sexual Attraction under Conditions of High Anxiety."
37. This wonderful phrase comes from Wilson, *Strangers to Ourselves*, 50.
38. Griffin, Dunning and Ross, "The Role of Construal Processes in Overconfident Predictions about the Self and Others."
39. Beck, *Prisoners of Hate*, 39.
40. Shah, "Thinking Past the Situation."
41. Quoted in Ross, "From the Fundamental Attribution Error," 765.
42. Ross, "From the Fundamental Attribution Error."
43. See the wonderful discussion, for example, in Ross and Ward, "Psychological Barriers to Dispute Resolution."
44. Bargh and Chartrand, "Studying the Mind in the Middle;" and Chartrand and

Bargh, "Automatic Activation of Impression Formation and Memorization Goals."

45. Shantz and Latham, "An Exploratory Field Experiment of the Effect of Subconscious and Conscious Goals on Employee Performance."

46. Duncker, "On Problem-Solving"; see also Öllinger and Goel, "Problem Solving."

47. See, for example, Dodge, "Social-Cognitive Mechanisms in the Development of Conduct Disorder and Depression."

48. Rozin, Markwith, and Ross show the tendency of people to confuse the name with the referent, "to treat the name as a nonarbitrary equivalent of its referent" ("The Sympathetic Magical Law of Similarity, Nominal Realism and Neglect of Negatives in Response to Negative Labels, 383").

49. Rozin, Millman, and Nemeroff, "Operation of the Laws of Sympathetic Magic in Disgust and Other Domains."

50. "The Town of Pullman—Pullman National Historical Park."

51. Milan, "Carlishia Hood + Witness Who FILMED SPEAK OUT."

52. Milan, "Carlishia Hood + Witness."

53. "Crossing Guard Salary in Chicago, Illinois."

54. NBC Chicago, "Details on Dropped Charges against Mom, Teen Son in Chicago Restaurant Shooting."

55. See, for example, Wilkinson et al., "Peers and Gun Use among Urban Adolescent Males"; Hemenway et al., "Gun Carrying among Adolescents"; and Cook and Ludwig, "Does Gun Prevalence Affect Teen Gun Carrying after All?"

56. Hemenway et al. "Gun Carrying by High School Students in Boston, MA."

57. Saunders, "Carlishia Hood Accepts Nicki Minaj's Offer to Pay for Son's College Education Following Viral Chicago Attack."

58. Hookah Anonymous, "Jeremy Brown GF Wears 'KnockOut King' T-Shirts & Curse Out the Internet!!"

59. Kahneman, Thinking, Fast and Slow, 55.

60. Wilson, Strangers to Ourselves.

CHAPTER SEVEN

1. Gopnik, "Jane Jacobs's Street Smarts."
2. Rich, "The Prophecies of Jane Jacobs."
3. Rich, "Prophecies of Jane Jacobs."
4. Gopnik, "Jane Jacobs's Street Smarts."
5. Jacobs, Death and Life of Great American Cities, 31.
6. Jacobs, Death and Life of Great American Cities, 38–39.
7. Jacobs actually seems to have used "eyes on the street" specifically in the context of the importance of having homes and commercial buildings with windows facing out on the street so that people could observe what was happening; she distinguished that factor from also having people physically out in public on streets and sidewalks to intervene. For convenience, I will refer to both neighborhood factors as "eyes on the street" in what follows.
8. Sampson, Raudenbush, and Earls, "Neighborhoods and Violent Crime."

9. Between three and four thousand police officers are assigned to patrol in Chicago, depending on whether we define that status based on the official HR classification or based on some activity measure like responding to some minimum number of 911 calls for service over some period of time. If the average officer works eight 8-hour shifts per week, and the department has to staff (3 shifts/day x 7 days/week = 21) shifts per week, there will be not more than fifty to seventy patrol officers in a given district at a point in time, almost surely less if we account for vacations, illnesses, and other regular absences.

10. Gratz, "Milestones: 100 Years of Jane Jacobs."

11. According to University of Chicago Crime Lab calculations, South Shore has 447 business licenses spread out over its 2.99 square miles. Greater Grand Crossing has 439 business licenses spread out over 3.56 square miles. (My thanks to Khoa Nguyen for these calculations.)

12. The share of housing units with four bedrooms is nearly twice as high in Greater Grand Crossing as in South Shore (9.9 percent versus 6.8 percent), as is the share of apartments with five or more bedrooms (4 percent versus 1.9 percent). Taken from the Chicago Metropolitan Agency for Planning, *Greater Grand Crossing* and *South Shore*.

13. Bradford Hunt, in his wonderful book *Blueprint for Disaster*, noted that one plausible reason crime rates were so high in Chicago's high-rise public-housing complexes is because of the well-intentioned decision to prioritize construction of multiple-bedroom apartments to help meet the housing needs of larger families, who typically have a harder time finding apartments in the private-housing market. Hunt argues that that decision led to an unusually high ratio of children to adults in many of Chicago's public-housing developments.

14. Data collected by the Chicago Metropolitan Agency for Planning suggest that in Greater Grand Crossing, 20.3 percent of the population is age 5–19 and 37.3 percent is age 20–49, for a ratio of prime-age adults to youth of 1.83. In South Shore, 16.9 percent of the neighborhood is ages 5–19, while 42.1 percent of the neighborhood is 20–49, for a ratio of adults to kids of 2.49. Compared to South Shore, Greater Grand Crossing also has a much higher share of kids growing up in single-parent households (22.4 percent versus 13.3 percent). See Chicago Metropolitan Agency for Planning, *Greater Grand Crossing* and *South Shore*.

15. Sampson and Raudenbush, "Systematic Social Observation of Public Spaces," 610.

16. Chicago Transit Authority, *Annual Ridership Report*.

17. The website *Chicago's Million Dollar Blocks* provides information on total state spending on people sentenced to prison over a five-year period, 2005–2009. The website takes data on sentence lengths and converts that to a cost figure by assuming spending of $22,000 per inmate per year prison costs; I convert their figure back into person-years of prison sentences by dividing the five-year cost figure by $22,000, and then turn that into a per-year figure (rather than a per-five-year figure) by dividing by five. The data imply 5,625 person-years of incarceration handed out in South Shore over a five-year period, or 1,125 per year, in a neighborhood of 53,971 residents, for a rate of 2.1 per 100 residents. For Greater Grand Crossing there are 4,207 person-years of incarceration handed

out over five years, or 841 per year, in a neighborhood of just 31,471 people, for a rate of 2.7 per 100 residents. See "Chicago's Million Dollar Blocks: Full Map."

18. Shen et al., "Locking Up My Generation."

19. To measure people's willingness to call the police, ideally we'd like to look at the ratio of 911 calls to criminal events in each neighborhood. The challenge here is in measuring the denominator; how do we know when crime events happen other than by people calling the police? To overcome that problem, I take advantage of the fact that Chicago has installed a system of directional microphones across the city to detect gunshots, the so-called Shotspotter system. With those data I can calculate the ratio of 911 calls for shots fired to gunfire detected by Shotspotter microphones. That ratio—the willingness of people to call 911—is about half again as high in South Shore as in Greater Grand Crossing (0.23 versus 0.17) (personal correspondence with David Leitson, March 30, 2023). One might worry that Shotspotter measures gunshots with some error; in principle such an error shouldn't affect my calculation because there is no reason to believe it would be systematically different across neighborhoods. But as a check, I can also calculate the ratio of 911 calls for shots fired to actual shooting incidents, and that figure is also substantially higher in South Shore than in Greater Grand Crossing (14.4 versus 10.1). Simultaneous to this analysis, Ang et al. used a similar idea in their study "Community Engagement with Law Enforcement after High-Profile Acts of Police Violence."

20. This measure is closely related to the definition of collective efficacy suggested by Robert Sampson and Steve Raudenbush—a neighborhood's capacity to solve "the task of maintaining order in public spaces" ("Systematic Social Observation of Public Spaces," 613).

21. Taken from the Chicago Metropolitan Planning Agency, *South Shore* and *Greater Grand Crossing*.

22. Our research team analyzed 311 calls to request that the city clean up graffiti, covering the period 2019 to 2022. Calculating 311 calls per year per 1,000 residents, the figures for Greater Grand Crossing and South Shore equal 2.35 vs. 1.28 (2019), 3.4 versus 1.37 (2020), and 3.27 vs. 1.96 (2022). See City of Chicago, "311 Service Requests"; and Chicago Metropolitan Agency for Planning, "Community Data Snapshots 2023."

23. Using data on licensed businesses in Chicago, we find there were six liquor stores in South Shore, a neighborhood of 53,971 people in 2022, for a per-100,000 rate of 11.1. By comparison, Greater Grand Crossing has ten liquor stores for a neighborhood of 31,471 people, for a per-100,000 rate of 31.8. See City of Chicago, "Active Business Licenses."

24. See, for example, Hogarth, Lejarraga, and Soyer, "The Two Settings of Kind and Wicked Learning Environments."

25. Baumeister and Tierney, *Willpower*.

26. See Black, "Crime as Social Control"; Anderson, *Code of the Street*; and Papachristos, "Murder by Structure."

27. As Anderson (*Code of the Street*, 66–67) put it: "As the problems of the inner city have become ever more acute, as the public authorities have seemingly abdicated their responsibilities, many of those residing in such communities feel that they are on their own, that especially in matters of personal defense, they

must assume the primary responsibility. . . . In the most socially isolated pockets of the inner city, this situation has given rise to a kind of people's law based on a peculiar form of social exchange that is perhaps best understood as a perversion of the Golden Rule, whose by-product in this case is respect and whose caveat is vengeance, or payback . . . one often learns the value of having a 'name,' a reputation for being willing and able to fight."

28. Beck, *Prisoners of Hate.*

29. Anderson, *Code of the Street,* 109: "As faith in the criminal justice system erodes, social behavior in public is organized around the code of the streets. Feeling they cannot depend on the police and other civil authorities to protect them from danger, residents often take personal responsibility for their security. They may yield, but often they are prepared to let others know in no uncertain terms that there will be dire consequences if they are violated. And they tend to teach their children to stand up for themselves physically or to meet violence with violence."

30. Black, "Crime as Social Control."

31. Anderson, *Code of the Street,* 26–27.

32. Hureau and Wilson ("The Co-Occurrence of Illegal Gun Carrying and Gun Violence Exposure," table 1) show that among the respondents who say on surveys that they "always carried a gun," the number of times they say they carried a gun over the past year was fifty-nine, or (given a year is 365 days) about once every six days.

33. Thaler and Sunstein, *Nudge.*

34. Bacher-Hicks, Billings, and Deming, "The School to Prison Pipeline." These impacts reflect the effects of a two-standard-deviation change in school suspension rates, i.e., a shift from the middle of the distribution to the tail of the distribution.

35. Tversky and Kahneman, "Belief in the Law of Small Numbers."

36. Agan, Doleac, and Harvey, "Misdemeanor Prosecution."

37. In table B.6 of their appendix, Agan, Doleac, and Harvey show that for violent crimes, the effect of being not prosecuted is −0.13, compared to a mean value for the "compliers" (marginal cases) on the bubble of prosecution or not—depending on who their ADA is—of 0.20 ("Misdemeanor Prosecution").

   In the same spirit, economists Anna Aizer of Brown and Joe Doyle of MIT showed that the effects of justice-system detention for teens is particularly damaging. Using the "natural experiment" of random assignment of juvenile arrestees to different juvenile-court judges with different propensities to detain teens in the Juvenile Temporary Detention Center—akin to an RCT testing the effects of detention—they found that teens who were detained had a high school graduation rate 13 percentage points lower than the rate for those not detained, and a risk of being incarcerated as an adult that was 23 percentage points higher (see Aizer and Doyle, "Juvenile Incarceration, Human Capital, and Future Crime").

38. Pandolfo, "School Discipline Records Show Racial Disparities."

39. It's hard to tell whether this trend has hit Greater Grand Crossing harder than South Shore, because the school attendance boundaries for the two neighborhoods aren't so cleanly defined.

40. "Economic Club of Chicago—Public Safety."

41. Mayson and Stevenson, "Misdemeanors by the Numbers," 1020. See also Natapoff, "Misdemeanors."
42. Figure created using arrest records from the Chicago PD; thanks to Javier Lopez. One might worry that overall deterrence varies across neighborhoods, as
a confounder for this behavioral-economics mechanism. That is, maybe police
make more misdemeanor arrests in Greater Grand Crossing and also make all
sorts of other arrests more often in Greater Grand Crossing—including for the
sort of serious violent crimes that drive the social harms of crime. What looks
like an effect of misdemeanor arrests in that case could as a logical matter be
due to a difference in the likelihood a violent-crime offender is arrested, which
would affect the likelihood that would-be violent offenders are deterred. But
that's not what's going on here; the violent-crime clearance rate is remarkably
similar across neighborhoods.
43. See, for example, Sampson, *Great American City*; Zen and Wu, "Neighborhood
Collective Efficacy in Stressful Events," and the citations therein; as well as
Butel and Braun, "The Role of Collective Efficacy in Reducing Health Disparities."
44. Not subtracting out years of potential life lost due to murder, the overall differences are 14,627 versus 16,563.
45. For example, one reason people carry guns is that they think everyone else
is carrying. As one commentator put it, "It's an arms race on the streets of
America. You only need one 12-year-old with a gun, then other 12-year-olds feel
they need a gun" (Terry, "Boy Sought in Teen-Ager's Death Is Latest Victim of
Chicago Guns"). But research shows that teenagers overestimate how often
everyone else is carrying (Hemenway et al., "Gun Carrying by High School
Students"). On college campuses, behavioral scientists have found that students binge-drink too often partly because they think all their peers are also
binge-drinking a lot. But giving them more accurate information about how
much their peers really drink reduces their own binge drinking. It's possible
that something similar could be done with gun carrying, too, which could
help get at least some guns off the streets. See also Kang, Ludwig, and Rasich,
"Intervention of Choice."
46. Cook et al., "Underground Gun Markets," F563.
47. In principle, one might worry that this result is an artifact of different stop
rates across neighborhoods, but that does not seem to be the case. The standard
economic model of enforcement from Gary Becker implies that "rational"
police should prioritize the most promising stops first—those with the highest
expected likelihood of resulting in the confiscation of some sort of contraband,
like a gun (Becker, *The Economics of Discrimination*; and Becker, "Nobel Lecture"). As the number of police stops increases, the hit rate (share of stops that
result in contraband) should fall. Some evidence consistent with this hypothesis is presented by Abrams, Fang, and Goonetilleke ("Police Frisks"). This phenomenon raises the hypothesis that the higher hit rate for gun confiscations
in Greater Grand Crossing could in principle be due not to a higher share of
people there carrying guns in public, but instead to a lower rate of police stop-
ping people in Greater Grand Crossing than in South Shore. But in practice
the data show the opposite: There are many more stops per capita in Greater

Grand Crossing, which suggests that if anything, our results may understate the degree to which there is more gun carrying in public in Greater Grand Crossing.

48. Alfred Blumstein and his colleagues have done work showing the age at which criminally involved people reach the population base rate of crime involvement risk; incarcerating people beyond that age has modest public safety value and is removing an "average citizen" from their community who could contribute to informal social control. (See, for example, Blumstein and Cohen, "Estimation of Individual Crime Rates from Arrest Records"; and Blumstein and Nakamura, "Redemption in the Presence of Widespread Criminal Background Checks.")

49. See Small, *Unexpected Gains*.

50. Alesina and Giuliano, "Preferences for Redistribution."

CHAPTER EIGHT

1. As one study of people's beliefs put it, "Americans think that people commit crimes as a result of something inherently wrong within the lawbreaker, such as lack of moral fiber, or due to ecological considerations that influence or force individuals to break the law, such as lack of money." (Bunten, Kendall-Taylor, and Lindland, *Caning, Context and Class*, 17).

2. Much of what follows is taken from the wonderful account of Dorothy Gautreaux and the Gautreaux case in Business and Professional People for the Public Interest, *What Is Gautreaux?*; as well as Rubinowitz and Rosenbaum, *Crossing the Class and Color Lines*; Ludwig, "Guest Editor's Introduction"; and Shroder and Orr, "Moving to Opportunity."

3. As Rubinowitz and Rosenbaum discuss, there was first a 1969 *Gautreaux* decision against CHA that required the agency to administer a scattered-site program, followed by debates within the federal courts about whether HUD was required to relocate CHA families to other parts of just the city of Chicago itself or whether other parts of the metropolitan area could be considered as relocation sites (*Crossing the Class and Color Lines*, 36–37). See also Keels et al., "Fifteen Years Later."

4. Rosenbaum, "Changing the Geography of Opportunity by Expanding Residential Choice"; and Rubinowitz and Rosenbaum, *Crossing the Class and Color Lines*.

5. For example, in 1982 Ken Auletta published a book, *The Underclass*, building on his three-part series in the *New Yorker*; the National Academy of Sciences in 1990 published a report by a blue-ribbon commission on the topic (Lynn and McGeary, *Inner-City Poverty in the United States*), and in 1991 the Brookings Institution published a volume edited by Christopher Jencks and Paul Peterson called *The Urban Underclass*.

6. This section draws from Shroder and Orr, "Moving to Opportunity."

7. In MTO there were actually three randomized "arms": a control group that kept eligibility for their initial public-housing unit, an "experimental" voucher group that could only redeem their housing voucher in a census tract with a

1990 poverty rate below 10 percent, and a traditional voucher group that could use a voucher to move to whatever neighborhood they wanted (see, for example, Ludwig, "Guest Editor's Introduction," for additional details). I focus here on the contrast between the control and experimental voucher groups, where the difference in neighborhood conditions is greatest.

8. Ludwig, "Guest Editor's Introduction."

9. Ludwig, "Guest Editor's Introduction."

10. The MTO data also showed that that property crime offending went up, particularly among male teens, when they moved to lower-poverty areas. That finding originally led me to be a little confused myself in how to think about whether MTO did or did not affect crime (see, for example, Harcourt and Ludwig, "Broken Windows"), but recognizing that the costs of violence wind up driving the total social harm of crime helps clarify that MTO moves reduced the harms of crime overall. Of course, there are other methodological issues you might worry about; for example, are the MTO movers just telling survey interviewers what they want to hear (a confounding factor known as "social desirability bias")? But our research team didn't just rely on surveys to measure violence involvement; we also looked at official government arrest records. You might worry that differences across neighborhoods in the willingness of police to make arrests, or in whom they single out for arrest, might make these results misleading. But if anything, the better police service in lower-poverty areas would suggest the MTO movers most likely faced a *higher* chance of being arrested if they committed a crime than people faced who stayed behind in the projects. That fact would lead these results to, if anything, *understate* neighborhood effects on violent behavior. See Kling, Ludwig, and Katz, "Neighborhood Effects on Crime for Female and Male Youth."

11. Sciandra et al., "Long-Term Effects of the Moving to Opportunity Residential Mobility Experiment on Crime and Delinquency."

12. See Bayer, Hjalmarsson, and Pozen, "Building Criminal Capital behind Bars," and Stevenson and Hjalmarsson, "Breaking Bad." See also Damm and Gorinas, "Prison as a Criminal School."

13. Billings and Hoekstra, "Schools, Neighborhoods, and the Long-Run Effect of Crime-Prone Peers."

14. Zeren, "Jane Jacobs, an Urban Ecologist."

15. Campanella, "Jane Jacobs and the Death and Life of American Planning."

16. Gratz, "Milestones: 100 Years of Jane Jacobs."

17. Sampson, Raudenbush, and Earls, "Neighborhoods and Violent Crime."

18. Chang and Jacobson, "Going to Pot?"

19. Chang and Jacobson ("Going to Pot?," table 4) show that within a one-eighth-mile radius around dispensaries, the effect of closures on property crime was 21 percent (standard error 11.3 percent) versus 18.8 percent for violent crime (standard error 27.4 percent). Within a quarter-mile radius the proportional effects were 10.7 percent (7 percent) for property crime and 17.7 percent (16.2 percent) for violent crime.

20. Chang and Jacobson ("Going to Pot?," table 6) show that, using the median closure period, within a quarter mile the effect is about one-quarter of the pre-closure mean (but imprecisely estimated) and about one-third of the pre-

closure mean within a third of a mile (statistically significant at 5 percent). Table 7 shows a larger effect of property than violent crimes within a quarter mile but a larger effect of violent than property crimes within a third of a mile (the flipping of the relative magnitudes being perhaps not so surprising given the size of the confidence intervals here).

21. See Chalfin et al., "Reducing Crime through Environmental Design"; and Mitre-Becerril et al., "Can Deterrence Persist?"

22. Branas et al., "Citywide Cluster Randomized Trial to Restore Blighted Vacant Land and Its Effects on Violence, Crime, and Fear." They report 3 million hectares of vacant land, which I convert to acres.

23. Branas et al., "Citywide Cluster Randomized Trial."

24. MacDonald et al. "Lessons Learned from a Citywide Abandoned Housing Experiment."

25. Sikora, "Hemingway Haunts."

26. Trice, "Village with a Vision."

27. "Columbus (Christopher) Park."

28. Associated Press, "Schools in Chicago Are Called the Worst by Education Chief."

29. Yousef, "What the West Side Lost."

30. Griffin, Dunning, and Ross, "Role of Construal Processes."

31. The department made a total of 41,449 arrests in 2022 (Chicago Police Department, 2022 Annual Report). The number of officers in the department is in the ballpark of ten thousand, which would imply around four arrests per year per officer, or one per officer every three months. Even if as many as, say, half of all officers were assigned to desk duties, the officers out on the street would still each only be making an arrest every month and a half.

32. Maciag, "Police Employment: Officers Per Capita Rates for U.S. Cities."

33. Evans and Owens, "COPS and Crime"; Braga et al., "Hot Spots Policing of Small Geographic Areas Effects on Crime"; Chalfin and McCrary, "Are U.S. Cities Underpoliced?"; Chalfin et al. "Police Force Size and Civilian Race"; MacDonald, Klick, and Grunwald, "The Effect of Private Police on Crime."

34. For example, Evans and Owens ("COPS and Crime," table 5) show that the elasticity of crime with respect to police (the percentage change in crime for a percentage change in police) is about four times as large for violent crimes as for property crimes, −0.99 versus −0.26.

35. For example, Evans and Owens use COPS funding allocations as a natural experiment and find that the elasticity of property crimes with respect to more police is −0.26, while for violent crime it's −0.99 ("COPS and Crime"). Chalfin and McCrary find that the elasticity is twice as large in absolute value for violent than property crimes, −0.344 versus −0.174 ("Are U.S. Cities Underpoliced?," table 3, column 9). See also Chalfin et al., "Police Force Size and Civilian Race"; and Mello, "More COPS, Less Crime," for additional findings using COPS funding. See Levitt, "Using Electoral Cycles in Police Hiring to Estimate the Effects of Police on Crime," for evidence using the tendency of cities to hire more or fewer municipal employees overall as a natural experiment. See Klick and Tabarrok, "Using Terror Alert Levels to Estimate the Effect of Police on Crime"; and Draca, Machin, and Witt, "Panic on the Streets

of London," for studies of the effects of police reallocations due to terror alerts. See MacDonald, Klick, and Grunwald, "Effect of Private Police on Crime"; and Heaton et al., "The Short- and Long-Run Effects of Private Law Enforcement," for studies of campus police across patrol boundaries. Weisburd ("Police Presence, Rapid Response Rates, and Crime Prevention") uses data from the Dallas PD to look at what happens when a call outside an officer's patrol area pulls them out of their normal beat. Cheng and Long ("Improving Police Services") look at what happens when the New Orleans police put more presence into the French Quarter. Mohler et al. ("Randomized Controlled Field Trials of Predictive Policing") report the results of a predictive policing algorithm (hot-spot policing) in Los Angeles and show that crime declines as a result of increased police presence; Brantingham, Valasik, and Mohler ("Does Predictive Policing Lead to Biased Arrests?") show that arrests (and/or arrests per crime) don't seem to increase and if anything may decline.

36. Owens, "COPS and Cuffs"; Chalfin et al., "Police Force Size and Civilian Race"; and Mello, "More COPS, Less Crime."

37. In the 2020 working-paper version of their article "Police Force Size and Civilian Race," Chalfin et al. note that the baseline clearance rate for index offenses is 16,349 arrests to 96,892 offenses (table 2). The effect of one additional police officer is to reduce the number of index offenses by 17.8 and the number of index crime arrests by 0.97 (using their "measurement error" instrument), or 23.5 fewer index crimes and 1.6 fewer index arrests (using the COPS funding instrument). In either case, the clearance rate stays at about 16.9 percent, with a chance at only something like the third decimal point. However, Cook ("The Clearance Rate as a Measure of Criminal Justice System Effectiveness") notes that the interpretation of the clearance rate as a probability of apprehension is complicated by the fact that criminals may endogenously choose crime opportunities that vary by the odds of getting caught, so a change in enforcement could as a logical matter lead to a clearance rate that increases, decreases, or does not change.

This clearance rate—the ratio of arrests to crimes—is usually interpreted as something like a probability of getting caught if you commit a crime, although Philip Cook has noted that reality may in practice be a little more complicated than that ("Clearance Rate").

38. One study by Chalfin et al finds that even though arrests for serious crimes decline alongside the number of serious-crime events, there also seems to be a concurrent increase in misdemeanor arrests (disproportionately concentrated among minority residents) ("Police Force Size and Civilian Race"). But that change in misdemeanor arrests seems to reflect enforcement activities with low public-safety value for serious crime, rather than a key mechanism through which police reduce serious crimes. See also Harcourt and Ludwig, "Broken Windows."

39. "Occupational Employment and Wage Statistics, May 2023."

40. "Law Enforcement Facts: Key Data about the Profession."

41. Cook and MacDonald ("Public Safety through Private Action," table 1) show a baseline clearance rate of 24/186 = 13 percent for all crimes; table 3 of the same study shows an effect of BIDs on total crimes of −28 and on arrests of −10, so

the new new clearance rate after that would be $(24–10)/(186–28) = 14/158 =$ 9 percent. If we look at assaults specifically (where we think disruption/de-escalation/interruption might be even more pronounced compared to crimes like robbery or burglary or car theft, etc.), the baseline clearance rate is $7.8/29.8 = 26$ percent, the effect on reported assault crimes is $–2.4$, and the effect on arrests for assault is $–3.8$, so the new clearance rate is $3.9/27.4 = 14$ percent.

42. Priks, "The Effects of Surveillance Cameras on Crime."

43. Rose, Schellenberg, and Shem-Tov, "The Effects of Teacher Quality on Adult Criminal Justice Contact."

44. Gunn, "Breaking the Code of the Street."

45. Heller et al., "Thinking, Fast and Slow?"

46. Levitt, "Understanding Why Crime Fell in the 1990s."

47. To see the issue, suppose that the rate of shootings (fatal plus nonfatal) in Chicago is something like 1 per 1,000. Because of limits to our research funding, when we do randomized controlled trials we may have only a thousand people getting BAM in a study, with a thousand "controls" getting whatever status quo services the schools normally offer. But far more young people will be engaging in the behaviors that are precursors to actual shootings, like assault or illegal gun carrying.

48. When the data are broken down into more fine-grained crime categories in this way, there's less information in the outcome and so statistical precision goes down. With this caveat in mind, when we pool data from the two BAM RCTs reported in Heller et al. ("Thinking, Fast and Slow?"). the effect of treatment on the treated (TOT) on assault is $–.0433$ (standard error 0.0215), with a control complier mean (CCM) of 0.12; for weapons offenses the results are $–0.0144$ (0.0136) and a CCM of 0.043.

49. For the two BAM RCTs reported in Heller et al. ("Thinking, Fast and Slow?") pooled together, the TOT estimate for robbery is $–.0183$ (standard error $–.013$), compared to a control mean of 0.035. So the point estimate is proportionately very large as a share of control mean but not quite statistically significant given the size of the standard error here. The robbery result is statistically significant and negative in study 1 but not in study 2.

50. Bhatt et al. ("Scope Challenges to Social Impact") show that as BAM expanded in Chicago, the point estimate for the effect on violent-crime arrests and graduation rates seems to get smaller and the confidence interval around that estimate now includes zero. So we can't reject the null hypothesis that the program has no effect at large scale. But at the same time it's also important to note that the standard error around the at-large-scale estimate is sizable; we can't reject the null hypothesis that the effect is the same as when the program was operating at much smaller scale.

51. Some programs, like Roca, emphasize "relentless engagement," never giving up on kids. C2C has an element of that attitude, too. As one participant put it, "They don't give up on kids, no matter how bad, no matter how snotty."

52. See Abdul-Razzak and Hallberg, "Unpacking the Impacts of a Youth Behavioral Health Intervention." Six months after baseline, 7.3 percent of the control group members who would have participated in the program had been arrested for a violent crime, compared to 3.8 percent of C2C participants, a difference

that is statistically significant at 5 percent in the pair-wise treatment-control comparison, and has a family-wise error rate (FWER) of 0.084 if we account for multiple testing across arrest outcomes for all crime categories. Through thirty-six months, the control complier mean is 17.9 percent arrested for a violent crime, with an estimated effect of treatment on the treated of −5.1 percentage points, statistically significant in the pair-wise comparison but now with a FWER of 0.134.

53. The effect for aggravated assault and battery through six months is 57 percent versus 33 percent for simple assault and battery.

54. Another said, "I'd say anybody who probably gets angry really easily should probably join the program to help calm down their anger, I would say." Another said: "I just feel like . . . everybody can change. It all just depends on the way you see it."

55. These next few paragraphs draw from Heller et al., "Thinking, Fast and Slow?"

56. Heller et al., "Thinking, Fast and Slow?"

57. The challenge is that this outcome is a very noisy one, and because the program is so expensive (jobs are combined with behavioral-economics programming, partly as an incentive to encourage participation) the sample size in the RCT is not as large as one might ideally like. See Bhatt et al., "Predicting and Preventing Gun Violence."

58. Another READI participant said: "I talk more. I asked, like, 'What's up?' I want to know why you got a problem with me or whatnot. Yeah, communicate. I want to know instead of doing what I usually do, just fighting."

59. See Strang et al., "Restorative Justice Conferencing (RJC) Using Face-to-Face Meetings of Offenders and Victims"; and Shem-Tov, Raphael, and Skog, "Can Restorative Justice Conferencing Reduce Recidivism?"

60. Adukia, Feigenberg, and Momeni, "From Retributive to Restorative."

61. Proctor, Hoffmann, and Allison, "Effectiveness of Interactive Journaling in Reducing Recidivism among Substance-Dependent Jail Inmates."

62. The "active ingredient" here could in principle come from morality training, although the conventional wisdom that crime and violence are committed by people who are so bad they can't be changed would predict such training shouldn't matter. The fact that other policies that do not include any explicit focus on morality per se also seem to reduce crime and violence involvement suggests a focus on morality may not be the key active ingredient in practice with this policy. See Seroczynski et al., "Reading for Life and Adolescent Re-Arrest."

63. "Lori E. Lightfoot."

64. See Stoddard, Fitzpatrick, and Ludwig, "Predicting Police Misconduct."

65. Spielman, "Lightfoot Comes Out Swinging Hours after Preckwinkle Fires Her Campaign Manager."

66. Spielman, "Lightfoot Delivers Tough-Love Anti-Crime Message."

67. Mackinnon, "One Year In, Chicago Mayor Lori Lightfoot's $1 Million Gun-Tip Line Has Rewarded Only One Tip for Just $10,000."

68. Ponce, "More than 10,000 Guns Recovered off Chicago's Streets in 2022."

69. In 2016, the latest year for which I can get comparable data from the three different cities, Chicago confiscated around seven thousand guns, versus six

thousand for LA and nearly four thousand for New York. See Chicago Office of the Mayor and Chicago Police Department, *Gun Trace Report 2017*.

70. Their research team collected the data for their paper (Abrams, Fang, and Goonetilleke, "Police Frisks") and then was kind enough to carry out a separate set of calculations for me using those data.

71. The Chicago PD make something like 60,000 stops a month, traffic plus pedestrian (Hausman and Kronick, "The Illusory End of Stop and Frisk in Chicago?"), and the baseline hit rate for guns—the share of stops resulting in guns—in Abrams, Fang, and Goonetilleke ("Police Frisks") is 5.8 percent, or roughly one in twenty stops resulting in an illegal gun. In the summer of 2020 in Chicago, the proxy for gun carrying—the share of stops resulting in a gun— rose by 2.6 percentage points, a 45 percent increase over the mean value of 5.8 percent. With 60,000 stops per month, if guns are confiscated at a higher rate by 2.6 percentage points, that would mean 1,560 more guns per month over this period. The Abrams paper implies that every four extra guns confiscated was associated with one more shooting; that implies the rise in gun carrying led to 390 extra shootings per month that summer. By way of comparison, there were something like four thousand shootings total (fatal plus nonfatal) in Chicago in 2020, so this figure reflects roughly a doubling of the number of shootings per month.

72. See Lott and Mustard, "Crime, Deterrence, and Right-to-Carry"; and Lott, *More Guns, Less Crime*.

73. Most people who are carrying guns in public at a point in time are doing so illegally. As discussed in Ludwig, "Gun Self-Defense and Deterrence," in most states that enact permissive right-to-carry laws, the number of permits issued is usually never more than 2 percent of the number of adults in the state. By comparison, nationally representative survey data suggests that something like 7 or 8 percent of American adults carried a gun with them or in their car at some point during the past year. Some data from North Carolina highlight the key point: In a survey of those who got a concealed-carry permit, 85 percent who carry in their car and 34 percent of those who carry on their person said they carried their gun around with them even before getting their permit.

74. While Lott and Mustard ("Crime, Deterrence, and Right-to-Carry") and Lott (*More Guns, Less Crime*) claimed more gun carrying reduces crime, more recent (and in my view more convincing) evidence suggests the opposite; see Dono- hue et al., "Why Does Right-to-Carry Cause Violent Crime to Increase?"; and Donohue, Aneja, and Weber, "Right-to-Carry Laws and Violent Crime." There is also a literature looking at the effects of police efforts to deter illegal gun car- rying; see Cook, "Great American Gun War."

75. This question remains open. In the BAM study, for instance, impacts on violent crime seemed to be concentrated during the program period (even though im- pacts on schooling attainment persisted over time). On the other hand, in the Choose 2 Change program, the data show substantial persistence of impacts on violent crime long after participants have left the program.

76. The BAM program is the only one of these programs that has tried to achieve scale; early indications are that program effectiveness might have declined, at least initially, when the number of students served in Chicago went from a

thousand or two up to seven thousand—although it should be noted that the standard errors around these impact estimates are quite sizable, so we cannot reject the null hypothesis that the impacts stayed the same as program scale increased. See Bhatt et al., "Scope Challenges to Social Impact."

CHAPTER NINE

1. There have been different spellings of his name reported; I use the spelling in the Cook County court transcripts. In March 2023, Ward's conviction was overturned, and he was ordered to be re-tried given problems the judge found with the interviews the Chicago PD detectives carried out with him, which led to his confession.
2. Taken from the transcript of the January 14, 2019, Circuit Court of Cook County sentencing hearing (no. 13 CR 052420-01): 79–80.
3. Average Chicago city salaries taken from Zip Recruiter, accessed June 5, 2024, https://www.ziprecruiter.com/Salaries/City-Worker-Salary-in-Chicago,IL#Yearly.
4. See Ziezulewicz, "Cops Vow Crackdown on SUWU Gang after Hadiya's Alleged Killers Charged."
5. See Gettinger and Belanger, "Harper Ave. Shooting Tuesday Leaves No Reported Injuries, Damage to Businesses and Cars."
6. "'I Ran for My Life.'"
7. Data taken from the Chicago Metropolitan Agency for Planning; for the period 2017–2021, per capita income equaled $21,077 for Woodlawn versus $41,821 for Chicago as a whole (Chicago Metropolitan Agency for Planning, *Woodlawn*), https://www.cmap.illinois.gov/documents/10180/126764/Woodlawn.pdf.
8. Schwartz, "Owens Pierced a Myth."
9. The current incarnation of the University of Chicago, founded by William Rainey Harper and John Rockefeller, was preceded by an earlier failed attempt; see Boyer, *The University of Chicago: A History*.
10. Baron, *Thinking and Deciding*, 197.
11. I should say "20 plus or minus a few years," because the exact peak of the age crime curve depends in part on exactly how one measures rates of gun crime involvement (what specific gun crime, and whether we look at offending versus victimization—the data are much more comprehensive for victims than offenders). The peak of the age crime curve for gun violence can also differ slightly depending on the time and place.
12. As people age, among other things their ability to determine what someone else is thinking and feeling—to come up with a "theory of mind" for someone else—gets better. Better theory of mind, fewer misunderstandings and conflict, less violence. See, for example, Dumontheil, Apperly, and Blakemore, "Online Usage of Theory of Mind Continues to Develop in Late Adolescence."
13. In 2010, life expectancy in Washington Park was sixty-nine years, ten years below Chicago's citywide average.
14. Ward during his interrogation claimed that Kenny Williams had threatened

to kill him if he didn't carry out the shooting. We have no way of knowing how seriously Ward took that threat in practice. But we do know that teenagers are enormously susceptible to peer influence more generally in all sorts of different circumstances. In fact, the vast majority of criminal activity carried out by teens is carried out in groups.

15. See Gramlich, "What the Data Says about Gun Deaths in the U.S."
16. See Centers for Disease Control and Prevention, "*QuickStats*: Age-Adjusted Rates of Firearm-Related Homicide."
17. See Giles, Hungerman, and Oostrom, "Opiates of the Masses?"
18. See Hollingsworth, Ruhm, and Simon, "Macroeconomic Conditions and Opioid Abuse"; and Pierce and Schott, "Trade Liberalization and Mortality."
19. See Karma, "'Deaths of Despair'"; and Case and Deaton, *Deaths of Despair and the Future of Capitalism*.
20. Case and Deaton, *Deaths of Despair*.
21. Owens, Horrocks, and House, "Fatal and Non-Fatal Repetition of Self-Harm."
22. Brody, "After a Suicide Attempt, the Risk of Another Try."
23. Coppersmith et al., "Mapping the Timescale of Suicidal Thinking."
24. Kernan, "What Two Men Who Survived Jumping Off the Golden Gate Bridge Learned."
25. Zouves, "Second Chances."
26. See, for example, the discussion in Baron, *Thinking and Deciding*, 201.
27. See Brown et al., "Cognitive Therapy for the Prevention of Suicide Attempts"; and Gøtzsche and Gøtzsche, "Cognitive Behavioural Therapy."
28. Law Enforcement Epidemiology Project, "U.S. Data on Police Shootings and Violence."
29. Hoekstra and Sloan, "Does Race Matter for Police Use of Force?"
30. Dube, MacArthur, and Shah, "A Cognitive View of Policing."
31. See Domma et al., *The Gang Book*, 286.
32. Engel, "Low Self-Control as a Source of Crime."
33. See, for example, Eriksson, Masche-No, and Dåderman, "Personality Traits of Prisoners as Compared to General Populations."
34. As part of one of our RCTS of BAM, we carried out surveys with teens in both the program group and the control group. We offered people a cash reward on the spot or a much larger cash reward in the future. The willingness to delay in exchange for a larger amount of cash was no different between the program and control groups, which is not what we'd expect if a change in self-control were the key mechanism through which BAM reduced violence.
35. Other examples include "multi-systemic therapy" or "functional family therapy." See, for example, the review in MacDonald, "Criminal Justice Reform Guided by Evidence."
36. Whewell wrote in 1840: "The Consilience of Inductions takes place when an Induction, obtained from one class of facts, coincides with an Induction, obtained from another different class. This Consilience is a test of the truth of the Theory in which it occurs" (quoted in Wilson, *Consilience*, 8–9).
    As Wilson writes in *Consilience*: "I had experienced the Ionian Enchantment. That recently coined expression I borrow from the physicist and historian Gerald Holton. It means a belief in the unity of the sciences—a conviction, far

deeper than a mere working proposition, that the world is orderly and can be explained by a small number of natural laws" (4–5). The same book includes a quote from Einstein: "It is a wonderful feeling to recognize the unity of a complex phenomena that to direct observation appear to be quite different things" (5).

37. Pinker, *Better Angels*, 84.
38. See, for example, Beck, *Prisoners of Hate*; and Fiske and Rai, *Virtuous Violence*.
39. See, for example, Cozens and Love, "A Review and Current Status of Crime Prevention through Environmental Design (CPTED)."
40. See Clarke, "Situational Crime Prevention."
41. For example, Jacob, Kapustin, and Ludwig ("The Impact of Housing Assistance on Child Outcomes") show that giving families housing vouchers that dramatically increase what families have to spend on their housing causes very modest if any change in the measurable characteristics of the neighborhoods in which people are living. See also, for example, Sharkey, Stuck in Place.
42. Pinker, *Better Angels*, 60.
43. See, for example, Golaszewski, "A Status Report."
44. See White, Cook, and Pollack, "Gunshot-Victim Cooperation with Police Investigations"; and Vallas, "The Protection of Chicago's Witnesses and Victims Must Be a Priority."
45. Cook and Ludwig, "Understanding Gun Violence" and "Response to Counterpoint," show that clearance rates decline in Chicago as the number of detectives declines, then increase again as the number of detectives increases.
46. Goldstein, *Problem-Oriented Policing*.
47. Muir, *Police*.
48. Braga et al. note that the mean "effect size" for simply putting more officers at high-crime hot spots was 0.108; having the extra officers at the hot spots engage in problem-oriented policing has an effect size of 0.164 ("Hot Spots Policing of Small Geographic Areas Effects on Crime," 39).
49. See, for example, Cordner and Biebel, "Problem-Oriented Policing in Practice."
50. "Budget Justice."
51. Heller et al., "Thinking, Fast and Slow?"
52. This and most of the examples that follow are taken from Flavell, "Metacognition and Cognitive Monitoring."
53. Taken from Verschaffel et al., "Learning to Solve Mathematical Application Problems."
54. Taken from Baron, Isler, and Yilmaz, "Actively Open-Minded Thinking and the Political Effects of Its Absence."
55. Oreopoulos and Salvanes, "Priceless"; Baron, "Actively Open-Minded Thinking (AOT) as Metacognition for Self and Others."
56. Harris, "Are America's Rising Graduation Rates Real—or Just an Accountability-Fueled Mirage?"
57. Lochner and Moretti, "The Effect of Education on Crime."
58. See Perkins, "Postprimary Education Has Little Impact on Informal Reasoning"; and Pithers and Soden, "Critical Thinking in Education."
59. Ander and Quinn, "Health Education."

60. See Baron, "Why Teach Thinking?" This essay also provides an excellent argument for what types of instruction might, and might not, achieve that goal.
61. See Deming, "Four Facts about Human Capital"; Weidmann and Deming, "Team Players"; and Deming, "The Growing Importance of Social Skills in the Labor Market."
62. See, for example, the Century Foundation's interactive data tool on public-education funding gaps ("Closing America's Education Funding Gaps").
63. Jackson and Foster, "Politics of Public Budgeting in Illinois."
64. Sanders, Pearson, and Macaraeg, "School Choice or a Drain on Public Education?"
65. Hanson, "U.S. Public Education."
66. Sharkey ("The Acute Effect of Local Homicides on Children's Cognitive Performance") shows that the short-term effect on achievement test scores is on the order of 0.5 to 0.66 standard deviations. Reardon ("The Widening Academic Achievement Gap between the Rich and the Poor") uses data from the National Assessment of Educational Progress to show that between 4th and 8th grades, students gain 1.2 to 1.5 standard deviations in their reading and math scores, or (if we did a simple, even allocation across years) roughly speaking about 0.3 to 0.375 standard deviations. Between 8th and 12th grades, test scores change by 0.6 to 0.7 standard deviations, or about 0.15 to 0.175 standard deviations per year. Schwartz et al. ("The Academic Effects of Chronic Exposure to Neighbourhood Violence") document a qualitatively similar effect using data from New York City; the estimated effects are smaller than those found in the Sharkey study, a difference that could be due in part to the fact that Schwartz et al.'s measure of violent crime includes an index of homicides and aggravated assaults together. For effects on children's attention levels and parental mental health, see Sharkey et al., "The Effect of Local Violence on Children's Attention and Impulse Control."
67. See Hong and Burnett-Zeigler, "The Frequency of PTSD and Subthreshold PTSD among African–American Women with Depressive Symptoms in a Disadvantaged Urban Neighborhood," and the citations therein.
68. Cullen and Levitt ("Crime, Urban Flight, and the Consequences for Cities") show that each serious UCR part 1 index crime reduces a city's population on net by one person. In a separate calculation that they were kind enough to do for a previous book I co-authored on the costs of gun violence (Cook and Ludwig, *Gun Violence: The Real Costs*), they looked at the effects of each murder specifically on a city's population, which was seventy people on net decline.
69. Chicago Mayor's Press Office, "Whole Foods Market and Mayor Emanuel Announce New Store in Chicago's Englewood Neighborhood."
70. Atavia, "Whole Foods Closes Englewood Store 6 Years after Promising to Fill a South Side Food Desert."
71. Stacy, Irvin-Erickson, and Tiry, "The Impact of Gunshots on Place-Level Business Activity."
72. "Chicago Public Schools Most Empty Schools."
73. Thanks to Alejandro Roemer for creating figures 9.1 and 9.2. Source: United States Census Bureau, "Decennial Census of Population and Housing by Decade."

74. Source: University of Chicago Crime Lab calculations. Chicago and New York City data taken from Ludwig, "Op-Ed: New York and Los Angeles." Detroit data for 1950 to 1985 taken from the Centers for Disease Control and Prevention, "Vital Statistics of the United States"; for 1985 to 2021, data taken from the UCR for the Detroit PD (see "Crime Data Explorer"); for 1951 and 1952, the homicide count was at the level of Wayne County, rather than Detroit. For all other years between 1950 and 2021, Detroit homicides accounted on average for 85 percent of Wayne County's homicides. Therefore, for 1951 and 1952, we estimated Detroit's homicide count as 85 percent of the available Wayne County data point.

75. Nissen, "Officials Tout Detroit's Falling Homicide Rate, Sees Results on Community Front and Hiring More Officers."

76. Karlinsky, "Making Detroit Home."

77. Roberts, "Infamous 'Drop Dead' Was Never Said by Ford."

78. University of Chicago calculation of United States census data. See decennial estimates at https://www.census.gov.

79. *Chicago Tribune* Editorial Board, "Killing Our Children."

80. *New York Times* Editorial Board, "To Restore New York City."

81. Klassen, "Mayor Bradley and L.A. Crime."

82. In 2009, the gap was 20 percentage points (Dillon, "Large Urban-Suburban Gap Seen in Graduation Rates"); today that figure is more like 10 percentage points (National Center for Education Statistics, "Condition of Education"). For a discussion of zero-tolerance policing, see chapter 7. For a discussion of the challenges for cities of both housing and educational policy, see, for example, Boustan, "Racial Residential Segregation in American Cities"; and Glaeser, "Urbanization and Its Discontents."

83. Cahill et al., "Evaluation of the Los Angeles Gang Reduction."

84. See Bratton, "New Strategies for Combatting Crime in New York City"; and "Transcript: Perspectives in Law Enforcement."

85. An article in the *Los Angeles Times* showed that public approval of the LAPD was 40 percent in 1991 and had increased to 77 percent by 2009 ("Citywide Survey of Los Angeles"). Later surveys, and surveys carried out by other news outlets, show different numbers that present a less clear trend, although the challenge with comparing numbers from different surveys is that different survey response rates and survey question wordings can lead to different answers.

86. "Republican Party Platforms: Republican Party Platform of 1932."

87. Roosevelt, address at the National Parole Conference.

BIBLIOGRAPHY

1970 Census of Population Supplementary Report: Race of the Population of the United States, by States: 1970. Washington, DC: US Department of Commerce, February 1972. https://www2.census.gov/library/publications /decennial/1970/pc-s1-supplementary-reports/pc-s1-11.pdf.

Abdul-Razzak, Nour, and Kelly Hallberg. "Unpacking the Impacts of a Youth Behavioral Health Intervention: Experimental Evidence from Chicago." Working paper. Chicago: University of Chicago Crime Lab, December 1, 2023. https://drive.google.com/file/d /1raJLqJbeT5pxY0EImTzkqF9wGT2ma57u/view.

Abelson, Robert P. "Psychological Status of the Script Concept." *American Psychologist* 36, no. 7 (1981): 715–29. https://doi.org/10.1037/0003 -066X.36.7.715.

Aborn, Richard M. "The Battle over the Brady Bill and the Future of Gun Control Advocacy." *Urban Law Journal* 22, no. 2 (1995): 417.

Abrams, David S., Hanming Fang, and Priyanka Goonetilleke. "Police Frisks." *AEA Papers and Proceedings* 112 (May 2022): 178–83. https://doi .org/10.1257/pandp.20221100.

"Achieving the Dream: Harold Washington." *WTTW News*. Accessed March 15, 2024. https://interactive.wttw.com/dusable-to-obama/ harold-washington.

Adams, Dani. "Democratizing Mental Health." *South Side Weekly*, February 4, 2020. https://southsideweekly.com/mental-health-advocates -put-public-services-back-on-table/.

Adukia, Anjali, Benjamin Feigenberg, and Fatemeh Momeni. "From Retributive to Restorative: An Alternative Approach to Justice." Becker Friedman Institute for Economics working paper no. 2023-117. Chicago: University of Chicago, Becker Friedman Institute for Economics, September 2023. https://doi.org/10.2139/ssrn.4566132.

Agan, Amanda Y., Jennifer L. Doleac, and Anna Harvey. "Misdemeanor Prosecution." *Quarterly Journal of Economics* 138, no. 3 (2023): 1453.

Agan, A. Y., and M. D. Makowsky. "The Minimum Wage, EITC, and Criminal Recidivism." *Journal of Human Resources* 58, no. 5 (2023): 1712–51.

Agnew, Robert. "Foundation for a General Strain Theory of Crime and Delinquency." *Criminology* 30 (1992): 47–88. https://doi.org/10.1111/j.1745 -9125.1992.tb01093.x.

Ahmad, Meha. "Arne Duncan on Violence Prevention in Chicago: 'It's Not Rocket Science.'" *WBEZ Chicago*, April 29, 2019. https://www.wbez.org /stories/arne-duncan-on-what-chicago-gets-wrong-about-violence -prevention/0977b1bd-57df-4897-b8b4-2aa7e789278e.

Aiello, Leslie C., and Peter Wheeler. "The Expensive-Tissue Hypothesis: The Brain and the Digestive System in Human and Primate Evolution." *Current Anthropology* 36, no. 2 (1995): 199–221.

Aizer, A. "The Gender Wage Gap and Domestic Violence." *American Economic Review* 100, no. 4 (2010): 1847–59.

Aizer, Anna, and Joseph J. Doyle. "Juvenile Incarceration, Human Capital, and Future Crime." *Quarterly Journal of Economics* 130, no. 2 (2015): 759–804.

Akee, Randall K. Q., William E. Copeland, Gordon Keeler, Adrian Angold, and E. Jane Costello. "Parents' Incomes and Children's Outcomes: A Quasi-Experiment Using Transfer Payments from Casino Profits." *American Economic Journal: Applied Economics* 2, no. 1 (2010): 86–115. http://www.jstor.org/stable/25760194.

Alder, Simeon, David Lagakos, and Lee Ohanian. "Competitive Pressure and the Decline of the Rust Belt: A Macroeconomic Analysis." NBER working paper no. 20538. Cambridge, MA: National Bureau of Economic Research, October 2014. https://doi.org/10.3386/w20538.

Alesina, Alberto, and Paola Giuliano. "Preferences for Redistribution."
NBER working paper no. 14825. Cambridge, MA: National Bureau of
Economic Research, March 2009. https://doi.org/10.3386/w14825.

Alesina, Alberto, Stefanie Stantcheva, and Edoardo Teso. "Intergenerational Mobility and Preferences for Redistribution." *American Economic Review* 108, no. 2 (2018): 521–54. https://doi.org/10.1257/aer
.20162015.

Allen, Bem P. "African Americans' and European Americans' Mutual Attributions: Adjective Generation Technique (AGT) Stereotyping." *Journal
of Applied Social Psychology* 26, no. 10 (1996): 884–912. https://doi.org/10
.1111/j.1559-1816.1996.tb01116.x.

Alund, Natalie Neysa. "Chicago Mom Accused of Telling Son to Shoot
Man Sues Police after Murder Charges Dropped." *USA Today*, June 28,
2023. https://www.usatoday.com/story/news/nation/2023/06/28
/carlisha-hood-chicago-mom-son-shooting-lawsuit/70364919007/.

Alvazzi del Frate, Anna, Eric G. Berman, Olivia Denonville, Emilia Dungel,
Russell Gasser, Fiona Mangan, and Glenn McDonald. *Small Arms Survey
Annual Report 2018*. Geneva: Small Arms Survey, May 2019. https://
www.smallarmssurvey.org/sites/default/files/resources/SAS-Annual
-Report-2018.pdf.

"The American Housing Survey: Then and Now." *PD&R Edge*, October 26,
2021. https://www.huduser.gov/portal/pdredge/pdr-edge-trending
-102621.html.

"Americans' Experiences, Concerns, and Views Related to Gun Violence."
AP-NORC Center for Public Affairs Research, 2022. https://apnorc
.org/projects/americans-experiences-concerns-and-views-related-to
-gun-violence/.

"An Anatomy of Hard Times in the City." *Economist*, September 12, 2022.
https://www.economist.com/special-report/2022/09/12/an-anatomy
-of-hard-times-in-the-city.

Ander, Roseanna, and Julia Quinn. "Health Education: The Missing Link
in Violence Prevention." *Education Week*, August 2, 2016. https://www
.edweek.org/leadership/opinion-health-education-the-missing-link-in
-violence-prevention/2016/08.

Anderson, Dennis B., and Randall E. Schumacker. "Assessment of Job

Training Programs." *Journal of Offender Counseling Services Rehabilitation* 10, no. 4 (1986): 41–48.

Anderson, Elijah. *Code of the Street: Decency, Violence, and the Moral Life of the Inner City.* New York: W. W. Norton and Company, 1999.

Ang, Desmond, Panka Bencsik, Jesse Bruhn, and Ellora Derenoncourt. "Community Engagement with Law Enforcement after High-Profile Acts of Police Violence." NBER working paper no. 32243. Cambridge, MA: National Bureau of Economic Research, March 2024. https://doi .org/10.3386/w32243.

Angrist, Joshua D., and Jörn-Steffen Pischke. "Undergraduate Economet- rics Instruction: Through Our Classes, Darkly." *Journal of Economic Per- spectives* 31, no. 2 (2017): 125–44. https://doi.org/10.1257/jep.31.2.125.

Anwar, Shamena, and Hanming Fang. "Testing for Racial Prejudice in the Parole Board Release Process: Theory and Evidence." *Journal of Legal Studies* 44, no. 1 (2015): 1–37. https://doi.org/10.1086/680994.

Aoraha, Claudia. "Democrat Chicago Treasurer Melissa Conyears-Ervin Is Accused of Forcing Taxpayer-Funded Staff to Plan Her Daughter's Birthday and Act as Her Personal Bodyguard." *Daily Mail*, September 6, 2023. https://www.dailymail.co.uk/news/article-12482825/Democrat -Chicago-treasurer-staff-daughter-BIRTHDAY.html.

Arendt, Hannah. *On Violence.* New York: Harcourt, Brace, and World, 1970.

"Arne Duncan." City Club of Chicago, October 4, 2022. https://www .cityclub-chicago.org/video/3534/arne-duncan.

Arnold, David, Will Dobbie, and Peter Hull. "Measuring Racial Discrim- ination in Bail Decisions." *American Economic Review* 112, no. 9 (2022): 2992–3038. https://doi.org/10.1257/aer.20201653.

Arruebo, Manuel, Nuria Vilaboa, Berta Sáez-Gutierrez, Julio Lambea, Alejandro Tres, Mónica Valladares, and África González-Fernández. "Assessment of the Evolution of Cancer Treatment Therapies." *Cancers* 3, no. 3 (2011): 3279–3330. https://doi.org/10.3390/cancers3033279.

Aspholm, Roberto R. *Views from the Streets.* New York: Columbia University Press, 2020.

"Assassination Attempt." Franklin D. Roosevelt Presidential Library and Museum. Accessed March 12, 2024. http://www.fdrlibraryvirtualtour .org/page03-06.asp.

Associated Press. "Schools in Chicago Are Called the Worst by Education Chief." *New York Times*. November 8, 1987. https://www.nytimes.com /1987/11/08/us/schools-in-chicago-are-called-the-worst-by-education -chief.html.

Auletta, Ken. *The Underclass*. New York: Overlook Press, 1999.

Azrael, Deborah, Lisa Hepburn, David Hemenway, and Matthew Miller. "The Stock and Flow of U.S. Firearms: Results from the 2015 National Firearms Survey." *RSF: The Russell Sage Foundation Journal of the Social Sciences* 3, no. 5 (2017): 38–57. https://doi.org/10.7758/rsf.2017.3.5.02.

Bacher-Hicks, Andrew, Stephen Billings, and David Deming. "The School to Prison Pipeline: Long-Run Impacts of School Suspensions on Adult Crime." NBER working paper no. 26257. Cambridge, MA: National Bureau of Economic Research, September 2019. http://www.nber.org /papers/w26257.pdf.

Bailey, Holly. "In Bodycam Footage, Nashville Police Seen Confronting School Shooter." *Washington Post*, March 28, 2023. https://www .washingtonpost.com/nation/2023/03/28/nashville-school-shooting -bodycam-footage/.

Balcetis, Emily, and David Dunning. "See What You Want to See: Motivational Influences on Visual Perception." *Journal of Personality and Social Psychology* 91, no. 4 (2006): 612–25. https://doi.org/10.1037/0022-3514 .91.4.612.

Ballantine, Ted. "Chicago's Per-Capita Pension Debt, Visualized (Gulp!)." *Wolf Street*, November 17, 2014. https://wolfstreet.com/2014/11/17 /chicagos-per-capita-pension-debt-visualized-gulp/.

Barbash, Fred. "Britain Votes to Ban Handguns." *Washington Post*, June 12, 1997. https://www.washingtonpost.com/archive/politics/1997/ 06/12/britain-votes-to-ban-handguns/928b2c18-67de-4082-ade8 -39f1aa6060de/.

Bargh, John A. "The Four Horsemen of Automaticity: Awareness, Intention, Efficiency, and Control in Social Cognition." In *Handbook of Social Cognition: Basic Processes; Applications*, 2nd ed., edited by Robert S. Wyer Jr. and Thomas K. Srull, 1–40. Hillsdale, NJ: Lawrence Erlbaum Associates, Inc., 1994.

Bargh, John A., and Tanya L. Chartrand. "Studying the Mind in the Middle: A Practical Guide to Priming and Automaticity Research." In *Handbook of Research Methods*, edited by Harry T. Reis and Charles Judd, 253–84. New York: Cambridge University Press, 2000.

Baron, Jonathan. "Actively Open-Minded Thinking (AOT) as Metacognition for Self and Others: A Review." Presented at the Psychonomic Society 62nd Annual Meeting, Philadelphia, PA, November 6, 2021. https://sjdm.org/~jbaron/ms/talks/ps21.pdf.

———. "A Brief History of Evidence-Based Policy." *Annals of the American Academy of Political and Social Science* 678, no. 1 (2018): 40–50. https://doi.org/10.1177/0002716218763128.

———. *Thinking and Deciding*. 5th ed. New York: Cambridge University Press, 2024.

———. "Why Teach Thinking?—An Essay." *Applied Psychology: An International Review* 42, no. 3 (1993): 191–237.

Baron, Jonathan, Ozan Isler, and Onurcan Yılmaz. "Actively Open-Minded Thinking and the Political Effects of Its Absence." In *Divided: Open-Mindedness and Dogmatism in a Polarized World*, edited by Victor Ottati and Chadly Stern, 162-C9P184. New York: Oxford University Press, 2023. https://doi.org/10.1093/oso/9780197655467.003.0009.

Barron, James, and Mary B. W. Tabor. "17 Killed, and a Life Is Searched for Clues." *New York Times*, August 4, 1991. https://www.nytimes.com/1991/08/04/us/17-killed-and-a-life-is-searched-for-clues.html.

Bastian, B., B. Tejada Vera, E. Arias, et al. "Mortality Trends in the United States, 1900–2018." National Center for Health Statistics, 2020. https://www.cdc.gov/nchs/data-visualization/mortality-trends/index.htm.

Baumeister, Roy F., Ellen Bratslavsky, Mark Muraven, and Dianne M. Tice. "Ego Depletion: Is the Active Self a Limited Resource?" *Journal of Personality and Social Psychology* 74, no. 5 (1998): 1252–65. https://doi.org/10.1037/0022-3514.74.5.1252.

Baumeister, Roy F., and John Tierney. *Willpower: Rediscovering the Greatest Human Strength*. New York: Penguin Books, 2012.

Bayer, Patrick, Randi Hjalmarsson, and David Pozen. "Building Criminal Capital behind Bars: Peer Effects in Juvenile Corrections." *Quarterly Journal of Economics* 124, no. 1 (2009): 105–47. https://doi.org/10.1162/qjec.2009.124.1.105.

Beall, Ross, and Bill McNary. "Nearly 90% of U.S. Households Used Air Conditioning in 2020." US Energy Information Administration, May 31, 2022. https://www.eia.gov/todayinenergy/detail.php?id=52558.

Beck, A. J. *Race and Ethnicity of Violent Crime Offenders and Arrestees, 2018.* NCJ report no. 255969. Washington, DC: US Department of Justice, Office of Justice Programs, January 2021. https://bjs.ojp.gov/library/publications/race-and-ethnicity-violent-crime-offenders-and-arrestees-2018.

Beck, Aaron T. *Prisoners of Hate: The Cognitive Basis of Anger, Hostility, and Violence.* New York: Harper Perennial, 2000.

Becker, Gary S. "Crime and Punishment: An Economic Approach." *Journal of Political Economy* 76, no. 2 (1968): 169–217.

———. *The Economics of Discrimination.* Chicago: University of Chicago Press, 1957.

———. "Nobel Lecture: The Economic Way of Looking at Behavior." *Journal of Political Economy* 101, no. 3 (1993): 385–409.

Belanger, Christian. "Shaoxiong 'Dennis' Zheng Remembered as 'Not Only a Promising Scholar, but a Wonderful Person' at Memorial Service." *Hyde Park Herald*, November 18, 2020. https://www.hpherald.com/evening_digest/shaoxiong-dennis-zheng-remembered-as-not-only-a-promising-scholar-but-a-wonderful-person-at/article_ab9645de-48c2-11ec-840d-b3b433d311e4.html.

Bennett, René. "Most Americans Are Significantly Stressed about Money—Here's How It Varies by Demographic." *Bankrate*, June 26, 2023. https://www.bankrate.com/banking/money-and-financial-stress-statistics/.

Bergant, Katharina, Anke Weber, and Andrea Medici. "Winning the War? New Evidence on the Measurement and the Determinants of Poverty in the United States." IMF working paper. Washington, DC: International Monetary Fund, January 14, 2022. https://www.imf.org/en/Publications/WP/Issues/2022/01/14/Winning-the-War-New-Evidence-on-the-Measurement-and-the-Determinants-of-Poverty-in-the-511832.

Berk, Richard A., Kenneth J. Lenihan, and Peter H. Rossi. "Crime and

Poverty: Some Experimental Evidence from Ex-Offenders." *American Sociological Review* 45, no. 5 (1980): 766–86. https://doi.org/10.2307/2094894.

Berman, Greg. "'Violence Is Contagious': A Conversation with Andrew Papachristos." Harry Frank Guggenheim Foundation, November 23, 2021. https://www.hfg.org/conversations/violence-is-contagious-a-conversation-with-andrew-papachristos/.

Bernard, Andrew B., Valerie Smeets, and Frederic Warzynski. "Rethinking Deindustrialization." *Economic Policy* 32, no. 89 (2017): 5–38. https://doi.org/10.1093/epolic/eiw016.

Beyer, James, ed. *Wound Ballistics.* Washington, DC: Department of the Army, Office of the Surgeon General, 1962. https://achh.army.mil/history/book-wwii-woundblstcs-default.

Bhatt, Monica, Jonathan Guryan, Jens Ludwig, and Anuj Shah. "Scope Challenges to Social Impact." NBER working paper no. 28406. Cambridge, MA: National Bureau of Economic Research, January 2021. https://doi.org/10.3386/w28406.

Bhatt, Monica, Sara B. Heller, Max Kapustin, Marianne Bertrand, and Christopher Blattman. "Predicting and Preventing Gun Violence: An Experimental Evaluation of READI Chicago." *Quarterly Journal of Economics* 139, no. 1 (2024): 1–56. https://doi.org/10.1093/qje/qjad031.

Biden, Joseph. "Remarks by President Biden at Signing of S.2938, the Bipartisan Safer Communities Act." Speech, Washington, DC, June 25, 2022. https://www.whitehouse.gov/briefing-room/speeches-remarks/2022/06/25/remarks-by-president-biden-at-signing-of-s-2938-the-bipartisan-safer-communities-act/.

Biles, Roger. "Machine Politics." *Electronic Encyclopedia of Chicago*, 2005. http://www.encyclopedia.chicagohistory.org/pages/774.html.

Billings, Stephen B., and Mark Hoekstra. "Schools, Neighborhoods, and the Long-Run Effect of Crime-Prone Peers." NBER working paper no. 25730. Cambridge, MA: National Bureau of Economic Research, April 2019. https://ssrn.com/abstract=3368020.

Black, Curtis. "Harold Washington's Legacy Provided Touchstones for Progressive Politics." *Chicago Reporter*, November 22, 2017. https://www.chicagoreporter.com/harold-washingtons-legacy-provided-touchstones-for-progressive-politics/.

Black, Donald. "Crime as Social Control." *American Sociological Review* 48, no. 1 (1983): 34–45. https://doi.org/10.2307/2095143.

Blais, Julie, Adelle E. Forth, and Robert D. Hare. "Examining the Inter-rater Reliability of the Hare Psychopathy Checklist—Revised across a Large Sample of Trained Raters." *Psychological Assessment* 29, no. 6 (2017): 762–75. https://doi.org/10.1037/pas0000455.

Blattman, Christopher, Donald P. Green, Daniel Ortega, and Santiago Tobón. "Place-Based Interventions at Scale: The Direct and Spillover Effects of Policing and City Services on Crime." *Journal of the European Economic Association* 19, no. 4 (2021): 2022–51. https://doi.org/10.1093/jeea/jvab002.

Block, Carolyn Rebecca, Richard L. Block, and Illinois Criminal Justice Information Authority. "Homicides in Chicago, 1965–1995: Version 5." Inter-University Consortium for Political and Social Research, July 6, 2005. https://doi.org/10.3886/ICPSR06399.V5.

Block, Carolyn Rebecca, and Antigone Christakos. "Intimate Partner Homicide in Chicago over 29 Years." *Crime and Delinquency* 41, no. 4 (1995): 496–526. https://doi.org/10.1177/0011128795041004008.

Blumstein, Alfred, and Jacqueline Cohen. "Estimation of Individual Crime Rates from Arrest Records." *Journal of Criminal Law and Criminology (1973–)* 70, no. 4 (1979): 561–85. https://doi.org/10.2307/1142642.

———. "A Theory of the Stability of Punishment." *Journal of Criminal Law and Criminology (1973–)* 64, no. 2 (1973): 198–207. https://doi.org/10.2307/1142990.

Blumstein, Alfred, Jacqueline Cohen, Daniel Nagin, and Franklin E. Zimring. *Deterrence and Incapacitation: Estimating the Effects of Criminal Sanctions on Crime Rates.* Panel on Research on Deterrent and Incapacitative Effects, NCJ report no. 44669. Washington, DC: National Academy of Sciences, 1978.

Blumstein, Alfred, and Kiminori Nakamura. "Redemption in the Presence of Widespread Criminal Background Checks." *Criminology* 47, no. 2 (2009): 327–59. https://doi.org/10.1111/j.1745-9125.2009.00155.x.

Blythe, Robert. "The Afro-American Patrolmen's League." Chicago History Museum (blog), February 8, 2017. https://www.chicagohistory.org/aapl/.

Bollinger, Christopher R., and Aaron Yelowitz. "Targeting Intensive Job

Assistance to Ex-Offenders by the Nature of Offense: Results from a Randomized Control Trial." *Economic Inquiry* 59, no. 3 (2021): 1308–27. https://doi.org/10.1111/ecin.12984.

Boustan, Leah Platt. "Racial Residential Segregation in American Cities." NBER working paper no. 19045. Cambridge, MA: National Bureau of Economic Research, May 2013. https://doi.org/10.3386/w19045.

———. "Was Postwar Suburbanization 'White Flight'? Evidence from the Black Migration." *Quarterly Journal of Economics* 125, no. 1 (2010): 417–43. https://doi.org/10.1162/qjec.2010.125.1.417.

Bowman, Karlyn, and Jennifer K. Marsico. "The Public's Verdict on the War on Poverty." *Fox News*, May 7, 2015. https://www.foxnews.com/opinion/the-publics-verdict-on-the-war-on-poverty.

Boyer, John W. *The University of Chicago: A History*. Chicago: University of Chicago Press, 2015.

Boyle, Greg. "On Being with Krista Tippett—The Calling of Delight: Gangs, Service, and Kinship." *On Being*, December 19, 2019. https://onbeing.org/programs/greg-boyle-the-calling-of-delight-gangs-service-and-kinship/.

Braga, Anthony A., Brandon Turchan, Andrew V. Papachristos, and David M. Hureau. "Hot Spots Policing of Small Geographic Areas Effects on Crime." *Campbell Systematic Reviews* 15, no. 3 (2019): e1046. https://doi.org/10.1002/cl2.1046.

Branas, Charles C., Eugenia South, Michelle C. Kondo, Bernadette C. Hohl, Philippe Bourgois, Douglas J. Wiebe, and John M. MacDonald. "Citywide Cluster Randomized Trial to Restore Blighted Vacant Land and Its Effects on Violence, Crime, and Fear." *Proceedings of the National Academy of Sciences* 115, no. 12 (2018): 2946–51. https://doi.org/10.1073/pnas.1718503115.

Brantingham, P. Jeffrey, Matthew Valasik, and George O. Mohler. "Does Predictive Policing Lead to Biased Arrests? Results from a Randomized Controlled Trial." *Statistics and Public Policy* 5, no. 1 (2018): 1–6. https://doi.org/10.1080/2330443X.2018.1438940.

Bratton, William J. "New Strategies for Combatting Crime in New York City." *Fordham Urban Law Journal* 23, no. 3 (1996): 781–95.

"A Brief History of the NRA." National Rifle Association. Accessed March 15, 2024. https://home.nra.org/about-the-nra/.

"British Lawmakers Vote for Total Handgun Ban." *CNN World News*, June 12, 1997. http://edition.cnn.com/WORLD/9706/12/britain .handgun/index.html.

Britt, Chester L., Gary Kleck, and David J. Bordua. "Avoidance and Misunderstanding: A Rejoinder to McDowall et al." *Law and Society Review* 30, no. 2 (1996): 393–97. https://doi.org/10.2307/3053965.

———. "A Reassessment of the D.C. Gun Law: Some Cautionary Notes on the Use of Interrupted Time Series Designs for Policy Impact Assessment." *Law and Society Review* 30, no. 2 (1996): 361–80. https://doi.org /10.2307/3053963.

Brody, Jane E. "After a Suicide Attempt, the Risk of Another Try." *New York Times*, November 7, 2016. https://www.nytimes.com/2016/11/08/well /live/after-a-suicide-attempt-the-risk-of-another-try.html.

Brosco, Jeffrey P. "The Early History of the Infant Mortality Rate in America: A Reflection upon the Past and a Prophecy of the Future." *Pediatrics* 103, no. 2 (1999): 478–85. https://doi.org/10.1542/peds.103.2.478.

Brown, Gregory K., Thomas Ten Have, Gregg R. Henriques, Sharon X. Xie, Judd E. Hollander, and Aaron T. Beck. "Cognitive Therapy for the Prevention of Suicide Attempts: A Randomized Controlled Trial." *JAMA* 294, no. 5 (2005): 563–70. https://doi.org/10.1001/jama.294.5 .563.

Bruner, J. S. "Going Beyond the Information Given." In *Contemporary Approaches to Cognition*, edited by H. Gruber, K. R. Hammond, and R. Jesser. Cambridge, MA: Harvard University Press, 1957.

Bryson, Bill. *At Home: A Short History of Private Life*. New York: Doubleday, 2010.

Buckley, Rosemary Sobol, and Sam Charles. "4 Teens Held without Bond in Slaying of Chicago Off-Duty Officer." *Chicago Tribune*, May 10, 2023. https://www.chicagotribune.com/2023/05/10/4-teens-held-without -bond-in-slaying-of-chicago-off-duty-officer/.

"Budget Justice." Vera Institute of Justice, 2020. https://www.vera.org /spotlights/election-2020/budget-justice.

Bump, Philip. "The Irreducible Problem for Gun-Control Activists: The Number of Guns." *Washington Post*, March 28, 2023. https:// www.washingtonpost.com/politics/2023/03/28/guns-united-states -shootings/.

Bunten, Alexis, Nathaniel Kendall-Taylor, and Eric Lindland. *Caning, Context and Class: Mapping the Gaps between Expert and Public Understandings of Public Safety.* Washington, DC: FrameWorks Institute, April 14, 2011. https://www.frameworksinstitute.org/publication/caning-context-and-class-mapping-the-gaps-between-expert-and-public-understandings-of-public-safety/.

Bunting, Glenn F. "Feinstein Faces Fight for Diluted Gun Bill." *Los Angeles Times*, November 9, 1993. https://www.latimes.com/archives/la-xpm-1993-11-09-mn-54844-story.html.

Bush, George, Brent A. Vogt, Jennifer Holmes, Anders M. Dale, Douglas Greve, Michael A. Jenike, and Bruce R. Rosen. "Dorsal Anterior Cingulate Cortex: A Role in Reward-Based Decision Making." *Proceedings of the National Academy of Sciences* 99, no. 1 (2002): 523–28. https://doi.org/10.1073/pnas.012470999.

Bushway, Shawn, Matthew Phillips, and Philip J. Cook. "The Overall Effect of the Business Cycle on Crime." *German Economic Review* 13, no. 4 (2012): 436–46. https://doi.org/10.1111/j.1468-0475.2012.00578.x.

Business and Professional People for the Public Interest. *What Is Gautreaux?* Chicago: BPI Chicago, 1991. https://www.bpichicago.org/wp-content/uploads/2013/12/what-is-gautreaux.pdf.

Butel, Jean, and Kathryn L. Braun. "The Role of Collective Efficacy in Reducing Health Disparities: A Systematic Review." *Family and Community Health* 42, no. 1 (2019): 8–19. https://doi.org/10.1097/FCH.0000000000000206.

Cahill, Meagan, Jesse Jannetta, Emily Tiry, Samantha Lowry, Miriam Becker-Cohen, Ellen Paddock, Maria Serakos, Loraine Park, and Karen Hennigan. *Evaluation of the Los Angeles Gang Reduction and Youth Development Program.* Washington, DC: Urban Institute, September 2015. https://www.urban.org/sites/default/files/publication/77956/2000622-Evaluation-of-the-Los-Angeles-Gang-Reduction-and-Youth-Development-Program-Year-4-Evaluation-Report.pdf.

Calmoret, John. "Racialized Space and the Culture of Segregation: 'Hewing a Stone of Hope from a Mountain of Despair.'" *UPenn Law Review* 143 (1995): 1233–73. https://scholarship.law.upenn.edu/cgi/viewcontent.cgi?article=3564&context=penn_law_review.

Camerer, Colin, George Loewenstein, and Matthew Rabin, eds. *Advances in Behavioral Economics*. Roundtable Series in Behavioral Economics. Princeton, NJ: Princeton University Press, 2003.

Campanella, Thomas J. "Jane Jacobs and the Death and Life of American Planning." *Places Journal*, April 2011. https://doi.org/10.22269/110425.

"Cancer Trends Progress Report: Survival." National Cancer Institute. Last reviewed March 2024. https://progressreport.cancer.gov/after /survival.

Carr, Jillian B., and Vijetha Koppa. "Housing Vouchers, Income Shocks and Crime: Evidence from a Lottery." *Journal of Economic Behavior and Organization* 177 (September 2020): 475–93.

Carr, Jillian B., and Analisa Packham. "SNAP Benefits and Crime: Evidence from Changing Disbursement Schedules." *Review of Economics and Statistics* 101, no. 2 (2019): 310–25. https://doi.org/10.1162/rest_a_00757.

———. "SNAP Schedules and Domestic Violence." *Journal of Policy Analysis and Management* 40, no. 2 (2021): 412–52. https://doi.org/10.1002/pam .22235.

Carroll, John S. "The Effect of Imagining an Event on Expectations for the Event: An Interpretation in Terms of the Availability Heuristic." *Journal of Experimental Social Psychology* 14, no. 1 (1978): 88–96. https://doi.org /10.1016/0022-1031(78)90062-8.

Carson, E. Ann. *Prisoners in 2019*. NCJ report no. 255115. Washington, DC: US Department of Justice, Office of Justice Programs, Bureau of Justice Statistics, October 2020. https://bjs.ojp.gov/content/pub/pdf/p19.pdf.

Casanova, Stephanie. "'They Are Somebody': Family Members, Advocates Push for Parole Bill That Would Give Longtime Prisoners a Second Chance at Life." *Chicago Tribune*, October 20, 2021. https://www .chicagotribune.com/2021/10/20/they-are-somebody-family-members -advocates-push-for-parole-bill-that-would-give-longtime-prisoners-a -second-chance-at-life/.

Case, Anne, and Angus Deaton. *Deaths of Despair and the Future of Capitalism*. Princeton, NJ: Princeton University Press, 2020.

Centers for Disease Control and Prevention. "Achievements in Public Health, 1900–1999: Healthier Mothers and Babies." *Morbidity and Mortality Weekly Report* 48, no. 38 (1999): 858.

————. "*QuickStats*: Age-Adjusted Rates of Firearm-Related Homicide, by Race, Hispanic Origin, and Sex—National Vital Statistics System, United States, 2019." *Morbidity and Mortality Weekly Report* 70, no. 42 (2021): 1491. https://doi.org/10.15585/mmwr.mm7042a6.

————. "Vital Statistics of the United States." National Center for Health Statistics, last reviewed November 6, 2015. https://www.cdc.gov/nchs /products/vsus.htm.

Chaiken, Shelly, and Yaacov Trope, eds. *Dual-Process Theories in Social Psychology*. New York: Guilford Press, 1999.

Chalfin, Aaron. "Economic Costs of Crime." In *The Encyclopedia of Crime and Punishment*, edited by Wesley G. Jennings, 1–12. Wiley, 2015. https:// doi.org/10.1002/9781118519639.wbecpx193.

Chalfin, Aaron, Benjamin Hansen, Jason Lerner, and Lucie Parker. "Reducing Crime through Environmental Design: Evidence from a Randomized Experiment of Street Lighting in New York City." *Journal of Quantitative Criminology* 38, no. 1 (2022): 127–57. https://doi.org/10 .1007/s10940-020-09490-6.

Chalfin, Aaron, Benjamin Hansen, Emily K. Weisburst, and Morgan C. Williams. "Police Force Size and Civilian Race." *American Economic Review: Insights* 4, no. 2 (2022): 139–58. https://doi.org/10.1257/aeri .20200792.

Chalfin, Aaron, and Justin McCrary. "Are U.S. Cities Underpoliced? Theory and Evidence." *Review of Economics and Statistics* 100, no. 1 (2018): 167–86. https://doi.org/10.1162/REST_a_00694.

————. "The Effect of Police on Crime: New Evidence from U.S. Cities, 1960–2010." NBER working paper no. 18815. Cambridge, MA: National Bureau of Economic Research, February 2013. https://doi.org /10.3386/w18815.

Chang, Tom Y., and Mireille Jacobson. "Going to Pot? The Impact of Dispensary Closures on Crime." *Journal of Urban Economics* 100 (July 2017): 120–36. https://doi.org/10.1016/j.jue.2017.04.001.

Chartrand, Tanya L., and John A. Bargh. "Automatic Activation of Impression Formation and Memorization Goals: Nonconscious Goal Priming Reproduces Effects of Explicit Task Instructions." *Journal of Personality and Social Psychology* 71, no. 3 (1996): 464–78. https://doi.org/10.1037 /0022-3514.71.3.464.

Chavis, Lakeidra. "The Problems with Chicago's Gang-Centric Narrative of Gun Violence." *Trace*, August 31, 2021. https://www.thetrace.org /2021/08/chicago-mayor-police-gang-database-shooting.

Cheng, Cheng, and Wei Long. "Improving Police Services: Evidence from the French Quarter Task Force." *Journal of Public Economics* 164 (August 2018): 1–18. https://doi.org/10.1016/j.jpubeco.2018.05.002.

Cherney, Samantha, Andrew R. Morral, Terry L. Schell, Sierra Smucker, and Emily Hoch. "Development of the RAND State Firearm Law Database and Supporting Materials." RAND Corporation, June 8, 2022. https://www.rand.org/pubs/tools/TLA243-2-v2.html.

"Chicago City Council Approves Citywide Lobbying Ban on Elected Officials," Illinois Policy, December 20, 2019. https://www.illinoispolicy .org/chicago-city-council-votes-to-ban-lobbying-by-elected-leaders/.

"Chicago Crime 2018." *HeyJackass!*, last updated January 21, 2022. https:// heyjackass.com/category/2018-stats/.

Chicago Mayor's Press Office. "Mayor Brandon Johnson Releases 'The People's Budget,' a Bold, Balanced Plan for FY2024." Press release, October 11, 2023. https://www.chicago.gov/city/en/depts/mayor/press _room/press_releases/2023/october/the-peoples-budget-fy2024.html.

———. "Whole Foods Market and Mayor Emanuel Announce New Store in Chicago's Englewood Neighborhood." Press release, September 4, 2013. https://www.chicago.gov/city/en/depts/mayor /press_room/press_releases/2013/september_2013/whole_foods _marketandmayoremanuelannouncenewstoreinchicagosengle.html.

Chicago Metropolitan Agency for Planning. "Community Data Snapshots 2023." Community Chicago Metropolitan Agency for Planning, last modified July 12, 2023. https://datahub.cmap.illinois.gov/maps /05831ce4f3064b3f8e26c85be10d9836/about.

———. *Greater Grand Crossing: Community Data Snapshot, Chicago Community Area Series*. Chicago: Chicago Metropolitan Agency for Planning, July 2023. https://www.cmap.illinois.gov/documents/10180/126764 /Greater+Grand+Crossing.pdf.

———. *South Shore: Community Data Snapshot, Chicago Community Area Series*. Chicago: Chicago Metropolitan Agency for Planning, July 2023. https://www.cmap.illinois.gov/documents/10180/126764/South +Shore.pdf.

———. *Woodlawn: Community Data Snapshot, Chicago Community Area Series*. Chicago: Chicago Metropolitan Agency for Planning, July 2023. https://cmap.illinois.gov/wp-content/uploads/dlm_uploads /Woodlawn.pdf.

Chicago Office of the Mayor and Chicago Police Department. *Gun Trace Report 2017*. Chicago: City of Chicago, 2017. https://www.chicago.gov /content/dam/city/depts/mayor/Press%20Room/Press%20Releases /2017/October/GTR2017.pdf.

Chicago Police Department. *2011 Chicago Murder Analysis*. Chicago: Chicago Police Department, Research and Development Division, 2012. https://home.chicagopolice.org/wp-content/uploads/2014/12/2011 -Murder-Report.pdf.

———. *2021 Annual Report*. Chicago: Chicago Police Department, Research and Development Division, 2022. https://home.chicagopolice .org/wp-content/uploads/2021-Annual-Report.pdf.

———. *2022 Annual Report*. Chicago: Chicago Police Department, Research and Development Division, 2023. https://home.chicagopolice.org/wp -content/uploads/2022-Annual-Report-FOR-PUBLICATION.pdf.

———. *Statistical Summary 1980*. Chicago: Chicago Police Department, August 1, 1981. https://home.chicagopolice.org/wp-content/uploads /2014/12/1980-Annual-Report.pdf.

"Chicago Public Schools Most Empty Schools." *Wirepoints*, August 5, 2022. https://wirepoints.org/more-failure-at-chicago-public-schools-about -one-third-of-traditional-schools-are-half-empty-or-worse-wirepoints /chicago-public-schools-most-empty-schools/.

Chicago Transit Authority. *Annual Ridership Report: Calendar Year 2022*. Chicago: Chicago Transit Authority, February 2, 2023. https://www .transitchicago.com/assets/1/6/2022_Annual_Report_-_FINAL.pdf.

Chicago Tribune Editorial Board. "Killing Our Children." *Chicago Tribune*, January 3, 1993. https://www.chicagotribune.com/1993/01/03/killing -our-children-2/.

"Chicago's Million Dollar Blocks: Full Map." *Chicago's Million Dollar Blocks*. Accessed March 15, 2024. https://chicagosmilliondollarblocks.com /map.html.

"Chicago's Recent Rating Upgrades." *Civic Federation* (blog), May 25, 2023.

https://www.civicfed.org/civic-federation/blog/chicagos-recent-rating
-upgrades.

Chioda, Laura, João M. P. De Mello, and Rodrigo R. Soares. "Spillovers
from Conditional Cash Transfer Programs: Bolsa Família and Crime in
Urban Brazil." *Economics of Education Review* 54 (2016): 306–20.

Churchill, Winston S. "My New York Misadventure." *Daily Mail*, January
4–5, 1932. https://winstonchurchill.org/publications/finest-hour
/finest-hour-136/my-new-york-misadventure/.

Chyn, Eric, Robert Collinson, and Danielle Sandler. "The Long-Run Ef-
fects of Residential Racial Desegregation Programs: Evidence from
Gautreaux." Working paper. Washington, DC: US Census Bureau,
March 29, 2023. https://robcollinson.github.io/RobWebsite/CCS
_Gautreaux.pdf.

Cialdini, Robert B. *Influence: The Psychology of Persuasion.* New York: Harper
Collins, 2006.

"Citywide Survey of Los Angeles." *Los Angeles Times*, September 16, 20014.
https://www.latimes.com/local/la-losangeles-poll-jun182009
-htmlstory.html.

City of Chicago. "311 Service Requests." Chicago Data Portal. Last
modified November 9, 2023. https://data.cityofchicago.org/Service
-Requests/311-Service-Requests/v6vf-nfxy.

City of Chicago. "Active Business Licenses." Chicago Data Portal. Last
updated July 3, 2024. https://data.cityofchicago.org/Community
-Economic-Development/Business-Licenses-Current-Active/uupf
-x98q/about_data.

Clark, K. B., and M. P. Clark. "Racial Identification and Racial Preference
in Negro Children." In *Readings in Social Psychology*, edited by T. M. New-
comb and E. L. Hartley, 169–78. New York: Holt, 1947.

Clarke, Ronald V. "Situational Crime Prevention." *Crime and Justice* 19
(1995): 91–150.

"Closing America's Education Funding Gaps." Century Foundation,
July 22, 2020. https://tcf.org/content/report/closing-americas
-education-funding/.

Cloward, Richard A., and Lloyd E. Ohlin. *Delinquency and Opportunity: A
Theory of Delinquent Gangs.* New York: Free Press, 1960.

Cloyne, James, Joseba Martinez, Haroon Mumtaz, and Paolo Surico. "Short-Term Tax Cuts, Long-Term Stimulus." NBER working paper no. 30246. Cambridge, MA: National Bureau of Economic Research, July 2022. https://doi.org/10.3386/w30246.

Cochran, John K., Denise Paquette Boots, and Kathleen M. Heide. "Attribution Styles and Attitudes toward Capital Punishment for Juveniles, the Mentally Incompetent, and the Mentally Retarded." *Justice Quarterly* 20, no. 1 (2003): 65–93. https://doi.org/10.1080/07418820300095461.

Cohen, Adam, and Elizabeth Taylor. *American Pharaoh: Mayor Richard J. Daley—His Battle for Chicago and the Nation.* Boston, MA: Little Brown and Company, 2000.

Cohn, Ellen G., and David P. Farrington. "Who Are the Most Influential Criminologists in the English-Speaking World?" *British Journal of Criminology* 34, no. 2 (1994): 204–25. https://doi.org/10.1093/oxfordjournals.bjc.a048403.

Collins, William, and Ariell Zimran. "Working Their Way Up? US Immigrants' Changing Labor Market Assimilation in the Age of Mass Migration." NBER working paper no. 26414. Cambridge, MA: National Bureau of Economic Research, revised December 2021. https://doi.org/10.3386/w26414.

"Columbus (Christopher) Park." Chicago Park District. Accessed March 1, 2024. https://www.chicagoparkdistrict.com/parks-facilities/columbus-christopher-park.

"Community Data Snapshots." Chicago Metropolitan Agency for Planning, 2024. https://www.cmap.illinois.gov/data/community-snapshots.

Congdon, William J., Jeffrey R. Kling, and Sendhil Mullainathan. *Policy and Choice: Public Finance through the Lens of Behavioral Economics.* Washington, DC: Brookings Institution Press, 2011.

Congressional Research Service. *Legal Sidebar: The Future of the Second Amendment: New York State Rifle & Pistol Association at the Supreme Court.* Washington, DC: Congressional Research Service, May 15, 2020. https://crsreports.congress.gov/product/pdf/LSB/LSB10468.

Cook, Philip J. "The Clearance Rate as a Measure of Criminal Justice System Effectiveness." *Journal of Public Economics* 11, no. 1 (1979): 135–42. https://doi.org/10.1016/0047-2727(79)90050-1.

———. "The Great American Gun War: Notes from Four Decades in the Trenches." *Crime and Justice* 42, no. 1 (2013): 19–73. https://doi.org/10.1086/670397.

———. "Is Robbery Becoming More Violent? An Analysis of Robbery Murder Trends since 1968." *Journal of Criminal Law and Criminology (1973–)* 76, no. 2 (1985): 480–89. https://doi.org/10.2307/1143614.

———. "Robbery." In *The Oxford Handbook of Crime and Public Policy*, edited by Michael Tonry, 102–14. Oxford University Press, 2011.

———. "The Technology of Personal Violence." *Crime and Justice* 14 (1991): 1–71.

Cook, Philip J., Songman Kang, Anthony A. Braga, Jens Ludwig, and Mallory E. O'Brien. "An Experimental Evaluation of a Comprehensive Employment-Oriented Prisoner Re-Entry Program." *Journal of Quantitative Criminology* 31, no. 3 (2014): 355–82. https://doi.org/10.1007/s10940-014-9242-5.

Cook, Philip J., and Jens Ludwig. "Does Gun Prevalence Affect Teen Gun Carrying after All?" *Criminology* 42, no. 1 (2004): 27–54. https://doi.org/10.1111/j.1745-9125.2004.tb00512.x.

———. "Aiming for Evidence-Based Gun Policy." *Journal of Policy Analysis and Management* 23, no. 3 (2006): 691–735.

———. *Gun Violence: The Real Costs*. New York: Oxford University Press, 2000.

———. *Guns in America: Results of a Comprehensive Survey on Private Firearms Ownership and Use*. Washington, DC: Police Foundation, 1997.

———. "Response to Counterpoint: Violence Itself Is a Root Cause of Violence." *Journal of Policy Analysis and Management* 38, no. 3 (2019): 802–4. https://doi.org/10.1002/pam.22142.

———. "The Social Costs of Gun Ownership." *Journal of Public Economics* 90, nos. 1–2 (2006): 379–91. https://doi.org/10.1016/j.jpubeco.2005.02.003.

———. "Understanding Gun Violence: Public Health vs. Public Policy." *Journal of Policy Analysis and Management* 38, no. 3 (2019): 788–95. https://doi.org/10.1002/pam.22141.

Cook, Philip J., Jens Ludwig, and David Hemenway. "The Gun Debate's New Mythical Number: How Many Defensive Uses Per Year?" *Journal of Policy Analysis and Management* 16, no. 3 (1997): 463–69.

Cook, Philip J., Jens Ludwig, Sudhir Venkatesh, and Anthony A. Braga. "Underground Gun Markets." *Economic Journal* 117, no. 524 (2007): F588–618.

Cook, Philip J., and John MacDonald. "Public Safety through Private Action: An Economic Assessment of BIDS." *Economic Journal* 121, no. 552 (2011): 445–62.

Cook, Philip J., Stephanie Molliconi, and Thomas B. Cole. "Regulating Gun Markets." *Journal of Law and Criminology* 86, no. 1 (1995): 59–92.

Cooper, Alexia D., and Erica L. Smith. *Homicide Trends in the United States, 1980–2008.* NCJ report no. 236018. Washington, DC: US Department of Justice, Office of Justice Programs, Bureau of Justice Statistics, November 2011. https://bjs.ojp.gov/library/publications/homicide-trends-united-states-1980-2008.

Coppersmith, Daniel D. L., Oisín Ryan, Rebecca G. Fortgang, Alexander J. Millner, Evan M. Kleiman, and Matthew K. Nock. "Mapping the Timescale of Suicidal Thinking." *Proceedings of the National Academy of Sciences* 120, no. 17 (2023): e2215434120. https://doi.org/10.1073/pnas.2215434120.

Cordery, Rachel. "UK PM May Holds Knife-Crime Summit with Teachers Ordered to Identify Violent Youths." *Yahoo News*, April 1, 2019. https://sg.news.yahoo.com/uk-pm-may-holds-knife-crime-summit-teachers-133634905.html.

Cordner, Gary, and Elizabeth Perkins Biebel. "Problem-Oriented Policing in Practice." *Criminology and Public Policy* 4, no. 2 (2005): 155–80. https://doi.org/10.1111/j.1745-9133.2005.00013.x.

Cornell, Dewey G., Janet Warren, Gary Hawk, Ed Stafford, Guy Oram, and Denise Pine. "Psychopathy in Instrumental and Reactive Violent Offenders." *Journal of Consulting and Clinical Psychology* 64, no. 4 (1996): 783–90. https://doi.org/10.1037/0022-006X.64.4.783.

"Corruption Convictions Decline Nationally but Chicago and Illinois Remain at, near Top." *UIC Today*, May 12, 2022. https://today.uic.edu/corruption-convictions-decline-nationally-but-chicago-and-illinois-remain-at-near-top/.

Costopoulos, Julie S., Amy M. Plewinski, Patricia L. Monaghan, and Vanessa A. Edkins. "The Impact of US Government Assistance on Recidivism." *Criminal Behaviour and Mental Health* 27, no. 4 (2017): 303–11. https://doi.org/10.1002/cbm.1997.

Coupland, Robin M., Markus A. Rothschild, and Michael J. Thali. *Wound Ballistics*. Edited by Beat P. Kneubuehl. Berlin, Heidelberg: Springer Berlin Heidelberg, 2011. https://doi.org/10.1007/978-3-642-20356-5.

Cox, Amanda. "Don't Be Surprised That People Still Say Racist Things." *New York Times*, April 30, 2014. https://www.nytimes.com/2014/04/30 /upshot/dont-be-surprised-that-people-still-say-racist-things.html.

Coy, Peter. "Goodhart's Law Rules the Modern World. Here Are Nine Examples." *Bloomberg*, March 26, 2021. https://www.bloomberg.com /news/articles/2021-03-26/goodhart-s-law-rules-the-modern-world -here-are-nine-examples.

Cozens, Paul, and Terence Love. "A Review and Current Status of Crime Prevention through Environmental Design (CPTED)." *Journal of Planning Literature* 30, no. 4 (2015): 393–412. https://doi.org/10.1177 /0885412215595440.

Crepeau, Megan, and Ray Long. "State Representative Takes Witness Stand at Perjury Trial of Madigan 'Gatekeeper' Tim Mapes." *Chicago Tribune*, August 10, 2023. https://www.chicagotribune.com/2023/08/10 /state-representative-takes-witness-stand-at-perjury-trial-of-madigan -gatekeeper-tim-mapes/.

"Crime Data Explorer." Federal Bureau of Investigation. Accessed May 7, 2024. https://cde.ucr.cjis.gov/LATEST/webapp/#/pages/explorer /crime/arrest.

Crimmins, Timothy. "Incarceration as Incapacitation: An Intellectual History." *American Affairs Journal* 2, no. 3 (2018). https://american affairsjournal.org/2018/08/incarceration-as-incapacitation-an -intellectual-history/.

"Crossing Guard Salary in Chicago, Illinois." *Salary.com*. Accessed May 2, 2024. https://www.salary.com/research/salary/benchmark/crossing -guard-salary/chicago-il.

Cullen, Francis T., Gregory A. Clark, John B. Cullen, and Richard A. Mathers. "Attribution, Salience, and Attitudes toward Criminal Sanctioning." *Criminal Justice and Behavior* 12, no. 3 (1985): 305–31. https://doi.org /10.1177/0093854885012003003.

Cullen, Julie Berry, and Steven D. Levitt. "Crime, Urban Flight, and the Consequences for Cities." *Review of Economics and Statistics* 82, no. 2 (1999): 159–69.

Curry, Theodore R. "Conservative Protestantism and the Perceived Wrongfulness of Crimes: A Research Note." *Criminology* 34, no. 3 (1996): 453–64. https://doi.org/10.1111/j.1745-9125.1996.tb01215.x.

Curry, Timothy. "Gun Owners More Likely to Distrust the Federal Government." *Ohio State News*, August 13, 2001. https://news.osu.edu/gun-owners-more-likely-to-distrust-the-federal-government/.

Cutler, David M., Edward L. Glaeser, and Jacob L. Vigdor. "The Rise and Decline of the American Ghetto." *Journal of Political Economy* 107, no. 3 (1999): 455–506. https://doi.org/10.1086/250069.

CWB Chicago. "Chicago Spree Killer Jason Nightengale Police Stop." YouTube, January 10, 2021. MP4 video, 0:20. https://www.youtube.com/watch?v=iDCCPigLNLw.

"Daley Pursuing Anti-Gang Law." *Chicago Tribune*, January 12, 2000. https://www.chicagotribune.com/news/ct-xpm-2000-01-12-0001120206-story.html.

Daley, Richard J. Inaugural address, April 20, 1955. Online at Chicago Public Library. https://www.chipublib.org/mayor-richard-j-daley-inaugural-address-1955/.

Damm, Anna Piil, and Cédric Gorinas. "Prison as a Criminal School: Peer Effects and Criminal Learning behind Bars." *Journal of Law and Economics* 63, no. 1 (2020): 149–80.

Darden, Michael, and Mario Macis. "Trust and Health Care-Seeking Behavior." NBER working paper no. 32028. Cambridge, MA: National Bureau of Economic Research, January 2024. https://doi.org/10.3386/w32028.

Darley, John M., and C. Daniel Batson. "'From Jerusalem to Jericho': A Study of Situational and Dispositional Variables in Helping Behavior." *Journal of Personality and Social Psychology* 27, no. 1 (1973): 100–108. https://doi.org/10.1037/h0034449.

Dattani, Saloni, Lucas Rodés-Guirao, Hannah Ritchie, Esteban Ortiz-Ospina, and Max Roser. "Life Expectancy." *Our World in Data*, 2023. https://ourworldindata.org/life-expectancy.

Decker, Scott H., David C. Pyrooz, and James A. Densley. *On Gangs*. Philadelphia, PA: Temple University Press, 2022.

DeLuca, Stefanie, Greg J. Duncan, Micere Keels, and Ruby M. Mendenhall. "*Gautreaux* Mothers and Their Children: An Update." *Housing Policy Debate* 20, no. 1 (2010): 7–25. https://doi.org/10.1080/10511481003599829.

Deming, D. J. "The Growing Importance of Social Skills in the Labor Market." *Quarterly Journal of Economics* 132, no. 4 (2017): 1593–640. https://doi.org/10.1093/qje/qjx022.

Deming, David J. "Four Facts about Human Capital." *Journal of Economic Perspectives* 36, no. 3 (2022): 75–102. https://doi.org/10.1257/jep.36.3.75.

Denning, Brannon P., and Glenn Harlan Reynolds. "Retconning Heller: Five Takes on New York Rifle & Pistol Association, Inc. v. Bruen." University of Tennessee Legal Studies research paper no. 446; *William and Mary Law Review* 65, no. 1 (2023). https://doi.org/10.2139/ssrn.4372216.

Deshpande, Manasi, and Michael Mueller-Smith. "Does Welfare Prevent Crime? The Criminal Justice Outcomes of Youth Removed from SSI." *Quarterly Journal of Economics* 137, no. 4 (2022): 2263–307. https://doi.org/10.1093/qje/qjac017.

Desmond, Ang, Panka Bencsik, Jesse Bruhn, and Ellora Derenoncourt. "Police Violence Reduces Civilian Cooperation and Engagement with Law Enforcement" HKS working paper no. RWP21-022. Cambridge, MA: Harvard Kennedy School, September 8, 2021. https://doi.org/10.2139/ssrn.3920493.

D'Este, Rocco, and Alex Harvey. "The Unintended Consequences of Welfare Reform: Universal Credit and Crime." *SSRN Electronic Journal*, April 5, 2022. https://doi.org/10.2139/ssrn.3642502.

Dewey, John. *Moral Principles in Education*. Boston, MA: Riverside Press Cambridge, 1909.

Dewey, John. *How We Think*. Boston, MA: DC Heath, 1910.

Deza, Monica, Catherine Maclean, and Keisha Solomon. "Local Access to Mental Healthcare and Crime." *Journal of Urban Economics* 129 (May 2022): 103410. https://doi.org/10.1016/j.jue.2021.103410.

Dickerson, Justin. "'Nothing Stops a Bullet Like a Job': Homeboy Industries and Restorative Justice." *Social Science Research Network*, May 14, 2010. https://doi.org/10.2139/ssrn.1827983.

DiIulio, John. "The Coming of the Super-Predators." *Weekly Standard*, November 27, 1995.

———. "What Happens in Real Bureaucracies." *Regulatory Review*, July 10, 2021. https://www.theregreview.org/2012/07/10/diiulio-wilson-real-bureaucracy/.

Dillon, Sam. "Large Urban-Suburban Gap Seen in Graduation Rates." *New York Times*, April 22, 2009. https://www.nytimes.com/2009/04/22/education/22dropout.html.

Dionne, E. J. "Milwaukee Mayor Tom Barrett's Battle against 'Slow-Motion Mass Murders.'" *Seattle Times*, May 13, 2013. https://www.seattletimes.com/opinion/milwaukee-mayor-tom-barrettlsquos-battle-against-lsquoslow-motion-mass-murdersrsquo/.

Djvlad. "Swagg Dinero on Lil Jojo's 'BDK' Starting War in Chicago, Jojo Getting Killed (Part 2)." YouTube, December 5, 2017. MP4 video, 9:27. https://www.youtube.com/watch?v=IjqNFp-OY4s.

Dodge, Kenneth A. "Social-Cognitive Mechanisms in the Development of Conduct Disorder and Depression." *Annual Review of Psychology* 44, no. 1 (1993): 559–84. https://doi.org/10.1146/annurev.ps.44.020193.003015.

Domma, Franco, Charito Romero, Elisabeth Saffell, and Chicago Crime Commission, eds. *The Gang Book: A Detailed Overview of Street Gangs in the Chicago Metropolitan Area*. Chicago: Chicago Crime Commission, 2018.

Donohue, John J. "Assessing the Relative Benefits of Incarceration: Overall Changes and the Benefits on the Margin." In *Do Prisons Make Us Safer? The Benefits and Costs of the Prison Boom*, edited by Steven Raphael and Michael A. Stoll, 269–342. New York: Russell Sage Foundation, 2009. http://www.jstor.org/stable/10.7758/9781610444651.13.

Donohue, John J., Abhay Aneja, and Kyle D. Weber. "Right-to-Carry Laws and Violent Crime: A Comprehensive Assessment Using Panel Data and a State-Level Synthetic Control Analysis." *Journal of Empirical Legal Studies* 16, no. 2 (2019): 198–247. https://doi.org/10.1111/jels.12219.

Donohue, John J., Samuel Cai, Matthew Bondy, and Philip Cook. "Why Does Right-to-Carry Cause Violent Crime to Increase?" NBER working paper no. 30190. Cambridge, MA: National Bureau of Economic Research, June 2022. https://doi.org/10.3386/w30190.

Draca, Mirko, Stephen Machin, and Robert Witt. "Panic on the Streets of London: Police, Crime, and the July 2005 Terror Attacks." *American Economic Review* 101, no. 5 (2011): 2157–81. https://doi.org/10.1257/aer.101.5.2157.

Drago, Francesco, Roberto Galbiati, and Pietro Vertova. "The Deterrent Effects of Prison: Evidence from a Natural Experiment." *Journal of Political Economy* 117, no. 2 (2009): 257–80. https://doi.org/10.1086/599286.

Drake, Patrick, Jennifer Tolbert, Robin Rudowitz, and Anthony Damico. "How Many Uninsured Are in the Coverage Gap and How Many Could Be Eligible if All States Adopted the Medicaid Expansion?" *KFF*, February 26, 2024. https://www.kff.org/medicaid/issue-brief/how-many-uninsured-are-in-the-coverage-gap-and-how-many-could-be-eligible-if-all-states-adopted-the-medicaid-expansion/.

Drug Enforcement Agency and Chicago Police Department. *Cartels and Gangs in Chicago: Joint Intelligence Report*. Report no. DEA-CHI-DIR-013-17. Chicago: DEA Chicago Field Division, May 2017. https://www.dea.gov/sites/default/files/2018-07/DIR-013-17%20Cartel%20and%20Gangs%20in%20Chicago%20-%20Unclassified.pdf.

Dube, Oeindrila, Sandy Jo MacArthur, and Anuj Shah. "A Cognitive View of Policing." NBER working paper no. 31651. Cambridge, MA: National Bureau of Economic Research, September 2023. https://doi.org/10.3386/w31651.

Duffy, Kevin. "Manor Tool & Manufacturing Co." *Manor Tool and Manufacturing* (blog), October 15, 2019. https://www.manortool.com/blog/history-of-chicagos-steel-mills-immigrants/.

Duis, Perry. "Chicago in History." *Perspectives on History*, November 1, 2002. https://www.historians.org/research-and-publications/perspectives-on-history/november-2002/chicago-in-history.

Duke, Lynne. "Summit Brings Together Gang Members, Black Elders." *Washington Post*, October 24, 1993. https://www.washingtonpost.com/archive/politics/1993/10/25/summit-brings-together-gang-members-black-elders/a8abc997-4b37-4367-ab64-0e76ef6ccd47/.

Dukes, Jesse. "'Poland Elsewhere': Why So Many Poles Came to Chicago."

WBEZ Chicago, October 30, 2015. https://www.wbez.org/stories
/poland-elsewhere-why-so-many-poles-came-to-chicago/b5576154
-6204-4c75-9ca1-ea3e85ba0b9a.

Dumontheil, Iroise, Ian A. Apperly, and Sarah-Jayne Blakemore. "Online
Usage of Theory of Mind Continues to Develop in Late Adolescence."
Developmental Science 13, no. 2 (2010): 331–38. https://doi.org/10.1111
/j.1467-7687.2009.00888.x.

Dunbar, Robin I. M. "The Social Brain Hypothesis." *Evolutionary Anthropology* 6, no. 5 (1998): 178–90.

Duncker, Karl. "On Problem-Solving." Translated by Lynne S. Lees. *Psychological Monographs* 58, no. 5 (1945): i–113. https://doi.org/10.1037
/h0093599.

Dutton, Donald G., and Arthur P. Aron. "Some Evidence for Heightened
Sexual Attraction under Conditions of High Anxiety." *Journal of Personality and Social Psychology* 30, no. 4 (1974): 510–17. https://doi.org/10
.1037/h0037031.

"Early Chicago, 1833–1871: A Selection of City Council Proceedings Files."
Office of the Illinois Secretary of State. Accessed May 1, 2024. https://
www.idaillinois.org/digital/collection/pshs/id/14792/rec/1.

Eckberg, D. L. "Estimates of Early Twentieth-Century U.S. Homicide
Rates: An Econometric Forecasting Approach." *Demography* 32, no. 1
(1995): 1–16.

"Economic Club of Chicago—Public Safety: A Call to Action for Business
(Recorded Remarks)." University of Chicago Crime Lab, September 26,
2023. https://crimelab.uchicago.edu/2023/09/public-safety-a-call-to
-action-for-business/.

Eggers, Frederick, and Alexander Thackeray. *32 Years of Housing Data*. Washington, DC: US Department of Housing and Urban Development, Office of Policy Development and Research, 2007. https://www.huduser
.gov/datasets/ahs/ahs_taskc.pdf.

Elving, Ron. "The NRA Wasn't Always against Gun Restrictions." *NPR*,
October 10, 2017. https://www.npr.org/2017/10/10/556578593/the
-nra-wasnt-always-against-gun-restrictions.

Emerson, Michael O., Karen J. Chai, and George Yancey. "Does Race
Matter in Residential Segregation? Exploring the Preferences of White

Americans." *American Sociological Review* 66, no. 6 (2001): 922–35. https://doi.org/10.2307/3088879.

Engel, Christoph. "Low Self-Control as a Source of Crime: A Meta-Study." Max Planck Institute for Research on Collective Goods, February 1, 2012. http://www.ssrn.com/abstract=2012381.

Ennis, Robert H. "Critical Thinking Across the Curriculum: A Vision." *Topoi* 37, no. 1 (2018): 165–84. https://doi.org/10.1007/s11245-016 -9401-4.

Enns, Peter K. *Incarceration Nation: How the United States Became the Most Punitive Democracy in the World.* 1st ed. New York: Cambridge University Press, 2016. https://doi.org/10.1017/CBO9781316471029.

Epley, Nicholas, Boaz Keysar, Leaf Van Boven, and Thomas Gilovich. "Perspective Taking as Egocentric Anchoring and Adjustment." *Journal of Personality and Social Psychology* 87, no. 3 (2004): 327–39. https://doi.org /10.1037/0022-3514.87.3.327.

Eriksson, Katherine, and Zachary Ward. "The Ethnic Segregation of Immigrants in the United States from 1850 to 1940." NBER working paper no. 24764. Cambridge, MA: National Bureau of Economic Research, June 2018. https://doi.org/10.3386/w24764.

Eriksson, T. Gerhard, Johanna G. Masche-No, and Anna M. Dåderman. "Personality Traits of Prisoners as Compared to General Populations: Signs of Adjustment to the Situation?" *Personality and Individual Differences* 107 (March 2017): 237–45. https://doi.org/10.1016/j.paid.2016 .11.030.

Erskine, Hazel. "The Polls: Causes of Crime." *Public Opinion Quarterly* 38, no. 2 (1974): 288–98.

Evans, Jonathan. "U.S. Adults Are More Religious than Western Europeans." Pew Research Center, September 5, 2018. https://www .pewresearch.org/short-reads/2018/09/05/u-s-adults-are-more -religious-than-western-europeans/.

Evans, Jonathan St. B. T. "Dual-Processing Accounts of Reasoning, Judgment, and Social Cognition." *Annual Review of Psychology* 59, no. 1 (2008): 255–78. https://doi.org/10.1146/annurev.psych.59.103006 .093629.

Evans, William N., and Emily G. Owens. "COPS and Crime." *Journal of*

Public Economics 91, no. 1 (2007): 181–201. https://doi.org/10.1016/j
.jpubeco.2006.05.014.

Fackler, Martin L. "Gunshot Wound Review." *Annals of Emergency Medicine*
28, no. 2 (1996): 194–203. https://doi.org/10.1016/s0196-0644(96)
70062-8.

Falco, Ed. "When Italian Immigrants Were 'the Other.'" *CNN*, July 10,
2012. https://edition.cnn.com/2012/07/10/opinion/falco-italian
-immigrants/.

Federal Bureau of Investigation. "Expanded Homicide Data Table 1—
Murder Victims by Race, Ethnicity, and Sex, 2019." Crime in the United
States, 2019. https://ucr.fbi.gov/crime-in-the-u.s/2019/crime-in-the
-u.s.-2019/topic-pages/tables/expanded-homicide-data-table-1.xls.

———. "Table 1—Crime in the United States by Volume and Rate per
100,000 Inhabitants, 2000-2019." Crime in the United States, 2019.
https://ucr.fbi.gov/crime-in-the-u.s/2019/crime-in-the-u.s.-2019
/tables/table-1.

———. "Table 19—Rate: Number of Crimes per 100,000 Inhabitants."
Crime in the United States, 2019. https://ucr.fbi.gov/crime-in-the-u.s
/2019/crime-in-the-u.s.-2019/tables/table-19.

———. "Table 23—Offense Analysis." Crime in the United States, 2019.
https://ucr.fbi.gov/crime-in-the-u.s/2019/crime-in-the-u.s.-2019
/tables/table-23.

Ferraz, Eduardo, Rodrigo R. Soares, and Juan Vargas. "Unbundling the Relationship between Economic Shocks and Crime." In *A Modern Guide to
the Economics of Crime*, edited by Paolo Buonanno, Paolo Vanin, and Juan
Vargas, 184–204. Northampton, MA: Edward Elgar Publishing, 2022.

Ferreira, Fernando, Jeanna Kenney, and Benjamin Smith. "Household
Mobility, Networks, and Gentrification of Minority Neighborhoods in
the US." NBER working paper no. 31480. Cambridge, MA: National
Bureau of Economic Research, July 2023. https://doi.org/10.3386
/w31480.

Feshbach, Seymour. "The Function of Aggression and the Regulation of
Aggressive Drive." *Psychological Review* 71, no. 4 (1964): 257–72. https://
doi.org/10.1037/h0043041.

Fishback, Price V., Ryan S. Johnson, and Shawn Kantor. "Striking at the

Roots of Crime: The Impact of Welfare Spending on Crime during the Great Depression." *Journal of Law and Economics* 53, no. 4 (2010): 715–40. https://doi.org/10.1086/655778.

Fiske, Alan Page, and Tage Shakti Rai. *Virtuous Violence: Hurting and Killing to Create, Sustain, End, and Honor Social Relationships.* 1st ed. New York: Cambridge University Press, 2014. https://doi.org/10.1017/CBO9781316104668.

Fitzgerald, John, and Robert Moffitt. "The Supplemental Poverty Measure: A New Method for Measuring Poverty." NBER working paper no. 30056. Cambridge, MA: National Bureau of Economic Research, May 2022. https://doi.org/10.3386/w30056.

FitzPatrick, Lauren. "Chicago Public Schools COO Steps Down amid PPP Fraud Finding by Inspector General." *Chicago Sun-Times*, September 6, 2023. https://chicago.suntimes.com/2023/9/6/23860469/ppp-payroll-protection-program-cps-will-fletcher-crystal-cooper.

Fitzsimmons, Emma G., and Dana Rubinstein. "Mayor Eric Adams Grapples with Two Shocking Acts of Violence." *New York Times*, March 26, 2024. https://www.nytimes.com/2024/03/26/nyregion/eric-adams-police-subway.html.

Flanagan, Timothy J. "Change and Influence in Popular Criminology: Public Attributions of Crime Causation." *Journal of Criminal Justice* 15 (1987): 231–43.

Flavell, John H. "Metacognition and Cognitive Monitoring: A New Area of Cognitive–Developmental Inquiry." *American Psychologist* 34, no. 10 (1979): 906–11. https://doi.org/10.1037/0003-066X.34.10.906.

Foley, C. Fritz. "Welfare Payments and Crime." *Review of Economics and Statistics* 93, no. 1 (2011): 97–112. https://doi.org/10.1162/REST_a_00068.

"Forged in Steel, Soon Forgotten." *Chicago Tribune*, March 30, 1995. https://www.chicagotribune.com/1995/03/30/forged-in-steel-soon-forgotten/.

Fowler, Katherine A., Rachel A. Leavitt, Carter J. Betz, Keming Yuan, and Linda L. Dahlberg. "Examining Differences between Mass, Multiple, and Single-Victim Homicides to Inform Prevention: Findings from the National Violent Death Reporting System." *Injury Epidemiology* 8, no. 1 (2021): 49. https://doi.org/10.1186/s40621-021-00345-7.

Frank, Robert H. *Microeconomics and Behavior*. 10th ed. New York: McGraw-Hill Education, 2021.

Freedman, Matthew, and Emily G. Owens. "Your Friends and Neighbors: Localized Economic Development and Criminal Activity." *Review of Economics and Statistics* 98, no. 2 (2016): 233–53.

Frey, William H. "Neighborhood Segregation Persists for Black, Latino or Hispanic, and Asian Americans." Brookings Institution, April 6, 2021. https://www.brookings.edu/articles/neighborhood-segregation -persists-for-black-latino-or-hispanic-and-asian-americans/.

Frey, William H., and Fred Dews. "White Decline and Increased Diversity in America's Aging Population." Brookings Institution, October 1, 2021. https://www.brookings.edu/articles/white-decline-and-increased -diversity-in-americas-aging-population/.

Fry, Richard, and Paul Taylor. "The Rise of Residential Segregation by Income." Pew Research Center, August 1, 2012. https://www.pewresearch .org/social-trends/2012/08/01/the-rise-of-residential-segregation-by -income/.

Fuchs, Lawrence H. "American Apartheid: Segregation and the Making of the Underclass." *American Journal of Sociology* 99, no. 5 (1993): 1342–43.

Gailey, Alex. "More than Half of Americans Say Money Negatively Impacts Their Mental Health, up Sharply from a Year Ago." *Bankrate*, May 8, 2023. https://www.bankrate.com/personal-finance/financial-wellness -survey/.

Gailliot, Matthew T., and Roy F. Baumeister. "The Physiology of Willpower: Linking Blood Glucose to Self-Control." *Personality and Social Psychology Review* 11, no. 4 (2007): 303–27. https://doi.org/10.1177 /1088868307303030.

Gailliot, Matthew T., Roy F. Baumeister, C. Nathan DeWall, Jon K. Maner, E. Ashby Plant, Dianne M. Tice, Lauren E. Brewer, and Brandon J. Schmeichel. "Self-Control Relies on Glucose as a Limited Energy Source: Willpower Is More Than a Metaphor." *Journal of Personality and Social Psychology* 92, no. 2 (2007): 325–36. https://doi.org/10.1037/0022 -3514.92.2.325.

Gale, Neil. "The History of the Union Stock Yards and Transit Company, Chicago (1865–1971)." *Digital Research Library of Illinois History Journal*,

August 2018. https://drloihjournal.blogspot.com/2018/08/history-of
-the-union-stock-yards-and-transit-company-chicago-1865-1971.html.

Garin, Andrew, Dmitri Koustas, Carl McPherson, Samuel Norris, Matthew Pecenco, Evan K. Rose, Yotam Shem-Tov, and Jeffrey Weaver. "The Impact of Incarceration on Employment, Earnings, and Tax Filing." Working paper no. 2023-108. Chicago: Becker Friedman Institute for Economics, August 9, 2023. https://dx.doi.org/10.2139/ssrn.4536659.

Gawronski, Bertram, and Laura A. Creighton. "Dual Process Theories." In *The Oxford Handbook of Social Cognition*, 282–312. New York: Oxford University Press, 2013.

Gee, Andre. "Lil Durk vs. NBA YoungBoy Is More Than Rap Beef." *Complex*, March 1, 2022. https://www.complex.com/music/a/andre-gee/lil
-durk-nba-youngboy-beef-essay.

Gelber, Alexander, Adam Isen, and Judd B. Kessler. "The Effects of Youth Employment: Evidence from New York City Lotteries." *Quarterly Journal of Economics* 131, no. 1 (2016): 423–60. https://doi.org/10.1093/qje
/qjv034.

Gettinger, Aaron, and Christian Belanger. "Harper Ave. Shooting Tuesday Leaves No Reported Injuries, Damage to Businesses and Cars." *Hyde Park Herald*, November 9, 2021. https://www.hpherald.com/evening
_digest/harper-ave-shooting-tuesday-leaves-no-reported-injuries
-damage-to-businesses-and-cars/article_9bbc1cc8-41a7-11ec-8e71
-abe6439f49be.html.

Ghandnoosh, Nazgol. "One in Five: Ending Racial Inequity in Incarceration." *Sentencing Project*, October 11, 2023. https://www
.sentencingproject.org/reports/one-in-five-ending-racial-inequity-in
-incarceration/.

Gibbs, Jack P. "Review Essay: Crime and Human Nature." *Criminology* 23, no. 2 (1985): 381–88.

Gilbert, Daniel T. "How Mental Systems Believe." *American Psychologist* 46, no. 2 (1991): 107–19. https://doi.org/10.1037/0003-066X.46.2.107.

Gilbert, Daniel T., Elizabeth C. Pinel, Timothy D. Wilson, Stephen J. Blumberg, and Thalia P. Wheatley. "Immune Neglect: A Source of Durability Bias in Affective Forecasting." *Journal of Personality and Social Psychology* 75, no. 3 (1998): 617–38. https://doi.org/10.1037/0022-3514.75.3.617.

Giles, Tyler, Daniel Hungerman, and Tamar Oostrom. "Opiates of the Masses? Deaths of Despair and the Decline of American Religion." NBER working paper no. 30840. Cambridge, MA: National Bureau of Economic Research, January 2023. https://doi.org/10.3386/w30840.

Girdwain, Alyssa. "11 Movies and TV Shows about Ted Bundy to Watch after 'Falling for a Killer.'" *Women's Health*, January 15, 2020. https://www.womenshealthmag.com/life/g27343777/ted-bundy-movies/.

Giulietti, Corrado, and Brendon McConnell. "Kicking You When You're Already Down: The Multipronged Impact of Austerity on Crime." ESRC working paper no. 104. Southampton: ESRC Centre for Population Change, 2020.

Glaeser, Edward. "Urbanization and Its Discontents." NBER working paper no. 26839. Cambridge, MA: National Bureau of Economic Research, March 2020. https://doi.org/10.3386/w26839.

Glaeser, Edward L., David M. Cutler, and Jacob L. Vigdor. "When Are Ghettos Bad? Lessons from Immigrant Segregation in the United States." Harvard Institute of Economic Research discussion paper no. 2152. Cambridge, MA: Harvard Institute of Economic Research, February 2008. http://www.ssrn.com/abstract=1095281.

Glaeser, Edward, and Joshua Gottlieb. "The Wealth of Cities: Agglomeration Economies and Spatial Equilibrium in the United States." NBER working paper no. 14806. Cambridge, MA: National Bureau of Economic Research, March 2009. https://doi.org/10.3386/w14806.

Glaeser, Edward, and Giacomo A. M. Ponzetto. "Did the Death of Distance Hurt Detroit and Help New York?" NBER working paper no. 13710. Cambridge, MA: National Bureau of Economic Research, December 2007. https://doi.org/10.3386/w13710.

Glaeser, Edward, and Kristina Tobio. "The Rise of the Sunbelt." NBER working paper no. 13071. Cambridge, MA: National Bureau of Economic Research, April 2007. https://doi.org/10.3386/w13071.

Glass, David C., Jerome E. Singer, and Lucy N. Friedman. "Psychic Cost of Adaptation to an Environmental Stressor." *Journal of Personality and Social Psychology* 12, no. 3 (1969): 200–10. https://doi.org/10.1037/h0027629.

Gneezy, Uri, and John A. List. *The Why Axis: Hidden Motives and the Undiscovered Economics of Everyday Life*. New York: PublicAffairs, 2013.

Golaszewski, Paul. "A Status Report: Reducing Prison Overcrowding in California." Legislative Analyst's Office, August 5, 2011. https://lao.ca .gov/reports/2011/crim/overcrowding_080511.aspx.

Goldstein, Herman. *Problem-Oriented Policing.* New York: McGraw-Hill, 2015.

Gopnik, Adam. "Jane Jacobs's Street Smarts." *New Yorker*, September 19, 2016. https://www.newyorker.com/magazine/2016/09/26/jane -jacobs-street-smarts.

Gordon, Robert J. "Back to the Future: European Unemployment Today Viewed from America in 1939." *Brookings Papers on Economic Activity* 19 (1988):·271–312. -https://www.brookings.edu/wp-content/uploads /1988/01/1988a_bpea_gordon_schultze.pdf.

Gorner, Jeremy. "Accused of Having His Officers Baby-Sit His Son, Chicago Police Commander Said It Was Really a Secret Study." *Chicago Tribune*, February 9, 2019. https://www.chicagotribune.com/2019/02 /09/accused-of-having-his-officers-baby-sit-his-son-chicago-police -commander-said-it-was-really-a-secret-study/.

———. "'We're Going After Gangs': Chicago Police Superintendent David Brown Redistributes Many Community Safety Team Officers." *Chicago Tribune*, September 10, 2021. https://www.chicagotribune.com/news /breaking/ct-cpd-superintendent-david-brown-deployment-20210910 -2szzyal3v5d3penyir6kz7gfyu-story.html.

Gotsch, Kara, and Vinay Basti. "Capitalizing on Mass Incarceration: U.S. Growth in Private Prisons." Sentencing Project, August 2, 2018. https://www.sentencingproject.org/reports/capitalizing-on-mass -incarceration-u-s-growth-in-private-prisons/.

Gottfredson, Michael R., and Travis Hirschi. *A General Theory of Crime.* Stanford, CA: Stanford University Press, 1990.

Gottschalk, Marie. "The Folly of Neoliberal Prison Reform." *Boston Review*, June 8, 2015. https://www.bostonreview.net/articles/marie-gottschalk -neoliberal-prison-reform-caught/.

Gøtzsche, Peter C., and Pernille K. Gøtzsche. "Cognitive Behavioural Therapy Halves the Risk of Repeated Suicide Attempts: Systematic Review." *Journal of the Royal Society of Medicine* 110, no. 10 (2017): 404–10. https:// doi.org/10.1177/0141076817731904.

Gould, Eric D., Bruce A. Weinberg, and David B. Mustard. "Crime Rates

and Local Labor Market Opportunities in the United States: 1979–
1997." *Review of Economics and Statistics* 84, no. 1 (2002): 45–61. https://
doi.org/10.1162/003465302317331919.

Gramlich, John. "The Gap between the Number of Blacks and Whites in
Prison Is Shrinking." Pew Research Center, April 30, 2019. https://www
.pewresearch.org/short-reads/2019/04/30/shrinking-gap-between
-number-of-blacks-and-whites-in-prison/.

———. "What the Data Says about Gun Deaths in the U.S." Pew Research
Center, April 26, 2023. https://www.pewresearch.org/short-reads
/2023/04/26/what-the-data-says-about-gun-deaths-in-the-u-s/.

Grasmick, Harold G., and Anne L. McGill. "Religion, Attribution Style,
and Punitiveness toward Juvenile Offenders." *Criminology* 32, no. 1
(1994): 23–46. https://doi.org/10.1111/j.1745-9125.1994.tb01145.x.

Gratz, Roberta Brandes. "Milestones: 100 Years of Jane Jacobs." *Architectural Record*, May 1, 2016. https://www.architecturalrecord.com/articles
/11631-milestones-100-years-of-jane-jacobs.

Griffin, Dale W., David Dunning, and Lee Ross. "The Role of Construal
Processes in Overconfident Predictions about the Self and Others."
Journal of Personality and Social Psychology 59 (January 1991): 1128–39.
https://doi.org/10.1037//0022-3514.59.6.1128.

Griffin, Dale W., and Lee Ross. "Subjective Construal, Social Inference,
and Human Misunderstanding." *Advances in Experimental Social Psychology* 24 (1991): 319–59. https://doi.org/10.1016/S0065-2601(08)60333-0.

Grimes, William. "Thomas C. Schelling, Master Theorist of Nuclear
Strategy, Dies at 95." *New York Times*, December 13, 2016. https://www
.nytimes.com/2016/12/13/business/economy/thomas-schelling-dead
-nobel-laureate.html.

Grossman, Ron. "As Black Leaders Pushed for 'Community Control of
Police' 50 Years Ago, One Activist Cop Was Assigned to Patrol an Alley."
Chicago Tribune, July 23, 2023. https://www.chicagotribune.com/2023
/07/23/as-black-leaders-pushed-for-community-control-of-police-50
-years-ago-one-activist-cop-was-assigned-to-patrol-an-alley/.

———. "Vintage Chicago Tribune: Dubbed a 'Toll Bridge' to Sidestep a
Legal Hurdle, Chicago Skyway Soon Became a White Elephant." *Chicago
Tribune*, September 25, 2022. https://www.chicagotribune.com/2022

/09/25/vintage-chicago-tribune-dubbed-a-toll-bridge-to-sidestep-a
-legal-hurdle-chicago-skyway-soon-became-a-white-elephant/.

———. "Symbols of Segregation." *Chicago Tribune*, August 6, 2023.
https://www.pressreader.com/usa/chicago-tribune-sunday/20230806
/281694029296914.

Gunn, Dwyer. "Breaking the Code of the Streets." *Psychology Today*, July 5,
2016. https://www.psychologytoday.com/us/articles/201607/breaking
-the-code-the-streets.

Haidt, Jonathan. "The Emotional Dog and Its Rational Tail: A Social In-
tuitionist Approach to Moral Judgment." *Psychological Review* 108, no. 4
(2001): 814–34. https://doi.org/10.1037/0033-295X.108.4.814.

Han, Jeehoon, Bruce D. Meyer, and James X. Sullivan. "Real-Time Poverty,
Material Well-Being, and the Child Tax Credit." NBER working paper
no. 30371. Cambridge, MA: National Bureau of Economic Research,
August 2022. https://doi.org/10.3386/w30371.

———. "Who Is Poor, How Poverty Has Changed, and Why It Matters:
Poverty Measurement in the U.S. and Its Implications for Policy." Working paper, September 30, 2022. https://sites.nd.edu/james-sullivan
/files/2023/04/Han_Meyer_Sullivan_Poverty_v21.pdf.

Haney, Craig. *Criminality in Context: The Psychological Foundations of Criminal
Justice Reform*. Psychology, Crime, and Justice Series. Washington, DC:
American Psychological Association, 2020.

———. "Solitary Confinement, Loneliness, and Psychological Harm." In
Solitary Confinement: Effects, Practices, and Pathways toward Reform, edited
by Jules Lobel and Peter Scharff, 129–52. Oxford University Press, 2019.
https://doi.org/10.1093/oso/9780190947927.003.0008.

Haney, Craig, and Susan Greene. "Capital Constructions: Newspaper Reporting in Death Penalty Cases." *Analyses of Social Issues and Public Policy*
4, no. 1 (2004): 129–50. https://doi.org/10.1111/j.1530-2415.2004
.00038.x.

Hansen, B. "Kids in Prison." *CQ Researcher* 27 (2001): 345–76.

Hanson, Melanie. "U.S. Public Education Spending Statistics." Education
Data Initiative, last updated September 8, 2023. https://educationdata
.org/public-education-spending-statistics.

Harcourt, Bernard E., and Jens Ludwig. "Broken Windows: New Evidence from New York City and a Five-City Social Experiment." *University of Chicago Law Review* 73, no. 1 (2006): 271–320.

Harlow, Caroline Wolf. *Robbery Victims*. Special report. Washington, DC: US Department of Justice, Bureau of Justice Statistics, April 1987. https://bjs.ojp.gov/content/pub/pdf/rv.pdf.

"The Harold Washington Story." DuSable Black History Museum and Education Center. Accessed March 15, 2024. https://www.dusable museum.org/exhibition/harold-washington-story.

Harris, Douglas N. "Are America's Rising Graduation Rates Real—or Just an Accountability-Fueled Mirage?" Brookings Institution, March 2, 2020. https://www.brookings.edu/articles/are-americas-rising-high -school-graduation-rates-real-or-just-an-accountability-fueled-mirage/.

Hasell, Joe, Max Roser, Esteban Ortiz-Ospina, and Pablo Arriagada. "Poverty." *Our World in Data*, 2022. https://ourworldindata.org/poverty.

Hastorf, Albert H., and Hadley Cantril. "They Saw a Game: A Case Study." *Journal of Abnormal and Social Psychology* 49, no. 1 (1954): 129–34. https://www.romolocapuano.com/wp-content/uploads/2013/06 /TheySawAGame.pdf.

Haushofer, Johannes, Charlotte Ringdal, Jeremy Shapiro, and Xiao Yu Wang. "Income Changes and Intimate Partner Violence: Evidence from Unconditional Cash Transfers in Kenya." NBER working paper no. 25627. Cambridge, MA: National Bureau of Economic Research, revised July 2019. http://www.nber.org/papers/w25627.pdf.

Hausman, David, and Dorothy Kronick. "The Illusory End of Stop and Frisk in Chicago?" *Science Advances* 9, no. 39 (2023): eadh3017. https:// doi.org/10.1126/sciadv.adh3017.

Hautzinger, Daniel. "The Olympic Athlete Who Became a Powerful Chicago Politician." *WTTW Chicago*, August 3, 2021. https://interactive .wttw.com/playlist/2021/08/03/ralph-metcalfe.

Havel, Václav, with Karel Hvínzndala. *Disturbing the Peace: A Conversation with Karel Hvínzndala*. New York: Knopf, 1990.

Haw, Camilla, Lesley Sutton, Sue Simkin, David Gunnell, Navneet Kapur, Mike Nowers, and Keith Hawton. "Suicide by Gunshot in the United Kingdom: A Review of the Literature." *Medicine, Science and the Law* 44, no. 4 (2004): 295–310. https://doi.org/10.1258/rsmmsl.44.4.295.

Heaton, Paul, Priscillia Hunt, John MacDonald, and Jessica Saunders. "The Short- and Long-Run Effects of Private Law Enforcement: Evidence from University Police." *Journal of Law and Economics* 59, no. 4 (2016): 889–912. https://doi.org/10.1086/690732.

Heckman, J. J., H. Ichimura, and P. E. Todd. "Matching as an Econometric Evaluation Estimator: Evidence from Evaluating a Job Training Programme." *Review of Economic Studies* 64, no. 4 (1997): 605–54. https://doi.org/10.2307/2971733.

Heckman, James, Hidehiko Ichimura, Jeffrey Smith, and Petra Todd. "Characterizing Selection Bias Using Experimental Data." *Econometrica* 66, no. 5 (1998): 1017. https://doi.org/10.2307/2999630.

Heider, Fritz. *The Psychology of Interpersonal Relations*. Hoboken, NJ: John Wiley and Sons Inc., 1958. https://doi.org/10.1037/10628-000.

Heller, Sara B. "Summer Jobs Reduce Violence among Disadvantaged Youth." *Science* 346, no. 6214 (2014): 1219–23. https://doi.org/10.1126/science.1257809.

Heller, Sara B., Benjamin Jakubowski, Zubin Jelveh, and Max Kapustin. "Machine Learning Can Predict Shooting Victimization Well Enough to Help Prevent It." NBER working paper no. 30170. Cambridge, MA: National Bureau of Economic Research, June 2022. https://doi.org/10.3386/w30170.

Heller, Sara B., Anuj K. Shah, Jonathan Guryan, Jens Ludwig, Sendhil Mullainathan, and Harold A. Pollack. "Thinking, Fast and Slow? Some Field Experiments to Reduce Crime and Dropout in Chicago." *Quarterly Journal of Economics* 132, no. 1 (2017): 1–54. https://doi.org/10.1093/qje/qjw033.

Hemenway, David, Deborah Prothrow-Stith, Jack M. Bergstein, Roseanna Ander, and Bruce P. Kennedy. "Gun Carrying among Adolescents." *Law and Contemporary Problems* 59, no. 1 (1996): 39–53. https://doi.org/10.2307/1192209.

Hemenway, David, Mary Vriniotis, Renee M. Johnson, Matthew Miller, and Deborah Azrael. "Gun Carrying by High School Students in Boston, MA: Does Overestimation of Peer Gun Carrying Matter?" *Journal of Adolescence* 34, no. 5 (2011): 997–1003. https://doi.org/10.1016/j.adolescence.2010.11.008.

Hemez, Paul, and Channel Washington. "Percentage and Number of Children Living with Two Parents Has Dropped since 1968." *US Census Bureau*, April 2021. https://www.census.gov/library/stories/2021/04/number-of-children-living-only-with-their-mothers-has-doubled-in-past-50-years.html.

Herrmann, Esther, Josep Call, María Victoria Hernàndez-Lloreda, Brian Hare, and Michael Tomasello. "Humans Have Evolved Specialized Skills of Social Cognition: The Cultural Intelligence Hypothesis." *Science* 317, no. 5843 (2007): 1360–66. https://doi.org/10.1126/science.1146282.

Hill, J. M. "The Impact of Liberalized Concealed Weapons Statutes on Rates of Violent Crime." BA thesis, Duke University, 1997.

Hirschi, Travis. *Causes of Delinquency*. Berkeley: University of California Press, 1969.

Hoekstra, Mark, and CarlyWill Sloan. "Does Race Matter for Police Use of Force? Evidence from 911 Calls." *American Economic Review* 112, no. 3 (2022): 827–60. https://doi.org/10.1257/aer.20201292.

Hogarth, Robin M., Tomás Lejarraga, and Emre Soyer. "The Two Settings of Kind and Wicked Learning Environments." *Current Directions in Psychological Science* 24, no. 5 (2015): 379–85. https://doi.org/10.1177/0963721415591878.

Holli, Melvin. "The Experts Choose Chicago's Greatest Mayors." *Public Perspective*, September 1995. https://ropercenter.cornell.edu/sites/default/files/2018-07/65054.pdf.

Hollingsworth, Alex, Christopher J. Ruhm, and Kosali Simon. "Macroeconomic Conditions and Opioid Abuse." *Journal of Health Economics* 56 (December 2017): 222–33. https://doi.org/10.1016/j.jhealeco.2017.07.009.

Holmes, Evelyn. "Chicago Holds Neighborhood Town Halls about Community Safety, Efforts to Reduce Violence." *ABC7 Chicago*, March 19, 2022. https://abc7chicago.com/city-of-chicago-town-hall-lori-lightfoot-police/11664623/.

Holmes, Steven A. "Gun Control Bill Backed by Reagan in Appeal to Bush." *New York Times*, March 29, 1991. https://www.nytimes.com/1991/03/29/us/gun-control-bill-backed-by-reagan-in-appeal-to-bush.html.

Home Office. "Statistics on Firearm and Shotgun Certificates, England and Wales: April 2022 to March 2023." Gov.uk, July 6, 2023. https://www.gov.uk/government/statistics/statistics-on-firearm-and-shotgun-certificates-england-and-wales-april-2022-to-march-2023/statistics-on-firearm-and-shotgun-certificates-england-and-wales-april-2022-to-march-2023.

Hong, Sunghyun, and Inger Burnett-Zeigler. "The Frequency of PTSD and Subthreshold PTSD among African-American Women with Depressive Symptoms in a Disadvantaged Urban Neighborhood: Pilot Study." *Journal of Racial and Ethnic Health Disparities* 4, no. 6 (2017): 1069–73. https://doi.org/10.1007/s40615-016-0311-3.

Hookah Anonymous. "Jeremy Brown GF Wears 'KnockOut King' T-Shirts & Curse Out the Internet!!" YouTube, July 4, 2023. MP4 video, 14:36. https://www.youtube.com/watch?v=fNxFW0M7cRM.

Horng, Eric, and ABC7 Chicago Digital Team. "Man Charged with Murder of University of Chicago Graduate Killed in Hyde Park Shooting." *ABC7 Chicago*, November 12, 2021. https://abc7chicago.com/chicago-shooting-hyde-park-shaoxiong-zheng-alton-spann/11229600/.

Horowitz, Julia Menasce, Anna Brown, and Kiana Cox. "Race in America 2019." Pew Research Center, April 9, 2019. https://www.pewresearch.org/social-trends/2019/04/09/race-in-america-2019/.

Hulse, Carl. "As Shootings Continue, Prospects for Gun Control Action in Congress Remain Dim." *New York Times*, December 2, 2022. https://www.nytimes.com/2022/12/02/us/gun-control-congress.html.

Hunkar, David. "Manufacturing Jobs as a Percentage of Total U.S. Workforce since 1939: Chart." *TopForeignStocks.com*, December 22, 2016. https://topforeignstocks.com/2016/12/22/manufacturing-jobs-as-a-percentage-of-total-u-s-workforce-since-1939-chart/.

Hunt, D. Bradford. *Blueprint for Disaster: The Unraveling of Chicago Public Housing*. Chicago: University of Chicago Press, 2009.

Hureau, David, and Theodore Wilson. "The Co-Occurrence of Illegal Gun Carrying and Gun Violence Exposure: Evidence for Practitioners from Young People Adjudicated for Serious Involvement in Crime." *American Journal of Epidemiology* 190, no. 12 (2021): 2544–51. https://doi.org/10.1093/aje/kwab188.

"'I Ran for My Life': Chicago Activist Describes Shooting in Hyde Park Just Hours before 24-Year-Old Man Killed Blocks Away." *CBS Chicago.* November 10, 2021. https://www.cbsnews.com/chicago/news/hyde -park-shootings/.

"Illinois Department of Corrections Inmate Status—Carter, Kalvin." State of Illinois Department of Corrections. Accessed March 15, 2024. https://www.idoc.state.il.us/subsections/search/inms_print.asp?idoc =M47424.

Inglot, Tomasz, and John P. Pelissero. "Ethnic Political Power in a Machine City: Chicago's Poles at Rainbow's End." *Urban Affairs Quarterly* 28, no. 4 (1993): 526–43. https://doi.org/10.1177/004208169302800402.

Ingraham, Christopher. "Americans Are Getting More Miserable, and There's Data to Prove It." *Washington Post*, March 22, 2019. https://www .washingtonpost.com/business/2019/03/22/americans-are-getting -more-miserable-theres-data-prove-it/.

International Monetary Fund. "GDP Based on PPP, Share of World." *IMF Datamapper*, 2024. https://www.imf.org/external/datamapper/PPPSH @WEO/WEOWORLD.

Issa, Nader. "Man, 27, Dies after Being Shot in Humboldt Park." *Chicago Sun-Times*, March 12, 2018. https://chicago.suntimes.com/2018/3/12 /18339787/man-27-dies-after-being-shot-in-humboldt-park.

"Jackson Calls Himself 'General' in Drug War." *Chicago Tribune*, May 23, 1988. https://www.chicagotribune.com/1988/05/23/jackson-calls -himself-general-in-drug-war/.

Jackson, John, and John Foster. "The Politics of Public Budgeting in Illinois (Second Edition)." *Simon Review (Occasional Papers of the Paul Simon Public Policy Institute)*, May 6, 2021. https://opensiuc.lib.siu.edu/cgi /viewcontent.cgi?article=1065&context=ppi_papers.

Jacob, Brian A., Max Kapustin, and Jens Ludwig. "The Impact of Housing Assistance on Child Outcomes: Evidence from a Randomized Housing Lottery." *Quarterly Journal of Economics* 130, no. 1 (2015): 465–506. https://doi.org/10.1093/qje/qju030.

Jacob, Brian A., and Jens Ludwig. "The Effects of Housing Assistance on Labor Supply: Evidence from a Voucher Lottery." *American Economic Review* 102, no. 1 (2012): 272–304.

Jacobs, Erin. "Returning to Work after Prison—Final Results from the Transitional Jobs Reentry Demonstration." *SSRN Electronic Journal*, May 10, 2012. https://doi.org/10.2139/ssrn.2056045.

Jacobs, Jane. *The Death and Life of Great American Cities*. New York: Random House, 1961.

Jacobs, Joel. "How Chicago's Controversial TIF Program Took Over a Third of the City." *Medill Reports Chicago*, February 2020. https://news .medill.northwestern.edu/chicago/how-chicagos-controversial-tif -program-took-over-a-third-of-the-city/.

Jacoby, Larry L. "A Process Dissociation Framework: Separating Automatic from Intentional Uses of Memory." *Journal of Memory and Language* 30, no. 5 (1991): 513–41. https://doi.org/10.1016/0749-596X (91)90025-F.

Jácome, Elisa. "Mental Health and Criminal Involvement: Evidence from Losing Medicaid Eligibility." Working paper, December 2022. https:// elisajacome.github.io/Jacome/Jacome_JMP.pdf.

Jamieson, Patrick E., and Daniel Romer. "The Association between the Rise of Gun Violence in Popular US Primetime Television Dramas and Homicides Attributable to Firearms, 2000–2018." Edited by M. Harvey Brenner. *PLoS One* 16, no. 3 (2021): e0247780. https://doi.org/10.1371 /journal.pone.0247780.

Jencks, Christopher, and Paul E. Peterson, eds. *The Urban Underclass*. 5th ed. Washington, DC: Brookings Institution, 1991.

"John Dillinger (1903–1934)." *PBS*. Accessed March 15, 2024. https://www .pbs.org/wgbh/americanexperience/features/dillinger-john-dillinger/#.

Johnson, Brandon. Inaugural address, May 15, 2023. Online at Chicago Public Library. https://www.chipublib.org/mayor-brandon-johnson -inaugural-address-2023/.

Johnson, Lyndon B. "Special Message to the Congress on Crime and Law Enforcement." March 9, 1966. https://www.presidency.ucsb.edu /documents/special-message-the-congress-crime-and-law-enforcement.

Johnson, Rucker, and Steven Raphael. "The Effect of Male Incarceration Dynamics on AIDS Infection Rates among African-American Women and Men." *Journal of Law and Economics* 52, no. 2 (2009): 251–93.

Jones, Edward E, and Victor A Harris. "The Attribution of Attitudes."

Journal of Experimental Social Psychology 3, no. 1 (1967): 1–24. https://doi .org/10.1016/0022-1031(67)90034-0.

Jones, Gareth, Richard W. Steketee, Robert E. Black, Zulfiqar A. Bhutta, and Saul S. Morris. "How Many Child Deaths Can We Prevent This Year?" *Lancet* 362, no. 9377 (2003): 65–71. https://doi.org/10.1016 /s0140-6736(03)13811-1.

Joravsky, Ben. "Chicago's TIF Scam Might Be Even More Crooked Than We Thought." *Chicago Reader*, July 2017. https://chicagoreader.com /columns-opinion/chicagos-tif-scam-might-be-even-more-crooked -than-we-thought/.

Kahneman, Daniel. "Maps of Bounded Rationality: Psychology for Behavioral Economics." *American Economic Review* 93, no. 5 (2003): 1449–75.

———. *Thinking, Fast and Slow*. New York: Farrar, Straus and Giroux, 2011.

Kahneman, Daniel, and Shane Frederick. "A Model of Heuristic Judgment." In *The Cambridge Handbook of Thinking and Reasoning*, edited by Keith J. Holyoak and Robert G. Morrison, 267–93. New York: Cambridge University Press, 2005.

Kang, Megan, Jens Ludwig, and Elizabeth Rasich. "Intervention of Choice: Behavioral Science and Gun Violence." *Quinnipiac Law Review* 39, no. 3 (2021): 409–18.

Kang, Megan, and Elizabeth Rasich. "Extending the Firearm Suicide Proxy for Household Gun Ownership." *American Journal of Preventative Medicine* 65, no. 5 (2023): 916–22. https://doi.org/10.1016/j.amepre .2023.05.003.

Kapustin, Max, Jens Ludwig, Marc Punkay, Kimberley Smith, Lauren Speigel, and David Welgus. *Gun Violence in Chicago, 2016*. Chicago: University of Chicago Crime Lab, January 2017. https://urbanlabs.uchicago.edu /attachments/c5b0b0b86b6b6a9309ed88a9f5bbe5bd892d4077/store /82f93d3e7c7cc4c5a29abca0d8bf5892b3a35c0c3253d1d24b3b9d1fa7b8 /UChicagoCrimeLab+Gun+Violence+in+Chicago+2016.pdf.

Karlinsky, Sarah. "Making Detroit Home: Addressing the Challenges of Housing Stability and Habitability." SPUR, July 17, 2023. https:// www.spur.org/news/2023-07-17/making-detroit-home-addressing -challenges-housing-stability-and-habitability.

Karma, Roge. "'Deaths of Despair': The Deadly Epidemic That Predated

Coronavirus." *Vox*, April 15, 2020. https://www.vox.com/2020/4/15
/21214734/deaths-of-despair-coronavirus-covid-19-angus-deaton
-anne-case-americans-deaths.

Karni, Annie. "Shooting Prompts a Shrug in Washington, as G.O.P. Rejects Pleas to Act." *New York Times*, March 29, 2023. https://www.nytimes .com/2023/03/29/us/politics/nashville-shooting-gop-action.html.

Kearney, Melissa S. *The Two-Parent Privilege*. Chicago: University of Chicago Press, 2023.

Keels, Micere, Greg J. Duncan, Stefanie Deluca, Ruby Mendenhall, and James Rosenbaum. "Fifteen Years Later: Can Residential Mobility Programs Provide a Long-Term Escape from Neighborhood Segregation, Crime, and Poverty?" *Demography* 42, no. 1 (2005): 51–73. https://doi .org/10.1353/dem.2005.0005.

Kena, Grace, and Jennifer Truman. *Trends and Patterns in Firearm Violence, 1993–2018*. NCJ report no. 251663. Washington, DC: US Department of Justice, Bureau of Justice Statistics, April 2022. https://bjs.ojp.gov /library/publications/trends-and-patterns-firearm-violence-1993 -2018.

Kernan, Sean. "What Two Men Who Survived Jumping Off the Golden Gate Bridge Learned." *Medium*, March 6, 2023. https://seanjkernan .medium.com/what-two-men-who-survived-jumping-off-the-golden -gate-bridge-learned-758e322117a8.

Kessler, Daniel, and Steven D. Levitt. "Using Sentence Enhancements to Distinguish between Deterrence and Incapacitation." *Journal of Law and Economics* 42, no. S1 (April 1999): 343–64. https://doi.org/10.1086 /467428.

Kessler, Judd B., Sarah Tahamont, Alexander Gelber, and Adam Isen. "The Effects of Youth Employment on Crime: Evidence from New York City Lotteries." *Journal of Policy Analysis and Management* 41, no. 3 (2022): 710–30. https://doi.org/10.1002/pam.22393.

Keysar, Boaz, Dale J. Barr, Jennifer A. Balin, and Jason S. Brauner. "Taking Perspective in Conversation: The Role of Mutual Knowledge in Comprehension." *Psychological Science* 11, no. 1 (2000): 32–38. https://doi.org /10.1111/1467-9280.00211.

Kiehl, Kent A., and Morris B. Hoffman. "The Criminal Psychopath:

History, Neuroscience, Treatment, and Economics." *Jurimetrics* 51 (2011): 355–97.

Kim, Hannah, Emily Hughes, Alice Cavanagh, Emily Norris, Angela Gao, Susan J. Bondy, Katherine E. McLeod, Tharsan Kanagalingam, and Fiona G. Kouyoumdjian. "The Health Impacts of the COVID-19 Pandemic on Adults Who Experience Imprisonment Globally: A Mixed Methods Systematic Review." Edited by Seth Blumberg. *PLoS One* 17, no. 5 (2022): e0268866. https://doi.org/10.1371/journal.pone .0268866.

Klarevas, Louis, Andrew Conner, and David Hemenway. "The Effect of Large-Capacity Magazine Bans on High-Fatality Mass Shootings, 1990–2017." *American Journal of Public Health* 109, no. 12 (2019): 1754– 61. https://doi.org/10.2105/AJPH.2019.305311.

Klassen, Tim. "Mayor Bradley and L.A. Crime: Letter to the Editor." *Los Angeles Times*, May 3, 1991. https://www.latimes.com/archives/la-xpm -1991-05-03-me-853-story.html.

Kleck, Gary, and Marc Gertz. "Armed Resistance to Crime: The Prevalence and Nature of Self-Defense with a Gun." *Journal of Criminal Law and Criminology* 86, no. 1 (1995): 150–87.

Kleck, Gary, and Karen McElrath. "The Effects of Weaponry on Human Violence." *Social Forces* 69, no. 3 (1991): 669–92. https://doi.org/10.2307 /2579469.

Klein, Michael. "'Headless Body in Topless Bar': 40 Years Later, the Story behind an Iconic Newspaper Headline." *Inquirer*, April 14, 2023. https://www.inquirer.com/opinion/commentary/headless-body -topless-bar-headline-40th-anniversary-20230414.html.

Klick, Jonathan, and Alexander Tabarrok. "Using Terror Alert Levels to Estimate the Effect of Police on Crime." *Journal of Law and Economics* 48, no. 1 (2005): 267–79. https://doi.org/10.1086/426877.

Kling, Jeffrey R., Jens Ludwig, and Lawrence F. Katz. "Neighborhood Effects on Crime for Female and Male Youth: Evidence from a Random-ized Housing Voucher Experiment." *Quarterly Journal of Economics* 120, no. 1 (2005): 87–130.

Kniesner, Thomas J., and W. Kip Viscusi. "The Value of a Statistical Life." In *Oxford Research Encyclopedia of Economics and Finance*, July 29, 2019. https://doi.org/10.1093/acrefore/9780190625979.013.138.

Knudsen, P. J. T. "Ballistic Trauma: Overview and Statistics—Wound Ballistics." *Encyclopedia of Forensic and Legal Medicine* 1 (2016): 413–24.

Koper, Christopher S. "Assessing the Potential to Reduce Deaths and Injuries from Mass Shootings through Restrictions on Assault Weapons and Other High-Capacity Semiautomatic Firearms." *Criminology and Public Policy* 19, no. 1 (2020): 147–70. https://doi.org/10.1111/1745-9133 .12485.

Koper, Christopher S., Dan Woods, and Jerry A. Roth. *An Updated Assessment of the Federal Assault Weapons Ban: Impacts on Gun Markets and Gun Violence, 1994–2003.* NCJ report no. 204431. Philadelphia, PA: Jerry Lee Center of Criminology, University of Pennsylvania, June 2004.

Kossowska, Małgorzata, Paulina Szwed, Miroslaw Wyczesany, Gabriela Czarnek, and Eligiusz Wronka. "Religious Fundamentalism Modulates Neural Responses to Error-Related Words: The Role of Motivation toward Closure." *Frontiers in Psychology* 9 (March 2018): 285. https://doi .org/10.3389/fpsyg.2018.00285.

Kotlowitz, Alex. *There Are No Children Here.* New York: Doubleday, 1992.

Kovaleski, Serge F., and Glenn Thrush. "A Craigslist for Guns, with No Background Checks." *New York Times*, August 1, 2023. https://www .nytimes.com/2023/08/01/us/gun-laws-private-sales-background -checks-armslist.html.

Kuziemko, Ilyana, and Steven D. Levitt. "An Empirical Analysis of Imprisoning Drug Offenders." *Journal of Public Economics* 88, no. 9–10 (2004): 2043–66. https://doi.org/10.1016/S0047-2727(03)00020-3.

LaLonde, Robert J. "Evaluating the Econometric Evaluations of Training Programs with Experimental Data." *American Economic Review* 76, no. 4 (1986): 604–20.

Larrimore, Jeff, Jacob Mortenson, and David Splinter. "Presence and Persistence of Poverty in U.S. Tax Data." NBER working paper no. 26966. Cambridge, MA: National Bureau of Economic Research, April 2020. https://doi.org/10.3386/w26966.

Latané, Bibb, and John M. Darley. "Group Inhibition of Bystander Intervention in Emergencies." *Journal of Personality and Social Psychology* 10, no. 3 (1968): 215–21. https://doi.org/10.1037/h0026570.

———. *The Unresponsive Bystander: Why Doesn't He Help?* New York: Appleton-Century Crofts, 1970.

Laurence, Justin. "Lightfoot's Plan to Sue Gang Members for Assets Clears Key Committee Hurdle, but Could Face a Tight Vote at City Council." *Block Club Chicago*, February 17, 2022. https://blockclubchicago.org /2022/02/17/lightfoots-plan-to-sue-gang-members-clears-key -committee-hurdle-but-a-tight-vote-looms-in-city-council/.

Law Enforcement Epidemiology Project. "U.S. Data on Police Shootings and Violence." University of Illinois Chicago School of Public Health. Accessed March 15, 2024. https://policeepi.uic.edu/u-s-data-on-police -shootings-and-violence/.

"Law Enforcement Facts: Key Data about the Profession." National Law Enforcement Officers Memorial Fund. Accessed March 1, 2024. https://nleomf.org/memorial/facts-figures/law-enforcement-facts/.

Leal, Wanda, Marc Gertz, and Alex R. Piquero. "The National Felon League? A Comparison of NFL Arrests to General Population Arrests." *Journal of Criminal Justice* 43, no. 5 (2015): 397–403. https://doi.org/10 .1016/j.jcrimjus.2015.08.001.

Leff, Carol Skalnik, and Mark H. Leff. "The Politics of Ineffectiveness: Federal Firearms Legislation, 1919–38." *Annals of the American Academy of Political and Social Science* 455 (1981): 48–62.

Lemann, Nicholas. *The Promised Land*. New York: Vintage Books, 1992.

Lescaze, Lee. "Reagan Blames Crime on 'Human Predator.'" *Washington Post*, September 28, 1981. https://www.washingtonpost.com/archive /politics/1981/09/29/reagan-blames-crime-on-human-predator /2892636f-d176-48fb-b06b-39012eace1f4/.

Levin, Sam. "These US Cities Defunded Police: 'We're Transferring Money to the Community.'" *Guardian*, March 11, 2021. https://www .theguardian.com/us-news/2021/mar/07/us-cities-defund-police -transferring-money-community.

Levitt, Steven D. "The Effect of Prison Population Size on Crime Rates: Evidence from Prison Overcrowding Litigation." *Quarterly Journal of Economics* 111, no. 2 (1996): 319–51. https://doi.org/10.2307/2946681.

———. "Understanding Why Crime Fell in the 1990s: Four Factors That Explain the Decline and Six That Do Not." *Journal of Economic Perspectives* 18, no. 1 (Winter 2004): 163–90. https://doi.org/10.1257 /089533004773563485.

———. "Using Electoral Cycles in Police Hiring to Estimate the Effects of Police on Crime: Reply." *American Economic Review* 92, no. 4 (2002): 1244–50. https://doi.org/10.1257/00028280260344777.

Levitt, Steven D., and Sudhir Alladi Venkatesh. "An Economic Analysis of a Drug-Selling Gang's Finances." *Quarterly Journal of Economics* 115, no. 3 (2000): 755–89. https://doi.org/10.1162/003355300554908.

Liberman, Varda, Steven M. Samuels, and Lee Ross. "The Name of the Game: Predictive Power of Reputations versus Situational Labels in Determining Prisoner's Dilemma Game Moves." *Personality and Social Psychology Bulletin* 30, no. 9 (2004): 1175–85. https://doi.org/10.1177/0146167204264004.

Lieberman, Matthew D. "Social Cognitive Neuroscience: A Review of Core Processes." *Annual Review of Psychology* 58, no. 1 (2007): 259–89. https://doi.org/10.1146/annurev.psych.58.110405.085654.

Lightfoot, Lori. "We Are Each Other's Business." Inaugural address, May 20, 2019. Online at Chicago Public Library. https://www.chipublib.org/mayor-lori-lightfoot-inaugural-address-2019/.

Liles, Alesa, and Stacy C. Moak. "Changing Juvenile Justice Policy in Response to the US Supreme Court: Implementing *Miller v. Alabama*." *Youth Justice* 15, no. 1 (2015): 76–92. https://doi.org/10.1177/1473225414529201.

Lin, Shuhong, Boaz Keysar, and Nicholas Epley. "Reflexively Mindblind: Using Theory of Mind to Interpret Behavior Requires Effortful Attention." *Journal of Experimental Social Psychology* 46, no. 3 (2010): 551–56. https://doi.org/10.1016/j.jesp.2009.12.019.

"A List of Chicago Aldermen Indicted, Raided or Implicated by the Feds, Criminally Charged or Convicted since 2019." *Block Club Chicago*, April 30, 2021. https://blockclubchicago.org/2021/04/30/a-list-of-chicago-aldermen-indicted-raided-or-implicated-by-the-feds-criminally-charged-or-convicted-since-2019/.

Lochner, Lance, and Enrico Moretti. "The Effect of Education on Crime: Evidence from Prison Inmates, Arrests, and Self-Reports." *American Economic Review* 92, no. 1 (2004): 155–89.

Loftin, Colin, David McDowall, Brian Wiersema, and Talbert J. Cottey. "Effects of Restrictive Licensing of Handguns on Homicide and Suicide in the District of Columbia." *New England Journal of Medicine* 325, no. 23 (1991): 1615–20. https://doi.org/10.1056/NEJM199112053252305.

Logan, John R., Andrew Foster, Hongwei Xu, and Wenquan Zhang. "Income Segregation: Up or Down, and for Whom?" *Demography* 57, no. 5 (2020): 1951–74. https://doi.org/10.1007/s13524-020-00917-0.

Logan, John R., and Brian Stults. *The Persistence of Segregation in the Metropolis: New Findings from the 2010 Census.* Census brief prepared for Project US2010. Washington, DC: US2010 Project, 2011. https://s4.ad.brown .edu/Projects/Diversity/Data/Report/report2.pdf.

Logan, Trevon, and John Parman. "The National Rise in Residential Segregation." *Journal of Economic History* 77, no. 1 (2017): 127–70.

"Lori E. Lightfoot." WHS Alumni Association. Accessed May 6, 2024. https://massillonwhsaa.org/awards/distinguished-citizens/lori -lightfoot/.

Lott, John. *More Guns, Less Crime.* 2nd ed. Chicago: University of Chicago Press, 2000.

Lott, John, and David B. Mustard. "Crime, Deterrence, and Right-to-Carry Concealed Handguns." *Journal of Legal Studies* 26, no. 1 (1997): 1–68. https://doi.org/10.1086/467988.

Luallen, Jeremy, Jared Edgerton, and Deirdre Rabideau. "A Quasi-Experimental Evaluation of the Impact of Public Assistance on Prisoner Recidivism." *Journal of Quantitative Criminology* 34, no. 3 (2018): 741–73. https://doi.org/10.1007/s10940-017-9353-x.

Ludwig, Jens. "Guest Editor's Introduction." *Cityscape* 14, no. 2 (2012): 1–28.

———. "Gun Self-Defense and Deterrence." *Crime and Justice* 27 (2000): 363–417.

———. "Op-Ed: New York and Los Angeles Got Their Gun Violence Under Control. Why Can't Chicago Do the Same?" *Chicago Tribune*, October 11, 2021. https://www.chicagotribune.com/2021/10/11/op-ed-new-york -and-los-angeles-got-their-gun-violence-under-control-why-cant -chicago-do-the-same/.

Ludwig, Jens, and Philip J. Cook. "Homicide and Suicide Rates Associated with Implementation of the Brady Handgun Violence Prevention Act." *JAMA* 284, no. 5 (2000): 585–91. https://doi.org/10.1001/jama.284.5 .585.

Ludwig, Jens, and Jacob Miller. "Jens Ludwig and Jacob Miller: We Are Seeing a Lethal Shift in America's Gun Violence Crisis." *Chicago Tribune*, March 24, 2024. https://www.chicagotribune.com/2024/03/24 /opinion-gun-violence-high-capacity-magazines-glock-swtiches/.

Ludwig, Jens, and Kevin Schnepel. "Does Nothing Stop a Bullet Like a Job? The Effects of Income on Crime." *Annual Review of Criminology* (forthcoming).

Lund, Nelson. "The Second Amendment and the War on Guns." In *Why We Are Losing the War on Gun Violence in the United States*, edited by Marie L. Crandall, Stephanie L. Bonne, Jennifer L. Bronson, and Woodie Kessel, 1st ed., 107–21. New York: Springer, 2021.

"Lynching in America." Equal Justice Initiative. Accessed May 1, 2024. https://lynchinginamerica.eji.org/explore/mississippi.

Lynn, Laurence E., and Michael G. H. McGeary. *Inner-City Poverty in the United States*. Washington, DC: National Academy Press, 1990.

MacDonald, John. "Criminal Justice Reform Guided by Evidence: Social Control Works—The Academy of Experimental Criminology 2022 Joan McCord Lecture." *Journal of Experimental Criminology*, February 27, 2023. https://doi.org/10.1007/s11292-023-09558-w.

MacDonald, John, Ahuva Jacobowitz, Jason Gravel, Mitchell Smith, Robert Stokes, Vicky Tam, Eugenia South, and Charles Branas. "Lessons Learned from a Citywide Abandoned Housing Experiment." *Journal of the American Planning Association* 90 (February 2023): 1–14. https://doi .org/10.1080/01944363.2022.2128855.

MacDonald, John, Jonathan Klick, and Ben Grunwald. "The Effect of Private Police on Crime: Evidence from a Geographic Regression Discontinuity Design." *Journal of the Royal Statistical Society Series A: Statistics in Society* 179, no. 3 (2016): 831–46. https://doi.org/10.1111/rssa.12142.

Maciag, Mike. "Police Employment, Officers Per Capita Rates for U.S. Cities." *Governing*, May 7, 2014. https://www.governing.com/archive /police-officers-per-capita-rates-employment-for-city-departments .html.

MacKinnon, Joseph. "One Year In, Chicago Mayor Lori Lightfoot's $1 Million Gun-Tip Line Has Rewarded Only One Tip for Just $10,000." *Blaze News*, August 19, 2022. https://www.theblaze.com/news/one-year-in

-chicago-mayor-lori-lightfoot-s-1-million-gun-tip-line-has-rewarded
-only-one-tip-for-just-10000.

Madonna, Anthony. "The National Firearms Act of 1934." *Congress Project*,
June 28, 2016. https://www.thecongressproject.com/national-firearms
-act-of-1934.

Main, Frank. "Goonie Gang Terrorized Englewood, Bragged on Facebook,
Made Goonie Gang T-Shirts, Feds Say." *Chicago Sun-Times*, March 17,
2023. https://chicago.suntimes.com/2023/3/17/23639713/goonie
-gang-boss-englewood-gangster-disciples-street-gangs-factions
-facebook-racketeering-rico.

———. "Gun Used in Hyde Park-to-Evanston Killing Spree Likely Used in
Prior South Side Shootings." *Chicago Sun-Times*, May 14, 2021. https://
chicago.suntimes.com/2021/5/14/22435118/jason-nightengale-hyde
-park-evanston-killing-spree-glock-chucks-gun-shop-south-side
-shootings.

———. "'O Block': The Most Dangerous Block in Chicago, Once Home
to Michelle Obama." *Chicago Sun-Times*, November 2, 2014. https://
chicago.suntimes.com/2014/11/2/18458059/o-block-most-dangerous
-block-in-chicago-michelle-obama-chief-keef-parkway-gardens-south
-king-drive.

———. "Rapper King Von's Killing Puts a Spotlight on Chicago Gang Ties
to Atlanta." *Chicago Sun-Times*, November 13, 2020. https://chicago
.suntimes.com/2020/11/13/21561328/king-von-atlanta-chicago-gang
-ties-black-disciples-oblock-o-block.

Malcom, Andrew H. "In the World of Chicago Politics, the Main Rule
Is There Are No Rules." *New York Times*, June 1, 1984. https://www
.nytimes.com/1984/06/01/us/in-the-world-of-chicago-politics-the
-main-rule-is-there-are-no-rules.html.

Malcolm, Joyce Lee. *Guns and Violence: The English Experience*. Cambridge,
MA: Harvard University Press, 2004.

———. *To Keep and Bear Arms: The Origins of an Anglo-American Right*. Cambridge, MA: Harvard University Press, 1994.

Mallar, Charles D., and Craig V. D. Thornton. "Transitional Aid for Released Prisoners: Evidence from the Life Experiment." *Journal of Human
Resources* 13, no. 2 (1978): 208–36. https://doi.org/10.2307/145359.

"Man Charged with Murder in Killing of UChicago Graduate in Hyde Park." *Block Club Chicago*, November 15, 2021. https://blockclubchicago .org/2021/11/15/man-charged-with-murder-in-killing-of-uchicago -graduate-in-hyde-park/.

Mankiw, N. Gregory, and Lawrence H. Summers. "Money Demand and the Effects of Fiscal Policies." *Journal of Money, Credit and Banking* 18, no. 4 (1986): 415–29.

Maragos, Alex. "Who Was Harold Washington? A Look Back at the Legacy of Chicago's First Black Mayor." *NBC Chicago*, April 15, 2022. https:// www.nbcchicago.com/news/local/chicago-politics/who-was-harold -washington-a-look-back-at-the-legacy-of-chicagos-first-black-mayor /2806193/.

Martens, Willem H. J. "The Problem with Robert Hare's Psychopathy Checklist: Incorrect Conclusions, High Risk of Misuse, and Lack of Reliability." *Medicine and Law* 27, no. 2 (2008): 449–62.

Maruna, Shadd, and Anna King. "Once a Criminal, Always a Criminal? 'Redeemability' and the Psychology of Punitive Public Attitudes." *European Journal on Criminal Policy and Research* 15, nos. 1–2 (2009): 7–24. https:// doi.org/10.1007/s10610-008-9088-1.

Masterson, Matt. "68 People Shot, 8 Killed in Shootings across Chicago over July 4th Weekend: Police." *WTTW News*, July 5, 2022. https:// news.wttw.com/2022/07/05/68-people-shot-8-killed-shootings-across -chicago-over-july-4th-weekend-police.

Maxfield, Michael G. "Circumstances in Supplementary Homicide Reports: Variety and Validity." *Criminology* 27, no. 4 (1989): 671–96. https:// doi.org/10.1111/j.1745-9125.1989.tb01050.x.

Mayson, Sandra G., and Megan T. Stevenson. "Misdemeanors by the Numbers." *Boston College Law Review* 61, no. 3 (2020): 971–1044.

Mazerov, Matthew. "Kansas Provides Compelling Evidence of Failure of 'Supply-Side' Tax Cuts." Center on Budget and Policy Priorities, January 22, 2018. https://www.cbpp.org/research/kansas-provides -compelling-evidence-of-failure-of-supply-side-tax-cuts.

McCarthy, Justin. "Perceptions of Increased U.S. Crime at Highest Since 1993." *Gallup*, November 13, 2020. https://news.gallup.com/poll /323996/perceptions-increased-crime-highest-1993.aspx.

McClelland, Edward. "Rahm Emanuel Has Not Been Good for Chicago." *Slate*, April 7, 2015. https://slate.com/news-and-politics/2015/04/rahm -emanuel-re-election-chicago-crime-tickets-hassle-libraries-gangster -rap.html.

McDonald, John F. *Chicago: An Economic History*. New York: Routledge, 2015.

McDowall, David, Colin Loftin, and Brian Wiersema. "Using Quasi-Experiments to Evaluate Firearm Laws: Comment on Britt et al.'s Reassessment of the D.C. Gun Law." *Law and Society Review* 30, no. 2 (1996): 381–91. https://doi.org/10.2307/3053964.

McVeigh, Karen. "Chicago Hip-Hop Feud Deepens after Death of Joseph 'Lil Jojo' Coleman." *Guardian*, September 13, 2012. https://amp .theguardian.com/world/2012/sep/13/chicago-hip-hop-feud-joseph -lil-jojo-coleman.

Mechoulan, Stéphane, and Nicolas Sahuguet. "Assessing Racial Disparities in Parole Release." *Journal of Legal Studies* 44, no. 1 (2015): 39–74. https://doi.org/10.1086/680988.

Meisner, Jason. "Founder of Chicago's 'Goonie' Gang Tells Federal Jury How It Morphed into Violent Faction Responsible for at Least 10 Slayings." *Chicago Tribune*, May 26, 2023. https://www.chicagotribune .com/2023/05/26/founder-of-chicagos-goonie-gang-tells-federal -jury-how-it-morphed-into-violent-faction-responsible-for-at-least-10 -slayings/.

Mello, Steven. "More COPS, Less Crime." *Journal of Public Economics* 172 (April 2019): 174–200. https://doi.org/10.1016/j.jpubeco.2018.12.003.

Meloni, Osvaldo. "Does Poverty Relief Spending Reduce Crime? Evidence from Argentina." *International Review of Law and Economics* 39 (August 2014): 28–38. https://doi.org/10.1016/j.irle.2014.05.002.

Mendenhall, Ruby, Stefanie DeLuca, and Greg Duncan. "Neighborhood Resources, Racial Segregation, and Economic Mobility: Results from the Gautreaux Program." *Social Science Research* 35 (December 2006): 892–923. https://doi.org/10.1016/j.ssresearch.2005.06.007.

Merton, Robert K. *Social Theory and Social Structure*. New York: Free Press, 1968.

Messinger, Sheldon L., and Richard A. Berk. "Review Essay: Dangerous People." *Criminology* 25, no. 3 (1987): 767–81.

Messner, Steven F., and Richard Rosenfeld. *Crime and the American Dream.* Belmont, CA: Wadsworth, 1994.

Mickelson, Roslyn Arlin, and Argun Saatcioglu. "Structure and Agency in Resistance to Schooling: Class, Race, and the Reproduction of Unequal Outcomes." *Social Science Research* 120 (May 2024). https://doi.org/10.1016/j.ssresearch.2023.102971.

Miethe, Terance D., Wendy C. Regoeczi, and Kriss A. Drass. *Rethinking Homicide.* New York: Cambridge University Press, 2004.

Milan, Paris. "Carlishia Hood + Witness Who FILMED SPEAK OUT." YouTube, June 29, 2023. MP4 video, 26:52. https://www.youtube.com/watch?v=PUjIaAepi7o.

Milgram, Stanley. "Behavioral Study of Obedience." *Journal of Abnormal and Social Psychology* 67, no. 4 (1963): 371–78. https://doi.org/10.1037/h0040525.

———. "Some Conditions of Obedience and Disobedience to Authority." *Human Relations* 18, no. 1 (1965): 57–76. https://doi.org/10.1177/001872676501800105.

"Milwaukee Homicide Review Commission." Medical College of Wisconsin, 2024. https://www.mcw.edu/departments/epidemiology/research/milwaukee-homicide-review-commission.

Mitre-Becerril, David, Sarah Tahamont, Jason Lerner, and Aaron Chalfin. "Can Deterrence Persist? Long-Term Evidence from a Randomized Experiment in Street Lighting." *Criminology and Public Policy* 21, no. 4 (2022): 865–91. https://doi.org/10.1111/1745-9133.12599.

Mittendorf, Brian. "Wayne LaPierre Leaves a Financial Mess Behind at the NRA." *Chronicle of Philanthropy*, January 16, 2024. https://www.philanthropy.com/article/wayne-lapierre-leaves-a-financial-mess-behind-at-the-nra.

Mizell, Jill. *An Overview of Public Opinion and Discourse on Criminal Justice Issues.* New York: Opportunity Agenda, August 2014. https://www.prisonpolicy.org/scans/2014.08.23-CriminalJusticeReport-FINAL_0.pdf.

Modestino, Alicia Sasser. "How Do Summer Youth Employment Programs Improve Criminal Justice Outcomes, and for Whom?" *Journal of Policy Analysis and Management* 38, no. 3 (2019): 600–28. https://doi.org/10.1002/pam.22138.

Moffitt, Terrie E. "Adolescence-Limited and Life-Course Persistent Anti-Social Behavior: A Developmental Taxonomy." *Psychological Review* 100, no. 4 (1993): 674–701.

Mohler, G. O., M. B. Short, Sean Malinowski, Mark Johnson, G. E. Tita, Andrea L. Bertozzi, and P. J. Brantingham. "Randomized Controlled Field Trials of Predictive Policing." *Journal of the American Statistical Association* 110, no. 512 (2015): 1399–411. https://doi.org/10.1080/01621459.2015.1077710.

Moore, David. "Developments in Constitutional Law: The Second Amendment." Wisconsin Legislative Council issue brief, November 2022. https://docs.legis.wisconsin.gov/misc/lc/issue_briefs/2022/constitutional_law/ib_secondamendment_dm_2022_11_28.

Morgan, Rachel E., and Alexandra Thompson. *Criminal Victimization, 2020.* NCJ report no. 301775. Washington, DC: US Department of Justice, Office of Justice Programs, Bureau of Justice Statistics, October 2021. https://bjs.ojp.gov/sites/g/files/xyckuh236/files/media/document/cv20.pdf.

Morley, Tony. "How Child Mortality Fell from 40% to 3.7% in 200 Years." *Big Think*, June 25, 2022. https://bigthink.com/health/child-mortality-progress/.

Morton, Robert J., ed. *Serial Murder: Multi-Disciplinary Perspectives for Investigators.* Washington, DC: United States Federal Bureau of Investigation Critical Incident Response Group, National Center for the Analysis of Violent Crime (US), Behavioral Analysis Unit-2, 2005. https://purl.fdlp.gov/GPO/gpo38709.

"Mother Allegedly Orders 14-Year-Old Son to Shoot Man at Fast Food Restaurant, Police Release Video." *NBC Chicago*, June 23, 2023. https://www.nbcchicago.com/top-videos-home/mother-allegedly-orders-14-year-old-son-to-shoot-man-at-fast-food-restaurant-police-release-video/3168637/.

Moura, Maria Cecilia P., Steven J. Smith, and David B. Belzer. "120 Years of U.S. Residential Housing Stock and Floor Space." Edited by Wei-Xing Zhou. *PLoS One* 10, no. 8 (2015): e0134135. https://doi.org/10.1371/journal.pone.0134135.

Moynihan, Daniel Patrick. "Defining Deviancy Down." *American Scholar* 62, no. 1 (1993): 17–30.

Mueller-Smith, Michael, James Reeves, Kevin Schnepel, and Caroline Walker. "The Direct and Intergenerational Effects of Criminal History-Based Safety Net Bans in the U.S." NBER working paper no. 31983. Cambridge, MA: National Bureau of Economic Research, December 2023. https://doi.org/10.3386/w31983.

Muir, William Kerr. *Police: Streetcorner Politicians*. Chicago: University of Chicago Press, 1979.

Mullainathan, Sendhil, and Eldar Shafir. *Scarcity: Why Having Too Little Means So Much*. New York: Times Books, 2013.

Natapoff, Alexandra. "Misdemeanors." *Annual Review of Law and Social Science* 11, no. 1 (2015): 255–67. https://doi.org/10.1146/annurev-lawsocsci-120814-121742.

National Advisory Commission on Civil Disorders. *Report of the National Advisory Commission on Civil Disorders*. Washington, DC: US GPO, 1968.

National Center for Education Statistics. "Condition of Education: Public High School Graduation Rates in Rural Areas." US Department of Education, Institute of Education Sciences, last updated August 2023. https://nces.ed.gov/programs/coe/indicator/lba/high-school-graduation-rates-rural.

NBC Chicago. "Details on Dropped Charges against Mom, Teen Son in Chicago Restaurant Shooting." YouTube, June 26, 2023. MP4 video, 3:46. https://www.youtube.com/watch?v=QkZR5Ci3jss.

"NCVS Dashboard." Bureau of Justice Statistics, US Department of Justice, last updated May 13, 2024. https://ncvs.bjs.ojp.gov/single-year-comparison/crimeType.

Neal, Derek, and Armin Rick. "The Prison Boom and Sentencing Policy." *Journal of Legal Studies* 45, no. 1 (2016): 1–41.

New York Times Editorial Board. "To Restore New York City—First, Reclaim the Streets; No Time to Give Up on Crime." *New York Times*, January 8, 1991. https://www.nytimes.com/1991/01/08/opinion/to-restore-new-york-city-first-reclaim-the-streets-no-time-to-give-up-on-crime.html?searchResultPosition=16.

Newell, Allen. "Duncker on Thinking: An Inquiry into Progress in Cognition." In *A Century of Psychology as Science: Retrospections and Assessments*, edited by Sigmond Koch and David Leary, 392–419. New York: McGraw-Hill, 1985.

Newman, George E., and Daylian M. Cain. "Tainted Altruism: When Doing Some Good Is Evaluated as Worse Than Doing No Good at All." *Psychological Science* 25, no. 3 (2014): 648–55.

Nickeas, Peter. "2 Dead, 15 Wounded in Shootings across the City." *Chicago Tribune*, June 3, 2012. https://www.chicagotribune.com/2012/06/03/2 -dead-15-wounded-in-shootings-across-the-city/.

———. "Riverdale Teen Charged with Killing Chicago Teen." *Chicago Tribune*, June 15, 2012. https://www.chicagotribune.com/2012/06/15 /riverdale-teen-charged-with-killing-chicago-teen-2/.

Nisbett, Richard E., and Timothy D. Wilson. "The Halo Effect: Evidence for Unconscious Alteration of Judgments." *Journal of Personality and Social Psychology* 35, no. 4 (1977): 250–56. https://doi.org/10.1037/0022 -3514.35.4.250.

———. "Telling More Than We Can Know: Verbal Reports on Mental Processes." *Psychological Review* 84, no. 3 (1977): 231–59. https://doi.org/10 .1037/0033-295X.84.3.231.

Nissen, Jack. "Officials Tout Detroit's Falling Homicide Rate, Sees Results on Community Front and Hiring More Officers." *Fox 2 Detroit*, January 3, 2024. https://www.fox2detroit.com/news/detroit-touts-lowest -homicide-rate-in-50-years-vows-further-work-to-quell-violence.

Norris, Samuel, Matthew Pecenco, and Jeffrey Weaver. "The Effects of Parental and Sibling Incarceration: Evidence from Ohio." *American Economic Review* 111, no. 9 (2021): 2926–63. https://doi.org/10.1257/aer .20190415.

Novak, Tim. "Vanecko's Life after the Punch, Moved to Hollywood." *Chicago Sun-Times*, December 4, 2012. https://projects.suntimes.com /koschman/latest-news/vaneckos-life-after-the-punch-moved-to -hollywood/.

"The NRA Is in Disarray: Here's What You Need to Know." *Giffords* (blog), May 2022. https://giffords.org/blog/2022/05/nra-in-disarray-what -you-need-to-know-blog/.

Nuwer, Rachel. "Mississippi Officially Ratifies Amendment to Ban Slavery, 148 Years Late." *Smithsonian Magazine*, February 20, 2013. https:// www.smithsonianmag.com/smart-news/mississippi-officially-ratifies -amendment-to-ban-slavery-148-years-late-21328041/.

"Occupational Employment and Wage Statistics, May 2023." US Bureau of Labor Statistics, 2023. https://www.bls.gov/oes/current/oes339032 .htm.

"October 1996 Weather History at Chicago/Rockford International Airport." *Weather Spark*. Accessed March 15, 2024. https://weatherspark .com/h/m/146414/1996/10/Historical-Weather-in-October-1996-at -Chicago-Rockford-International-Airport-Illinois-United-States.

Office of the New York State Comptroller. "New York Continues to Send More Federal Tax Dollars to Washington Than It Gets in Return." Press release, January 14, 2020. https://www.osc.ny.gov/press/releases/2020 /01/new-york-continues-send-more-federal-tax-dollars-washington-it -gets-return.

Öllinger, Michael, and Vinod Goel. "Problem Solving." In *Towards a Theory of Thinking*, edited by Britt Glatzeder, Vinod Goel, and Albrecht Müller, 3–21. On Thinking. Berlin: Springer, 2010. https://doi.org/10.1007 /978-3-642-03129-8_1.

O'Neill, Tom. "The Manson Murders May Have Something to Do with CIA Mind-Control Experiments: Interview with Tom O'Neill." *Jacobin*, May 3, 2023. https://jacobin.com/2023/05/the-manson-murders-may -have-something-to-do-with-cia-mind-control-experiments.

Oreopoulos, Philip, and Kjell G. Salvanes. "Priceless: The Nonpecuniary Benefits of Schooling." *Journal of Economic Perspectives* 25, no. 1 (2011): 159–84. https://doi.org/10.1257/jep.25.1.159.

Owens, David, Judith Horrocks, and Allan House. "Fatal and Non-Fatal Repetition of Self-Harm: Systematic Review." *British Journal of Psychiatry* 181, no. 3 (2002): 193–99. https://doi.org/10.1192/bjp.181.3.193.

Owens, Emily Greene. "COPS and Cuffs." In *Lessons from the Economics of Crime*, edited by Philip J. Cook, Stephen Machin, Olivier Marie, and Giovanni Mastrobuoni, 17–44. Cambridge, MA: MIT Press, 2013. https://doi.org/10.7551/mitpress/9780262019613.003.0004.

Pacyga, Dominic A. "Czechs and Poles in Chicago: Pan-Slavism and the Origins of the Cermak Democratic Machine, 1860–1931." *Studia Migracyjne—Przeglad Polonijny* 4 (2015): 55–68.

Pain in the Nation 2022: U.S. Experienced Highest Ever Combined Rates of Deaths Due to Alcohol, Drugs, and Suicide during the First Year of the COVID-19 Pan-

demic. Annual report. Washington, DC: Trust for America's Health and Well Being Trust, May 24, 2022. https://www.tfah.org/report-details/pain-in-the-nation-2022/.

Palmer, Caroline, David C. Phillips, and James X. Sullivan. "Does Emergency Financial Assistance Reduce Crime?" *Journal of Public Economics* 169 (January 2019): 34–51. https://doi.org/10.1016/j.jpubeco.2018.10.012.

Paluck, Elizabeth Levy, Roni Porat, Chelsey S. Clark, and Donald P. Green. "Prejudice Reduction: Progress and Challenges." *Annual Review of Psychology* 72, no. 1 (2021): 533–60. https://doi.org/10.1146/annurev-psych-071620-030619.

Pandolfo, Nick. "School Discipline Records Show Racial Disparities." *Hechinger Report*, October 5, 2011. http://hechingered.org/content/school-discipline-policies-show-racial-disparities_4359/.

Papachristos, Andrew V. "48 Years of Crime in Chicago: A Descriptive Analysis of Serious Crime Trends from 1965 to 2013." ISPS working paper no. ISPS13-023. New Haven, CT: Institution for Social and Policy Studies, 2013. https://isps.yale.edu/research/publications/isps13-023.

———. "Murder by Structure: Dominance Relations and the Social Structure of Gang Homicide." *American Journal of Sociology* 115, no. 1 (2009): 74–128. https://doi.org/10.1086/597791.

Paral, Rob. "Chicago Community Area Data." Rob Paral and Associates. Accessed May 1, 2024. https://robparal.com/chicago-data/.

Parrish, Madeleine, and Chima Ikoro. "Chicago Public Schools and Segregation: A Historical View of How Education Decisions Have Perpetuated Segregation." *WTTW Chicago*, February 2022. https://interactive.wttw.com/firsthand/segregation/chicago-public-schools-and-segregation.

"Percentage of Households by Number of Vehicles, 1960–2020." *Geography of Transport Systems*. Accessed March 15, 2024. https://transportgeography.org/contents/chapter8/urban-transport-challenges/household-vehicles-united-states/.

Perkins, Craig. *Weapon Use and Violent Crime*. NCJ report no. 194820. Washington, DC: US Department of Justice, Office of Justice Programs, September 2003. https://bjs.ojp.gov/content/pub/pdf/wuvc01.pdf.

Perkins, D. N. "Postprimary Education Has Little Impact on Informal Reasoning." *Journal of Educational Psychology* 77, no. 5 (1985): 562–71. https://doi.org/10.1037/0022-0663.77.5.562.

Pfaff, John. *Locked In: The True Causes of Mass Incarceration and How to Achieve Real Reform*. New York: Basic Books, 2017.

Phinney, Jean S., Debra L. Ferguson, and Jerry D. Tate. "Intergroup Attitudes among Ethnic Minority Adolescents: A Causal Model." *Child Development* 68, no. 5 (1997): 955–69. https://doi.org/10.2307/1132044.

Pierce, Justin R., and Peter K. Schott. "Trade Liberalization and Mortality: Evidence from US Counties." *American Economic Review: Insights* 2, no. 1 (2020): 47–63. https://doi.org/10.1257/aeri.20180396.

Pinker, Steven. *The Better Angels of Our Nature: Why Violence Has Declined*. New York: Penguin Books, 2011.

Pinto, Antonio, Anna Russo, Alfonso Reginelli, Francesca Iacobellis, Marco Di Serafino, Sabrina Giovine, and Luigia Romano. "Gunshot Wounds: Ballistics and Imaging Findings." *Seminars in Ultrasound, CT and MRI* 40, no. 1 (2019): 25–35. https://doi.org/10.1053/j.sult.2018.10.018.

Pithers, R. T., and Rebecca Soden. "Critical Thinking in Education: A Review." *Educational Research* 42, no. 3 (2000): 237–49. https://doi.org/10.1080/001318800440579.

"Poland's Double-Edged Vodka Tradition." *France 24*, July 13, 2018. https://www.france24.com/en/20180713-polands-double-edged-vodka-tradition.

Police Executive Research Forum. *New National Commitment Required: The Changing Nature of Crime and Criminal Investigations*. Critical Issues in Policing. Washington, DC: Police Executive Research Forum, January 2018. https://www.policeforum.org/assets/ChangingNatureofCrime.pdf.

Ponce, Anthony. "More than 10,000 Guns Recovered off Chicago's Streets in 2022: Police." *Fox32 Chicago*, October 11, 2022. https://www.fox32chicago.com/news/more-than-10000-guns-recovered-off-chicagos-streets-in-2022-police.

Pozzi, Lucia, and Diego Ramiro Fariñas. "Infant and Child Mortality in the Past." *Annales de Démographie Historique* 129, no. 1 (2015): 55–75.

Priks, Mikael. "The Effects of Surveillance Cameras on Crime: Evidence from the Stockholm Subway." *Economic Journal* 125, no. 588 (2015): F289–305. https://doi.org/10.1111/ecoj.12327.

Proctor, Steven L., Norman G. Hoffmann, and Steve Allison. "The Effectiveness of Interactive Journaling in Reducing Recidivism among Substance-Dependent Jail Inmates." *International Journal of Offender Therapy and Comparative Criminology* 56, no. 2 (2012): 317–32. https://doi.org/10.1177/0306624X11399274.

Raphael, Steven. "Explaining the Rise in U.S. Incarceration Rates." *Criminology and Public Policy* 8, no. 1 (2009): 87–95. https://doi.org/10.1111/j.1745-9133.2009.00550.x.

Raphael, Steven, and Rudolf Winter-Ebmer. "Identifying the Effect of Unemployment on Crime." *Journal of Law and Economics* 44, no. 1 (2001): 259–83. https://doi.org/10.1086/320275.

Razzell, Peter, and Christine Spence. "The History of Infant, Child and Adult Mortality in London, 1550–1850." *London Journal* 32, no. 3 (2007): 271–92. https://doi.org/10.1179/174963207X227578.

"The Reagan Presidency." Ronald Reagan Presidential Library and Museum. Accessed March 15, 2024. https://www.reaganlibrary.gov/reagans/reagan-administration/reagan-presidency.

Reagan, Ronald. "Why I'm for the Brady Bill." *New York Times*, March 29, 1991. https://www.nytimes.com/1991/03/29/opinion/why-i-m-for-the-brady-bill.html.

Reardon, Sean F. "The Widening Academic Achievement Gap between the Rich and the Poor: New Evidence and Possible Explanations." In *Whither Opportunity? Rising Inequality and the Uncertain Life Chances of Low-Income Children*, edited by Richard Murnane and Greg Duncan, 91–116. New York: Russell Sage Foundation Press, 2011.

Reardon, Sean F., and Kendra Bischoff. *Growth in the Residential Segregation of Families by Income, 1970–2009*. US 2010 Project report. New York: Russell Sage Foundation and American Communities Project of Brown University, November 2011. https://s4.ad.brown.edu/Projects/Diversity/Data/Report/report111111.pdf.

Reardon, Sean F., Kendra Bischoff, Ann Owens, and Joseph B. Townsend. "Has Income Segregation Really Increased? Bias and Bias Correction in Sample-Based Segregation Estimates." *Demography* 55, no. 6 (2018): 2129–60.

"Recidivism and Reentry." Prison Policy Initiative. Accessed March 15, 2024. https://www.prisonpolicy.org/research/recidivism_and _reentry/.

Redcross, Cindy, Megan Millenky, Timothy Rudd, and Valerie Levshin. *More Than a Job: Final Results from the Evaluation of the Center for Employment Opportunities (CEO) Transitional Jobs Program.* NCJ report no. 238357. Washington, DC: US Department of Justice, Office of Justice Programs, 2012. https://www.ojp.gov/ncjrs/virtual-library/abstracts /more-job-final-results-evaluation-center-employment-opportunities.

Reed, Atavia. "Whole Foods Closes Englewood Store 6 Years after Promising to Fill a South Side Food Desert." *Block Club Chicago*, November 14, 2022. https://blockclubchicago.org/2022/11/14/whole-foods-closes -englewood-store-6-years-after-promising-to-bring-fresh-food-to-the -south-side/.

Reinhardt, Loren. "Loren Reinhardt: An Uptick in Robberies Has Made Chicagoans Feel Unsafe. Drop the Politics and Take Action." *Chicago Tribune*, October 6, 2023. https://www.chicagotribune.com/2023/10 /06/loren-reinhardt-an-uptick-in-robberies-has-made-chicagoans-feel -unsafe-drop-the-politics-and-take-action/.

"Republican Party Platforms: Republican Party Platform of 1932." June 14, 1932. Online at the *American Presidency Project*, edited by Gerhard Peters and John T. Wooley. https://www.presidency.ucsb.edu/documents /republican-party-platform-1932.

Rhodes, William, Gerald Gaes, Jeremy Luallen, Ryan Kling, Tom Rich, and Michael Shively. "Following Incarceration, Most Released Offenders Never Return to Prison." *Crime and Delinquency* 62, no. 8 (2016): 1003–25. https://doi.org/10.1177/0011128714549655.

Rich, Nathaniel. "The Prophecies of Jane Jacobs." *Atlantic*, November 2016.

"Robert Martinson and Nothing Works." *Communicating with Prisoners*. Accessed March 15, 2024. https://www.acrosswalls.org/robert-martinson -nothing-works/.

Roberts, Julian V. "Public Opinion and Youth Justice." *Crime and Justice* 31 (2004): 495–542.

Roberts, Sam. "Infamous 'Drop Dead' Was Never Said by Ford." *New York Times*, December 28, 2006. https://www.nytimes.com/2006/12/28 /nyregion/28veto.html.

Robertson, Sheena. "READI Chicago Offers a New Lease on Life." *Chicago Leader*, June 5, 2022. https://chicagoleader.com/readi-chicago-offers-a -new-lease-on-life/.

Robuck-Mangum, G. "A Descriptive Study of Handgun-Carrying Behavior." MSc thesis, University of North Carolina, School of Public Health, 1997.

Rohlfs, Chris, Ryan Sullivan, and Thomas Kniesner. "New Estimates of the Value of a Statistical Life Using Air Bag Regulations as a Quasi-Experiment." *American Economic Journal: Economic Policy* 7, no. 1 (2015): 331–59.

Roosevelt, Franklin D. Address at the National Parole Conference, White House, Washington, DC, April 17, 1939. Online at the *American Presidency Project*, edited by Gerhard Peters and John T. Wooley. https:// www.presidency.ucsb.edu/documents/address-the-national-parole -conference-white-house-washington-dc.

Rose, Evan K. "The Effects of Job Loss on Crime: Evidence from Administrative Data." *Social Science Research Network*, June 15, 2018. https://ssrn .com/abstract=2991317.

Rose, Evan, Jonathan Schellenberg, and Yotam Shem-Tov. "The Effects of Teacher Quality on Adult Criminal Justice Contact." NBER working paper no. 30274. Cambridge, MA: National Bureau of Economic Research, revised September 2022. https://doi.org/10.3386/w30274.

Rosenbaum, James E. "Changing the Geography of Opportunity by Expanding Residential Choice: Lessons from the Gautreaux Program." *Housing Policy Debate* 6, no. 1 (1995): 231–69. https://doi.org/10.1080 /10511482.1995.9521186.

Rosenberg-Douglas, Katherine, and Sylvia Goodman. "'I Arrived a Few Minutes Too Late,' Says Doctor Who Tried to Save International Student Killed in Hyde Park." *Chicago Tribune*, November 10, 2021. https:// www.chicagotribune.com/2021/11/10/i-arrived-a-few-minutes-too -late-says-doctor-who-tried-to-save-international-student-killed-in -hyde-park/.

Ross, Lee. "From the Fundamental Attribution Error to the Truly Fundamental Attribution Error and Beyond: My Research Journey." *Perspectives on Psychological Science* 13, no. 6 (2018): 750–69. https://doi.org/10
.1177/1745691618769855.

Ross, Lee, and Richard E. Nisbett. *The Person and the Situation: Perspectives of
Social Psychology*. New York: McGraw-Hill, 1991.

Ross, Lee, and Andrew Ward. "Psychological Barriers to Dispute Resolution." In *Advances in Experimental Social Psychology* 27 (1995): 255–304.
https://doi.org/10.1016/S0065-2601(08)60407-4.

Ross, Michael, and Fiore Sicoly. "Egocentric Biases in Availability and Attribution." *Journal of Personality and Social Psychology* 37, no. 3 (1979): 322–
36. https://doi.org/10.1037/0022-3514.37.3.322.

Ross, Trap Lore, dir. *Trap Lore Ross on "Gangs of Chicago—300 vs JoJo
World."* HipHopCanada, January 24, 2021. MP4 video, 34:32. https://
hiphopcanada.com/trap-lore-ross-300-v-jojo-world/.

Rossi, Peter H., Richard A. Berk, and Kenneth J. Lenihan. *Money, Work, and
Crime*. New York: Academic Press, Inc., 1980.

Rossman, Shelli, Caterina Gouvis, Janeen Buck, and Elaine Morley. *Confronting Relapse and Recidivism: Case Management and Aftercare Services
in the OPTS Programs*. Washington, DC: Urban Institute, February 18,
2000. https://www.ojp.gov/pdffiles1/nij/grants/181047.pdf.

Rossman, Shelli, Sanjeev Sridharan, Caterina Gouvis, Janeen Buck, and
Elaine Morley. *Impact of the Opportunity to Succeed (OPTS) Aftercare Program for Substance-Abusing Felons: Comprehensive Final Report*. NCJ report
no. 181046. Washington, DC: Urban Institute, 1999.

Royko, Mike. *Boss: Richard J. Daley of Chicago*. New York: Plume, 1988.

Rozin, Paul, Maureen Markwith, and Bonnie Ross. "The Sympathetic
Magical Law of Similarity, Nominal Realism and Neglect of Negatives
in Response to Negative Labels." *Psychological Science* 1, no. 6 (1990):
383–84. https://doi.org/10.1111/j.1467-9280.1990.tb00246.x.

Rozin, Paul, Linda Millman, and Carol Nemeroff. "Operation of the Laws
of Sympathetic Magic in Disgust and Other Domains." *Journal of Personality and Social Psychology* 50, no. 4 (1986): 703–12. https://doi.org/10
.1037/0022-3514.50.4.703.

Rozin, Paul, and Edward B. Royzman. "Negativity Bias, Negativity Dominance, and Contagion." *Personality and Social Psychology Review* 5, no. 4 (2001): 296–320. https://doi.org/10.1207/S15327957PSPR0504_2.

Rubinowitz, Leonard S., and James E. Rosenbaum. *Crossing the Class and Color Lines: From Public Housing to White Suburbia.* Chicago: University of Chicago Press, 2000.

Ruhm, Christopher J. "Are Recessions Good for Your Health?" *Quarterly Journal of Economics* 115, no. 2 (2000): 617–50. https://doi.org/10.1162/003355300554872.

———. "Health Effects of Economic Crises." *Health Economics* 25, S2 (2016): 6–24. https://doi.org/10.1002/hec.3373.

———. "Recessions, Healthy No More?" *Journal of Health Economics* 42 (July 2015): 17–28. https://doi.org/10.1016/j.jhealeco.2015.03.004.

Rury, John L. "School Desegregation." *Electronic Encyclopedia of Chicago.* Accessed March 15, 2024. http://www.encyclopedia.chicagohistory.org/pages/1121.html.

Ryan, Elisabeth J. "The History of Gun Law and the Second Amendment in the United States." In *Why We Are Losing the War on Gun Violence in the United States*, edited by Marie L. Crandall, Stephanie L. Bonne, Jennifer L. Bronson, and Woodie Kessel, 1st ed., 123–36. New York: Springer, 2021.

Sabino, Pascal. "The City Closed Many of Its Free Mental Health Clinics, so West Siders Opened Their Own." *Block Club Chicago*, November 1, 2019. https://blockclubchicago.org/2019/11/01/the-city-closed-many-of-its-free-mental-health-clinics-so-west-siders-opened-their-own/.

Sahgal, Neha, and Besheer Mohamed. "In the U.S. and Western Europe, People Say They Accept Muslims, but Opinions Are Divided on Islam." Pew Research Center, October 8, 2019. https://www.pewresearch.org/short-reads/2019/10/08/in-the-u-s-and-western-europe-people-say-they-accept-muslims-but-opinions-are-divided-on-islam.

Salmassi, Mithra. "Survey: People Have More Negative Opinions about Drug Addiction Than Mental Illness." Partnership to End Addiction, October 2014. https://drugfree.org/drug-and-alcohol-news/survey-people-negative-opinions-drug-addiction-mental-illness/.

Sampson, Robert J. "Collective Efficacy Theory: Lessons Learned and Directions for Future Inquiry." In *Taking Stock*, edited by Francis T. Cullen,

John Paul Wright, and Kristie R. Blevins, 1st ed., 149–67. New York: Routledge, 2008.

———. *Great American City: Chicago and the Enduring Neighborhood Effect.* Chicago: University of Chicago Press, 2013.

Sampson, Robert J., and Stephen W. Raudenbush. "Systematic Social Observation of Public Spaces: A New Look at Disorder in Urban Neighborhoods." *American Journal of Sociology* 105, no. 3 (1999): 603–51. https://doi.org/10.1086/210356.

Sampson, Robert J., Stephen W. Raudenbush, and Felton Earls. "Neighborhoods and Violent Crime: A Multilevel Study of Collective Efficacy." *Science* 277, no. 5328 (1997): 918–24. https://doi.org/10.1126/science.277.5328.918.

Sampson, Robert J., William Julius Wilson, and Hanna Katz. "Reassessing 'Toward a Theory of Race, Crime, and Urban Inequality.'" *Du Bois Review* 15, no. 1 (2018): 13–34. https://doi.org/10.1017/S1742058X18000140.

Sanchez, Angelica. "'I Wasn't Trying to Kill Her': Milwaukee Man Charged with Death of Woman Found Stuffed in Tote." *Fox 6 Milwaukee*, October 28, 2016. https://www.fox6now.com/news/i-wasnt-trying-to-kill-her-milwaukee-man-charged-with-death-of-woman-found-stuffed-in-tote.

Sanchez, Jose Antonio, Scott H. Decker, and David C. Pyrooz. "Gang Homicide: The Road so Far and a Map for the Future." *Homicide Studies* 26, no. 1 (2022): 68–90. https://doi.org/10.1177/10887679211043804.

Sandel, Michael J., Sidney Verba, and Harvey C. Mansfield. "James Q. Wilson." *Harvard Gazette*, February 6, 2013. https://news.harvard.edu/gazette/story/2013/02/james-q-wilson/.

Sander, Richard Henry, Yana A. Kucheva, and Jonathan M. Zasloff. *Moving toward Integration: The Past and Future of Fair Housing.* Cambridge, MA: Harvard University Press, 2018.

Sanders, Hank, Rick Pearson, and Sarah Macaraeg. "School Choice or a Drain on Public Education? Backers Aim to Save Controversial Private School Tax Credit Left Out of New Illinois Budget." *Chicago Tribune*, June 19, 2023. https://www.chicagotribune.com/2023/06/11/school-choice-or-a-drain-on-public-education-backers-aim-to

-save-controversial-private-school-tax-credit-left-out-of-new-illinois
-budget/.

Saunders, Angel. "Carlishia Hood Accepts Nicki Minaj's Offer to Pay for
Son's College Education Following Viral Chicago Attack." *Yahoo Entertainment*, June 28, 2023. www.yahoo.com/entertainment/carlishia
-hood-accepts-nicki-minaj-131430973.html?guccounter=1.

Sawyer, Wendy, and Peter Wagner. "Mass Incarceration: The Whole Pie
2023." Prison Policy Initiative, March 14, 2023. https://www.prison
policy.org/reports/pie2023.html.

Schlikerman, Becky. "South Shore Teen Killed Blocks from His Home."
DNA Info, November 20, 2012. https://www.dnainfo.com/chicago
/20121120/south-shore-above-79th/south-shore-teen-killed-blocks
-from-his-home.

Schmid, Hannah. "4 of Illinois' Past 10 Governors Went to Prison." *Illinois
Policy*, April 11, 2022. https://www.illinoispolicy.org/4-of-illinois-past
-10-governors-went-to-prison/.

Schmidt, John. "John Schmidt: Illinois Should Restore the 10% Local
Share of State Income Tax to Chicago, Other Municipalities." *Chicago
Tribune*, April 11, 2023. https://www.chicagotribune.com/2023/04
/11/john-schmidt-illinois-should-restore-the-10-local-share-of-state
-income-tax-to-chicago-other-municipalities/.

Schnepel, Kevin T. "Good Jobs and Recidivism." *Economic Journal* 128, no.
608 (2018): 447–69. https://doi.org/10.1111/ecoj.12415.

Schwartz, Amy Ellen, Agustina Laurito, Johanna Lacoe, Patrick Sharkey,
and Ingrid Gould Ellen. "The Academic Effects of Chronic Exposure
to Neighbourhood Violence." *Urban Studies* 59, no. 14 (2022): 3005–21.
https://doi.org/10.1177/00420980211052149.

Schwartz, Larry. "Owens Pierced a Myth." *ESPN SportsCentury*, 2000.
https://www.espn.com/sportscentury/features/00016393.html.

Sciandra, Matthew, Lisa Sanbonmatsu, Greg J. Duncan, Lisa A. Gennet-
ian, Lawrence F. Katz, Ronald C. Kessler, Jeffrey R. Kling, and Jens
Ludwig. "Long-Term Effects of the Moving to Opportunity Residential
Mobility Experiment on Crime and Delinquency." *Journal of Experimental Criminology* 9, no. 4 (2013): 451–89. https://doi.org/10.1007/s11292
-013-9189-9.

Seroczynski, A. D., William N. Evans, Amy D. Jobst, Luke Horvath, and Giuliana Carozza. "Reading for Life and Adolescent Re-Arrest: Evaluating a Unique Juvenile Diversion Program." *Journal of Policy Analysis and Management* 35, no. 3 (2016): 662–82. https://doi.org/10.1002/pam.21916.

Seto, Christopher H., and Iman Said. "Religious Perceptions of Crime and Implications for Punitiveness." *Punishment and Society* 24, no. 1 (2022): 46–68. https://doi.org/10.1177/1462474520960038.

Shafer, Ronald G. "They Were Killers with Powerful Guns. The President Went after Their Weapons." *Washington Post*, May 26, 2022. https://www.washingtonpost.com/history/2022/05/26/fdr-machine-gun-control-dillinger/.

Shah, Anuj. "Thinking Past the Situation." Unpublished paper, 2015.

Shantz, Amanda, and Gary P. Latham. "An Exploratory Field Experiment of the Effect of Subconscious and Conscious Goals on Employee Performance." *Organizational Behavior and Human Decision Processes* 109, no. 1 (2009): 9–17. https://doi.org/10.1016/j.obhdp.2009.01.001.

Sharkey, Patrick. "The Acute Effect of Local Homicides on Children's Cognitive Performance." *Proceedings of the National Academy of Sciences* 107, no. 26 (2010): 11733–38. https://doi.org/10.1073/pnas.1000690107.

———. *Stuck in Place: Urban Neighborhoods and the End of Progress toward Racial Equality*. Chicago: University of Chicago Press, 2013.

Sharkey, Patrick, Nicole Tirado-Strayer, Andrew V. Papachristos, and C. Cybele Raver. "The Effect of Local Violence on Children's Attention and Impulse Control." *American Journal of Public Health* 102, no. 12 (2012): 2287–93. https://doi.org/10.2105/AJPH.2012.300789.

Sharkey, Patrick, Gerard Torrats-Espinosa, and Delaram Takyar. "Community and the Crime Decline: The Causal Effect of Local Nonprofits on Violent Crime." *American Sociological Review* 82, no. 6 (2017): 1214–40. https://doi.org/10.1177/0003122417736289.

Shaw, C. R., and H. D. McKay. *Juvenile Delinquency in Urban Areas*. Chicago: University of Chicago Press, 1942.

Shem-Tov, Yotam, Steven Raphael, and Alissa Skog. "Can Restorative Justice Conferencing Reduce Recidivism? Evidence from the Make-it-

Right Program." *Econometrica* 92, no. 1 (2024): 61–78. https://doi.org
/10.3982/ECTA20996.

Shen, Yinzhi, Shawn D. Bushway, Lucy C. Sorensen, and Herbert L. Smith.
"Locking Up My Generation: Cohort Differences in Prison Spells over
the Life Course." *Criminology* 58, no. 4 (2020): 645–77. https://doi.org
/10.1111/1745-9125.12256.

Sherif, Muzafer, O. J. Harvey, B. Jack White, William R. Hood, and Carolyn W. Sherif. *Intergroup Conflict and Cooperation: The Robbers Cave Experiment*. Norman: University of Oklahoma Book Exchange, 1961.

Shiller, Robert J. *Irrational Exuberance*. 2nd ed. New York: Currency/
Doubleday, 2005.

Shroder, Mark D., and Larry L. Orr. "Moving to Opportunity: Why, How,
and What Next?" *Cityscape* 14, no. 2 (2012): 31–56.

Sikora, Lacey. "Hemingway Haunts." *Wednesday Journal of Oak Park and
River Forest*, July 12, 2016. https://www.oakpark.com/2016/07/12
/hemingway-haunts/.

Silver, Laura, Janell Fetterolf, and Aidan Connaughton. "Diversity and
Division in Advanced Economies." Pew Research Center, October 13,
2021. https://www.pewresearch.org/global/2021/10/13/diversity-and
-division-in-advanced-economies/.

Simpson, Dick, Marco Rosaire Rossi, and Thomas J. Gradel. *Corruption
Continues through the COVID-19 Pandemic*. Anti-Corruption Report no.
14. Chicago: University of Illinois at Chicago, Department of Political
Science, May 11, 2022. https://pols.uic.edu/wp-content/uploads/sites
/273/2022/05/Corruption-Rpt-14-on-5-7-22-final.pdf.

Sims, Barbara, and Eric Johnston. "Examining Public Opinion about
Crime and Justice: A Statewide Study." *Criminal Justice Policy Review* 15,
no. 3 (2004): 270–93. https://doi.org/10.1177/0887403403252668.

Skelley, Geoffrey, and Holly Fuong. "How Democrats and Republicans
Think Differently about Crime and Gun Violence." *FiveThirtyEight*, August 10, 2022. https://fivethirtyeight.com/features/how-democrats
-and-republicans-think-differently-about-crime-and-gun-violence/.

Slovic, Paul, Melissa L. Finucane, Ellen Peters, and Donald G. MacGregor.
"The Affect Heuristic." *European Journal of Operational Research* 177, no. 3
(2007): 1333–52. https://doi.org/10.1016/j.ejor.2005.04.006.

Small, Mario Luis. *Unexpected Gains*. New York: Oxford University Press, 2009.

Smith, Jeffrey A., and Petra E. Todd. "Does Matching Overcome LaLonde's Critique of Nonexperimental Estimators?" *Journal of Econometrics* 125, no. 1–2 (2005): 305–53. https://doi.org/10.1016/j.jeconom.2004.04 .011.

Smith, Tom W. *Classifying Protestant Denominations*. General Social Survey Methodological Report no. 43. Chicago: National Opinion Research Center, revised July 1987. https://gss.norc.org/Documents/reports /methodological-reports/MR043.pdf.

Smylie, Samantha, and Becky Vevea. "Chicago Will Get Smaller Share of State's Increased K-12 Education Budget for Second Year in a Row." *Chalkbeat Chicago*, August 10, 2023. https://www.chalkbeat.org/chicago /2023/8/9/23826279/chicago-schools-funding-enrollment-state -board/.

Sotomayor, Marianna, and Liz Goodwin. "In Congress, Little Urgency to Address Gun Violence with Legislation." *Washington Post*, March 29, 2023. https://www.washingtonpost.com/politics/2023/03/29 /congress-little-urgency-address-gun-violence-with-legislation/.

Spelman, William. "Crime, Cash, and Limited Options: Explaining the Prison Boom." *Criminology and Public Policy* 8, no. 1 (2009): 29–77. https://doi.org/10.1111/j.1745-9133.2009.00546.x.

Spielman, Fran. "Lightfoot Comes out Swinging Hours after Preckwinkle Fires Her Campaign Manager." *Chicago Sun-Times*, February 22, 2019. https://chicago.suntimes.com/2019/2/22/18328222/lightfoot-comes -out-swinging-hours-after-preckwinkle-fires-her-campaign-manager.

———. "Lightfoot Delivers Tough-Love Anti-Crime Message: Young People, 'Put Down the Guns,' and Adults, 'Be Better.'" *Chicago Sun-Times*, February 21, 2020. https://chicago.suntimes.com/politics/2020/2/21 /21147532/lightfoots-tough-love-anti-crime-message-young-people -put-down-guns-adults-better.

———. "Mayoral Challenger Ja'Mal Green Unveils $5 Billion Public Safety Plan." *Chicago Sun-Times*, January 3, 2023. https://chicago.suntimes.com /2023/1/3/23537661/chiacgo-mayor-election-2023-jamal-green-public -safety-police-reform-housing-basic-income.

———. "Worst-Case Scenario: Chicago Budget Gap Could Reach $1.9 Billion by 2026." *Chicago Sun-Times*, September 13, 2023. https://chicago .suntimes.com/2023/9/13/23871924/chicago-budget-gap-deficit-2026 -three-year-forecast-city-council-mayor-johnson-ervin-lightfoot.

Srull, Thomas K., and Robert S. Wyer. "The Role of Category Accessibility in the Interpretation of Information about Persons: Some Determinants and Implications." *Journal of Personality and Social Psychology* 37, no. 10 (1979): 1660–72. https://doi.org/10.1037/0022-3514.37.10.1660.

Stacy, Christina, Yasemin Irvin-Erickson, and Emily Tiry. "The Impact of Gunshots on Place-Level Business Activity." *Crime Science* 10, no. 1 (2021): 10. https://doi.org/10.1186/s40163-021-00146-9.

Stanovich, Keith E. "The Cognitive Miser: Ways to Avoid Thinking." In *What Intelligence Tests Miss*, 70–85. New Haven, CT: Yale University Press, 2017. https://doi.org/10.12987/9780300142532-008.

Stanovich, Keith E., and Richard F. West. "Individual Differences in Reasoning: Implications for the Rationality Debate?" *Behavioral and Brain Sciences* 23, no. 5 (2000): 645–65. https://doi.org/10.1017 /S0140525X00003435.

Stefanopoulos, P. K., D. E. Pinialidis, G. F. Hadjigeorgiou, and K. N. Filippakis. "Wound Ballistics 101: The Mechanisms of Soft Tissue Wounding by Bullets." *European Journal of Trauma and Emergency Surgery* 43, no. 5 (2017): 579–86. https://doi.org/10.1007/s00068-015-0581-1.

Steiner, Jacob E. "Human Facial Expressions in Response to Taste and Smell Stimulation." *Advances in Child Development and Behavior* 13 (1979): 257–95. https://doi.org/10.1016/S0065-2407(08)60349-3.

Stevenson, Betsey, and Justin Wolfers. "Subjective and Objective Indicators of Racial Progress." *SSRN Electronic Journal*, July 2011. https://doi.org /10.2139/ssrn.1884635.

Stevenson, Megan, and Jennifer L. Doleac. "Algorithmic Risk Assessment in the Hands of Humans." IZA discussion paper no. 12853. Bonn: IZA Institute of Labor Economics, 2019. http://dx.doi.org/10.2139/ssrn .3513695.

Stevenson, Megan, and Randi Hjalmarsson. "Breaking Bad: Mechanisms of Social Influence and the Path to Criminality in Juvenile Jails." *Review of Economics and Statistics* 99, no. 5 (2017): 824–38.

Stoddard, Greg, Dylan Fitzpatrick, and Jens Ludwig. "Predicting Police Misconduct." Working paper no. 32432. Cambridge, MA: National Bureau of Economic Research, May 2024. https://www.nber.org/papers/w32432.

Strang, Heather, Lawrence W. Sherman, Evan Mayo-Wilson, Daniel Woods, and Barak Ariel. "Restorative Justice Conferencing (RJC) Using Face-to-Face Meetings of Offenders and Victims: Effects on Offender Recidivism and Victim Satisfaction. A Systematic Review." *Campbell Systematic Reviews* 9, no. 1 (2013): 1–59. https://doi.org/10.4073/csr.2013.12.

Struett, David, and Madeline Kenney. "Violent Death of Chinese Student in Hyde Park Sparks Calls for Action—but Few Specifics on How to Combat City's Rising Crime." *Chicago Sun-Times*, November 10, 2021. https://chicago.suntimes.com/crime/2021/11/9/22772821/university-chicago-shooting-dennis-shaoxiong-zheng-hyde-park.

Sulski, Jim. "Riding High." *Chicago Tribune*, November 10, 2002. https://www.chicagotribune.com/2002/11/10/riding-high-34/.

"Sunday, June 28, 1998: Questions For; Ozzy Osbourne." *New York Times*, June 28, 1998. https://www.nytimes.com/1998/06/28/magazine/sunday-june-28-1998-questions-for-ozzy-osbourne.html.

Suneson, A., H. A. Hansson, and T. Seeman. "Peripheral High-Energy Missile Hits Cause Pressure Changes and Damage to the Nervous System: Experimental Studies on Pigs." *Journal of Trauma* 27, no. 7 (1987): 782–89. https://doi.org/10.1097/00005373-198707000-00016.

Sunstein, Cass R. "Are Poor People Worth Less Than Rich People? Disaggregating the Value of Statistical Lives." John M. Olin Program in Law and Economics working paper no. 207. Chicago: Coase-Sandor Institute for Law and Economics, 2004.

———. *How Change Happens*. Cambridge, MA: MIT Press, 2019.

Sutherland, Edwin H., and Donald R. Cressy. *Principles of Criminology*. 7th ed. Philadelphia, PA: J. B, Lippincott and Co., 1966.

Sweeney, Annie, and Jason Meisner. "Federal Authorities Announce Sweeping Conspiracy Case against Chicago Street Gang Involving 19 Slayings." *Chicago Tribune*, November 1, 2021. https://www.chicagotribune.com/2021/11/01/federal-authorities-announce-sweeping-conspiracy-case-against-chicago-street-gang-involving-19-slayings/.

"Synthetic Identity Theft: The New ID Fraud." Wexler, Boley, and El-gersma, LLP (blog), December 15, 2016, https://wbe-llp.com/synthetic -identity-theft/.

Terry, Don. "Boy Sought in Teen-Ager's Death Is Latest Victim of Chicago Guns." *New York Times*, September 2, 1994. https://www.nytimes.com /1994/09/02/us/boy-sought-in-teen-ager-s-death-is-latest-victim-of -chicago-guns.html.

Thaler, Richard H. *Misbehaving: The Making of Behavioral Economics*. New York: W. W. Norton, 2016.

———. "Prize Lecture." December 8, 2017. https://www.nobelprize.org /prizes/economic-sciences/2017/thaler/lecture/.

Thaler, Richard H., and Cass R. Sunstein. *Nudge: Improving Decisions about Health, Wealth, and Happiness*. New Haven, CT: Yale University Press, 2008.

———. *Nudge: Improving Decisions about Health, Wealth, and Happiness*. Rev. ed. New York: Penguin Books, 2009.

"Thatcher and Atlee Top PM List." *BBC News*, August 29, 2006. http:// news.bbc.co.uk/2/hi/uk_news/politics/5294024.stm.

Thompson, Victor R., and Lawrence D. Bobo. "Thinking about Crime: Race and Lay Accounts of Lawbreaking Behavior." *Annals of the American Academy of Political and Social Science* 634 (2011): 16–38.

Thrasher, Frederic Milton. *The Gang: A Study of 1,313 Gangs in Chicago*. Chicago: University of Chicago Press, 1927.

Tiwari, A. K., and H. K. Roy. "Progress against Cancer (1971–2011): How Far Have We Come?" *Journal of Internal Medicine* 271, no. 4 (2012): 392– 99. https://doi.org/10.1111/j.1365-2796.2011.02462.x.

Tomasello, Michael. "The Ultra-Social Animal." *European Journal of Social Psychology* 44, no. 3 (2014): 187–94. https://doi.org/10.1002/ejsp .2015.

Tonry, Michael. "Explanations of American Punishment Policies: A National History." *Punishment and Society* 11, no. 3 (2009): 377–94. https:// doi.org/10.1177/1462474509334609.

"The Town of Pullman—Pullman National Historical Park." National Park Service, January 8, 2023. https://www.nps.gov/pull/learn/history culture/the-town-of-pullman.htm.

"Transcript: Perspectives in Law Enforcement—The Concept of Predictive Policing: An Interview with Chief William Bratton." US Department of Justice, Bureau of Justice Assistance, November 2009.

Travis, Dempsey. *Harold, the People's Mayor: The Biography of Harold Washington*. Evanston, IL: Agate Bolden, 2017.

Travis, Jeremy, Bruce Western, and Steve Redburn, eds. *The Growth of Incarceration in the United States: Exploring Causes and Consequences*. Washington, DC: National Academy of Sciences, 2014.

Trice, Dawn Turner. "Village with a Vision." *Chicago Tribune*, June 27, 2014. https://www.chicagotribune.com/2014/06/27/village-with-a-vision-2/.

Trisi, Danilo, and Matt Saenz. "Economic Security Programs Reduce Overall Poverty, Racial and Ethnic Inequities." Center on Budget and Policy Priorities, updated July 1, 2021. https://www.cbpp.org/research/poverty-and-inequality/more-than-4-in-10-children-in-renter-households-face-food-andor.

Trussell, Jacqueline. "Building Leaders for Today's World: The Legacy of Harold L. Washington." *Roosevelt Review* (blog), May 9, 2022. https://blogs.roosevelt.edu/review/2022/05/09/building-leaders-for-todays-world-the-legacy-of-harold-l-washington-2/.

Tugade, F. Amanda. "Breaking the Cycle." *Chicago Reader*, May 12, 2021. https://chicagoreader.com/news-politics/breaking-the-cycle/.

Turner, R. Jay, Blair Wheaton, and Donald A. Lloyd. "The Epidemiology of Social Stress." *American Sociological Review* 60, no. 1 (1995): 104. https://doi.org/10.2307/2096348.

Tuttle, Cody. "Snapping Back: Food Stamp Bans and Criminal Recidivism." *American Economic Journal: Economic Policy* 11, no. 2 (2019): 301–27. https://doi.org/10.1257/pol.20170490.

Tversky, Amos, and Daniel Kahneman. "Belief in the Law of Small Numbers." *Psychological Bulletin* 76, no. 2 (1971): 105–10. https://doi.org/10.1037/h0031322.

Uggen, Christopher. "Work as a Turning Point in the Life Course of Criminals: A Duration Model of Age, Employment, and Recidivism." *American Sociological Review* 65, no. 4 (2000): 529–46. https://doi.org/10.2307/2657381.

United States Census Bureau. "Decennial Census of Population and Hous-

ing by Decade." *Census.gov*, last revised August 4, 2023. https://www
.census.gov/programs-surveys/decennial-census/decade.1930.html.

———. "QuickFacts: United States." *Census.gov*. Accessed May 7, 2024.
https://www.census.gov/quickfacts/fact/table/US/PST045219.

———. "Why We Ask Questions about . . . Vehicles Available." *Census.gov*.
Accessed May 7, 2022. https://www.census.gov/acs/www/about/why
-we-ask-each-question/vehicles/.

"University of Chicago Graduate Who Was Shot and Killed in Robbery
Is Identified as Dennis Shaoxiong Zheng; Vigil Held at Site of His
Murder." *CBS News*, November 10, 2021. https://www.cbsnews.com
/chicago/news/university-of-chicago-student-killed-in-robbery
-shaoxiong-zheng/.

US Attorney's Office, Northern District of Illinois. "Leader of Violent
Chicago Street Gang Convicted on Federal Racketeering Charge."
Press release, November 15, 2022. https://www.justice.gov/usao-ndil
/pr/leader-violent-chicago-street-gang-convicted-federal-racketeering
-charge.

———. "Superseding Federal Indictment against Former Illinois Speaker
of the House Adds Charge for Alleged Corruption Scheme Related to
AT&T Illinois." Press release, October 14, 2022. https://www.justice
.gov/usao-ndil/pr/superseding-federal-indictment-against-former
-illinois-speaker-house-adds-charge.

US Burden of Disease Collaborators, Ali H. Mokdad, Katherine Ballestros,
Michelle Echko, Scott Glenn, Helen E. Olsen, Erin Mullany, et al. "The
State of US Health, 1990–2016: Burden of Diseases, Injuries, and Risk
Factors Among US States." *JAMA* 319, no. 14 (2018): 1444–72. https://
doi.org/10.1001/jama.2018.0158.

Valentino, Nicholas A., and David O. Sears. "Old Times There Are Not Forgotten: Race and Partisan Realignment in the Contemporary South."
American Journal of Political Science 49, no. 3 (2005): 672–88. https://doi
.org/10.1111/j.1540-5907.2005.00136.x.

Vallas, Paul. "The Protection of Chicago's Witnesses and Victims Must
Be a Priority." *Chicago Tribune*, February 27, 2024. https://www
.chicagotribune.com/2024/02/27/opinion-witness-protection
-misdemeantor-weapons-charges-chicago/.

Verdugo, Eduardo. "Drug Gang Kills 20 in Town Hall Massacre in Southern Mexico." *PBS NewsHour*, October 7, 2022. https://www.pbs.org/newshour/world/drug-gang-kills-20-in-town-hall-massacre-in-southern-mexico.

Verschaffel, Lieven, Erik De Corte, Sabien Lasure, Griet Van Vaerenbergh, Hedwig Bogaerts, and Elie Ratinckx. "Learning to Solve Mathematical Application Problems: A Design Experiment with Fifth Graders." *Mathematical Thinking and Learning* 1, no. 3 (1999): 195–229. https://doi.org/10.1207/s15327833mtl0103_2.

"Victims of Identity Theft, 2021." Bureau of Justice Statistics, US Department of Justice, 2021. https://bjs.ojp.gov/press-release/victims-identity-theft-2021#:~:text=As%20of%202021%2C%20about%201,email%20or%20social%20media%20account.

"Video Shows Moments before Mom Allegedly Encouraged Teen Son to Shoot Man in Chicago Restaurant." *NBC Chicago*, June 26, 2023. https://www.nbcchicago.com/news/local/video-shows-moments-before-mom-allegedly-encouraged-teen-son-to-shoot-man-in-chicago-restaurant/3171535/.

"The Views of White Americans," *New York Times* interactive graphic, April 30, 2014, https://www.nytimes.com/interactive/2014/04/30/upshot/100000002853274.embedded.html.

Vigdor, Elizabeth Richardson, and James A. Mercy. "Do Laws Restricting Access to Firearms by Domestic Violence Offenders Prevent Intimate Partner Homicide?" *Evaluation Review* 30, no. 3 (2006): 313–46. https://doi.org/10.1177/0193841X06287307.

Villagomez, Jessica. "University of Chicago Scholar Killed in Shooting Spree Remembered as 'a Kind Individual and an Extraordinary Student.'" *Chicago Tribune*, January 14, 2021. https://www.chicagotribune.com/2021/01/14/university-of-chicago-scholar-killed-in-shooting-spree-remembered-as-a-kind-individual-and-an-extraordinary-student/.

Vold, George B., and Thomas Bernard. *Theoretical Criminology*. 3rd ed. New York: Oxford University Press, 1986.

Votruba, Mark, and Jeffrey Kling. "Effects of Neighborhood Characteristics on the Mortality of Black Male Youth: Evidence from Gautreaux,

Chicago." *Social Science and Medicine (1982)* 68 (February 2009): 814–23. https://doi.org/10.1016/j.socscimed.2008.12.018.

Wall Street Journal Editorial Board. "Another Shoot-'Em-Up Memorial Day Weekend in Chicago." *Wall Street Journal*, May 31, 2023. https://www .wsj.com/articles/chicago-memorial-day-weekend-shootings-brandon -johnson-275ef812.

"Washington Post Fatal Force Tracker." *Washington Post*. Accessed March 15, 2024. https://www.washingtonpost.com/graphics/investigations /police-shootings-database/.

Washington, Harold. Inaugural address, April 29, 1983. Online at Chicago Public Library, https://www.chipublib.org/mayor-harold-washington -inaugural-address-1983/.

Washington, Harold. Inaugural address, May 4, 1987. Online at Chicago Public Library, https://www.chipublib.org/mayor-harold-washington -inaugural-address-1987/.

Watson, Brett, Mouhcine Guettabi, and Matthew Reimer. "Universal Cash and Crime." *Review of Economics and Statistics* 102, no. 4 (2020): 678–89. https://doi.org/10.1162/rest_a_00834.

Watson, Tara. "Inequality and the Measurement of Residential Segregation by Income in American Neighborhoods." *Review of Income and Wealth* 55, no. 3 (2009): 820–44. https://doi.org/10.1111/j.1475-4991.2009 .00346.x.

Webb, Dan K. *The Death of David Koschmann: Report of the Special Prosecutor*. Chicago: Winston and Strawn, LLC, September 18, 2013. https://news .wttw.com/sites/default/files/article/file-attachments/The%20Death %20of%20David%20Koschman%20-%20Report%20of%20the %20Special%20Prosecutor.pdf.

Weber, Bruce. "James Q. Wilson Dies at 80; Originated 'Broken Windows' Policing Strategy." *New York Times*, March 2, 2012. https:// www.nytimes.com/2012/03/03/nyregion/james-q-wilson-dies-at-80 -originated-broken-windows-policing-strategy.html.

Webster, Daniel W., Alexander D. McCourt, Cassandra K. Crifasi, Marisa D. Booty, and Elizabeth A. Stuart. "Evidence Concerning the Regula- tion of Firearms Design, Sale, and Carrying on Fatal Mass Shootings in the United States." *Criminology and Public Policy* 19, no. 1 (2020): 171– 212. https://doi.org/10.1111/1745-9133.12487.

Weidmann, Ben, and David J. Deming. "Team Players: How Social Skills Improve Team Performance." *Econometrica* 89, no. 6 (2021): 2637–57. https://doi.org/10.3982/ECTA18461.

Weisburd, Sarit. "Police Presence, Rapid Response Rates, and Crime Prevention." *Review of Economics and Statistics* 103, no. 2 (2021): 280–93. https://doi.org/10.1162/rest_a_00889.

Western, Bruce. "Inside the Box: Safety, Health, and Isolation in Prison." *Journal of Economic Perspectives* 35, no. 4 (Fall 2021): 97–122. https://doi .org/10.1257/jep.35.4.97.

———. *Punishment and Inequality in America*. New York: Russell Sage Foundation, 2006.

Western, Bruce, and Becky Pettit. "Incarceration and Racial Inequality in Men's Employment." *Industrial and Labor Relations Review* 54, no. 1 (2000): 3. https://doi.org/10.2307/2696029.

WGN News. "55 Shot, 11 Fatally over Labor Day Weekend in Chicago." YouTube, September 6, 2022. MP4 video, 3:10. https://www.youtube .com/watch?v=AktofoDAYPQ.

"Where'd They Get Their Guns? An Analysis of the Firearms Used in High-Profile Shootings, 1963 to 2001." Violence Policy Center, 2001. https:// www.vpc.org/studies/wgun810330.htm.

White, Kailey, Philip J. Cook, and Harold A. Pollack. "Gunshot-Victim Cooperation with Police Investigations: Results from the Chicago Inmate Survey." *Preventive Medicine* 143 (February 2021): 106381. https://doi .org/10.1016/j.ypmed.2020.106381.

Wihbey, John. "White Racial Attitudes over Time: Data from the General Social Survey." *Journalist's Resource*, August 14, 2014. https:// journalistsresource.org/criminal-justice/white-racial-attitudes-over -time-data-general-social-survey/.

Wilkinson, Deanna L., Marquette S. McBryde, Brice Williams, Shelly Bloom, and Kerryn Bell. "Peers and Gun Use among Urban Adolescent Males: An Examination of Social Embeddedness." *Journal of Contemporary Criminal Justice* 25, no. 1 (2009): 20–44. https://doi.org/10.1177/ 1043986208328449.

Will, George F. "James Q. Wilson, Honored Prophet." *Washington Post*, March 2, 2012. https://www.washingtonpost.com/opinions/james-q -wilson-americas-prophet/2012/03/02/gIQAtEWGnR_story.html.

Wilson, Edward O. *Consilience: The Unity of Knowledge.* 1st ed. New York: Vintage Books, 1999.

Wilson, James Q. "Lock 'Em Up and Other Thoughts on Crime." *New York Times*, March 9, 1975. https://www.nytimes.com/1975/03/09/archives /lock-em-up-and-other-thoughts-on-crime-lock-em-up.html.

———. *Thinking about Crime.* 2nd ed. New York: Basic Books, 1983.

———. "Thinking about Crime." *Atlantic*, September 1983. https://www .theatlantic.com/past/docs/politics/crime/wilson.htm.

Wilson, James Q., and Richard J. Herrnstein. *Crime and Human Nature.* New York: Simon and Schuster, 1985.

Wilson, Timothy D. *Strangers to Ourselves: Discovering the Adaptive Unconscious.* Cambridge, MA: Belknap Press of Harvard University Press, 2002.

Wilson, William J. *The Truly Disadvantaged: The Inner City, the Underclass, and Public Policy.* Chicago: University of Chicago Press, 1987.

Wingrove, Sara, Jessica Jee Won Paek, Rebecca Ponce de Leon, and Gráinne M. Fitzsimons. "Tying the Value of Goals to Social Class." *Journal of Personality and Social Psychology* 125, no. 4 (2023): 699–719. https:// doi.org/10.1037/pspa0000346.

Wohl, Anthony S. "Racism and Anti-Irish Prejudice in Victorian England." *Victorian Web*, last modified 1990. https://www.victorianweb.org /history/race/Racism.html.

World Bank. "Population Estimates and Projections." *DataBank*, 2020. https://databank.worldbank.org/source/population-estimates-and -projections.

Wright, James D., Peter H. Rossi, and Kathleen Daly. *Under the Gun: Weapons, Crime, and Violence in America.* 1st ed. New York: Routledge, 1993.

Yamagishi, Toshio. "The Provision of a Sanctioning System as a Public Good." *Journal of Personality and Social Psychology* 51, no. 1 (1986): 110–16.

Yamane, David. "The Sociology of U.S. Gun Culture." *Sociology Compass* 11, no. 7 (2017): e12497. https://doi.org/10.1111/soc4.12497.

Yang, Crystal S. "Local Labor Markets and Criminal Recidivism." *Journal of Public Economics* 147, C (2017): 16–29. https://doi.org/10.1016/j .jpubeco.2016.12.003.

———. "Does Public Assistance Reduce Recidivism?" *American Economic Review* 107, no. 5 (2017): 551–55. https://doi.org/10.1257/aer.p20171001.

Yelderman, Logan A., and Monica K. Miller. "Religious Fundamentalism and Attitudes toward the Insanity Defense: The Mediating Roles of Criminal Attributions and Attitudes toward the Mentally Ill." *Psychiatry, Psychology and Law* 23, no. 6 (2016): 872–84. https://doi.org/10.1080/13218719.2016.1160005.

Young, Yolanda. "Analysis: Black Leaders Supported Clinton's Crime Bill." *NBC News*, April 8, 2016. https://www.nbcnews.com/news/nbcblk/analysis-black-leaders-supported-clinton-s-crime-bill-n552961.

Yousef, Odette. "What the West Side Lost." *WBEZ Chicago*, October 28, 2019. https://interactive.wbez.org/2019/manufacturing/overview/.

Zeng, Donglin, and Xiaogang Wu. "Neighborhood Collective Efficacy in Stressful Events: The Stress-Buffering Effect." *Social Science and Medicine* 306 (August 2022): 115154. https://doi.org/10.1016/j.socscimed.2022.115154.

Zeren, Seth. "Jane Jacobs, an Urban Ecologist." *Strong Towns*, May 6, 2016. https://www.strongtowns.org/journal/2016/5/4/the-value-of-old-buildings.

Zidar, Owen. "Tax Cuts for Whom? Heterogeneous Effects of Income Tax Changes on Growth and Employment." *Journal of Political Economy* 127, no. 3 (2019): 1437–72. https://doi.org/10.1086/701424.

Ziezulewicz, Geoff. "Cops Vow Crackdown on SUWU Gang after Hadiya's Alleged Killers Charged." *DNA Info*, February 15, 2013. https://www.dnainfo.com/chicago/20130215/kenwood/cops-vow-crackdown-on-suwu-gang-after-hadiyas-alleged-killers-charged/.

Zimring, Franklin E. *The City That Became Safe: New York's Lessons for Urban Crime and Its Control.* New York: Oxford University Press, 2011.

———. "Firearms and Federal Law: The Gun Control Act of 1968." *Journal of Legal Studies* 4, no. 1 (1975): 133–98. https://doi.org/10.1086/467528.

———. "Is Gun Control Likely to Reduce Violent Killings?" *University of Chicago Law Review* 35, no. 4 (1968): 721. https://doi.org/10.2307/1598883.

———. "Will Success Spoil James Q. Wilson?" *Journal of Criminal Law and Criminology* 85, no. 3 (1995): 828–32.

Zimring, Franklin E., and Gordon Hawkins. *Crime Is Not the Problem: Lethal Violence in America*. New York: Oxford University Press, 1999.

Zouves, Natasha. "Second Chances: 'I Survived Jumping Off the Golden Gate Bridge.'" *ABC7 Chicago*, May 18, 2017. https://abc7news.com/golden-gate-bridge-suicides-suicide-survivors-jump-survive/2010562/.

Index

Page numbers set in italics refer to figures or tables.